William Walton: Music and Literature

To
Raymond Monk

William Walton:
Music and Literature

Edited by

Stewart R. Craggs

Ashgate

Aldershot • Brookfield USA • Singapore • Sydney

WITHDRAWN

© The individual contributors, 1999

The editor and contributors have asserted their moral rights under the Copyright, Designs and Patents Act, 1988, to be identified as the authors of this work.

Published by
Ashgate Publishing Limited
Gower House
Croft Road
Aldershot
Hants GU11 3HR
England

Ashgate Publishing Company
Old Post Road
Brookfield
Vermont 05036-9704
USA

British Library Cataloguing-in-Publication data

William Walton: music and literature
    1. Walton, William, 1902–1983 – Criticism and interpretation
    I. Craggs, Stewart R. (Stewart Roger)
    780.9'2

Library of Congress Cataloging-in-Publication data

William Walton: music and literature / edited by Stewart R. Craggs.
    Includes index.
    1. Walton, William, 1902–1983 – Criticism and interpretation
2. Music and literature.   I. Craggs, Stewart R.
ML410.W292W53   1999
780'.92—dc21   98–42921
                CIP
                MN

ISBN 1 85928 190 7

Typeset in Sabon by Midlands Book Typesetting Company
Printed and bound in Great Britain by MPG Books Ltd, Bodmin, Cornwall

Contents

Notes on Contributors

John Coggrave, born in 1928, is the former Head of English in the Humanities Faculty of Sunderland Polytechnic (now the University of Sunderland). He began listening to Walton in 1940 and remembers the excitement, in a wartime with little new recorded music, of finding in a provincial music shop the original 78 discs of the *First Symphony* in the Harty recording with the LSO, Frederick Riddle's performance of the *Viola Concerto* and *Belshazzar's Feast* in the Walton performance of 1943. He has since discovered that the Trio sections of *Crown Imperial*, *Orb and Sceptre* and the *Spitfire Prelude* make magnificent wedding marches and has used them for the bridal processions of each of his three daughters.

Stewart Craggs, editor of this book, is an author, editor and bibliographer, with a special interest in British music of the nineteenth and twentieth centuries. He has spent the last 35 years researching the music of Sir William Walton. His Walton thematic catalogue was first published by Oxford University Press in 1977, and a second edition appeared in 1990. This was awarded the McColvin medal by the Library Association for the outstanding reference book of that year. A third edition is planned as part of the Walton Edition. His *Walton Source Book* was published by Scolar Press in 1993. Professor Craggs is currently consultant to the William Walton Edition to be published by Oxford University Press.

Alan Cuckston is a professional keyboard player. Born in Yorkshire, he attended a Methodist school near Bradford and read Music at King's College, Cambridge, 1959–1963, studying composition with Patrick Hadley and musicology with Thurston Dart. For more than 30 years he has performed as harpsichordist, pianist and organist, giving solo recitals and broadcasts and touring worldwide with such ensembles as the Academy of St Martin-in-the-Fields, and the vocal consort Pro Cantione Antiqua. Amongst his many recordings are several of British music ranging from Thomas Tallis to Alan Rawsthorne, via performances on historic instruments of George Frederick Pinto and Sterndale Bennett to William Baines and Cyril Scott. He has worked on a great deal of twentieth-century English songs with many singers, making the first recordings of the songs of Alan Rawsthorne and giving several early performances, in the 1960s, of the Walton *Songs for the Lord Mayor's Table*. In the world of Baroque music, Alan Cuckston's recording of harpsichord music by François Couperin has recently been selected as one of the '1000 Best CDs' (BBC Publications). He is also active as a lecturer in the field of adult education and has conducted amateur choirs since he was in his teens. He directed the first performance of Gerald Finzi's *Requiem da Camera* in a concert marking the centenary of the Great War composer Ernest Farrar.

Lewis Foreman has written and edited many books about music, with a particular interest in British music of the twentieth century. He is the biographer of Sir Arnold Bax; most recently he edited the symposium *Ralph Vaughan Williams in Perspective*. He is also known as a broadcaster, for his CD booklet and programme notes, and reviews in many journals. Over many years he has assisted a variety of performing organizations, researched unknown repertoire, and as the Music Trustee of the Sir Arnold Bax Trust has directed the Trust's funding of recordings of Bax's music, particularly on the Chandos label.

Lyndon Jenkins is a writer, lecturer and broadcaster on music. From 1972–1987 he wrote on music for *The Birmingham Post* before becoming a regular contributor to BBC Radio 3, World Service and the Independent Radio Network, specializing in British music, British artists, and British musical history through documentary programmes on Beecham, Sargent, Maggie Teyte, Eric Fenby, E.J. Moeran, Glyndebourne and many others. He lectures widely on these and a range of other subjects. He gave the first Adrian Boult Lecture in Birmingham (1986). Outside Britain he is especially interested in Scandinavian composers and has been heard on Finnish and Danish radio speaking about Sibelius and Nielsen. His wide-ranging musical enthusiasms are currently reflected in his being Chairman of the Delius Society, a consultant to the record industry, and Special Projects Manager at Symphony Hall, Birmingham. Publications: *Sir Adrian Boult's Birmingham Years* (1980); *The Birmingham 78s* (1983).

Michael Kennedy OBE was born in Manchester and educated at Berkhamstead. He has been staff music critic on *The Daily Telegraph* since 1950, northern editor from 1960 to 1986 and joint chief critic from 1987. He has written biographical studies of many composers and conductors including Elgar, Walton, Britten, Vaughan Williams, Boult and Barbirolli.

Zelda Lawrence-Curran was born in Kent and studied music at Trevelyan College, University of Durham. She is currently writing her doctoral thesis on William Walton's music at Worcester College, University of Oxford. She became an unashamed Walton devotee after being taken to hear *Belshazzar's Feast* at the tender age of 14. Once her thesis is complete she intends to research other British twentieth-century composers and also music for films, particularly those made in the UK.

Stephen Lloyd, a teacher by profession, has had a lifelong passion for British music. From 1980 to 1996 he was Editor of *The Delius Society Journal*. He has written a biography of *H Balfour Gardiner* (CUP 1984) and a history of Sir Dan Godfrey and the Bournemouth Municipal Orchestra (Thames 1994). He edited *Edmund Rubbra's collected essays on Holst* (Triad Press 1964) and more recently a comprehensive collection of Eric Fenby's writings on Delius for his 90th birthday (Thames 1996). He contributed to *The Percy Grainger Companion* (Thames 1981), the *Studies in Music* Grainger Centennial Volume (1982), *An Elgar Companion* (Sequoia Publishing 1982), as well as to companion Ashgate volumes on Delius (1998) and Bliss (forthcoming). He has recently completed a biography of Sir William Walton.

Kevin McBeath was born in 1924 and began his career with the Australian Broadcasting Corporation as an announcer. Later he joined the Music Presentation Staff and became well-known for his programmes of contemporary music. He introduced the first live performances of *Façade* to Australian audiences in 1952. He also produced and narrated three successful performances of the work at the Union Theatre, Melbourne University, with members of the Victorian Symphony Orchestra. These performances led to the recording of *Façade* with the VSO which were released in December 1953, and which earned praise from Sir William Walton.

Robert Meikle was born in Derbyshire, and completed his M.A. and B.Mus. degrees at Glasgow University. He took his Ph.D. (on eighteenth-century Italian opera) at Cornell University, where he studied under Donald Grout. He has taught at the Universities of Glasgow and Leicester (where he was Director of Music for 15 years), and is now head of the music department at the University of Birmingham. His particular research interests are in the classical era and in English music of the twentieth century – whose repertoires he has also been fortunate in encountering as a conductor – and all aspects of opera.

Michael Pope was born in London in 1927 and educated at Wellington College and the Guildhall School of Music and Drama, where his studies included singing with Howard Fry and Reinhold Gerhardt, conducting with Joseph Lewis, and musical history under Peter Latham and Alec Robertson. From 1954 to 1980 he was on the staff of the BBC, where he planned and produced many revivals of eighteenth- to twentieth-century British music, and worked closely with the BBC Chorus. He was responsible for programmes celebrating Walton's 65th and 70th birthdays, and for the rebroadcast of Dallas Bower's 1942 production of *Christopher Columbus* in 1973. He was music director of the London Motet & Madrigal Club 1954–93, and has written, lectured, and broadcast on various aspects of the English music heritage.

Scott Price was born in South Wales in 1972 and went up to Oxford in 1990. There his passion for the music of William Walton resulted in a dissertation on the composer's film music. The present essay is based on a thesis written for the Master of Studies degree which the author took in 1995. Scott Price is currently a teacher in London.

Acknowledgements

This volume of essays, like the first in the series (*Edward Elgar: Music and Literature*, Scolar Press, 1990) seeks to reflect aspects of the life and work of Sir William Walton. Each essay is self-contained but it is hoped that the reader will discern a literary thread running through many of them – strong enough to justify the choice of title for this collection.

It has been a pleasure to edit this symposium and friendships (old and new) have again played an important part in its production. My thanks are first extended to the contributors themselves. I must also thank Lady Walton and the Walton Trust for continuing support; Raymond Monk for his kind suggestions and invaluable help, particularly in the planning stage of the volume (hence the dedication); Michael Pope for writing the Foreword and help in other ways, and Evelyn Hendy, Copyright Manager at OUP's Music Department, for her kind help and guidance.

Last, but not least, my thanks go to Ellen Keeling and Rachel Lynch at Ashgate Publishing for their guidance and help, and my wife, Valerie, for her support.

Stewart R. Craggs

Foreword
Michael Pope

How does it happen that a partial view of a great composer's work can acquire the virtual status of received opinion? So far as the evaluation of Walton's music is concerned, there has for some time been a tendency to focus attention on the earlier stages of his development. It is of course true that the phase concerned included the first performances of three major masterpieces, the Viola Concerto (C 22 in Professor Craggs's chronological Catalogue), *Belshazzar's Feast* (C 23), and the First Symphony (C 27). But what are we to say of a view which limits recognition of his genius to works produced before the outbreak of the Second World War in September 1939?

Despite Walton's remarkable achievements by the age of thirty-three, it is important to appreciate that he was not one of those composers, so vividly described by Sir Hubert Parry, 'whose main spur is facility of diction, who come to the point of production early, and do not grow much afterwards'. The subsequent development of his style indicates that his rightful place is with the other, gradually maturing, type of artist, the kind appraised by Parry in his 1909 study of Bach: 'the composer who combines musical gift with a great temperament and a great personality keenly alive to things external to music itself, only by degrees hammers out of himself the fullest and most unalloyed expression in his musical ideas'.

The general musical situation during Walton's early years as a composer was in a state of flux and ferment which was perhaps without parallel. It is a sign of his enquiring mind that he experimented with at least five of the different 'schools' of music which were then active; clear too that the test of performance led him to reject four of them as being unsuited to express what he wanted to say. What this was became evident in 1929, when he conducted the first performance of his Viola Concerto at a Queen's Hall Promenade Concert, with Paul Hindemith as the soloist. The Concerto proved to be a masterpiece, and it may be said to have begun Walton's second period. One of the most prescient of critics, Frank Howes, later wrote that it was this work which revealed the composer 'as a romantic, as an adherent of modernity in so far as it meant a dissonant harmony but a basic adherence to tonality'. With this may be balanced the composer's description of himself as 'a classical composer with a strong feeling for lyricism'.

The distinguished violist Bernard Shore, who played in that première, was subsequently the soloist in the second performance of the Concerto, and he regarded it as 'the finest of all compositions of that form and combination'. His knowledge of Walton's music was extensive, and his comments on individual works are of great significance, for they come from a musician who spoke from first-hand experience. It is enlightening, for instance, to recall his remarks on *Façade* (C 12): 'Humorous, witty and charming, this 'Façade' is an untiring joy to play. It must also be said to have misled a good many people as to the composer's essential nature – his essential seriousness'. This is certainly true, and it is valuable to hear Walton's own comments made during a 1964 television interview in Adelaide: 'I like *Façade* up to a point – I like the other works more'.

It seems clear that the changing circumstances of Walton's life around 1935 had an animating influence on his musical development. It is as though, having achieved a masterly command of artistic resources, he was now inspired to attain those higher levels of expression where great music becomes a fresh revelation of spirit. An increasing melodiousness is now apparent: one has only to think of the radiantly beautiful second subject in the Finale of the Violin Concerto (C 37), the work which is the key to a deeper appreciation of the warmly poetical third period after the end of the war. Furthermore, how many other composers, since Elgar, have enriched the form of the March with such memorable melodic invention? Several of these pieces were for incidental music to films, culminating in the magnificent March for *The Battle of Britain* (C 81). Is it too much to hope that one day a version will be prepared which restores this to its due place in the film? It is good, at any rate, to read in the following pages a comprehensive account of Walton's notable music for the cinema (see Chapter 6), and to see him placed at the pinnacle of film composers, with three of the finest scores ever written.

Works of a dramatic cast occupied much of Walton's attention during the period when he was attached to the Films Division of the Ministry of Information, and these included two large scores for the radio drama *Christopher Columbus* (C 46) and for the ballet *The Quest* (C 49). Both contain some fine, though little-known, music, and it is certainly to be hoped that in the fullness of time there will be renewed opportunities to hear more of it.

Walton's first two compositions after the war deserve special mention. The motet *Where does the Uttered Music go?* (C 52) is perhaps the composer's most striking work for unaccompanied choir. My mind goes back to February 1967, when the BBC Chorus, conducted by Alan G. Melville, were rehearsing in the Waldegrave studio for a 65th birthday broadcast the following month. As they sang the final pages, where the choir divides into sixteen parts, and the sopranos climb to top A, it seemed as though one was hearing the music of the spheres. Masefield's tribute to Sir Henry Wood needs study and reflection before its inner meaning becomes clear; but the Poet Laureate's words are certainly attuned to the vital essence of Walton's music – 'The living Sun-Ray entering the heart / Touching the Life with that which cannot die. . .'.

In May 1947 the BBC Third Programme broadcast the first performance of the String Quartet in A minor (C 53). A little later, Shore expressed the view that 'This glorious music represents Walton's full maturity'. Even so, he discerningly asked whether the composer's finely distinguished compositions, at that stage, each rather partially represented a mind that had not, as a whole, realized itself in art. I venture to suggest that this complete realization of all Walton's finest and most characteristic qualities was to come seven years later, in a work originally commissioned by the BBC in 1947, and produced at the Royal Opera House in 1954, the three-act opera *Troilus and Cressida* (C 62).

How well I remember going into a studio on Friday, 3 December 1954, to hear the broadcast of the first Act; and what an impression it made! After attending the third performance at Covent Garden a week later, I felt it to be the work for which we had long been waiting, perhaps the finest English tragic opera since Purcell. Repeated hearings of it have served to confirm such a view. This is music which rises to the height of the tragic theme with no trace of morbidity, sounds the deepest chords in our nature, and enhances the experience of life. Its new richness of language fertilized each of the three major orchestral works which followed: the Cello Concerto (C 65), the Second Symphony (C 68), and the Variations on a Theme of Hindemith (C 76).

Among the qualities which have made Walton's music endure are his masterly treatment of form and tonality, and they receive detailed examination in this book, as do many other aspects of his art. It is much to be hoped that the following essays will stimulate a wider interest in the whole range of Walton's compositions; for I believe the time is right for them to come into their own. This century has seen much experimentation, and by no means all of it has proved fruitful. During the course of human evolution there have been various dead-ends, and many of these experiments may prove to be blind alleys. To quote a leading authority on the theory of evolution, Professor Karl Pearson, 'The final touchstone is equal validity for all normally constituted minds'. At the end of a comprehensive examination in his *Aesthetics of Music*, Dr Roger Scruton concludes: 'The possibility remains that tonal music is the only music that will ever really mean anything to us . . .'. Croce wrote that great artists and great work can be called neither classicist nor romantic, for they are both; 'they are sheer emotion absolutely identified with the most lucid imagery'. Judged by these standards, is not Walton one of the great masters of the twentieth century?

Music examples

Ashgate gratefully acknowledges the assistance of the following publishers in granting their permission to reproduce extracts from the music of Walton and others:

Oxford University Press: examples 1.12, The Winds and 1.13, Tritons, © transferred to Oxford University Press 1985; 1.14, Daphne (from Façade), © Oxford University Press 1951; 1.15, Daphne (from Three Songs), © Oxford University Press 1932; 1.16, Anon in Love, © Oxford University Press 1960; 1.17, A Song for the Lord Mayor's Table, © Oxford University Press 1963; 5.1 and 5.13, Concerto for Violin and Orchestra, © Oxford University Press 1945; 5.2a and 5.6, Symphony No. 1, © Oxford University Press 1936; 5.5a, Concerto for Viola and Orchestra, © Oxford University Press 1930; 5.8 and 5.16, Symphony No. 2, © Oxford University Press 1958; 5.14 and 5.15, Concerto for Cello and Orchestra, © Oxford University Press 1957; 7.1, 7.2, 7.14, 7.15, 7.17 and 7.18, Christopher Columbus, © Oxford University Press; 7.7, Belshazzar's Feast, © Oxford University Press 1931; 7.6, The Foreman went to France and 7.11, Henry V, © Oxford University Press 1990; 7.20a and b, Gloria, © Oxford University Press 1961; 7.20c, The Twelve, © Oxford University Press 1966.

Robert Lienau Musikverlag for Example 5.2b, Sibelius Symphony No. 3. Reproduced by kind permission of the publishers.

Schott & Co. Ltd for Examples 5.3a and b, Hindemith Kammermusik No. 5. © B. Schott's Söhne, Mainz, 1927. © renewed 1955.

Boosey & Hawkes Music Publishers Ltd for Example 5.4, Prokofiev Violin Concerto No. 1, copyright © 1921 by Hawkes & Son (London Ltd) and an extract from Prokofiev's Violin Concerto No. 2 in note 44 on page 105, copyright © 1937 by Hawkes & Son (London) Ltd.

Every effort has been made to trace all copyright holders but if any have been inadvertently missed the publishers will be pleased to add an acknowledgement in any future editions.

1   The Songs

Alan Cuckston

I would wager that if you asked the average lover of Walton's music to sing his favourite tunes from the composer's work, the selections would come from instrumental rather than vocal pieces. The openings of the Violin Concerto and the Cello Concerto, themes from the Scapino and Johannesburg Festival Overtures and the Coronation Marches, fugue subjects of the First Symphony and for the 'Spitfire' – though we may not be able physically to encompass them all through the voice, their melodic stamp is such that they can be readily recalled by the mind's ear, which has learned to identify them as indelibly Waltonian.

Although in some respects Walton received the mantle of Elgar, he did not add to our store of what we once used to call our British National Airs in the way that Vaughan Williams and Holst did. Indeed, the whole art of writing popular songs of mass appeal during Walton's lifetime passed to Irving Berlin, Gershwin, Kern, Cole Porter and Co., and their colleagues in the Broadway theatres, as well as their British successors like Noel Coward and Ivor Novello. The name of Eric Coates is most often invoked whenever Walton achieves a broad tune in the old tradition, as though to excuse it. A brave man these days would it be who dared set such melodies to words of stirring sentiment. Much more typical to find Maxwell Davies turning *Crown Imperial* into a foxtrot (though Holst's 'Jupiter' melody from *The Planets* has once again found contemporary celebration in connection with football's World Cup!).

The fact is that when it came to writing solo songs, Walton wrote chiefly for other musicians and connoisseurs rather than for the wider public, which is more or less the case for all the best composers of song in the twentieth century, including Poulenc, Britten, Ives, Messiaen and Barber. A couple of centuries ago the popular song and the serious art song had no clear dividing line and little change of musical idiom was needed to pass from one to the other. James Hook's 'The Lass of Richmond Hill' or Charles Dibdin's 'Tom Bowling' were appreciated quite readily by a population that was both musically educated and uneducated, but was willing and able to pay for musical entertainment.

Popular or otherwise, in the nineteenth century the song with piano accompaniment was chiefly performed in private – at a family gathering or in the tavern, or (shades of *Façade* in the 1920s) in the salon, before invited guests. Song recitals were unknown, singers at public concerts up to about 1840 being accompanied by an orchestra in what were known as 'Ballads'. Such songs were straightforward in terms of their musical treatment and sentiment, and were thus separate from 'serious' art in which progressive innovations might occur, though a few ballads did attain to a higher artistic quality. The boy Walton, whose father taught singing in Oldham during his Edwardian childhood, would doubtless have been acquainted with the whole gamut of this repertoire, running from Balfe and Wallace, via Gilbert and Sullivan, to Liza Lehmann and Amy Woodforde-Finden. Walton's earliest surviving examples of song-writing date from his teenage years at Oxford, passing from chorister to undergraduate during the Great War, setting texts by Shakespeare and Swinburne, as well as Matthew Arnold in a cantata, and Phineas Fletcher in an anthem.

Although it is accorded the initial entry in Stewart Craggs's catalogue of Walton's works, the SATB setting of Fletcher's 'Drop, drop, slow tear', attributed to Easter 1916, with its affective use of diminished intervals and harmony, seems considerably in advance of the second catalogued work 'Tell me where is fancy bred', dated July 1916.[1] Some Masters of the Choristers, however, might see it as a sort of chorister's prank to begin a piece with what sounds like an out-of-tune chord in E minor![2]

Walton's Shakespeare setting is scored for soprano and tenor voices, with three violins and piano, with text taken from *The Merchant of Venice*. Peter Warlock set the same text two years later (now lost) and so did Norman O'Neill in 1922, with accompaniment for small orchestra – 'all 7ths and sentimentality' (Banfield).[3] And how significant, wrote Christopher Palmer, that one of the very first works of a composer later to become so celebrated for his Shakespeare music should be this piece. Just why these particular forces are prescribed may be attributed perhaps to local conditions prevailing at Christchurch that summer, using talent from fellow choristers (and choir-men?).

'Tell me where is fancy bred' is a clearly tonal setting in E flat major, strong and purposeful, with a straightforward rhythmic stride and simple modulations. The phrases fall into 2-bar patterns with echoes and elisions, the piano doubling most of the vocal and instrumental material (Ex. 1.1). The violins echo, sometimes with simultaneous *arco* and *pizzicato* replies. Mostly the textures are homophonic, although the three string players sometimes suggest counterpoint by occasional independent movement.

The tenor voice enters for the second verse, and here the word setting reveals a certain awkwardness, the musical and metrical accents a little contradictory (Ex. 1.2). The barring loses its natural force here and young Walton has to hurry the last phrase into a bar of quavers. And if the second voice really is a tenor, and not an alto, there are some odd moments of curious harmonic movement if one makes the necessary octave transpositions, especially where the piano leaves off and this voice becomes the 'bass' of the texture, below the violins and soprano, at the ringing of 'fancy's knell'.

Ex. 1.1 'Tell me where is fancy bred'

Ex. 1.2 'Tell me where is fancy bred'

The final bars of 'Ding dong bell' naturally bring back those quoted in the opening, to good effect, as well as recalling the Christmas carol 'Up good Christen folk!' in the final *tutti*. This bright diatonic setting must surely have given pleasure when first performed, and could do so again in the context of a school concert or competitive festival class, the melody instruments being substituted, if necessary, by woodwind.

In that same summer of 1916 William Walton tried his hand at a much more extended and ambitious piece of word setting, producing a cantata, *The Forsaken Merman*. Nearly half of Matthew Arnold's poem is here composed 'for Tenor and Soprano Solo, Chorus and Orchestra', as the surviving manuscript short-score reads. However, the accompaniment is conceived almost entirely in pianistic terms, the sustaining pedal an essential, the watery effect of repeated sweeping arpeggios recalling Ravel's *Jeux d'eau* (Ex. 1.3). The soloist's opening invocations are set against the alternating time signatures of 2/4 and 6/16, the latter used to enliven and excite the basic F minor tonality (Ex. 1.4). A double chorus

Ex. 1.3   The Forsaken Merman

Ex. 1.4   The Forsaken Merman – opening solo

call the mother's name in the impressionist manners of Debussy and, contemporaneously with Walton, employed by Holst in his *Planets Suite*. The calling of the first chorus is pre-echoed by the second, singing 'Bouche fermée' (Ex. 1.5). The effect is also of course found in Verdi and Puccini, composers by whom Walton's later music was not untouched.

'The far off sound of a silver bell' is evoked in Cyril Scott-like whole tones at the beginning of an atmospheric passage whose orchestral garb is the more readily imaginable. The winds 'sleep' in deeply resonant caverns of parallel secondary

Ex. 1.5   The Forsaken Merman – double chorus

seventh chords; the 'spent lights quiver' in high tremolandi. The sea beasts are manifest in firm brazen fanfares, *fortissimo*. And great whales voyage in a 7/8 motion (Ex. 1.6).

The piece ends with a shattering climax, *con tutta forza*, the soprano soloist rising through a crescendo, *con passione*, to a top B flat. But again, the experimental nature of the writing and the scale of the conception are difficult to reconcile with the naive straightforwardness of the previous Shakespeare setting, which bears a precise date.[4] Walton's work is a fascinating documentation of an early interest in taking a dramatic setting of a romantic subject on a grand scale.

From two years later come three Swinburne settings for voice and piano, dated July 1918. These are much more disciplined compositions, eschewing technical display, the voice part having little more than an octave compass. Although none has a tempo marking, they are easy to gauge from the simple conventions of the rhythmical styles adopted. The first, entitled *Child's Song*, bears an E flat major signature though harmonically it relies on seventh and eleventh chords in parallel motion, the accompaniment doubling much of the vocal line (Ex. 1.7). The gentle triple rhythm is initiated in the piano part, a basically homophonic movement in four-part texture. The simple two-bar phrases have melodic figures going stepwise or in thirds. It is an entirely syllabic setting, with Swinburne's verses and their internal rhythms mirrored in occasional bars of duple time. These changing rhythmic metres allow for a seamless setting of the words (Ex. 1.8). Occasional chromaticisms are reminiscent of Delius.

The second of these early Swinburne settings is simply entitled *Song* – the verse beginning 'Love laid his sleepless head on a thorny rosy bed'. The piano sets up a gently rocking 6/8 accompaniment for the first Aeolian-inflected vocal phrases. Walton pares down the notes to a minimum, reducing the piano soon to only a Debussian syncopated major second (Ex. 1.9). This acts as a 'pedal point' to the melody, which rotates around A, until the moment of Swinburne's daybreak, 'when the day was merry with morn'. Here the rhythms are suddenly enlivened with Scotch snaps and the piano writing expands into the treble and bass with stark dissonances culminating in a Scriabinesque 'mystic chord' before melting away again into a tolling high treble E flat (Ex. 1.10).

Ex. 1.6   The Forsaken Merman

Ex. 1.7   Child's Song

Ex. 1.8   Child's Song 'Lady when I behold the roses'

Ex. 1.9   Song

The third Swinburne number is *A Lyke Wake Song*, recalling the famous Lyke Wake Dirge most famously set by Benjamin Britten in his Serenade for tenor, horn and strings over 20 years later. Swinburne, himself from the Borders whence the original medieval Ballad came, attempts the mock-antique here, but does not achieve the horrid fascination of the original incantations with his cod-Scots terminology:

> Fine gold and blithe fair face,
> Ye are come to a grimly place.
> Gold hair and glad grey een,
> Nae man kens if ye had been.

As in the first setting, Walton chooses a gentle triple rhythm with falling vocal phrases, the accompaniment doubling up most of the time. The melodic figures are folk-like, symmetrical patterns, an ostinato beginning at the top of the compass, the word setting syllabic. The same music is used for each of the four strophes, the harmonies initially consisting of sequences of inversions of the seventh, with chromatic Warlock-like chords containing dissonant appoggiaturas in the second and third strophes. The key signature is as for F minor, the voice part employing

Ex. 1.10 Song

#a 'gapped' scale (no D flat – that is, no sixth degree, and with a flattened seventh), but the ending is an unequivocal F major. In a way, the descending bass, featured as an ostinato, is reminiscent somewhat of an English baroque ground (Ex. 1.11). And this new lucidity of texture calls to mind contemporary pieces by Frank Bridge and Rebecca Clarke.

A fourth Swinburne setting, *The Winds*, also from 1918, proved to be Walton's first published composition, issued by Curwen in 1921, along with *Tritons*. A strange distinction for a man who later described himself as 'the world's worst pianist and second worst singer'! As in the Lyke Wake Song, *The Winds*, though through-composed, sets the four strophes to quite similar music, each heralded by the same couple of bars of murmuring accompaniment, the first two beginning with an impassioned octave leap in the voice (Ex. 1.12). Each commences with the vocal phrases pivoting around E, forming a sharp seventh to the bass whose F natural immediately contradicts the key signature. The patterns of seventh chords continue, the bass rising to B flat and then dropping back to G flat as an augmented fourth, imparting a modal quality to underline perhaps the medieval style of Swinburne's alliteration:

Ex. 1.11 A Lyke Wake Song (Swinburne)

Ex. 1.12 The Winds

And gin I were under the wan waves wide
I wot weel wad I rest.

For the third verse, Walton screws up the pitch a little more, the bass rising now
to a C sharp rather than a B flat, but cadencing yet again on C natural as the left
hand falls back from a *fortissimo* in powerful octaves to take the final straight,
the voice ascending to its top A in decorating the initial phrase. The singer's final
unaccompanied peroration, *ad libitum*, is heralded by six accented chords rising
towards a huge A flat minor seventh climax, *fff*:

And weary fa'ye, mariners a',
And weary fa' the sea:
It might hae taken an hundred men,
And let my ae love be.

The piano plays the last three bars alone, taking its cue from the opening and
reinforcing E as the tonal centre.

Curwen's companion publication, *Tritons*, was completed in 1920, and is set
in an entirely different style. Its text is by the seventeenth-century Scot, William
Drummond of Hawthornden, of whose poems Ben Jonson said they 'smelled too
much of the schools'. Although both these first published songs have a common
link via their marine subject matter, *Tritons* reveals its young composer's continuing
awareness of contemporary developments in musical thinking.

A first superficial glance at the opening of *Tritons* has one thinking that the
composer has invented the twelve-note row. It certainly partakes of the then
current atonalist's style. With rhythmic gestures deriving from baroque models,
particularly the dotted manner of the French Overture, the writing bears all the
hallmarks of post-war neoclassicism. This was spearheaded by Stravinsky's
Pulcinella and is manifest in 1920s' works like Poulenc's *Concert Champêtre*
and other celebrations of the Grand Siècle, of Lully and Couperin and all those
pieces with fanciful titles which pay homage to the characters of the *Commedia
dell'Arte*.

In his Piano Quartet and the (First) String Quartet, whose first two movements
we are told were originally written for Walton's Exhibition at Oxford, 'more as

a technical exercise than with a view to performance', the young composer introduced fugal procedures to certain movements. Indeed, the String Quartet's second movement was said by its first commentator to be closely modelled on the B flat Fugue (op.133) of Beethoven. Here in *Tritons* is yet another example of Walton's contrapuntal ingenuity. The whole central section consists of a four-voiced canon for the piano to accompany the singer's words:

> Whenas ye shall arrive
> With tilting tides where silver Ora plays
> And to your King his watry tribute pays.

(Ex. 1.13)

The vocal writing is similarly angular in this song, not what one might call 'grateful'. In the final section, as in *The Winds*, the singer rises to the top note at a double *fortissimo* climax, preceded by rumbling *tremolandi* from the accompaniment, building over a pedal D, with quotations from the opening material interjecting. The voice is then left unaccompanied for an *ad libitum* recitative-like moment of declamation, before the piano makes a final contribution, affirming an A major tonality with a combination of references both to the opening and the canonic theme, certain notes suitably sharpened. Any contrapuntal artifice in this song certainly does not 'smell of the schools' – it is carried off with the conviction of creative vitality.

A further composition, dating from the same period as these first two published songs, a setting for tenor voice and ten instruments of Christopher Marlowe's *The Passionate Shepherd*, was withdrawn and never performed. Perhaps, given Walton's talent for pastiche (soon to be so enjoyably evident in *Façade*), the music contained episodes of 'real Elizabethan counterpoint', like those Angus Morrison recalled seeing in another piece from the same time, *Dr Syntax*, which the composer similarly abandoned. Sadly, there seems to be no chance of ever discovering just what place these works have in the shaping of Walton's emerging idiom and technique. The conventional idea of song, as such, was mostly to take a back seat for the next ten years.

Ex. 1.13   *Tritons*

Michael Kennedy has written of the original notion of *Façade* as being 'a highbrow extension of country-house charades', with Edith Sitwell's poems being 'studies in word rhythms and onomatopoeia'. The *Façade Entertainment* then denies the voice its traditional melodic function, not even allowing it the kind of 'sung speech' inflections which Schöenberg had adopted in his *Pierrot Lunaire* of 1912. There was of course a strong tradition of accompanied poetic recitation in England, which Elgar had successfully exploited in patriotic works during the Great War. But the Sitwell poems are abstract, the music detached from its traditional role of underlining or illustrating the poetry in parallel. As Walton was to discover, his work is quite self-sufficient, standing very successfully on its own in the form of orchestral suites, quite divorced from any verbal associations, though aficionados may still attach odd lingering phrases, like 'Do not take a bath in Jordan, Gordon', to their concomitant musical tags.

During the composition of *Façade*, the composer himself may have felt some dissatisfaction with the recited form, as he made five settings from Edith's collection of verses entitled *Bucolic Comedies* (1923–4). Three of these had an accompaniment for six instruments, but the score is lost. However, revised versions appeared as *Three Songs* for voice and piano in 1932, and the late Christopher Palmer produced a reconstruction of the original instrumentation in the late 1980s.

The first song in the published order, 'Daphne', was the last to be composed, and the one which gave the composer the most trouble. He told the dedicatee, soprano Dora Stevens, that he 'could not get it satisfactory – this is the third version – all I can say about it is that it is better than the other two'. Angus Morrison recalled Walton saying that he felt this particular poem really needed the singing voice.

In the *Façade Entertainment* 'Daphne' opens with diatonic duetting for clarinet and flute over a pedal C on the saxophone (Ex. 1.14), the recitation commencing

Ex. 1.14   'Daphne' (*Façade*)

in the fourth bar – the trumpet remains silent, with just the three woodwind and the cello taking part. Despite the passing of years between the different versions it is fascinating to note the thematic connection between the rising clarinet phrase in the third and fourth bars and the same motif a tone lower in the vocal part (Ex. 1.15). Walton himself thought of the song as 'the "Lydian" one, which is proving a little obstreperous'. Certainly it begins and ends on the note F, which serves as an initial pivot, the accompaniment commencing with a two-bar phrase, four times stated. The tonal centre soon rises a semitone, to F sharp, the timbre of Hindemith-like fourths replaced by major seconds. At the climax the voice is left unaccompanied, with expressive rising sevenths, before the accompaniment returns with its opening patterns, the right hand's G's initially flattened.

This song is one of Walton's loveliest lyric inspirations in the English pastoral style – he marked it originally 'Nello Stile Inglese'. Frank Howes remarks of the accompaniment that its airy texture is 'of the sort Stanford used to urge on his pupils'. Insofar as it is originally conceived, it differs from that of the other two songs whose accompaniments are directly fashioned out of the substance of the chamber textures of the *Façade* score. So in the second song 'Through gilded trellises' the pianist's hands initially share the opening clarinet solo, and then the left engages with the cello's pizzicato bass line whilst the right conflates the accompanying arabesques of flute and clarinet. When the voice enters, it is with the music of the saxophone solo, in sinuous, lilting Spanish rhythms, fitting the words so well that one is tempted to wonder whether Walton in fact conceived a melodic setting of Edith's words initially and then added in the monotone version later. In the new version Walton allows himself some extra moments of expansiveness, where the voice will pause on a sustained high note, underpinned with pedalled *arpeggiandos* of glittering piano harmonies. And at the final words, 'Time dies', the voice is left unaccompanied in a little sinewy roulade, drawn from the clarinet's notes, but now a couple of octaves higher. The pianist then has an extended epilogue, gently meditating on the singer's phrase, dying away before a last flicker sparks up and a final 'flick of the jingles' brings this sultry erotic dance to a close.

Just as Walton drew his vocal part from the instrumental lines of the Spanish-like style 'Through gilded trellises', so the foxtrot 'Old Sir Faulk' draws most of its melodic material from the trumpet and saxophone parts of the chamber sextet. But he has had to supply further invention in a number of places, especially the little jazz 'breaks' which enliven the very authentic flavour of this spoof. Walton shows himself very capable of aping the jazz idiom – much more so than, say, Lambert or Britten. His year of working with the Savoy Orpheans apparently

Ex. 1.15 'Daphne' (Three Songs)

ended in 'a fit of disgust', with Walton admitting in later life that he 'wasn't slick enough, somehow'. (How tantalizing is the loss of his *Fantasia Concertante* for two pianos, jazz band and orchestra of 1923–4.) A certain Englishness of approach can be discerned in Walton's adoption in his piano writing of the Billy Mayerl left hand stride style, in tenths, at the words 'Sally, Mary, Mattie, what's the matter, why cry?' Perhaps this is the way the composer himself played in those times. He teasingly told Dora Stevens that the piano part of 'Through gilded trellises' 'sounds difficult, but is in reality as easy as Sydney Smith and I may say not unlike', and that 'Old Sir Faulk' 'ought to evoke a touch of lunacy in any programme'.

Between the Sitwell songs and the *Anon in Love* cycle of 1959 are only two published numbers, which lie outside the chronology of the composer's art-songs. *Under the Greenwood Tree*, though not eventually used, was actually written for the 1936 film of *As You Like It*. It can never replace in our affections the elegant tunefulness of Thomas Arne's setting, though it has a kind of antique melancholy all its own. The names of Morley and Dowland have been evoked in connection with its pastiche qualities, the spare piano textures recalling the lute style of those early masters. The opening phrase of the introduction is the vocal roulade of the 'rough weather' which ends both verses. Otherwise, this is a generally syllabic setting, the treble part of the piano doubling the voice for much of the course, coming to each close with a written-out mordent.

Another item drawn from incidental music has also achieved separate publication. This is 'Beatriz's Song' from Louis MacNeice's 1942 radio play *Christopher Columbus*, written to celebrate the 450th anniversary of the discovery of the New World, and for which Walton provided a massive score, given the full resources of the BBC Music Department, its Orchestra and Chorus. An interesting feature here is the composer's exploitation of the guitar (along with Latin American percussion instruments like the maracas and rumba sticks), in anticipation of the accompaniment of the later *Anon in Love*.

'Beatriz's Song' is conceived in terms of Renaissance dance measures, like a stately sarabande, such as had been explored by Warlock in his *Capriol Suite*, or Respighi in his *Ancient Airs and Dances*, and was to captivate Alan Rawsthorne in his use of *Les Folies d'Espagne*. The simple balanced vocal phrases are modal in feeling, the harmonization making special play with the sharp ascending and flattened descending characteristics of the melodic minor scale. Eventually these chromatic twists give rise to final harmonizations which might themselves be straight out of a Warlock song, at the words 'When will he return? Only to depart'. The accompaniment was originally scored for strings and, as Christopher Palmer suggests, should therefore be played as smoothly and gently as possible.

Walton's late adoption of the song sequence as a congenial medium, with *Anon in Love* and *A Song for the Lord Mayor's Table*, reveals the composer's disposition in middle life to explore the more lyrical and the more humorous aspects of his personality which, since *Façade*, had not been so much in evidence. These are extended essays in wordsetting for a man for whom words did not always offer the kind of stimulus to the musical imagination that they did for Britten. 'The trouble is, I wasn't properly trained', said Walton of himself, when speaking of Britten's particular gifts, though Britten said that he (Britten) felt not to measure up to the standards Frank Bridge had set him.

Anon in Love was the result of a commission in 1959 from Britten's partner, the tenor Peter Pears, and the guitarist Julian Bream, who were giving duo recitals at that time and were anxious to enlarge their repertoire. Pears showed his mastery of the English lute song repertory of the Dowland school, and Walton here sets six sixteenth- and seventeenth-century lyrics. These were chosen by Christopher Hassall from Gerald Bullett's 'The English Galaxy of Shorter Poems', for which sequence Walton himself gave the brilliant title of *Anon in Love*. The first performance was given as part of the Aldeburgh Festival in June 1960. The composer arranged the work for strings, harp and percussion in 1971, and, to give it perhaps even further currency, the guitar part was arranged for the piano by Christopher Palmer in 1989. Despite the obviously 'manly' qualities in the words – such as 'I thought she was a-fear'd till she stroaked my Beard' – the cycle can be successfully sung by a soprano.

The first number of the cycle, 'Fair would I change that note', takes its text from the 'Musicall Humors' of 1605 of Captain Tobias Hume, exponent of the lyra viol, and author of the famous celebration in song of *Tobacco*. Roger Quilter's 1907 setting of these words must be embedded in the consciousness of all lovers of English song, with its ecstatic climax at 'Fair House of Joy and Bliss'. The intimate medium of the guitar accompaniment in the Walton perhaps inhibits a little the intensity of the singer's delivery, though Palmer's piano transcription opens up the dynamic possibilities. He does, however, provide a caveat, suggesting that the player use the una corda pedal quite freely and reserves a true *fortissimo* only for the end of the last song. Palmer has also drawn on the orchestral version in making his piano arrangement, though he seems keen that a guitar-like approximation be achieved where possible, as for example in the strummed chords of 'Fain would I change that note'.

Ostensibly in G major, this first song reveals an initial musical paragraph whose vocal range spans an octave and a half, often in the contradictory minor mode, with clashing false relations. Indulging his propensity for wide-intervalled melody, Walton creates a line which would sit just as well on the cello as the tenor voice. Generally set syllabically, only an occasional word is awarded a brief roulade, with the words 'adore thee' and 'before thee', chosen for repetition. The example of Purcell, which was such a powerful stimulus to the songs of Britten and Tippett and their verbal illustrations, is not evident in Walton's vocal writing, though Frank Howes has suggested that the minor ninth on 'change' might here be regarded as an example, tiny though it is, of such illustration. There is nothing Brittenish about the music, nor does the voice part lie in such a way as to tempt any parody of the Peter Pears manner. This is indeed, as Palmer points out, 'one of the first fruits of Walton's *rapprochement* with Britten'.[5]

Christopher Hassall – librettist of Walton's opera *Troilus and Cressida* – in selecting the verses for *Anon in Love* may be seen to choose the plain and unpretentious as opposed to the allusive or emblematic. The choice of the first three numbers comes then from the Elizabethan, the rest from the Restoration Age are much saucier, bawdier.

'O stay, sweet love' comes from John Farmer's *First Set of Madrigals* of 1599. Walton's tonal centre here is A, the sharpened seventh serving enharmonically as minor third to a delightful F minor with which it occasionally alternates. The guitar accompaniment, which requires some variable tuning of the sixth string, is mostly chordal and syncopatedly rhythmic, with some downward arpeggios. Semiquaver patterns in the voice part are imitated in the guitar, or anticipated by it, the figuration at the words 'I never meant to live and die a maid', revealing its Elizabethan prototypes.

Although the voice again overall encompasses nearly an octave and a half, the melodic intervals show more stepwise movement than was encountered in Walton's no.1 with some delicious staccato articulations and acciaccaturas at the chirping of the birds. Each strophe is introduced by the same melodic pattern. A few notes, briefly a semitone lower, for the words 'Whereat she smiled, and kindly to me said' make their point as they echo the former phrase 'Then stay, dear love, for tho' thou run from me, and the pattern of 'Run ne'er so fast, yet I will follow thee' is later developed by the imitations between voice and accompaniment, as quoted in Ex. 1.16a.

Ex. 1.16a 'O stay sweet love'

Christopher Palmer called no.3, 'Lady when I behold the roses', 'one of English music's most glorious love songs'. The words originate in John Wilbye's *First Book of Madrigals* of 1598, wherein he set them twice. (Incidentally, Pears called his madrigal group the Wilbye Consort.)

The tonal anchor here is D, and there is tonic-dominant motion as well as downward stepping movement in the bass by scalewise descent. Though generally eschewing such things, Walton reserves a special harmonic moment for the last reference to the lady's lips. Rhythmic fluidity is achieved by oft-changing time-signatures, the voice holding forward progression in check by the use of duple patterns against the triple values in the accompaniment. Beginning with the smaller melodic intervals, Walton's line eventually encompasses an overall range of an octave and a sixth, the leaps increasing gradually with each semiquaver roulade. The guitar arpeggios mark out triads with appoggiaturas, the chords being at their simplest as outlined by the voice in rising sequence to its top A, where the words state the point of ambiguity in its basic terms (Ex. 1.16b). This top note is marked *piano*, after a crescendo on the penultimate mention of the lips.

Ex. 1.16b 'Lady when I behold the roses'

After such contemplativeness, Walton lightens the mood with the brisk 'My love in her attire', the accompaniment imitating evenly articulated semiquaver patterns in C major and closely related tonalities, the voice in even quavers with some *portamento* effects specified. Teasing bars of 5/8 and 7/8 refer to the seasonal changes of wardrobe of the beloved through a rising figure in thirds and fifths across a major ninth, an interval employed soon to characterize 'Beauty's self'. Triadic patterns are found too in the chatter of the accompaniment of this syllabic quasi-patter song, whose function is chiefly harmonic, occasionally imitative, with wit in its brief upward motif before the voice falls through its last A minor chord at 'When all her robes are gone'.

In its original seventeenth-century manifestation as a male-voice Catch, 'I gave her cakes and I gave her ale' can bring down the house in a concert performance today. For suitably inebriated effect, Walton embellishes the voice with acciaccaturas, mordents and slides, gradually exciting it to a state of whooping delirium across the total compass of an octave and a sixth up to top B flat. The interval of a fourth plays a strong part in both the melodic and harmonic detail within a basic tonal basis of a conflation of E minor and its relative major. The brilliant guitar writing combines – in all its exuberantly teeming detail – chords and arpeggios with grace notes and tapping on the belly of the instrument (*tamburo*). The lilting 6/8 metre, in less riotous circumstances, might be otherwise described as a Siciliano. The accompaniment at certain moments echoes the voice, the moment of beard-stroking an especial delight. At 'Merry my Hearts, merry my Cocks' the accompaniment recalls the first phrase of the song simultaneously with its harmonies.

As a Finale to the cycle, 'To couple is a custom' is the most folk-like in its basic melody shapes, reminiscent, with its phrase 'Since love to all is free', of 'Come you not from Newcastle'. It is also the most basically diatonic, with its preponderance of white-note A minor. The guitarist sets up the 'oom-pah' style of a guitar pattern beloved of latter-day 'folk' entertainers, of whom perhaps Jake Thackray is the most talented. A recurring tag of syncopated notation spices up the otherwise plain rhythm patterns in the voice part. A couple of bars of semiquavers form the roulade to the word 'scrape' in the phrase 'Come fiddler scrape thy crowd'.[6] Here fiddle tuning is mimicked by the open fifths on the guitar, which are outlined in the vocal part.

To bring the song and the cycle to a brilliant close, Walton drives singer and accompanist towards a frenzied climax of verbal repetitions, with rising fourths and chromatic shifts propelled by the pace-making rhythms to a final octave swoop for the voice and an emphatic A minor chord for the accompanist.

Two choral pieces only – the *Gloria* for Huddersfield, and the carol *What Cheer?* for David Willcocks's *Carols for Choirs* – separate *Anon in Love* from Walton's last song cycle, the six settings of texts collected by Christopher Hassall entitled *A Song for the Lord Mayor's Table*. This was a commission from the Worshipful Company of Goldsmiths for the 1962 Festival of the City of London. Although the publication bears the inscription 'In honour of the City of London', Walton had wanted to dedicate the songs to the 75-year-old Edith Sitwell, who was nearing the end of her days, her reputation, after being attacked by F.R. Leavis, sustained by her poems inspired by the Blitz and the Atom Bomb, but even then beginning to wane. All the texts are drawn from seventeenth- and eighteenth-century sources, though the gem of the cycle sets Wordsworth's 'Glide gently, thus for ever, O Thames'. First performed by Elisabeth Schwarzkopf and Gerald Moore, the cycle was scored for small orchestra eight years later, which version was premièred by Janet Baker in the Mansion House in July 1970. Back in February 1962 the composer had written to Alan Frank to say that although he was busy on the songs he found 'writing for the pfte very irksome' and had 'spent a lot of time on no. 1 which was really for orch.'.

This very first item, whose title lends itself to the whole cycle, *The Lord Mayor's Table*, a poem of 1674 by Thomas Jordan, elicited from Frank Howes the concern that 'it might almost be a coronation instead of a banquet, being quite in the vein of *Orb and Sceptre*'. For a Lancastrian with an Oxford education who made his home on an Italian island, it is astonishing how successfully Walton celebrated the British capital, its royal occasions and its Shakespearean associations with such musical relish. Here the opening is tailor-made for a brass fanfare, its rhythm taken up by the voice which invokes 'all the nine Muses to pen a ditty in praise of the City', with ensuing characteristic syncopated accents, rests and repetitions in that unmistakable vein (Ex. 1.17a).

When 'in bountiful bowls they do succour their souls with claret, Canary and Rhenish', the musical shapes become graceful and elegant, the voices of oboe and clarinet rounding out the pandiatonic arabesques in the orchestral version, the harmonies in lush sevenths, the vocal roulade outlining a ninth (Ex. 1.17b). The popping corks of these libations have been seen to be depicted in the accompanying rhythmic repeated thirds driving forward to an accented fifth. They produce this fizz more effectively in the *martellato* piano style than in their orchestral garb. But the woodwind colouring is very beautiful for 'The Promised Land's in a Londoner's hand', where the roulade now expands to an eleventh. The fourths of 'the flowing bowls' contract to thirds for 'wallowing in milk and honey', though the melodic shapes are distinctly derived. At the 'recapitulation' and return to the original A flat signature, where the fourth verse repeats the first, the voice enters instead on the supertonic, for extra harmonic piquancy. It ends with a couple of unaccompanied bars, in relief, before the final chatter of the fanfare figures, *Allargando*, after a bubbling *Presto* of sequence and repetition.

Ex. 1.17a 'The Lord Mayor's Table'

Ex. 1.17b

Wordsworth's 'Glide Gently' comes second, with every kind of contrast to the first number, evoking the Thames from perhaps more of a pre-Industrial standpoint, and seeking from its fair stream the inspiration of lovely visions, a quietness of soul and depth of mind. Most of the vocal line glides gently too in a stepwise motion, *Adagio tranquillo*, in a sostenuto cantabile. The piano part is meticulously pedalled through its initial thirteen bars of pedal B flat, a kind of flattened supertonic which then drops stepwise to the low A. The opening looks like a slowly arpeggiated B flat major chord, with Baroque acciaccaturas of sharpened thirds, unfolding in support of the long-sustained vocal phrases, and echoing the final vocal motifs of the words 'come to me', and 'flowing' (at the *meno mosso)*. A similarly Baroque spread of the A major chord rises up in to the high treble above a B flat bass. Flute and clarinet tones alternate in the lovely accompaniment, figures briefly resting the voice between verses. And in the setting of those words

> Till all our minds for ever flow
> As thy deep waters now are flowing,

which commence with a long slow scale-wise descent, one is irresistibly reminded of the Cello Concerto as the line turns back and ascends again (Ex 1.17c).

Ex. 1.17c

From the B flat we move to the G minor of the anonymous 'Wapping Old Stairs', and again the semitonal bite of acciaccaturas informs the accompaniment in its strumming guitar style. The words run on that constant theme of sea-songs – the inconstant sailor. At its first performance it was accurately defined as 'a wry half-teasing complaint of the jilted girl' from Wapping. Above the piano's *una corda* with an expressive *mezza voce* the singer has the rhythmic delight of teasing the hearer with alternations of two, sometimes three, crotchets within the unusual time signature of one minim per bar. When Molly gives the names of two of her Tom's inamorata, Susan and Sal, the accompaniment abandons the crushing seconds in favour of more widely spaced fourths and fifths, standing to hear his unkindness with sparser seventh chords. A rising appoggiatura, C sharp to D, which Purcell's generation would know as a Forefall, marks out Tom's own name and the tear with which she upbraids him. At a broadening out of the tempo, where Sal and Susan are named again, the emotion is forcefully underlined by the side drum in the orchestral version.

Blake's 'Holy Thursday' forms the main slow movement of the cycle which Christopher Palmer has suggested is virtually symphonic, beginning with a first movement of broad design on an important scale and following it with two contrasting intermezzi ('Glide gently' and 'Wapping Old Stairs'). The poem describes one of the Charity Children's services at St Paul's and Frank Howes reminds us how impressed was the composer Berlioz by such an event during his London visit in the Great Exhibition year. Christopher Hassall has cleverly linked the Thames of Wordsworth to Blake's picture of the Procession flowing into the high dome, like Thames waters. The accompaniment lilts in 6/4 time against the voice's more measured 2/2 (the children walking two and two), though the voice falls also into an occasional triplet pattern. Its interval in this first verse is principally the fourth, whilst the accompaniment features major seconds, eventually juxtaposing fourths and fifths as the music descends into the bass. The piano's melodic phrase which links the first two verses is given to the french horn most memorably in the orchestral scoring (Ex. 1.17d):

Ex. 1.17d

The marking now changes from the *Lento* of the first verse to *Maestoso* of the second, the piano assuming the voice's 2/2 time. Adopting something akin to the dotted rhythmic style of the Baroque French Overture, the piano writing here takes on the sweeping arpeggiations, rising scale patterns and trillings of harpsichord playing. There is more movement in the vocal part as it takes in quavers and dotted patterns and leaps across broader intervals of fifths, sevenths and octaves, all underpinned by the regular processional pace.

Another two-bar interlude of falling fourths separates the end of the second from the beginning of the third verse, where the accompaniment initiates a further two bars of yet another type of figuration, the pulse marked as regularly as before, but decorated by runs passing upwards from left to right hand. These are the undercurrents stirring that 'mighty wind' which raises to heaven 'the voice of song', building to a *fortissimo* climax 'like harmonious thunderings the seats of heaven among'. The orchestration introduces the angelic harp colour to underscore the final words 'Then cherish, pity, lest you drive an angel from your door'. Oboe and flute echo the voice's last roulade, the glint of a glockenspiel touched in to the final *pianissimo* string chords.

Number 5, 'The Contrast', sets a Charles Morris poem of 1798 which, in Christopher Palmer's symphonic scheme, might be seen as the main Scherzo. The poet compares the Londoner who is bored in the country with its rural calm and solitude, preferring the hurly-burly of the seething masses, and the promiscuous birds flirting in their bucolic groves, when one might dally amongst London's 'good grove of chimneys'. As Christopher Palmer remarks, 'The coda, one of Walton's funniest inventions, seemingly looks back to those pre-war, high society London days when "devils" (in female guise) were in plentiful supply.' As the poet concludes:

> I know love's a devil, too subtle to spy,
> That shoots through the soul, from the beam of an eye;
> But in London these devils so quick fly about,
> That a new devil still drives an old devil out.

For this London thesis Walton's accompaniment is all staccato, sometimes broken chord patterns in single notes shared by the hands, sometimes in contrary motion in two voices or else in two octaves. The singer's enthusiasm is heightened by the use of baroque style ornament on the word 'enraptured' (Ex. 1.17e) such as Tippett and Britten had developed. In the orchestration Walton even adds trills and mordents to the interlude which links to the second verse, left plain in the piano version, but slightly glittering in the woodwind.

Ex. 1.17e

To enhance the ironic stance of the Country verse, the singer is directed to exaggerate with *portamento* and a soulful expression by the word '*noiosamente*'. The yawning, punning reference to composing here (Ex. 1.17f) could be an autobiographical *cri de coeur*:

> But the country, Lord help me! sets all matters right,
> So calm and composing from morning to night.

Ex. 1.17f

Walton remarked in an interview with Tony Palmer that, once confined on Ischia he composed, principally because there was nothing else to do!

Trilling strings initiate the thought of a good grove of chimneys, the bassoon plaintively colours the idea of Cupid finding a man out in the country, the harp's arpeggios accompanying the 'poor tortured victim'. The high treble toccata 6/8 patterns in the piano for those 'London devils' are heightened in effect by flute and xylophone.

The whole of the last page is 'white-note' diatonic; the voice, rising through the mixolydian mode, the tempo accelerating, the dynamic gradually softening to a pianissimo parlando as 'a new devil still drives an old devil out'. C major is finally asserted *fortissimo* on dominant and tonic by the accompaniment. This coda ranks high in Walton's humorous musical moments.

'White-note', too, is the music for the opening of the song cycle's quicksilver Finale, the french horns barking out the ostinato two-bar bass figure, G-A-E-G-D-E, as we ring the bells of London town. Using the traditional nursery-rhyme motif of 'Oranges and lemons', Walton sets a longer version of the text as found in the 1810 publication *Gammer Gurton's Garland*. In this are named a good many more bell towers, and the chopper of the singing-game with its bloody imagery is omitted. The rising and falling, however, in the old rhyme of 'Gay go up and gay go down' is well mirrored in the hiccupping vocal style and its acciaccaturas (Ex. 1.17g). Twinkling accompaniment patterns in chains of rising and falling thirds sustain in the piano to produce chords of the eleventh.

Ex. 1.17g

The numerous textual repetitions draw from the composer many adroit key changes, the palette of woodwind colours shading the kaleidoscopic scoring. Additionally, Walton employs rhythmic augmentation for:

> Old father bald-pate
> Say the slow bells of Aldgate

Here the bite of ninths in the resonating piano chords is enhanced by the tubular bells of the orchestra, whilst the elongated rhythm-values are further enlivened by the syncopation of a 5/4 accentuation. The introduction of the trumpet heralds further augmentation at 'I do not know, says the great bell of Bow', where the greatly broadening tempo and the sinking of the vocal *tessitura* is orchestrally reinforced by trombones and the vibrant crash of the tamtam. Then into the final straight for a last 'Gay go up' – the same music as before, the light tintinnabulation of the diatonic quaver patterns pedal-sustained over a dozen bars. The fourth modal note, C, is then sharpened, as the pealing bells of London Town dissolve into a resolving chord on G, in a triumph of tonal celebration.

Notes

1. The *printed* copy of the Litany, however, is marked 1917.
2. The short-lived William Hurlstone had set the Fletcher, though as a boy Walton would know it as set for Anglican use to Gibbons' madrigal *The Silver Swan*.
3. That inveterate Shakespeare setter, Roger Quilter, did not choose these particular words until 1951.
4. Arthur Somervell set the same text for the Leeds Festival in 1895. Robin Milford also took it later for a work completed in 1950, also requiring tenor and soprano soloists and female chorus.
5. In former times Walton had difficulty in coming to terms with the rising fortunes of his younger colleague – even going so far as to brandish his (Walton's) cheque stubs at him as proof of his superior commercial viability.
6. 'Crowd' is a medieval word for a fiddle.

2 Sacred Music
John Coggrave

Walton's musical life began in the church in Oldham where his father was choirmaster. To judge from his comments to Tony Palmer in the television presentation *At the Haunted End of the Day*, his lasting memories were of being rapped on the knuckles for faulty singing.[1] However unpleasant the experience, his time there laid the foundations for his later choral music. Later in the same interview he attempted Marcello's anthem *O Lord Our Governor* which he had been required to sing on entry to the Christ Church Choir School at Oxford. There he was steeped in the Anglican choral tradition which then consisted largely of nineteenth-century works which displayed solid craftsmanship even when they lacked any particularly distinctive melodic or harmonic invention.

In 1932, while wrestling with a seemingly intractable First Symphony, Walton wrote to Hubert Foss about his first compositions:

> First signs of composition 'Variations for violin and pf. on a chorale by J.S.B' didn't progress [like his latest composition] more than a dozen bars. Not very interesting and wisely decided to stop. However broke loose again about 13 and wrote two 4-part songs, 'Tell me where is fancy bred' and 'Where the bee sucks'. After that, fairly went in for it and produced about 30 very bad works of various species, songs, motets, Magnificats etc.[2]

His musical experience as a choral scholar was like that of Geoffrey Bush, once a youthful chorister at Salisbury Cathedral, who is quoted as follows by Christopher Palmer in a sleeve note to Conifer's recording of Walton's Sacred Music:

> Music was around us all the time; we absorbed it as children absorb a foreign language when they live abroad, effortlessly. We did not need to be taught, for instance, as some first-year harmony students at university have to be taught, the normal spacing of 4-part chords; we knew which was the right and which the wrong way just from the look of the page.[3]

This familiarity may go some way to explain the astonishing maturity of Walton's first published choral setting, *A Litany*, to words by the Jacobean poet Phineas Fletcher, dated Easter 1916 (though an erasure on the manuscript indicates that the Christmas of 1915 had been the first indication of the compositional date).[4] It is an extremely accomplished work for a schoolboy of fourteen. Michael

Kennedy has confessed that the cliché 'bitter-sweet' is inevitable in any discussion of Walton's distinctive melodic and harmonic idiom and its persuasive presence in this brief motet is, surprisingly, more prophetic of his later style than in subsequent instrumental compositions such as the Piano Quartet and the first (and later withdrawn) String Quartet.[5] Walton's musical experience was not limited to Victorian anthems; we know that Hugh Allen, the organist of New College, had played a piano reduction of *Petrushka* to the young chorister and that when on holiday in Oldham Walton had, according to his brother Noel, made a 'horrible din' by playing through *Le Sacre du Printemps* and Bartók's *Allegro Barbaro*.[6]

Mendelssohn, Wesley, Stanford and Parry were not the only composers who were being assimilated. Perhaps his experience in the choir had given him the assurance that in the task of writing a choral setting his inner ear could be trusted to find his own voice regardless of other contemporary models, whereas the early chamber works had to rely more heavily on stylistic influences such as Ravel, Bartók and Schöenberg.

Throughout his life other choral compositions of all kinds were invited and sometimes entertained but never proceeded with. Sacred settings might have included an oratorio on the subject of Moses and Pharaoh (another *Israel in Egypt* in fact), other *Te Deums* and settings of Psalms. The projected one of *Psalm 150* with organ and brass would have made a fascinating comparison with the third movement of Stravinsky's *Symphony of Psalms*.[7]

Although one thinks of Walton as primarily an orchestral composer, his published works begin with a choral setting and his last projected work before his death in 1983 was for the 150th anniversary of the Huddersfield Choral Society in 1986. On 7 March 1983 he telephoned Owain Arwel Hughes, the Huddersfield conductor, to accept the commission for a *Stabat Mater*. Two days later he died.[8] Earlier in the year he had told Alan Frank that he was studying Palestrina, who had bored him in his choirboy days but now delighted him.[9] What new development the *Stabat Mater* would have shown is conjectural, but a combination of a study of Palestrina together with recollections of one of Walton's favourite composers, Rossini (whose own *Stabat Mater* is a masterpiece of Italian operatic sacred music, as well as a possible study both of the versions by Verdi in his *Four Sacred Pieces* and by Poulenc as recently as 1960) leads us to speculate on one of the lost possibilities of twentieth-century music.

Walton's musical preferences are fairly clear; like his friend Constant Lambert he preferred English, French, Russian and Italian music to the Germanic tradition. For both of them the Wagnerian *melos* was something to be shunned (Walton claimed that he contrived to sleep when taken to a Wagner performance). But in other than musical matters he was a man who guarded intensely his emotional privacy; nothing that one reads about him either in the biographical accounts already written by Michael Kennedy and Susana Walton or in the many reminiscences scattered in the writings and reported conversations of friends and acquaintances such as Osbert and Sacheverell Sitwell, Constant Lambert, Spike

Hughes, Roy Campbell, Alice Wimborne, Alan Frank and Hubert Foss gives any hint that religion had any place in his life; in fact he wrote disparagingly on several occasions of his dislike for the liturgical texts he was setting.

Walton made clear his attitude towards musical idiom and style when he said that he was a romantic composer with a strong preference for classical structures. His orchestral and instrumental music bears this out, though in the second half of his life this led to increasingly deprecating comment from critics who felt that he had not kept up with the times – the dreaded phrase 'the mixture as before', once used in a purely descriptive and quite non-judgmental sense by Desmond Shawe-Taylor after the first performance of the String Quartet in 1947 – which became increasingly irksome to him as a sign of his relegation to the class of epigones among composers.[10]

From first to last his idiom reflected his very personal eclecticism. Bartók, Stravinsky (especially the Stravinsky of *Petrushka*), Ravel and, among *Les Six*, Honegger and Poulenc with their very different idioms (sometimes brutally abrasive in the case of Honegger, elegiac and nose-thumbingly flippant in that of Poulenc), together with the all-pervading lyricism of nineteenth-century Italian opera, with Rossini as a model of scintillating brio, seem to me to be the outstanding influences. Add to these Elgar's mixture of melancholy and *nobilmente* dignity (a composer whom Spike Hughes discovered was much admired by the young Walton when they listened to his Second Symphony together in the early Twenties), which comes out strongly in his ceremonial marches, together with more than a hint of Delius (as Christopher Palmer has pointed out in his book on that composer and his influence[11]) and one is left with a seemingly disparate collection of admirations and influences which nevertheless coalesce into an extremely personal style, one at least as distinctive after the hearing of a few bars as those of Elgar, Vaughan Williams, Holst or Delius, to name but four of his contemporaries. He discovered his personal voice very early – some of the more reflective movements in *Façade* have already that note of melancholy nostalgia which permeates his later slow movements – and the crackling brio with its syncopation and displaced accents is likewise there from the start. What does mark a certain division is the difference between the music which seems to have come from deep personal roots (even if in response to commissions) such as the Viola Concerto, First Symphony and Violin Concerto, which seem to have been deeply influenced by his personal feelings for Lady Christabel Aberconway, Baroness Imma Doernberg and Viscountess Alice Wimborne respectively and those which are the works of a master-craftsman writing not in a different idiom but donning an appropriate mask of public celebrant. Not that there is a stylistic division as in the case of Aaron Copland, who wrote fine music in two completely different styles (the pan-diatonic popular ballets like *Appalachian Spring* and *Billy the Kid* and the serial-influenced music of *Connotations* and *Inscape*); rather, at least in the Coronation Marches, film music and some (not all) of the works for Church or Cathedral performance, there is a highlighting of the extrovert diatonicism that was only one element among others in more complex works such as the

First Symphony and *Belshazzar's Feast*. This can be seen in the opening of the First Symphony's finale and the march motif which follows the injunction to praise the god of gold. *Belshazzar's Feast*, his most considerable choral work, fits uneasily into the category of sacred music. Its huge public success in 1931 was not sufficient for its acceptance by the Three Choirs Festival as a piece suitable for performance in what was the accepted tradition of Festival works. It was obviously an overwhelmingly original masterpiece; the fact that its agonized lamentations and bloodthirsty rejoicings were the exact musical parallel of the ferociously vindictive texts from *Daniel, Psalms* and *The Book of Revelation* seems to have been lost on the festival organizers. Leaving it aside, there are some fifteen choral settings of religious texts, dating from 1916 to 1977:

1. A Litany: 1916
2. Carol: Make we Joy now in this Fest: 1931
3. Set Me as a Seal upon thine Heart: 1938
4. Secular motet: Where Does The Uttered Music Go?: 1945/6
5. Coronation Te Deum: 1952
6. Gloria: 1960/1
7. Carol: What Cheer?: 1961
8. The Twelve: 1964/5
9. Missa Brevis: 1965/6
10. Carol: All This Time: 1970
11. Jubilate Deo: 1972
12. Cantico del Sole: 1973/4
13. Magnificat and Nunc Dimittis: 1974
14. Antiphon: 1977
15. Carol: King Herod and the Cock: 1977

The pieces fall into three groups: settings of medieval carol texts in an idiom similar to that of Peter Warlock whom Walton had known in the Twenties; full-scale settings of liturgical texts; and treatments of poetic or biblical material. All were commissioned – Walton was always spurred by a definite invitation which produced in him the desire to write a crafted piece of work with specific aims and demarcations. A commission for a cello concerto lasting 30 minutes produced no quibbles about the time-span. (Stravinsky, equally professional, happily accepted the same limitations for *Apollon Musagètes*.) Walton was quick to say:

> Well, I'm a professional composer. I write anything for anybody if they pay me. Naturally, I write much better if I am paid in American dollars.[12]

The four carols which span 46 years of composition are delightful examples of neo-medieval pastiche, as invigorating and accomplished as Walton's neo-Elizabethan pastiche in his Shakespearian film scores. They are over in a flash but they dance and radiate a simple joy which is what carols should do.

Apart from a setting of lines from *The Song of Solomon* – *Set Me as a Seal upon thine Heart* – which was written in 1938 as an anthem for a friend's wedding and which only a dedicated allegorist could construe as a 'sacred' text (the Hebrew words being a totally secular erotic poem despite the interpretations of Rabbinical and Christian commentators), Walton's major choral work after *Belshazzar's Feast* of 1931 and *In Honour of the City of London* in 1937 was *Where Does the Uttered Music Go?* This was designed for performance at the unveiling of a memorial window to Sir Henry Wood at St Sepulchre's Church in Holborn on 26 April 1946.[13] But while quite willing to honour the dead conductor for whom he had already written a ceremonial fanfare to be played at a memorial concert, Walton was unhappy with the text that John Masefield, the Poet Laureate, had prepared for the occasion, saying that he would much rather write a piece for strings. His words to Wood's widow as reported by Michael Kennedy were:

> It is not possible, for me at any rate, to make a worthy work out of it. I am *loth* to make this decision as I have so much respect for Mr Masefield and the last thing I want to do is to offend or hurt his feelings.[14]

Whatever the further discussions, Masefield submitted a new poem. What the original submission would have been is unknown but it cannot be said that the text finally given to Walton was very inspiring. Alone among Walton's choral works it has a text of threadbare banality, a proof – if one were needed – that in a post-Romantic era the writing of public verse (such as Tennyson's *Ode on the Death of the Duke of Wellington*) is no longer an artistic possibility. Not that poor verse precludes the writing of good music; Elgar was able to rise above O'Shaughnessy's feeble efforts in *The Music Makers* and Newman's *The Dream of Gerontius* would hardly be remembered as poetry if it were not by a great writer in other genres, but at least these texts were representative of the idiom of the period – second-rate Victorian verse in fact. Masefield's poem is a tired pastiche of an earlier style. In spite of this, Walton succeeded in writing a grave celebratory motet.

The *Coronation Te Deum*, performed in Westminster Abbey on 2 June 1953, brought out Walton's total professionalism. He was invited to write both the setting and a march, *Orb and Sceptre*, for the ceremony in Westminster Abbey. In fact, in the Coronation year 1953 he became the virtual *de facto* Master of the Queen's Music. Sir Arnold Bax, who held the title, was a fine composer who had little inclination by that time (if he ever had) to provide examples of what Frank Howes, referring to Walton's contributions, called 'shatteringly apt displays of pomp and circumstance'[15] but who did write a march for the occasion which, coming after Walton's flamboyant contribution, has now been quite forgotten. Walton visited the Abbey on several occasions before the ceremony and paid careful attention to the sizes of choir and orchestra and their layout during the Coronation Service. Innumerable settings of the *Te Deum* would have been familiar since childhood, as would the *Magnificat*, *Jubilate* and *Nunc Dimittis* which he later set and which were then still regular features of Matins and Evensong, increasingly perhaps unfamiliar to any Christians of any denomination since the jettisoning of Cranmer's *Book of Common Prayer*. He may also have reflected on the structural problems involved in setting the text. Elgar, who wrote a *Te Deum* two years before the *Enigma Variations*, is said to have commented that it presented an ungrateful text to a composer as its alternations between ecstatic glorification and humble petitioning are such as to make difficult any extended musical sequences and developments. Given Walton's known habit of studying closely the scores of other composers when tackling a new work in a particular genre,[16] it is quite possible that he looked at the great nineteenth-century settings by Berlioz and Verdi who solved the structural problems in two very different ways. Berlioz, hoping that his setting might be played at the Coronation of Napoleon III, wrote a work lasting just under an hour which included antiphonal effects where organ alternated with full orchestra; Verdi confined himself to just over 16 minutes. Although his setting is much less spectacular he made great play with brass fanfares immediately before the section beginning 'Tu Rex Gloriae Christe'. Walton's coronation anthem, like that of Berlioz, also makes considerable play with alternating organ and orchestra and, like Verdi, has an exciting brass fanfare before 'Thou art the King of Glory, O Christ'. Sir Adrian Boult, who conducted at the Abbey Ceremony, said later that he thought the setting too pagan. Such unrestrained exultation was obviously not to the taste of a distinguished but highly reticent member of the musical establishment who on another occasion said that *Le Sacre du Printemps* celebrated the less desirable aspects of the season.[17] Walton himself wrote to Christopher Hassall of the work in progress with his usual detachment and habitual impropriety:

> I've got cracking on the *Te Deum*. You will like it, I think, and I hope he will too. Lots of counter-tenors and little boys Holy-holying, not to mention all the Queen's trumpeters and side-drum.

and the following day wrote:

> After a spot of bother with the 'Virgin's Womb' (the kind of trouble I always seem to get into – don't tell the Archbishop!) the *Te Deum* is complete and both full and piano scores dispatched. Quite a lot of work. It is not too bad for an occasional piece and should be right for the ceremony.[18]

It is a truly magnificent setting and captures to perfection the spirit of 1953 when in the immediate post-war years (which in many ways had been even more drab and dispiriting than the war years themselves), the Coronation of the young Queen was perceived as a heartening episode in English history. Watching and listening on the new television network at the time, many were thrilled with the exuberance and total mastery of the medium which were displayed. Walton's slightly depreciatory description of it somewhat underrates its success. If, inevitably, it lacks the inner tensions of his more personally inspired music, it can still take its place in a great line of English ceremonial anthems which puts it in the society of Purcell and Handel.

His other large-scale work, the *Gloria*, was written for the 125th anniversary of the Huddersfield Choral Society, the body which made under Walton the first recording of *Belshazzar's Feast*, and received its first performance in the November of 1961. Another non-liturgical and detached setting, by Poulenc, was first performed in January 1961, some ten months earlier. I owe to Dr Stewart Craggs the information that Walton had, in his own words, 'A lot of time for Poulenc' and once again speculate that he may have looked at his contemporary's score. But where Poulenc's setting is in various places proclamatory, cheeky and elegiac, Walton's is both more assertive and more anguished and quite without the gamin flavour which led Poulenc to say that in parts of his work he had in mind

> those frescoes by Gozzoli where the angels are sticking out their tongues, and also those serious Benedictine monks I spotted one day playing soccer.[19]

The text does not present such problems to a composer as that of the *Te Deum*. After an exultant opening, ascribing all praise and honour to God, comes a middle section of appeal to the incarnate and atoning Saviour to have mercy on the petitioners, after which exultation returns in the final praise of the Holy Trinity – a three-part structure which gives convenient alternations of mood and in the central section a clear invitation to use solo voices within the choral and orchestral web. The practical-minded Walton took advantage of the fact that at the same festival celebrations the Society was performing one of its special favourites, Elgar's *Dream of Gerontius*, with solo parts for tenor, bass and alto. Richard Lewis, John Cameron and Marjorie Thomas were accordingly at hand for both works. Walton wrote to the Society during its composition and after sending the opening section promised that it got better as it went on, a judgment with which I agree, though I disagree with Michael Kennedy when he writes in his *Portrait of Walton* that the invention simmers on a low light. If the opening ascriptions of praise do not match similar ones in *Belshazzar's Feast* the anguished middle section with solo voices proclaiming Christ's atoning sacrifice is Walton at his finest. Often in his music for solo voices Walton writes with the wide intervals which are the mark of his orchestral melodic phrases. It concludes with a magnificent swinging finale whose ultimate added 'Gloria' was perhaps inspired by Beethoven's similar addition at the end of the section in the *Missa Solemnis*.

The other liturgical settings comprise a *Missa Brevis, Magnificat, Nunc Dimittis* and *Jubilate Deo*. Settings of the Ordinary of the Mass in this century have been frequent, despite the trend towards an increasingly secular culture. Stravinsky, Janáček, Poulenc, Vaughan Williams and Kodály, among others, have all written Masses, either designed for or capable of liturgical performance, not to speak of such musical (if non-liturgical) sports as Bernstein's eclectic concoction. Their settings raise the question of the possible congruence of musical idiom in a post-Romantic era with a text which is rooted in a theological and devotional ambience, now increasingly remote from many listeners' experience. Indeed, the Mass settings are only one aspect of a problem which is going to become increasingly apparent in the next century: how a text which springs from a worshipping community which has found its central need for worship in a liturgical rite is going to maintain its impact and centrality in a secularist ethos. Earlier centuries with an accepted musical idiom did not experience this tension; hence Mozart's masses, which Stravinsky called 'rococo-operatic sweets of sin', were still perfectly acceptable to his contemporaries.[20] Austrian ecclesiastical decor and performance *were* operatic and no incongruity was discerned. Today, however, we have the problem of a composer being impelled to write in a style capable of immediate public comprehension but which may differ from that employed in his other works. Stravinsky solved the problem typically by deliberately seeking a new idiom for each and every work so that, far from writing a pastiche Mass in imitation of medieval modes, he merely continued the practice of choosing and then dominating an earlier model, in this case Machaut, as he had with Bach, Tchaikovsky, Beethoven, Rossini and Mozart in the Piano Concerto, *Apollo*, Symphony in C, *Jeu de Cartes* and *The Rake's Progress*. Similarly Vaughan Williams in his *Mass in G Minor* eschewed the element of folk-song idiom which had always been present in his work and drew from another inspirational stream, the Tudor sacred music which had also formed part of the totality of his idiom. Walton was quite capable of producing enjoyable Elizabethan pastiche as his Shakespearian film scores show but in the *Missa Brevis* he comes close to the spirit which marks Poulenc's work after his return to the Catholic faith and practice. It is an extremely concentrated work – the Credo is omitted and seven minutes suffice for the Kyrie, Sanctus, Benedictus, Agnus Dei and Gloria. This last, placed as it is in the Common Prayer sequence necessitated by its commission for performance in Coventry Cathedral, enables Walton to move from the austerity of the earlier sections to a vigorously joyful conclusion in which the organ makes its only contribution, something denied to a setting of the Roman liturgy which has musically to fade out with the pathos of the Agnus Dei.

Walton wrote scathingly about the text in a letter to Alan Frank during its composition:

> I'm also on to the Missa Brevissima. I doubt if there will be more than 8 to 10 minutes of it. Remembering the boredom I suffered as a dear little choirboy, I've made it or am making it as brevissima as poss. It should be v. popular among Communion takers. But how uninspiring are the words![21]

All the more surprising is the effect of simple devotional concentration which is heard in its cool and balanced austerity.

As a chorister Walton must have sung in innumerable performances, of the *Jubilate Deo, Magnificat* and *Nunc Dimittis* at Matins and Evensong. Perhaps it was a similar memory of overexposure that prompted another dismissive comment to Frank some nine years later when engaged on a new commission to set the last two for performance in Chichester Cathedral:

> How I dislike the words of Mag. & Nunc, most uninspiring. But as the queer dean has been very generous, I feel I must try to do something at least respectably good.[22]

After these dismissive comments one might expect, not a perfunctory setting – that would not fit with Walton's professionalism – but perhaps one that failed to match the ebb and flow of the text. But in both the result is very satisfying; in the *Magnificat* the contrast between the exultation and the consolation is managed perfectly; in the *Nunc Dimittis* the words of a tired old man who has finally been vouchsafed his hoped-for vision is also rendered with a sure insight – (did Walton know Eliot's poem, *A Song for Simeon?*) – the music catches perfectly the slow and rather painful utterance of the old visionary, and both pieces illustrate what is a constant feature of all Walton's settings of words, whether in sacred or secular contexts: his sensitivity to the spoken rhythm and cadence of the speech. In a letter written to his librettist Christopher Hassall, during the composition of *Troilus and Cressida*, Walton expresses pleasure in Alan Frank's judgment that he showed acute responsiveness to the text.[23] In this he differed totally from Stravinsky who quite explicitly claimed the right to override pronunciation and speech patterns, regarding syllables as the foundation of his musical structures, or even Britten who – surprisingly for a composer with a wide knowledge of English poetry – could be insensitive to verbal inflections if intent on carrying out a musical cadence. (A case in point would be the emphasis on 'the' in the line 'In the cool air to sit and chat' in the Charles Cotton poem which comes at the beginning of the *Serenade for Tenor, Horn and Strings*.) Walton had little of Britten's omnivorous interest in poetry; his texts were either established ecclesiastical ones or, as in *Anon in Love* and *A Song for the Lord Mayor's Table*, were chosen for him from standard anthologies by colleagues like Christopher Hassall. Indeed, in the case of *Belshazzar's Feast* he is on record as saying that he was taken aback by Osbert Sitwell's belief that in choosing this episode from *Daniel* he would be setting something familiar to everyone. He claimed that he had no idea of the story save for a vague memory that someone had been sent out to eat grass. How much of this is an example of Walton's protective self-mockery is open to question; what remains is the evidence everywhere of his wish to fit the musical phrase to the verbal cadence. The *Magnificat* is a case in point. In many Magnificats the word 'generations' is equally apportioned between the musical accents. Not so in Walton's setting; the third syllable leaps out in the musical phrase just as it does in the spoken word.

The other major settings (leaving aside the *Jubilate* and *Antiphon*) are the *Cantico del Sole* and, finest of all in its penetration of Auden's admittedly difficult but stimulating text, *The Twelve, an Anthem for the Feast of any Apostle*, which inspired one of his finest choral pieces. The idea for the anthem came from Dr Cuthbert Simpson, Dean of Christ Church Cathedral. Walton's letter to Alan Frank describes its genesis:

> Wystan Auden sometime last year at Oxford let himself and me in for writing an Anthem for Ch. Ch. Choir. He said he must have been in his cups! Anyhow a few days ago what he calls 'this bloody anthem' arrived, so I suppose I must do it. It is a somewhat obscure and difficult-to-set text . . . [and a few days later] . . . difficult to keep from being difficult to sing and I know b***** all about the Organ![24]

The result was Walton's finest short occasional choral work. The text is eminently settable – not great poetry certainly but, as Auden has argued in his prose commentaries on writing for music, the richest poetical texts such as Shakespeare's sonnets are simply self-defeating as musical offerings. Auden had had plenty of experience as librettist to Britten, Stravinsky and Henze and knew how to provide the kind of high camp libretto which in this half-century is perhaps the only alternative to the drab or the impossibly grand manner.

Auden has some interesting speculations on the problems of writing words for music in an age when the 'drab', in C. S. Lewis's sense, is the only possible style for most poets. His attitude towards a possible speech for contemporary poetry is expressed by these lines from *We Too Had Known Golden Hours*, written in 1950:

> . . . And would in the old grand manner
> Have sung from a resonant heart,
> But, pawed-at and gossiped-over
> By the promiscuous crowd,
> Concocted by editors
> Into spells to befuddle the crowd,
> All words like Peace and Love,
> All sane affirmative speech,
> Had been soiled, profaned, debased
> To a horrid mechanical screech.
> No civil style survived
> That pandemonium
> But the wry, the sotto-voce,
> Ironic and monochrome . . . .[25]

Auden's solution to the problem of his own provision of words for music is contained in his T.S. Eliot Memorial lecture entitled *The World of Opera*.[26] It throws an interesting light on his approach to a commission for a sacred anthem:

> Judging by the poetry they have written, all the modern poets whom I admire seem to share my conviction that in this age poetry intended to be spoken or read can no longer be written in a High, even in a golden style, only in a Drab one, to use these terms as Professor C.S. Lewis has used them. By a Drab style I mean a quiet tone of voice which deliberately avoids drawing attention to itself as Poetry with a capital P, and a modesty of gesture. Whenever a modern poet raises his voice, he makes me feel embarrassed, like a man wearing a wig or elevator shoes.
> . . . For non-dramatic poetry this raises no problem; for verse drama it does. In writing his verse plays Mr Eliot took, I believe, the only possible line. Except for a few unusual moments, he kept the style Drab. I cannot think, however, that he was altogether happy at having to do this, for to perform in public is, as we say, 'to put on an act'; this a High style can unashamedly do, but a Drab style has to pretend it is not 'making a scene'. What I have tried to show you is that, as an art-form involving words, opera is the last refuge of the High style, the only art to which a poet with a nostalgia for those times past, when poets could write in the grand manner all by themselves, can still contribute, provided he will take the pains to learn the *métier* and is lucky enough to find a composer he can believe in.

Charles Williams, a now somewhat neglected writer greatly admired by Auden, is the model for much of the text. In fiction, historical exposition and verse he adumbrated a vision of Christendom as an incarnational entity which announced a new vision of the union of the divine and human. Auden had been deeply impressed and imitated Williams's poetic idiom in poems like *Memorial for the*

City in 1945 and testified that Williams's *Descent of the Dove* (a history of the work of the Holy Spirit in the Church) had been decisive in his own intellectual and spiritual development. The vision of a community charged with world-regeneration in defiance of all hitherto accepted systems and, in that commission, regarded by its contemporaries as hardly worthy of intellectual credence, but which after persecution became the accepted metaphysical, doctrinal and ethical code for our civilization appealed to Auden. Having accepted a Marxist/Freudian ethos as the true diagnosis of the ills of personal and public life in the 1930s Auden, from the 1940s onwards, had been drawn towards orthodox Christianity which in the 1960s could credibly be presented not as an unacceptable and outdated inheritance from a discredited past but as a counter-creed to current secularist values. Hence his attachment to Williams's books, which appear to be interesting but disturbing examples of what C.S. Lewis, his friend and admirer, called the cult of the 'Inner Ring'. In them Christianity becomes a new semi-agnostic cult and elements of Yeats's Society of the Golden Dawn, of which Williams had been a member, mix oddly with orthodox affirmations of the Nicene Creed.

Whatever Walton's puzzlement when presented with the text, he produced a brilliantly constructed anthem whose three-part structure echoes the wonder and darkness of Auden's first section, through the dragging petitions of the second to the cheerful celebration of the third. Internal rhymes are laced throughout the prose text (with somewhat unfortunate reminiscences of Tolkien's *Lord of the Rings* in its references to 'The Dark Lord') but they afford Walton convenient points for musical demarcation and stress. Whatever his bafflement at this rather esoteric commission he provided a tense and invigorating setting.

This is perhaps more than can be said for his last major choral commission in 1973 (leaving aside the contemporaneous *Magnificat and Nunc Dimittis*), the setting of St Francis of Assisi's *Cantico del Sole*, a hymn of praise to God's creation of the sun, moon, stars, wind, fire, earth and its fruits and death, written in response to a commission from Lady Mayer for the 1974 Cork International Choral Festival. Walton spoke of it during its composition with his usual reservations:

> The 'Cantico' has worked out as a deplorably dull and unexciting piece and one for which I need doctoring in the other sense.[27]

While allowing for his habitual self-depreciation and the undoubted feeling that in any case his creative powers were flagging (he wrote some years later to André Previn that he found that anything which he was writing had been done better before), it is fair to say that the piece is 'well-made Walton' without being particularly memorable.

No-one would claim that the works discussed are Walton's finest compositions. They are workshop productions of a very high quality – in most cases tailored for a public who could reasonably expect a piece which made an impact without requiring close study or repetition for its full appreciation and understanding. They are the work of an honest *kappelmeister* and sometimes (as in the case of the *Coronation Te Deum*, the *Missa Brevis* and *The Twelve*) accomplish the level of his larger works. They form an interesting and valuable addition to a choral tradition which shaped the young composer and is now perhaps coming to an end.

Notes

1. Palmer, T. (1981) *At the Haunted End of the Day* – 'Profile of the Life and Work of William Walton', transmitted on the ITN Network, 19 April.
2. Kennedy, M. (1989) *Portrait of Walton*, Oxford: OUP, pp. 7–8.
3. Palmer, C. (1989) Programme Note to Conifer Recording, 'William Walton – The Sacred Choral Music', CDCF 164.
4. Craggs, S. (1990) *William Walton: A Catalogue*, Oxford: OUP, p. 13.
5. Kennedy, M., op. cit., p. 51.
6. Kennedy, M., ibid., p. 8.
7. Craggs, S., *William Walton: A Catalogue*, Oxford: OUP, p. 163.
8. Craggs, S., ibid., p. 165.
9. Craggs, S., ibid.
10. Kennedy, M., op. cit., p. 135.
11. Palmer, C. (1976) *Delius – Portrait of a Cosmopolitan*, London: Duckworth, pp. 162–5.
12. Walton, S. (1989) *William Walton – Behind the Façade*, Oxford: OUP, p. 162.
13. Walton had good reason to be grateful to Wood who had included his Viola Concerto in his Promenade Season of 1929. In a television interview with Wood's widow Walton maintained that he had conducted the work himself since Wood would not have been able to negotiate the tricky rhythmic problems with their unpredictable syncopations. Lady Wood seemed somewhat indignant and replied that Sir Henry would have been a complete master of the score. Walton smiled sardonically.
14. Kennedy, M. (1989) *Portrait of Walton*, Oxford: OUP, pp. 127–8.
15. Howes, R. (1974) *The Music of William Walton*, Oxford: OUP, p. 176.
16. Such as his study of the three movements of Prokofiev's First Violin Concerto with their then unusual choice of tempi when writing his Viola Concerto and his virtual plagiarization of Roussel's *Suite in F* in the finale of his *Partita*.
17. Kennedy, M. (1987) *Adrian Boult*, London: Hamish Hamilton, p. 281.
18. Kennedy, M. (1989) *Portrait of Walton*, Oxford: OUP, p. 163.
19. Ramey, P. (1978) Programme Note to CBS recording 'Poulenc – Gloria and Stravinsky – Symphony of Psalms', CBS 76670.
20. Ramey, P. (1991) Programme Note to Sony Classical recording 'Stravinsky – Sacred Works', SM2K 46301.
21. Kennedy, M. (1989) *Portrait of Walton*, Oxford: OUP, p. 228.
22. Kennedy, M., ibid., pp. 262–3.
23. Kennedy, M., ibid., p. 173.
24. Kennedy, M., ibid., p. 227.
25. Auden, W. H. (1976) *Collected Poems*, London: Faber & Faber, p. 472.
26. Auden, W. H. (1968) *Secondary Worlds*, London: Faber & Faber, p. 102.
27. Kennedy, M. (1989) *Portrait of Walton*, Oxford: OUP, p. 259.

3   *Façade* – 'a Noise like Amber'
Kevin McBeath

It can be argued that *Façade* is a unique achievement in British music and in the world's repertoire of works for speaker and instruments. The work brought William Walton's name before the English public, earned him the reputation of an *enfant terrible* and marked the emergence from an apprenticeship of a great composer. He was to focus much attention on *Façade* from time to time throughout his life, even just five years before his death in 1983 when he prepared *Façade 2* for publication. The rhythmic exuberance of the words matches and is enhanced by the music as Walton's genius to parody manifests itself for the first time in some of the numbers. Another manifestation is Walton's gallic lyricism in several other numbers, which was to re-emerge initially in the slow movement of the *Sinfonia Concertante* and in *Siesta*, both works written within six years of *Façade*.

As the music is unique and unmatched as regards Walton's output, so are the poems to Edith Sitwell's. From her earliest essays and 'notes' on her own poetry, Edith Sitwell drew attention to her 'virtuoso exercises' in *Façade* – experiments into the effect upon rhythm and upon speed 'of the use of rhymes, assonances and dissonances . . . in the most elaborate patterns'.[1] Of the original musical settings Hugo Cole found it 'hard to believe that earlier notebooks were not raided'. The same might well be construed of some of the poems 'hurried into music during December 1921 and early January 1922', as intimated by Sir Sacheverell in an essay written in 1972 to celebrate the work's 50th anniversary.[2] 'The notebook habit became the keystone of her working life', as Victoria Glendinning revealed in her extensive biography *Edith Sitwell – a Unicorn among Lions*.[3] Dame Edith had been drawn on this subject by John Freeman in 'Face to Face' in 1959:

> 'Do you revise your work many times?'
> 'Oh yes – when I write poetry – you see, I mean I will sometimes have a whole notebook full of quite a short poem.'
> 'You're writing many drafts?'
> 'Oh yes – and sometimes I would put them aside . . .'[4]

Edith Sitwell's very first poem was published in the London *Daily Mirror* in March 1913 – a poem called 'Drowned Suns'. Already we encounter some of the images and symbols which were to pervade her work for the rest of her life –

gold, stars, bees and flowers; her 'patterns of the world, the images of wonder' as she described them to her father-confessor later in life.[5] 'The sun, the rose, water, gold, are invoked again and again', observed Stephen Spender, and John Lehmann and many others have written in admiration of this most personal characteristic. In re-reading the early poetry one also discovers how many of the Sitwell 'images' were drawn from life – from childhood, often spent at the homes of her grandparents on the Yorkshire coast; the seaside, the Pierrots, the tropical birds flying free in the gigantic aviary of Lady Louisa Sitwell; also from the ancestral estate of Renishaw in Derbyshire, her true home, with its ornamental lake, its fairy-tale 'Wilderness', large tapestries and the toy theatre from 'Mr Pollock's shop'.[6] A distant family home in Wales, called 'Troy Park', was never seen by Edith but 'the name had a great effect on me'.[7] Did she share Osbert's memory of a wretched Negro beggar selling flowers in the seaside resort of Scarborough, where she was born? It surely would have remained as exotic and profound an influence as anything she may have discovered in Rimbaud, to whose work she was early introduced by Helen Rootham, niece of the Cambridge composer and Edith's close companion of many years.[8]

Edith Sitwell's first book *The Mother and Other Poems* was printed in 1915 at her own expense – 500 copies, to be sold for sixpence. 'It cannot be bought for sixpence now', she was able to claim many years later; only occasionally is this slim collector's item offered for sale today. Her last book was published posthumously in 1965 – a collection of 'memoirs' which was to have been called 'More in Sorrow'; commenced late in life, and under strain, it was finally put together 'with scissors and paste' by Elizabeth Salter, and retitled 'Taken Care Of' – a phrase from the text preferred by the publishers. With each successive publication of the *Façade* cycle, the poet presents us with an amended table of contents – revisions, in much the same way as the 'entertainment' progressively developed with each new recital, though by no means identically. Over a period of 20 years, both texts and music were regrouped and reshaped in many ways. It is common, for instance, to encounter a phrase such as 'baskets of ripe fruit' appearing over and over again in unrelated sequences – even whole lines and couplets being transplanted from one poem to another. By 1950, Dr Sitwell (her damehood came in 1954) had chosen 33 of her early poems collectively to represent *Façade* on the printed page; previously there had been 9 in 1922, 19 in 1923, 27 in 1930, 18 in 1936, 23 in 1949; the 1950 edition was represented by a thoroughly revised cycle with an illuminating introduction by Jack Lindsay, Australian friend and champion.[9] There were still further reshuffles – but by 1950 Dr Walton (his knighthood was soon to come) had finally been persuaded by Alan Frank, his publisher, to allow the release of the settings which had been collected together for a 'wartime revival' in 1942 and an 'American Première' seven years later, but not without further attention to detail (*vide* 'Old Sir Faulk', 'Popular Song' and 'Something Lies' in recordings pre- and post-publication). At Constant Lambert's suggestion, the 21 settings – now considered musically sufficient – were sorted and divided into seven groups as a Parthian shot at *Pierrot Lunaire*. Walton, if

Lambert is to believed, had interpolated a passage from Schöenberg's melodrama into one of the early settings; indeed, the musical jokes in *Façade* are many, rivalling in number those to be detected – and suspected – in his later 'extravaganza', *The Bear*. Two thousand copies of a full score were printed the following year, 1951, by Oxford University Press and carried a reproduction of John Piper's striking design for a drop curtain, replacing Frank Dobson's original and an apparently 'lost' one used in Siena and Paris and elsewhere by Gino Severini. Walton dedicated the work to Constant Lambert. It is thanks to the efforts and enthusiasm of Lina Lalandi, Richard Baker, Sir Charles Mackerras and others that *Façade 2* appeared nearly 30 years later, assembled from discarded settings and 're-workings'. It, in turn, was dedicated to that adventurous *artiste*, Cathy Berberian – a supplement unprecedented in all twentieth-century music.

* * *

'Tell me Osbert – was it an advantage or a drawback to have a brother and a sister who were also writers?', asked Samuel Chozinoff for NBC Television during the early 1950s.

Osbert replied: 'It was a great advantage except that we were sometimes treated rather as if we were three branches on one tree instead of three separate trees; but we were able to work together in launching our works.' Edith, likewise, in a letter to her publisher expressed a preference that they not be lumped together – 'as if we were an aggregate Indian god'.[10] 'The Sitwells can all write. They are educated in words. They are interested in words; they have an affection for words', Arnold Bennett had long since declared.[11] Edith, 'in disgrace for being a female' as she once described herself, having failed to arrive as her eccentric father's anticipated 'son and heir', was the eldest. Sacheverell was the youngest, a 'miraculous baby from the void' in Osbert's eyes and his closest friend and companion, five years separating the ages of each sibling. 'You couldn't find a more devoted trio', declared the first-born.[12]

Accustomed to servants and domestics of every kind in an early, comfortable, baronial isolation, the Sitwell siblings found that independence in war-time London – when finally gained – had to be purchased in certain ways. Thus ensconced as adults – the brothers in Bohemian Chelsea, their sister lodged in a 'spartan flat' in Bayswater with her governess-turned-companion, Helen Rootham – income became a necessity rather than a birthright, and 'servants' such as gardeners and footmen belonged, mostly, to the past. But it is to a London 'charlady' (or was it 'housekeeper'? – recollections having conflicted over the years) to whom credit must be given for so instinctively dropping the right word at the right time . . . and in French too!

* * *

'Who is this Walton?' exclaimed Herman Scherchen into the silence of a score-reading panel in faraway Winterthür, perusing hopeful submissions for the first – official – ISCM Festival to be held in Salzburg in a matter of weeks. William Turner Walton, whose youthful *Quartet for Strings* had already been heard in London, was a 16-year-old choirboy from Lancashire when first introduced to the Sitwells, some years his seniors, particularly Edith. The young composer had been 'discovered' at Oxford in February 1919, just prior to his 17th birthday, by Osbert and Sacheverell and was presently inducted into the family circle. At age 17 we find Walton as dedicatee of a poem entitled 'What the Goosegirl said about the Dean', which appeared in Edith's 'Wheels' anthology later that same year (Dean Strong from Oxford, one wonders?).[13] By 19 Walton had come to live, and travel, with the Sitwell brothers and to be exposed unremittingly to the arts; by 21 he was hearing one of his own works in a foreign country. In the interim he had 'produced some rather bad works in various styles now mercifully in the fire', among which, one suspects, were some pages for a ballet that Sacheverell and Percy Wyndham Lewis had in mind.[14] *Dr Syntax*, however, like Percy's new painting of Edith, was never completed (for vastly different reasons) as far more pressing plans had taken over at Carlyle Square.[15]

'I wonder what punishment Ena has thought up for us this time?', an old Etonian friend of Osbert's asked his outgoing, party-going wife Viva King, mindful of the charades, impromptu plays, fancy-dress affairs and 'cabarets' he preferred to avoid from Belgravia to Bloomsbury. Mrs Robert Mathias ('Ena'), famous Mayfair patroness of the arts, friend of Goossens, Diaghilev and Lady Cunard – painted, as was Edith as a young girl, by Sargent – was to discover her New Year 'surprise' for 1922 at Osbert's house in Chelsea, and would soon demand a repetition for her own drawing-room in Montagu Square. At Carlyle Square, all other work including *Dr Syntax* had come to a halt; a projected 'Omnibus' of prose, poems and drawings at 'sixpence a run' was put aside – sadly, forever. Something 'new and original' had taken shape over Christmas 1921.

* * *

'Sometimes I wrote the poems and he put the music to them and sometimes it was the other way round, he showed me the rhythm I wanted. We made it bit by bit', Dame Edith told a small press contingent in a muted stateroom on the *Arcadia*, passing through the port of Melbourne, Australia, in April 1963. She was travelling in the joint care of a nursing sister and her Australian-born secretary-companion of later years, Elizabeth Salter – a near-fatal cruise, as it happened. And it was Elizabeth Salter, in her fine memoir *The Last Years of a Rebel* who confirmed Dame Edith's *modus operandi*: 'Willie gave me certain rhythms . . .'.[16] The dance measures in *Façade* would speak for themselves, though the majority of these were to come later – there was but one 'dance' to begin with, the

Hornpipe; the later *Fox Trot, Tango, Waltz, Polka* and *Tarantella* together providing the essence of what *Façade* represents today. Among the displaced settings we find a *March* and a *Gallop*, both happily preserved in an unpublished supplement, and a *Mazurka*, of which only fragments survive. A 'working page' illustrates how Walton scanned the poem for bar-lines (Ex. 3.1). It is an awkward poem to declaim to speed (Sir Sacheverell 'preferred the music to the poem') and seems to have enjoyed only a single try-out, in June 1926.

Ex. 3.1

Wind-sor   Bal - mor - al   high - er   feather-ed   pots

Dame Edith, at different times, recorded some of her *Façade* poems unaccompanied. 'The Wind's Bastinado', which she once described as a 'ghostly march tune', was originally 'No. 5', but for some reason abandoned. Her *Caedmon* record, made during an American visit in the 1950s, preserves an echo of what she may have remembered from 1922 (Ex. 3.2).

Ex. 3.2

This mel-on   Sir Mam-mon   comes out of   Ba-by-lon   Buy for a   pa - ta-coon   Sir you must buy.

Helen Rootham's translations into English of Rimbaud's *Illuminations*, though not published until 1932, would have been some years in the preparation.[18] Edith Sitwell's participation in this exercise may well have extended beyond the long introductory essay she provided for the book, and it is not surprising that we encounter some of her own favourite 'images' emerging from her companion's pages; blood, flowers, fire and gems, dreams, forests, colours, crystal. Rimbaud's 'beffrois' and 'cloches' become Edith's 'bell-towers', his 'clochettes' her 'bell-flowers'; similarly a 'white satin bouquet' in Rimbaud's *Fleurs* – through Helen – can be found in the *Tango Pasodoblé*. Many such 'rumeurs et visions' held great sway over Edith's imagination, and both Rimbaud and Rootham received abundant credit, acknowledgement and gratitude in much of her early work:

> Des chalets de crystal et de bois se meuvent sur des rails et des poulies
>   invisibles (Rimbaud)
> Castles of crystal and wood move on rails and invisible pulleys (Rootham)
> Castles of crystal,
> Castles of wood,
> Moving on pulleys
> Just as you should! (Sitwell)

Trams was in print long before *Façade* was ever contemplated, as were several others. John Pearson (*Façades*) quotes Walton on this: 'Edith had written a number of poems already which were calling out for music'. Ernest Newman must have enjoyed *Trams* at the New Chenil Galleries in April 1926, before it, in turn, was replaced by a trial *Mazurka*. 'The jolliest entertainment of the season', he concluded in the *Sunday Times*.[19] How did it scan?

Ex. 3.3

Cast-les of cry-stal,   cast-les of wood,   mov-ing on pul-leys   just as you should!

*   *   *

As stage-manager for the early performances of *Façade*, Osbert Sitwell appeared before the front curtain, which would soon rise to reveal an enormous painted face, to prepare his audience for a 'New and Original Musical Entertainment'; later, unseen, he would announce 'eight groups' of his sister's poems from behind a smaller face. 'You will meet strange people', he warned, not referring to the handful of nervous performers huddled behind the painted face (a representation of 'Venus', as Osbert explained, executed by the well-known sculptor Frank Dobson of Chelsea). To the majority of those present, 'Miss Edith Sitwell' ('perched presumably on a stepladder', remarked Percy Scholes of *The Observer*) was by now an established poet and known as the editor of the controversial arts annual, *Wheels*.

'If there had not been an Osbert Sitwell in modern London, it would have been necessary to invent one', proclaimed Beverley Nicols in one of his lively 'bouquets' of the Twenties.[20] A 'born impresario', Osbert had exhibited a flair for showman-ship from an early age: he had learned to dance the Hornpipe at three or four; had discovered a shy protégée in Frieda, the housemaid, who could entertain the family with a *Swiss Yodelling Song* and was able to provide a one-woman cabaret as a certain 'Mrs Haynesworth' for a political supper, to the delight of Lord Asquith. With his brother Sacheverell, he managed to provoke the post-war art connoisseurs of London into the correspondence columns with a challenging exhibition of modern French art. A keen ballroom-dancer, he soon discovered the Foxtrot and published one – a poem.[21] Foxtrots had crossed the Atlantic with The Original Dixieland Jazz Band, and were now the rage of London, from Osbert's club in Beak Street in 'The Black Mile' down to the Savoy, where he danced to 'The Havana Band' and was a close friend of the management.[22] Osbert Sitwell was soon to earn the sobriquet of 'The Charles B Cochran of the Muse' from no less a man of letters than Arnold Bennett: 'Osbert "presents" the family, and does it with originality'.[23] And it was Arnold Bennett to whom sister Edith had latterly dedicated *her* new book of poems called *Bucolic Comedies* containing, as she explained to him in a letter, 'a good many new poems, as well as the whole of *Façade*' – the fourth poem of which happened, also, to be a *Fox Trot*.

CONCERTS, &c.

ÆOLIAN HALL, Tuesday, June 12, 3.15 p.m.
OSBERT SITWELL
presents
MISS EDITH SITWELL and W. T. WALTON in FACADE,
A New and Original Musical Entertainment.
Tickets :—Usual Agents, usual prices.

24

Bucolic Comedies went on sale in April 1923 in good time for the advertised concert, an occasion for which texts could *not* be printed 'owing to copyright' (Gerald Duckworth's). *Façade as published* had by now grown from 9 titles the previous year – privately printed by the Favil Press – to 19, a total somewhat at odds with the '24 facets' advertised on a concert flier, or the 'twenty-eight Sitwell lyrics' endured with obvious impatience by Dr Scholes ('. . . let me say regretfully that it failed'.[25] 'Blanket press invitations' had not yielded much praise and as no copy of the printed programme seems to have survived, exactly what the 'half-filled hall' actually heard that afternoon remains something of a mystery. 'In the main', Sir Osbert Sitwell recalled in his famous autobiography many years later, 'the programme was identical' [to the January 1922 programme]. By this, he was almost certainly confusing recitals which occurred three years apart, during which time much had changed. Professor Stewart Craggs has put together an imaginative reconstruction, from all known sources, of this elusive musical landmark (see Appendix 2). It is of particular interest that his research has determined the first item on the programme: *Gardener Janus catches a Naiad.*[26]

*   *   *

'All this carry-on is just one big *Façade*', someone must have uttered in or around Carlyle Square (or was it Moscow Road?) towards the end of 1921.[27] Sir Osbert, rising to the defence of his sister, attributed the remark to 'a painter, with the side-whiskers of the period but with a name which, as it proved, has not attached

ÆOLIAN HALL

NEW BOND STREET, W.

———

Tuesday Afternoon, June 12th, 1923, at 3.15.

Poems by

EDITH SITWELL

Music by

W. T. WALTON

Curtain by FRANK DOBSON

———

Sengerphone	-	EDITH SITWELL
Flute	-	R. MURCHIE
Clarionet	-	P. DRAPER
Saxophone	-	F. MOSS
Trumpet	-	H. BARR
'Cello	-	A. GAUNTLETT
Percussion	-	C. BENDER

Conductor :

W. T. WALTON

Programme
Sixpence

itself to the epoch'.[28] Might this have been one Rowley Smart, knockabout friend of Roy Campbell, that adventurous South African poet, and one-time protector of Edith? Rowley, in his sudden rise from rough to rich, is described by Campbell as having grown side-whiskers ('We called him Lord Washmore . . . a really fine painter . . . a loyal friend . . . Later he became rich as an art teacher in the Midlands, and owned a car and a titled lady, who had previously owned the car . . .'). No, Sir Sacheverell, who seems to have had the last word on the matter, attributed it to 'our charlady'. All were delighted with this *mot juste* so obliviously uttered around the house, yet so synonymous with Cocteau's 'Parade' which they had all attended during Diaghilev's season at the Alhambra in 1919, with its 'bellowing megaphone' and 'fairground curtain' which had so impressed Sacheverell. Edith's poem 'Clowns' Luck', 'vaguely suggested' by 'Parade', presents the reader with a remarkable inventory of that ballet's surreal components, in addition to providing a rich source for a 'Scotch Rhapsody' to come. 'It is difficult to say which of us thought of the various parts of the production', wrote Sir Osbert a quarter of a century later. Curtain there certainly was, originally to screen the unsightly musical paraphernalia from the view of the invited guests; megaphone, to balance the speaking voice against the unforeseen clamour of the music . . . and some hot rum punch downstairs afterwards, to restore the faint-hearted.

*   *   *

'The pace was set, so to speak, with "Long Steel Grass" ', Sir Sacheverell recounts, remembering a 'haunting and sinister fanfare' which their young composer friend Walton had copied down 'note for note'. Walton's first visit abroad was 'in the spring of 1920' with his 'adopted, or elected' brothers each retaining his own impression of one particular adventure. Osbert, in *The Chapbook* for 1924, wrote:

> The life of Catania throbs and shrills noisily outside the hotel, for as befits the second largest, and far the richest, city in Sicily, in clamour it is second to none . . . . In among the tortuous lanes wandered ragged children buying prickly pears . . . or hurrying to find the fortune-teller whose trumpet could be heard in the distance. A young man, dark as a gypsy, he holds in one hand his trumpet, in the other a large glass bottle or square box full of clear water, balanced on the end of a wooden pole. You give him money and he presses a button. A small black devil, with horns and tail, made of celluloid or a similar substance, can then be seen diving through the water, and you are presented with a printed form which foretells the happenings of your life . . . .[29] (By kind permission of Frank Magro.)

For Sacheverell, the episode remained indelibly fascinating throughout his life. In *Sacred and Profane Love* (1940) he remembered *two* men – 'one playing a trumpet, the other carrying a hooded black box upon a stick' – further, 'a pair of small black imps, or devils, not more than two inches high' diving down through the water. Their trumpet call 'of peculiar and military import . . . spoke of spectral soldiers, moonlight sentries . . . and cats serenading upon tiles'. Later, in a broadcast, the same tune was 'portentous and wonderful', and in his farewell to poetry, *An Indian Summer*, published when his 80th birthday was approaching in 1977 – Sacheverell remembered again 'that magical fanfare'. His sister's poem, originally and coincidentally entitled 'Serenade for Two Cats and a Trombone', made its first appearance in *The Saturday Westminster Gazette* during September 1921; within four months it would be spoken to music, introduced by 'an itinerant fortune-teller's trumpet call' from Sicily:

Ex. 3.4

Dame Edith objected to the setting being published as 'Long Steel Grass' (its opening line): 'It is about a couple of cats, do you see, having a love affair. It is extremely impertinent of them to have altered it', not realizing, perhaps, that Sir William himself had supplied the contents page for the final score, in his own hand. 'In fact it is called "Trio for Two Cats and a Trombone" ', Dame Edith insisted, having meanwhile amended the word 'Serenade' to 'Trio'. 'None of these instruments actually appear in the score', quipped an early Walton historian.[31]

* * *

As has been well documented over the years, in programme notes and record sleeves the world over, the original intention behind *Façade* was to screen the performers from view, to create as abstract a presentation as possible of words and music, to raise the level of the speaking voice to that of another instrument in the small ensemble, and to avoid 'the inevitable blush-rose shame' which the presence of a reciter can entail upon an audience – a modesty no longer fashionable in recitals of *Façade* today.[32] As the loud-hailer had yet to be invented and amplification was in its infancy, a particular type of megaphone was selected for the purpose – the Sengerphone. But attempts fully to document the inventor, a certain 'Herr Senger', do not draw a clear picture of a musician/inventor who may have appeared as Fafner at the Metropolitan but not at Bayreuth. Was he, in fact, Herr Alexander Senger – actor-husband of Katerina Senger-Bettaque, who *did* sing at the Met (Wagner, to be sure) and whose voice is preserved in the famous 'Record of Singing'?[33]

Certainly, Barbara Cartland well remembered the 'Sengerphone', which, she reminded readers, was taken up by the Admiralty and used by sea captains for short orders from the bridge. Sir Osbert's long footnote on this elusive Swiss who lived in Hampstead and died in 1936, makes enjoyable, if sad, reading.[34] Herr Senger, along with Rowley Smart – together with an apparently lost 'sipario' from 1928 by Gino Severini – must, for the present, remain mysterious. His Wagnerian invention certainly gained for the Sitwells a reputation for trumpeting their poetry through London streets, *Façade* and company quickly becoming targets for caricature in the press and on the London stage. The Family Sitwell became 'The Swiss Family Whittlebot'[35] and their 'Wheels' became 'Cranks'. The *Sunday Express* felt that *Façade* had 'raised the status of the megaphone' which the 'bright young people' at university were quick to endorse.[36] An undergraduate Harold Acton could be heard declaiming from a windowsill to a supportive quad below, and Tom Driberg – with the help of Eric Walter White and others – collaborated on a 'Megaphone Concerto' not only as a 'homage' to Beethoven but also as a 'tribute' to Edith. Not to be outdone, Osbert Sitwell, from a rooftop in Chelsea, bellowed the arrival of ficti- tious guests to a respectable party – someone else's – being given nearby.

*   *   *

'. . . the perfect instrument of this performance'

(Sir Osbert Sitwell)

The arrival of a teenage Constant Lambert 'on Osbert Sitwell's doorstep' is difficult to pinpoint exactly from published information; his involvement in *Façade* may well have begun much earlier than is generally believed. He was born in August 1905 and was therefore 16 at the time of *Façade*'s first private recitals. It was in that year, 1922, that Lambert entered the Royal College of Music with a scholarship in composition and within a year or two was asking the Sitwell brothers to hear a performance of two of his songs – settings of Sacheverell's early poems 'Serenade' and 'The Moon' (otherwise 'The White Nightingale'). In an article for *The Monthly Musical Record* a few years later, Beryl de Zoete (joint- translator of *The Rio Grande* and *Belshazzar's Feast*) named several of Lambert's 'college' works which owed their existence to further Sitwell texts: an 'overture' *The Bird Actors* (Sacheverell); a symphonic poem *Argonaut and Juggernaut* and a song *Proud Fountains* (Osbert); and, perhaps most surprising of all, Edith's earliest poem *Serenade*, and – from 'Wheels' 1916 – *The King of China's Daughter*, misprinted somewhere along the way as *The Queen of China's Daughter*.[37] Evidence in private hands also reveals Lambert's later intention to set to music Dame Edith's most famous war poem *Still Falls the Rain*. 'Nothing could possibly give me greater real pleasure and happiness', came the message from Renishaw on 22 May 1946, 'it will be a deeply impressive and beautiful work on your part.'[38] Britten's 'Canticle III' appeared early in 1954 dedicated to the pianist Noel Mewton-Wood who had recently died. Lambert died two days before his forty-sixth birthday in 1951; however, no manuscript of *Still Falls the Rain* has come to light. His association with the Sitwells was immediate and lasting, as was his friendship with Walton, not quite three years his senior; in her autobiography Dame Edith referred to Lambert as her 'young and robust friend'. *Popular Song* bears the dedication 'For Constant Lambert' and Lambert, dedicatee of Walton's score, lived long enough to see his ghostly ostinato for 'No. 14' in print at last, and requiring all future performances to pause in his memory, to enable the cellist to retune.

* * *

The well-known soloist and ensemble-player Ambrose Gauntlett was *Façade*'s first cellist, in both the private performances of 1922 and the Aeolian Hall première the following year. In a letter to Stewart Craggs – at the time preparing his first Walton thesis in 1972 – Gauntlett reveals some surprising information, at other times on occasion 'speaking from memory', at other times quoting from his diary:

> The very first rehearsal for *Façade* took place at the Sitwell's house in Carlyle Square, Chelsea on Sunday 22nd of January 1922 – this is from a very dilapidated diary of mine – at 11 a.m. and 2 more rehearsals on the Tuesday January 24th.' [the date of the performance]

A little later, whether from diary or memory is not clear, Gauntlett writes:

> At the early rehearsals there were of course Sir William, Dame Edith, Constant Lambert and once or twice Eugene Goossens (Jun) looked in with an avuncular interest.[39]

* * *

'A fine 19th century town house' – 'Historic former Chelsea home of the Sitwells' – these were captions appearing in *Country Life* at different times.

'I hope that many of you will look round the house and inspect the small exhibition of family furniture and pictures which we have assembled in the drawing-room where the first performance took place on 24th January, 1922'; this was the invitation extended by Francis Sitwell on Tuesday 14 October 1986. On that evening, a plaque bearing the name of Sir Osbert Sitwell was unveiled near a doorway in Carlyle Square, SW3, by Her Royal Highness the Princess Alexandra. Under a protective marquee in the gardens opposite, a special celebration – with music, poetry, champagne and hot rum punch – marked the occasion. The poetry was, of course, the late Dame Edith's; the music, the late Sir William's; the Fifth Baronet Sir Francis Osbert Sacheverell Sitwell had died abroad these many years, a Companion of Honour, and the house had passed into other hands. Sacheverell, Sixth Baronet, was too frail to travel to London from his home in Northamptonshire to enjoy the tribute which his son Francis – Dame Edith's 'cheerful, unhaunted nephew' – had so imaginatively prepared. It was Sacheverell who, upon listening to his sister recite a new poem after dinner one night so long ago, had remarked 'You see this would sound much better if you had some music to it' – and they had all turned to face their unconvinced 19-year-old house-guest.[40] Sixty-five years had passed; outside No 2 Carlyle Square, Chelsea, 'Façade – An Entertainment' was given a unique reading by a special company of six reciters with The Park Lane Group, and with a *Prologue* devised with great theatrical skill by the Australian-born actress and musician Pamela Hunter, restoring early material which had long since been discarded.

* * *

'One of the wonder-works of the twentieth century' is how *The Sunday Times* heralded the completion of Sir Osbert Sitwell's autobiography *Left Hand, Right Hand* which he commenced on the eve of his 50th year in 1941, and completed on 29 March 1950. It was a massive work of nine books, published progressively between 1945 and 1950, in five volumes. His entertaining chapter on *Façade* has rightly been the source for all subsequent and responsible accounts.[41] In recalling the occasion of the first private performance, however, Sir Osbert refers to a 'sextet' of instrumentalists, the required complement in performances today. In a broadcast celebrating the composer's 75th birthday in 1977, Sir William remembered four only: 'clarinet, trumpet and drums, and cello – yes'. This he further confirmed in the Tony Palmer/Reiner Moritz profile 'At the Haunted End of the Day' for London Weekend Television in 1981.[42] 'So there we were – four musicians and myself, and Edith recited and Osbert sort of chipped in . . . a mixed reception; they thought *I* was off my head – *she* was off *her* head. But we persevered and decided to try a public performance at the Aeolian Hall . . . this time with six instruments, plus Edith and myself.' And now coming from a posthumous source (Edith Sitwell: see Appendix 1) though much closer to the times, the poet's own account would appear to set the record straight.

* * *

Neil Ritchie is a collector of Sitwelliana *sans pareil*, if we may borrow a phrase from Sir Osbert. His *Annotated and Descriptive Bibliography of Sacheverell Sitwell* is the standard reference in libraries around the world, as is his previous volume on Sir Harold Acton. Sir Sacheverell lived to witness this remarkably detailed compilation of his own work, which was published for the occasion of his birthday, 15 November 1987.[43] The book represents Ritchie's devotion of 15 years, researching and documenting the Sitwell *oeuvre*, of which he possesses a collection second to none in private hands. It extends – in the case of *Façade* – from letters, handbills and actual holographs of the poems (with, in Constant Lambert's hand, an occasional alteration!) to the rare and remarkable first edition of *The Legion Book*, 1929, which was limited to 100 copies, all in the gift of the then Prince of Wales, and which contains the first printing of *Scotch Rhapsody* (revealing two minor variations in text), along with the autographs of upwards of 100 of its famous contributors. Long retired from diplomatic life, Neil Ritchie continues to supplement his library and to devote himself to 'miscellaneous writings'. His 'FOOTNOTE TO FAÇADE' published in *The Book Collector*, Vol. 45 No. 2, Summer 1996, is an exciting addition to the chronology of the work, and is now reprinted here, with permission, as Appendix 1.

*　*　*

Details of the original typewritten programme appear in the chapter on *Façade* in the fourth volume of Sir Osbert's autobiography, *Laughter in the Next Room*. Sir Osbert relates that Mrs Robert Mathias ('Ena') 'was so pleased and stimulated by it' that a further production was given in her house two weeks later. This may well account for: (a) a shorter programme for Montagu Square, (b) the re-positioning of four titles, (c) Constant Lambert's 'assistance'.

Gauntlett recalls:

> The instruments for the first 2 performances, if I remember rightly, were five, Trumpet, Tymps, Clarinet and Sax, Cello and was it Flute? . . . For the performances in 1923, if I remember correctly, we had one more player . . . It was great fun doing the rehearsals and it took some time with Dame Edith (Edith in those days) to settle down with some of the more tricky rhythms through her trumpet or "Sengerphone" as it was named in the programmes and in fact, Constant Lambert eventually spoke some of the faster poems such as "Hornpipe". The Sengerphone was in fact a megaphone supported in such a way in the centre of a drop curtain so that all the audience saw was this round large hole – the front part of the megaphone. The speaker and players not visible.

Nowhere in the several accounts of the 1923 performance is there mention of Lambert having participated in any way; handbills, advertisements and reviews all attest to the singular delivery of her poems by Miss Sitwell herself: 'Miss Sitwell half spoke, half shouted'; 'One-note concert by Miss Sitwell'; 'Miss Sitwell was there, it is true, unseen to recite'. Constant Lambert came into his own in 1926, and became thereafter its interpreter *sans pareil*, as Sir Osbert wrote. Andrew Motion's triple biography *The Lamberts* clearly places Lambert's 'first performance' of *Façade* at the Chenil Galleries, Chelsea, in April 1926, a 'restructured and revitalised' *Façade* at which Ambrose Gauntlett did not assist.[44]

*　*　*

'Strange people,' Osbert had announced, 'Queen Victoria and Venus, Circe and Lord Tennyson.'[45] 'Strange glimpses of fate, of mortals and immortals,' he would later add. Of the mortals, 'Gordon Macpherson' was actually Edith's grandmother's gardener at Scarborough where she was born; 'Old Sir Faulk' was in reality a Colonel Hume, whose young daughters would visit for nursery tea when Edith was a girl; two of Edith's aunts were the 'Tall Pagodas' in *By the Lake*; Sir Joshua Jebb was not an admiral, but a military engineer and surveyor of prisons, reminding Edith perhaps of the 'good works' undertaken by her forbear 'The Wicked Lady Conyngham'. 'Marvellous things are constantly being revealed,' observed Paul Driver in a detailed re-evaluation of *Façade 1* and 2, '. . . strange objects, vistas, emotions.'[46] But mention of 'Circe' in Osbert's original Aeolian Hall introduction is mystifying, for there is no provision in *Façade* today for this legendary sorceress. In the *Hornpipe*, Lady Venus, Lord Tennyson and Queen Victoria are subtly introduced by Britannia, the first of Walton's many brilliant 'asides'. But Circe? 'Queen Circe, the farmer's wife at the Fair' belongs to one of Edith's *Bucolic Comedies* called 'The Higher Sensualism'. Could this have been one of *Façade*'s early casualties? It is curious that Gerald Cumberland in his review for *Vogue* in July 1923 quotes two lines from this very poem, while Percy Scholes, somewhat less enthusiastically in *The Observer*, chooses as illustration the closing lines from another poem 'Fête Galante'. Had these diligent critics acquired 'Bucolic Comedies' well in advance of the recital, for they were given no help from the printed programme? Could it be that 'Queen Circe', 'Fête Galante' and others were in fact given at Aeolian Hall and – like so many early settings – subsequently abandoned? Known to be missing today are the scores for 'The Wind's Bastinado', 'Small Talk II', 'Switchback', 'Bank Holiday I and II', 'Springing Jack', 'Ass Face', 'Trams' and a complete 'Mazurka'. 'Gardener Janus' ('Baskets of ripe fruit') re-appeared in 1979 – but from manuscript or memory? The poem 'Trams', though written before 1916, was not spoken to music until 1926, when it was given a solitary hearing – withdrawn, one gathers, as being 'too derivative' and excluded from the *Collected Poems* of 1930.[47] The short jingle was an affectionate paraphrase of those lines, quoted earlier, from Rimbaud: 'in some ways my closest spiritual relation'. Until a documented chronology of all early performances is made possible, we must remain in ignorance of certain numberings and alterations on the surviving manuscripts, such as 'Herodiade's Flea' as 'No. 11', and how 'Numbers 7, 8, 9' came to be re-positioned as '4, 5, 6' in April 1926.

*   *   *

'How much would we recognise of the original version . . .? Not very much', concludes Michael Kennedy in his careful chronology of *Façade* from 1921 to 1979.[48] The 18 'numbers' given before a chattering assemblage of 'painters, musicians and poets' (16 poems to music, with an 'overture' and 'interlude') bear little resemblance to the score which Sir William Walton allowed finally to be published.

Mᴿ C. PITT, AS CHARLY WAG.

Between the first private 'soirées' and ultimate printing(s), *Façade* had undergone constant change; 'There were a number of experimental performances', writes John Pearson in his splendid volume *Façades*.[49] No two recitals – private or otherwise – appear to have been the same, with the result that many choice and unusual settings were put aside in favour of new ones, and others – lamentably – lost. A possible 45 individual numbers existed between 1921 and 1928, and only 21 chosen for publication by a composer unwilling to witness, so finally in print, a work which had suffered so many revisions. In later years he was to be observed still 'tinkering' with his masterpiece, cutting two bars here, putting trumpet up an octave there.[50] *Façade*, if totally restored today, would take twice as long to perform; Pamela Hunter's recording comes closest to this ideal, with her dedicated tribute to a completed cycle which she has called 'Something lies beyond the Scene'. Walton's original manuscripts (those so far salvaged) are lodged in the USA, with one or two in private hands. The remainder? – 'auctioned off', the composer once confided to a persistent enquirer.[51]

Acknowledgements

For their kind co-operation, I have to thank Francis Sitwell, Frank Magro, Neil Ritchie, Stewart Craggs, the Arts, Music and Performing Arts Library of the State Library of Victoria, the Performing Arts Museum of the Victorian Arts Centre, Oxford University Press and my fellow enthusiasts Naomi Woods, James Murdoch and James Collins.

Notes

1.   Sitwell, E. (1954) Sleeve notes for *Façade*: Decca LP recording LXT 2977.
2.   Sitwell, S. (1972) '*Façade*' deluxe edition of the score, Oxford, OUP.
3.   Glendinning, V. (1981) *A Unicorn Among Lions,* Weidenfeld & Nicholson.
4.   BBC 'Face to Face' interview: Dame Edith Sitwell with John Freeman (May 1959); also available on Pye LP record FTF38502.
5.   Sitwell, E. (1970) *Selected Letters,* ed. J. Lehman and D. Parker, Macmillan.
6.   Wilson, A. E. (1932) *Penny Plain & Twopence Coloured: A History of the Juvenile Drama*, Harrap.
7.   E. Sitwell in BBC 'Candidates for Greatness', BBC Tape CXP572.
8.   Elborn, G. (1981) *Edith Sitwell: a biography*, Sheldon Press.
9.   Lindsay, J. (1950) 'Edith Sitwell' in *Façade*, Duckworth.
10. Sitwell, E. (1970) *Selected Letters*, op. cit.
11. A. Bennett in *The Adelphi* (August 1923) reprinted in Sitwell, O. (1924) *Triple Figure*, Grant Richards Ltd.
12. E. Sitwell in BBC 'Face to Face' interview (May 1959).
13. Sitwell, E. (ed.) (1919) *Wheels*, 4th cycle, Blackwell.
14. Kennedy, M. (1989) *Portrait of Walton*, Oxford: OUP.
15. Craggs, S. R. (1990) *William Walton: a Catalogue*, Oxford: OUP.
16. Salter, E. (1967) *The Last Years of a Rebel*, Bodley Head.
17. E. Sitwell reciting *The Wind's Bastinado* on *Caedmon LP 1016*.
18. Rootham, H. (trans.) (1932) *Les Illuminations* by Artur Rimbaud, Faber.
19. Newman, E. (1926) 'Façade', *The Sunday Times*, 2 May, p.7.
20. Nichols, B. (1927) *Are They the Same at Home?*, Jonathan Cape.
21. Fifoot, R. (1971) *Edith, Osbert and Sacheverell Sitwell*, 2nd edn., Rupert Hart-Davis.
22. Osbert Sitwell introduced Walton to Richmond Temple, Manager of the Savoy, which resulted in his arranging jazz pieces for the Savoy Orpheans.
23. A. Bennett in *The Adelphi* (August 1923).
24. *The Times*, 11 June 1923, p.10.
25. P. Scholes in *The Observer*, 17 June 1923.
26. Craggs, S. R. (1990) *William Walton: a Catalogue*, Oxford: OUP.
27. Pearson, J. (1978) *Façades*, Macmillan.

28. Sitwell, O. (1949) *Laughter in the Next Room*, Macmillan.
29. Sitwell, O. (1924) 'Catania' in *The Chapbook*, No. 39.
30. Opening bars of 'Long Steel Grass' from the Vocal score of Walton's *Façade*, OUP (1951).
31. Howes, F. (1942) *The Music of William Walton*, vol. 1, Oxford: OUP.
32. Sitwell, O. (1927) *All at Sea*, Duckworth.
33. HMV Record Set RLS 725 with booklet 'The Record of Singing'.
34. Sitwell, O. (1949) *Laughter in the Next Room*, Macmillan.
35. Coward, N. (n.d.) *Collected Sketches and Lyrics*, Hutchinson.
36. *Sunday Express* quoted in Glendinning, V. (1981) *A Unicorn among Lions*, Weidenfeld and Nicholson.
37. de Zoete, B. (1929) 'William Walton', *Monthly Musical Record*, 59, 321–23 and 356.
38. Letter to Constant Lambert dated 22 May 1946 (Ritchie archive).
39. Letter to S. R. Craggs dated 15/16 May 1972 (Craggs archive).
40. BBC (Radio 3), 'A Portrait of Sir William Walton' (4 June 1977).
41. Sitwell, O. (1949) *Laughter in the Next Room*, Macmillan.
42. Sir William Walton in LWT 'At the Haunted End of the Day', produced by Tony Palmer (19 April 1981).
43. Ritchie, N. (1987) *Sacheverell Sitwell – An Annotated and Descriptive Bibliography*, The Giardo Press.
44. Motion, A. (1986) *The Lamberts*, Chatto & Windus.
45. Cumberland, G. (1923) 'Façade: a new entertainment', *Vogue*, 62 (early July), 36 and 70.
46. Driver, P. (1980) 'Façade Re-visited', *Tempo*, Nos 133–134 (September), 3–9.
47. E. Sitwell's essay in *Les Illuminations* (trans. Helen Rootham), op. cit.
48. Kennedy, M. (1989) *Portrait of Walton*, Oxford: OUP.
49. Pearson, J. (1978) *Façades*, Macmillan.
50. Sir William Walton rehearsing *Façade*, Adelaide, Australia (1964).
51. Walton in conversation with Kevin McBeath, 1964.
52. Lambert, C. (1936) 'Some Angles of the Compleat Walton', *Radio Times*, 7 August, 13.
53. Sitwell, E. (1927) *Rustic Elegies*, Duckworth.
54. Planché, J. R. (1879) 'The Seven Champions of Christendom' from *Extravaganzas* (1825–71), Vol III, ed. T. F. Dillon Croker and Stephen Tucker, French.

APPENDIX 1

By Neil Ritchie, from *The Book Collector*, 45(2), (Summer 1996).

NOTE 557. FOOTNOTE TO *FAÇADE*

In March 1922 Edith Sitwell while living at 22 Pembridge Mansions, Moscow Road, W2, paid a visit to Oxford where she stayed with Mrs Louisa Grace Hughes, mother of Richard (1900–76), then an undergraduate poet. In thanking Mrs Hughes for her hospitality Edith praised young Richard's poem which had appeared in *The Weekly Westminster Gazette (The Bird's-Nester* on 18 March) and said she would be sending her hostess one of her own books of poems.

Edith Sitwell wrote again on 4 April to announce she was posting her book *Façade. Façade*, the entertainment, was first performed privately in Osbert Sitwell's house at 2 Carlyle Square, Chelsea, on 24 January 1922 and subsequently at Mrs Robert Mathias's residence in Montagu Square, W1, on 7 February. The first public performance took place on 12 June 1923 in the Aeolian Hall, W1. Edith's book *Façade*, privately printed and limited to 150 signed copies, became available for distribution during February 1922 or shortly afterwards and the copy Edith sent Mrs Hughes was No 87 with the holograph inscription 'For Mrs Hughes with all best wishes from Edith Sitwell'.

For the first public performance of *Façade* in the Aeolian Hall an orchestra of six players was used and such an ensemble has been used for performances of the entertainment ever since. The composition of the orchestra for the two private performances in 1922 has been the subject of much debate, but leading musicologists today, basing themselves on a BBC interview William Walton gave in 1977 at the age of 75 in which he mentioned four players only, accept that it consisted of four instrumentalists: *see*, for example, Michael Kennedy, *Portrait of Walton* (OUP, 1989).

When Edith Sitwell wrote to Mrs Hughes on 4 April 1922 sending the copy of *Façade* (the text of which is divided into two sections, one entitled *Winter* and the other *Façade*) she expanded a little on the genesis of the work:

> A good deal of the section called 'Façade' was written for music; and it was set by a youth called Walton – (whom I believe most strongly to be the best composer we've had since Purcell, though he is only just twenty) and I recited them down a kind of megaphone to this accompaniment, consisting of trumpet, clarinet, flute, drum and cello. It was very curious, and it was great fun doing it.

Given that Edith was herself no mean musician, her letter would appear to settle the question of the composition of the original orchestra for *Façade*.

I am grateful to Kevin McBeath, an authority on *Façade*, for drawing my attention to the musical importance of my Edith Sitwell letters to Mrs Hughes.

APPENDIX 2

An alphabetical list of titles from *Façade* with dates of performance. For further details see Craggs, S. R. (1990) *A Walton Catalogue*, Oxford: OUP.

Poem	1922	1923[1]	1926 (a)	1926 (b)	1928	1929	1942	1951	1977	1979
Ass-face	*									
Aubade (Jane, Jane)		*	*	*			*		*	*
Bank Holiday (1&2)	*									
Black Mrs Behemoth		*	*	*	*	*	*	8		
By the Lake			*	*	*		*	11		
Country Dance		*	*	*	*			12		
Daphne		*	*	*					*	
En famille	*	*	*	*	*		*	2		
Fanfare and Introduction										
Flourish										*
Four in the Morning		*	*	*	*		*	14		
Fox-Trot: Old Sir Faulk		*	*	*	*	*	*	20		
Gardener Janus		*								*
General Salute and prologue	*	*								
Herodiade's Flea		*							*	*
Hornpipe	*	*	*	*	*		*	1		
Interlude	*									
The Last Galop		*	*	*	*	*	*		*	
Long Steel Grass	*	*	*	*	*	*	*	4		
Lullaby for Jumbo	*	*	*	*	*		*	7		
Madam Mouse Trots	*	*	*	*						*
A Man from a Far Countree		*	*	*	*	*	*	10		
March		*	*		*		*		*	*

[1] reconstruction

53

APPENDIX 2—Cont.

An alphabetical list of titles from *Façade* with dates of performance. For further details see Craggs, S. R. (1990) *A Walton Catalogue*, Oxford: OUP.

Poem	1922	1923[1]	1926 (a)	1926 (b)	1928	1929	1942	1951	1977	1979
Mariner Man	*	*	*	*	*		*	3		
Mazurka				*						*
The Octogenerian	*	*	*	*					*	
Overture	*									
Polka		*	*	*	*	*	*	13		
Popular Song					*	*	*	19		*
Said King Pompey	*	*	*	*	*	*	*		*	
Scotch Rhapsody		*	*	*	*	*	*	18		
Small Talk (1&2)	*	*	*							
Something lies beyond		*	*	*	*		*	15		
Springing Jack	*	*	*	*	*	*	*			
(Swiss) Jodelling Song				*	*		*	17		
Switchback	*	*	*	*	*	*	*			
Tango-Pasodoblé		*	*	*	*	*	*	6		
Tarantella		*	*	*	*	*	*	9		
Thro' gilded trellises		*	*	*	*		*	5		
Trams		*	*							
Valse		*	*	*	*	*	*	16		
Water Party (Rose Castles)	*	*	*	*	*					*
(When) Sir Beelzebub	*	*	*	*	*		*	21		
The White Owl		*							*	
The Wind's Bastinado	*									

[1] reconstruction

54

APPENDIX 3

FAÇADE – towards a permanent calendar . . .

1922 *24 JANUARY* 9.30 pm 2 Carlyle Square, SW3, at the London home of the Sitwell brothers. '*Miss Edith Sitwell* on her *Sengerphone*'

7 FEBRUARY Montagu Square, W1 'another production' at the home of 'The Late Mrs Robert Mathias' (O Sitwell: *Laughter in the Next Room*)

'a number of experimental performances'

'several private performances'

'further private performances followed in 1923'

1923 'first in sundry Mayfair drawing-rooms and then at the Aeolian Hall'

12 JUNE 3.15 pm Aeolian Hall, New Bond Street, W

'Miss Edith Sitwell presents FAÇADE' – first public performance

1926 *27 APRIL* 8.45 pm The New Chenil Galleries, Chelsea 'second public performance', 'Jolliest entertainment'

29 JUNE 8.45 pm The New Chenil Galleries, Chelsea 'repeat performance'

3 SEPTEMBER 11.15pm BBC 2LO London, Savoy Hill first broadcast, in radio fantasy 'The Wheel of Time'

3 DECEMBER Lyceum Theatre, London. Orchestral SUITE of *four* movements, during Diaghilev's season of 'The Triumph of Neptune'

1927 *28 NOVEMBER* 8.30 pm Arts Theatre Club, Great Newport Street, London
'Osbert Sitwell will introduce FAÇADE' during 'First Class Passengers Only' season

1928 *5 JULY* Arts Theatre Club, Great Newport Street, London
First performance of *complete* SUITE, conducted by Edward Clark. BBC broadcast

'Orchestral Suite . . . put into the programme of the Leeds Festival'

14 SEPTEMBER Teatro dei Rozzi, Siena

Two morning performances, for the Sixth I.S.C.M. Festival, conducted by Walton

1929   *? JANUARY* Paris? unidentified news cutting ex Sassoon '. . . booked for Paris, Berlin, Vienna and Warsaw. Paris is seeing it this month . . .'

? APRIL Paris performance by 'Pro Musica Society'
Walton to Sassoon. (Reviewed by Lennox Berkeley in *Monthly Musical Record*, June 1929)

22 SEPTEMBER 11.15 am. Stadttheater Hagen, Westphalia
Ballet première 'Fassade' by Chamber Dance Theatre, Gunter Hess choreographer

28 NOVEMBER The New Chenil Galleries, Chelsea
3rd and final recording session for 'Decca' first world recording

'Where are you going?' . . . 'To Hammersmith, to hear you perform in Façade'
(Elizabeth Frank quoted in 'The Lamberts' re 'late 1920s')

1930   *FEBRUARY* Release of Decca T 124/5 records

3 MARCH 10.00 pm. Central Hall, Westminster, first complete broadcast; Contemporary Music Concert, relayed to 5GB Daventry

'. . . Paris in 1930 when Edith Sitwell and Constant Lambert performed it there'
(Frederick Ashton)

'late March . . . early April' Bath Contemporary Arts Festival
'where he (Lambert) recited Façade'

1931   *26 APRIL* Cambridge Theatre, London
Première of Frederick Ashton's ballet for the Carmargo Society conducted by Lambert

1933   Paris? Salle Playel? '. . . un fondale per Façade, rappresentato alla Salle Pleyel di Parigi nel 1933' (Severini Exhibition, Florence 1983)

30 SEPTEMBER Queen's Hall, London: BBC Promenade Concert
Orchestral SUITE, Sir Henry Wood conducting

1935   *8 OCTOBER* Ashton's 'Façade' taken up by the Vic-Wells Ballet at Sadler's Wells, Constant Lambert conducting

1936   *8 & 10 DECEMBER* Walton conducts Vic-Wells 'Façade' for BBC TV

1938 *30 MARCH* Carnegie Hall, New York
Barbirolli premières Second Orchestral Suite

1 JUNE BBC Orchestra broadcast includes Suite conducted by Clarence Raybould

10 SEPTEMBER Queen's Hall, London: BBC Promenade Concert
Sir Henry Wood conducts Second Orchestral Suite, London première

1939 *26 AUGUST* Queen's Hall, London: BBC Promenade Concert
William Walton conducts Second Orchestral Suite, BBC broadcast

1940 *MAY* Ballet scenery and costumes lost in evacuation from Holland

23 JULY Ballet re-staged with new decor

1941 *17 DECEMBER* Arts Theatre, Cambridge: BBC broadcast
Walton conducts Second Orchestral Suite

1942 *29 MAY* Aeolian Hall, London
'war-time revival' coupled with 'Pierrot Lunaire'.
'definitive version', Walton conducting, Lambert reciting

1949 *19 JANUARY* Museum of Modern Art, New York
American première of the Entertainment

1951 *26 JULY*
Publication of the score by Oxford University Press

1953 *DECEMBER* First complete recording of published order.
New Music Ensemble, Australia.

1954 *JULY/AUGUST* Recording of Decca LP record (LXT 2977)
Released in October 1954

1972 *MARCH* Publication of the deluxe limited edition by Oxford University Press to mark the composer's 70th birthday and the 50th anniversary of the first performance

1977 *25 MARCH* Plaisteners' Hall, London
Charles Mackerras conducts *Façade Revised* at a special birthday concert organized by Lina Lalandi

1979 *19 JUNE* The Maltings, Snape (Aldeburgh Festival)
Premiere of *Façade 2: A further Entertainment* conducted by Steuart Bedford.
Facsimile score published 28 June 1979 by Oxford University Press

1980   Cathy Berberian – Façade 2, Melbourne, Australia

Other early venues mentioned in various texts:

Paris, The Hague, London, Siena, Osbert Sitwell

New York, London, Edinburgh, Prague, The Hague, India. Osbert Sitwell, New York, 19/1/49

Paris, Berlin, Vienna, Warsaw, Siegfried Sassoon quoted in press 'January 1929'

Belfast projected performance by 'Ronald Marshall of Methodist College' 1937

Singapore 'pirated' wartime performance quoted in Melbourne *Herald*, 11/12/52

Editor's note: as this book went to press, a copy of the programme for the June 1923 performance of *Façade*, for which I have been searching for over 30 years, emerged. See page 41 for details of the programme's cover. It reveals that 28 poems were performed in eight groups with a Fanfare, a Preface given by Osbert Sitwell and Overture prefacing the performance. It also reveals that four settings, unknown until now, were performed: 'Clown Argheb's Song' [from *Wheels 5*], 'Serenade' [from *Daily Mirror*, 22 November 1913], 'Gone Dry' [source unknown] and 'Dark Song' [from *Bucolic Comedies*, 1923].

4 Belshazzar and BBC Bureaucracy: the Origins of a Masterpiece

Michael Kennedy

At some time in 1929, after completion of his Viola Concerto, William Walton decided that his next composition would be choral. Osbert Sitwell suggested the subject of the Writing on the Wall at Belshazzar's feast in Babylon, and in December 1929 he was working on the libretto in Venice. Another of Walton's and Sitwell's friends, Christabel McLaren (later Christabel, Lady Aberconway) later claimed that she did most of the research on the text, by which she presumably meant that she selected the biblical passages. No matter who helped him, Sitwell produced a magnificent piece of work: the section of the *Book of Daniel* dealing with the feast is given extra impact by the excision of the episode concerning Daniel's interpretation of the writing on the wall, and the central drama is 'topped and tailed' by choruses taken from Psalms 137 and 81 and preceded by an adaptation from *Revelations* of the description of Babylon in all its affluence. The whole is introduced by Isaiah's prophecy of doom for the inhabitants of Babylon – 'Howl ye, howl ye, therefore, for the day of the Lord is at hand'. In an interview which he gave to the *Yorkshire Evening News* of 7 October 1931, Sitwell said: 'When the libretto was, as I thought, complete, I handed it over to Mr Walton. At his suggestion various passages were altered and other passages were substituted.' Walton's friend, the pianist Angus Morrison, said[1] that Sitwell's first intention was to end the libretto with the nursery-rhyme

> How many miles to Babylon?
> Threescore miles and ten.
> Can I get there by candlelight?
> Yes, and back again.

Fortunately Walton would have none of this whimsy, which it might have been possible (as Morrison said) for a Mahler to have brought off. In the end, this collaboration between Lancashire and Yorkshire resulted in a model example of a text for music.

59

Coincidental with the early stages of the collaboration was the emergence of the BBC as an influential patron of music. In 1929 alone, 50 works received first performances, or first performances in Britain, under BBC auspices. There were plans to establish the Corporation's own symphony orchestra under the newly-appointed Director of Music, Adrian Boult, and the orchestra gave its first performance on 22 October 1930. Equally important, and chiefly through the enterprise of Edward Clark (1888–1962), a member of the music staff, compositions were commissioned. A BBC internal memorandum from Clark and Julian Herbage dated 12 January 1930 discloses that three English composers had been approached: Walton, Constant Lambert and Victor Hely-Hutchinson. All three, it was stated, 'would be willing to accept the limitations of apparatus we have in mind, i.e. small chorus, small orchestra of not exceeding 15 and soloist'. Their subjects would be: Walton 'Nebuchadnezzar or the Writing on the Wall', text by Osbert Sitwell; Lambert 'Black Majesty (The Emperor of Haiti)', text by Lambert from the book of the same name; and Hely-Hutchinson 'The Town', to a text by Cecil Lewis. Fees of 50 guineas were agreed for Walton and Lambert. Kenneth Wright, the BBC's Music Executive, repeated these facts to Boult in a memorandum dated 13 March, adding:

> Thus, the works we shall obtain will be on similar lines to the successful ones in Germany (e.g. *Lindbergh's Flight*[2]). The works provided should be musically entertaining and usable fairly extensively and not merely rarely, as in the case of an oratorio like *The Pilgrim's Progress*.[3] They should, further, be more of the type that continental stations would like to broadcast as indicative of our work in this sphere. Immediately Clark had discussed matters with Walton, he 'spilled the beans' to the press, stating that he had been definitely commissioned – at least that is the story in the papers. We do not want to quarrel with him, and by the time these suggestions have been approved, and letters sent to the composers, it will be almost a new story.

The next development was a memorandum from Boult to Roger Eckersley, Director of Programmes. 'I should very much like to talk over the whole question with you', he wrote. 'In the meantime, as Walton and Lambert have gone ahead with their works, though they are aware that proper sanction has not been given to the commission, I might perhaps suggest that you would be good enough to sanction these two in order that notice of this might be issued at the time when [Hermann] Scherchen conducts for us a concert of German works specially written for broadcasting (May 7th, 9:40–11pm).' Eckersley scribbled a reply: 'All right – but let's discuss future policy.'

On 30 May, Edward Clark, as Music Programme Builder, wrote to Boult:

> I saw William Walton on Wednesday who has just returned from abroad where he has completed the composition of 'Belshazzar'. . . It is for two soloists, small chorus, small orchestra. While abroad he has shown this work to various people whom it has evidently much impressed, and has been told by Berlin that they wish to broadcast the performance of this work, and also by Volkmar Andreae that he proposes to give it a public performance during the course of next season at Zürich.[4] Part of the arrangement being that the first performance should, of course, be given by the BBC, Walton is asking us to let him know when he may expect this to take place in order

that he may make arrangements for subsequent performances abroad. I presume that we have also a financial, to say nothing of an artistic, interest in as many performances taking place as possible'.

Boult's comment was: 'We must get clear about the finance of this: has it been sanctioned yet? We should arrange the performance as soon as possible.'

The upshot was that on 6 June, R. J. F. Howgill, then working in the copyright section of the Director of Programmes, wrote to Walton at Osbert Sitwell's address, 2 Carlyle Square, regretting that 'we have been so long in giving you formal notification'. He continued:

> We gather that the work has already been completed under the title *Belshazzar* and that it is for two soloists, small chorus and small orchestra. The payment we would suggest is £50 for the sole broadcasting rights to cover the interests of both yourself and your collaborator, and this leaves the mechanical rights and all other performing rights in your hands. We shall be glad to hear that you are agreeable to these terms in order that we can complete the matter and arrange for the first performance.

No reply from Walton has been preserved. Nearly three weeks later, on 26 June, Howgill reported to Cecil Graves, Assistant Controller of Programmes, and Boult the result of a discussion about *Belshazzar* with Hubert Foss, head of the Oxford University Press's music department and Walton's publisher. 'The work is to be called *Belshazzar's Feast*', he wrote,

> and will take between thirty and forty minutes in performance. It is for two soloists, chorus and small orchestra and the text has been written by one of the Sitwells. I offered £50 which is considered inadequate and I am not at all surprised in the circumstances, but when I mentioned this amount at a meeting some months ago I gathered that we did not require a work written on such a large scale. The payment required by Walton is £100 and for this he would let us have the British broadcasting rights for a period of ten years. In all the circumstances this is not unreasonable.
>
> I must mention that we seem to be very definitely committed over the matter although I did not write to Walton until the 6th of this month when the composition of the work had been in train apparently for some time. Walton refers to having been commissioned to do the work and states that he definitely refused a better offer in order to get on with it, which points to his having been asked to go ahead before arrangements were ready. I do not think the matter ought to have been mentioned to him in such a way as to give him a reason for starting before we were able to agree about the payment and the nature and length of the work required. If it was, our hands are tied as regards negotiation and it seems that all we can do now is to endeavour to get it for, say, £80 instead of £100. It is, I understand half completed but there is no possibility of its being ready for the first performance until the New Year. The commissioning of new works is not, in my opinion, very satisfactory and you will probably agree that unless the initial stages of negotiation are properly handled, it is even less so.

So what was going on? Walton wrote to his mother from 2 Carlyle Square in December 1929: 'I am off tonight to Amalfi to join Osbert. I am sorry not to be with you all over Xmas but I must get away to begin work on this thing for the BBC.'[5] Osbert Sitwell, in a letter from Amalfi on 17 January 1930 to Siegfried Sassoon, described Walton as 'rather depressed' and that he was sitting long at the piano 'and does little work. But it is a stage through which he always passes, if he could only recognise it.' It was after returning from this visit to Italy that Walton told Edward Clark he had 'completed' *Belshazzar* for two soloists, small chorus and small orchestra. It is intriguing to contemplate a chamber-cantata *Belshazzar's Feast*. When I asked Walton about it in 1976 he replied: 'I recollect vaguely that I did start on a version for 2 soloists, but it went down the drain.' Foss, we have seen, was telling the BBC late in 1930 that the work existed in this form. Yet Walton, writing to Foss early in 1933, recalled that 'in *Belshazzar* I got landed on the word "gold" – I was there from May to December (1930), perched, unable to move to either right or left or up or down.' That is a typically Waltonian story. It may be true. Or was that when the original version was scrapped and work begun on the larger version we know? If that was the prosaic truth, Walton also preferred to say that his mental block had been intensified when he read a joke by the humorist 'Beachcomber' (J. B. Morton) in the *Daily Express* that the Writing on the Wall was not 'Mene, mene, tekel Upharsin' but 'Aimeé, Aimeé, Semple McPherson', who was a much-publicized American evangelist of the day.

In the meantime the BBC internal row over the commission continued to rage. One cannot avoid the impression that a piece of music was being treated rather as if it was the requisite amount of carpet for a BBC mandarin's office. On 14 July 1930 Kenneth Wright told Cecil Graves that he had:

> taken it up hot and strong with Clark and Herbage [a programme planner], and Clark assured me that nothing was ever said to Walton that implied a definite commission. On the contrary, when he was going away to Italy early this year and asked if he could get on with it, he was told that that was a matter for himself to decide and that although this department was recommending the commissioning of the work, it had not had any official sanction whatsoever. When he returned from Italy, the work was half written. I might add that the subject was well in his mind as an attractive possibility at the time that we first approached him with regard to a commission of some kind. It is obvious therefore that the facts as quoted by Foss are not strictly accurate. The delay has been unfortunate and I cannot quite trace how it arose . . .
>
> With regard to the time and price for *Belshazzar's Feast*, Mr Howgill agreed with Clark, Herbage and myself that the work should be from 20 minutes to half an hour, which is still of the magnitude envisaged by Mr Howgill for the £50 figure. If Walton has found 40 minutes necessary, it is his concern and in fact we view it with disfavour, having felt always that 30 minutes should be the maximum for broadcasting purposes. If Mr Howgill has to go higher than £50, I submit that it should be on the intrinsic value of the work considered on the half-hour basis still and not because Walton on his own account has gone well beyond the limits first discussed.

Howgill now wrote on 30 July to Foss to claim that no commission had been offered to Walton before 6 June. He ended with a broadside:

> If Mr Walton thinks that *Belshazzar's Feast* is too large a work for these terms, the matter must be dropped entirely, but in this event perhaps we can discuss the question of his writing another. As far as we are concerned, we shall not mind as *Belshazzar's Feast* is apparently a bigger work than we wanted.

All this was communicated to Boult who replied to Howgill on 20 August:

> D.P. [i.e. Eckersley] agrees that there is no question that we have been committed
> and must stand by it. A further complication, however, has cropped up in the fact
> that *Belshazzar's Feast* has grown to such proportions that both Clark and the
> composer considered it inappropriate for the studio. Walton, therefore, proposes to
> write us something else as his commissioned work and offer us, quite independent
> of commission, the first performance of *Belshazzar's Feast*. . . I hope this will mean
> the end of commissioned works.

Walton never composed 'something else' for the BBC, and when the BBC in 1948
commissioned his opera *Troilus and Cressida*, it eventually yielded it to Covent
Garden for stage performance. Nor did the BBC give the first performance of
Belshazzar's Feast. Progress on its composition was faster during 1931. Writing
to Siegfried Sassoon (dedicatee of *Portsmouth Point*) on 8 March 1931, Walton
remarked what a 'frightful nuisance' it was that he would have to leave Ascona,
Switzerland, on 23 March to hear Lionel Tertis's performance of the Viola
Concerto at a Royal Philharmonic Society concert in London on 26 March:

> It is heavenly here and am enjoying it very much and am immensely happy. Also I
> am doing a vast amount of work as you prophesied I would. I am now on the last
> chorus – unfortunately at the moment it doesn't progress too well, but I hope to
> complete it or practically do so before I leave.

Evidently this mood of happiness was sustained, because Walton told Peter Lewis
of the *Daily Mail*, in an interview published on 28 March 1972, the eve of his
70th birthday, that 'I do get moments of great exhilaration when things are going
well. I remember the excitement of getting towards the end of *Belshazzar's Feast*,
and I still feel it when I hear it now'. (He incomparably conveyed this exhilaration and excitement in the two *Belshazzar* recordings he conducted.) Early in
1931, it had been announced that the work was destined for the Leeds Festival,
which was being run by Beecham, who had assigned *Belshazzar's Feast* to Malcolm
Sargent. Walton told Lewis that Beecham said to him: 'Well, my boy, as you will
probably never hear this work again, you might as well chuck in a couple of brass
bands. I've always liked brass bands, so I did.' Brass bands in this context meant
two extra brass sections comprising three trumpets, three trombones and tuba.

The first performance, in the Town Hall, Leeds, on Thursday, 8 October 1931,
conducted by Sargent with Dennis Noble the baritone soloist, was a tumultuous
success, although Walton was privately dissatisfied with it, complaining that
Sargent took it too slowly. The festival chorus had liked the work once they had
mastered its difficulties and they joined wholeheartedly in the ovation for the
29-year-old composer. With scarcely a dissenting voice, the critics, swept off their
feet by the brazen splendour of the choral and orchestral sound, acclaimed it as
a landmark in British choral music, perhaps the greatest work in its genre since
Elgar's *The Dream of Gerontius* in 1900. The first London performance, on 25
November 1931, was at a BBC Symphony Orchestra concert in Queen's Hall
conducted by Boult. In the seven weeks after Leeds, Walton re-scored several
passages and himself copied the revised orchestral parts. He revised it again in

1948 when Roy Douglas pointed out 80 errors in the published full score. He eliminated some percussion and made various other adjustments to the scoring. Later, in 1957, he entirely re-scored the last 14 bars, extending them to 18, using full orchestra, adding the upper octaves instead of only the lower instruments, and adding a full organ chord halfway through the very last chord. Incidentally, the autograph full score has been lost. Since its first performance, the work has maintained a regular place in the repertory and has been performed all over the world. Edward Clark informed Walton in March 1934 that 'Prokofiev is going to Russia in a few days' time and would like to take a vocal score of *Belshazzar* with him. Will you send him one direct?' It was once conducted by Herbert von Karajan[6] – to Walton's admiration – and has been recorded several times. Walton himself conducted it in Israel in 1963 in a Hebrew translation. As his recordings of it prove, he was a magnificent interpreter. Susana Walton tells a bizarre story[7] of Walter Legge informing Walton the night before the composer was to conduct the work for EMI in 1961 that he had engaged a young German conductor for the sessions although Walton's name would still appear on the records. Walton responded: 'Well, in that case there will be no recording.' Legge capitulated. It was also in 1961 that he conducted an extract from *Belshazzar's Feast* for one of Gerard Hoffnung's entertainments in the Royal Festival Hall. He told his publisher in advance: 'After the chorus and orch. pompously filing in, including myself, I bring them all in on the word "Slain". Nothing more. It might be rather funny. [It was.] Anyhow it will be the easiest £20 I shall have earned ever!'

His more serious views on the problems of conducting *Belshazzar's Feast* were expressed in October 1972 to his friend Malcolm Arnold. He had just heard André Previn's recording.

> Conductors never seem to realise that in B.'s F. there is no need to add to the excitement – on the contrary, it should be kept on a very tight rein, otherwise it becomes a shambles, as unfortunately this recording often does. It just shows how necessary it is for the composer to be present for a recording. . . I couldn't be there, but I just had the time to instruct him about the "trumpeters and pipers" and the very end which had been completely wrong at the perf. the previous night. These bits are O.K. but the speed in other places completely defeats its object.[8]

It should be added that when Previn conducted the work ten years later for Walton's eightieth birthday, the audience's reception moved the frail and ill composer to tears – 'they have gone mad', he said to his wife.

Belshazzar's Feast is now a classic. Its difficulties have grown no less formidable, but choirs and conductors enjoy meeting and overcoming its challenges. With his customary flair for the apt summing-up, Neville Cardus in October 1931 described it as 'a clear case of red-hot conception instinctively finding the right and equally red-hot means of expression'.

What Cardus did not say was how remarkable it was that Walton should have displayed such mastery of choral technique in his first major choral work. He had written nothing for voices since his boyhood at Christ Church, Oxford, 14 years earlier. He seemed to be developing into a purely instrumental composer, yet suddenly he produced a work in which all the training of his choir-school days and all his North Country background of massed voices and sounding brass fused to bring into existence a masterpiece, a choral symphonic-poem of a unique kind. Not, of course, a religious or a mystical masterpiece, although the human compassion of 'By the Waters of Babylon' is music which probes deep spiritual emotions. 'Stark Judaism from first to last', said *The Times* of 10 October 1931. 'It culminates in ecstatic gloating over the fallen enemy, the utter negation of Christianity' – words that made their mark on the ecclesiastical authorities of the Three Choirs Festival who refused to admit *Belshazzar's Feast* into their cathedrals until 1957. Perhaps it was not for clerics to salute Walton's musical achievement in eroding the largely artificial boundary between sacred and secular. Moreover, too much emphasis has always been laid on the 'barbaric dissonance' of this great score. The foreign listeners to the International Society of Contemporary Music performance in Amsterdam (10 June 1933, conducted by Lambert) who found it 'conventional' were wrong in one respect but right in another. So exciting is the impression made in 35 short minutes that one is bamboozled by the delightful confidence-trick that the composer has played: *Belshazzar's Feast* sounds so perennially 'modern' that one does not notice that much of its harmony is of nineteenth-century vintage and that diatonicism is at the root of the matter as the string tremolandi, brass fanfares and masterly use of unaccompanied declamation work their customary magic. The rhythmical energy and momentum are irresistible, the lyrical melodies are enticing, the sense of timing and contrast is infallible, the use of the large exotic orchestra is brilliant and restrained, the infusion of jazzy rhythms is piquant enough never to pall. Did Walton, I wonder, take another short oratorio dealing with the destruction of Babylon – Vaughan Williams's *Sancta Civitas* of 1926 – as his model? Maybe. His sense of the dramatic is equally unerring. There is no elaboration, no repetition, and the only ornamentation is in the pungent orchestral descriptions of gold, silver, iron, wood, stone and brass. Walton's solution to being 'stuck on "gold"' was a splendid march tune of the kind that served him also for the crown imperial and the flight of the Spitfire aircraft. *Gerontius* and *Belshazzar's Feast* were revolutionary works in their time, not because they crossed frontiers but because they took the conventions of a genre and idiom and revivified them by imaginative genius. *Belshazzar's Feast* has now passed the test of all great and enduring art: it is impossible to imagine a time when it did not exist.

Notes

1. *Willie: the Young Walton and his Four Masterpieces*, talk given in London, 31 January 1984, reprinted in *RCM Magazine*, 80/3 (1984), pp. 119–27.
2. *Der Lindberghflug*, a radio cantata by Kurt Weill in collaboration with Hindemith, for tenor, baritone, bass, chorus and orchestra (1928). It was re-scored by Weill in 1929 and revised a year later as *Der Flug des Lindberghs*. Charles Lindbergh was the first man to fly the Atlantic solo in May 1927.

3. Sir Granville Bantock's work had been performed in 1928.
4. Andreae (1879–1962) was conductor of the Tonhalle Orchestra, Zürich. He conducted the first performance of Walton's *Portsmouth Point* in Zürich on 22 June 1926 and also conducted the Viola Concerto with Lionel Tertis as soloist, in Zürich in 1931.
5. Kennedy, M. (1989) *Portrait of Walton*, Oxford: OUP, pp. 54–5.
6. Karajan also conducted Walton's First Symphony in Rome.
7. Walton, S. (1988) *Behind the Façade*, Oxford: OUP, pp. 145–6.
8. *Portrait of Walton*, op. cit., p. 257.

5 The Symphonies and Concertos

Robert Meikle

Traditional, tonal, romantic, even conservative, are the epithets which have attached themselves to Walton's music ever since the dust settled on the initially outrageous rhythms and dissonances of – in particular – *Belshazzar's Feast* and the First Symphony. And growing familiarity with the music brought the realization that such epithets have some justification. Rhythmic effects, for instance, at once idiosyncratic and recognizable, are often just a momentary, if exhilarating, disruption of a fundamentally simple underlying pulse. Arthur Hutchings, though more trenchant than most, is not alone in discerning a certain arbitrariness in the placing of the 5/4 bars in the First Symphony's Scherzo: he writes of '. . . the recalcitrant interplay of metrical stress and cross-accent. Where rhythm is almost entirely accentual, and phrasing allows caprice to stop or resume at will, a resourceful composer has little difficulty'.[1] Kenneth Avery is more respectful but equally perceptive: '. . . the "malicious" tunes are rapped out in angry cross-rhythms, the most frequent *distortions* being the changing of the 3/4 time-signature to 5/4, and two 3/4 bars being treated as if they were three separate 2/4 bars.'[2] This characteristic treatment of rhythm lies in the creation of a regular pulse with which Walton beguiles the listener, only to destroy any possible complacency with a sudden extension or – more frequently – compression of an expected rhythmic shape, as in the principal scherzo theme of the Viola Concerto, on whose time-signature changes Tovey anticipates Hutchings:

> The listener need not worry too much about these changes; an odd bar of 3/4, 3/8 or 5/8 is merely a practical necessity for conductor and players; it happens whenever the composer has found that his groups of 3 or 5 quavers across his 4-quaver bars will land him on a main beat either too soon or too late for his whim.[3]

Again a degree of spur-of-the-moment impulse is assumed by Frank Howes, in a typical attribution of Walton's rhythmic heritage: 'Walton inherited from Stravinsky the method of scattering bar-lines and drumming away at gritty chords on all the wrong beats.'[4] Such a remark is, however, an oversimplification which does little service to Stravinsky, and misinterprets the relationship between the two composers. For there is nothing in Walton to compare with a piece of typical Stravinsky such as, say, the first five bars of *Petrushka*, barred in the simplest 3/4 time, yet refusing to yield any underlying, regular pulse, whether 3/4 or not. A comparison with an equally typical passage from Walton – the *Allegro spiritoso* theme from the *Sinfonia Concertante*, shows that, despite the initial groupings of the theme into five quavers, its treatment in canon between piano and horns, the duple, 2/8 grouping of the upper strings and the 3/4 placing of the woodwind chords, the overall 6/8 is never in any danger.[5] Even in *Portsmouth Point*, if we cannot always pin down an underlying pulse, we sense that there is one, and that it is being pummelled like a piece of plasticine. And, given the ubiquitous twists and turns he applies to rhythm and the at times violent energy thereby generated, it is surprising to discover a fondness for regular four-bar and eight-bar phrases. The beginning of the *Brioso ed ardentemente* in the last movement of the First Symphony is typical.

At the same time Walton's harmony, even in its most acerbic moments, is grounded in western tonal procedures, almost invariably heavily spiced with a selection of added sevenths, ninths and modal dissonances. From this follows his treatment of tonality:

> that notes should be related according to their function in the tonal scale (tonic, dominant, and so on), that movements should be constructed on the principle of thematic and harmonic contrast, and that the logical movement of the music should be decided mainly by the harmony, and the answering of phrase with phrase.[6]

From time to time there are moments where a key may be unclear, as for example in the *Brioso* passage (beginning at bar 172) in the first movement of the Second Symphony, though in such cases coherence is preserved through devices such as clearly-phrased sequential progressions, often, as here, at the upper minor third.[7] Pedals (as, famously, in the First Symphony) also provide anchors for the most piercing of dissonances (see for example the passage beginning at 94 in the slow movement), though their frequency in this work has led to exaggerated claims for their presence elsewhere: in no other work are they as persistent as here.[8] At times his treatment of harmony is reminiscent of Hindemith's, though without the counterpoint: the direction of a particular passage may be ambiguous or quite unclear until, at the end of the phrase, it settles onto a triad which, if decorated, is never so veiled as to be indecipherable. Ex. 5.1 shows the harmonic structure of the beginning of the Violin Concerto, and its clearly articulated bass line moves from i-vii-ivb-v-i-bii-ii-iii-biv.

Ex. 5.1   Violin Concerto

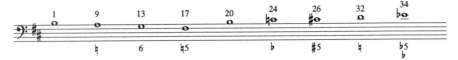

Even when he writes a serial theme (in the finale of the Second Symphony), Walton treats it tonally, as we shall see. Critics have identified both these and other characteristics of Walton's harmonic and rhythmic fingerprints, but little has been written about his treatment of form and, related to it, of tonality. There have been a few observations about sonata form, most notably in Howes,[9] and generalizations concerning his liking for compressed recapitulations, but there is little detailed study, and virtually no consideration of the effect that a compressed (and often understated at that) recapitulation may have on the dimensions of a sonata-form movement. Writers have scurried past his most problematic movements, the scherzos, apparently relieved to reach the safer ground of the slow movements and finales where, even if again in an adapted sonata form, their reminiscences of earlier movements can be confidently noted.

Howes gives up on the scherzo of the First Symphony about a quarter of the way through it, and has little to say beyond figure 53: 'there is no formal recapitulation, but both [the main theme] and [the theme at 51] are heard more than once in the headlong course of the movement and at one point (76) they occur together'.[10] Even Tovey is uncharacteristically vague when discussing the Scherzo from the Viola Concerto:

> As in the other movements . . . the orchestra eventually arises in its might, bringing the development to its climax, and leading, at its own leisure, to the final return of the main theme in the tonic.[11]

Yet Walton's use in his symphonies and concertos of the traditional forms – particularly sonata and scherzo – is as personal as are his harmony and rhythm, and it is to these two forms that we must presently turn. It is impossible to discuss these works, however, without encountering and summarizing the influences which helped shape them. Most notable and notorious among these is of course Sibelius; the first subject of Walton's First Symphony (Ex. 5.2a) could almost have been written by him, as a comparison with the second subject of his Third Symphony will show (Ex. 5.2b).

Ex. 5.2a   Walton Symphony No. 1

Ex. 5.2b   Sibelius Symphony No. 3, 1st movement

Moreover, Sibelius, like Walton, is exploring the potential of ostinati and pedals; the Third Symphony is set in motion by an ostinato, and its second movement consists almost entirely of variants of one simple melodic figure, while pedals of some 20–30 bars in length are common in the first and last movements. The slow pendulum of the brass at the end of Sibelius's Fifth Symphony, against fragments of melody and an off-beat crescendo in the strings, is directly echoed in the recapitulation of the first movement of the Walton, and he seems indebted also to Sibelius's liking for modal inflections and figures heavily dependent on fourths. Two further influences are apparent in the Viola Concerto – those of Hindemith and Prokofiev. Geoffrey Skelton[12] recounts Walton's acknowledgement of his debt to Hindemith's *Kammermusik* No. 5 (also a Viola Concerto, op.36 no. 4), and his surprise that Hindemith agreed to play it. 'One or two bars are almost identical', he said, and indeed they are. In addition to the fact that Hindemith's first movement is a sonata form with shortened recapitulation (and, like Walton's scherzo, is a toccata for the soloist), Ex. 5.3 indicates the most striking thematic correspondences; Ex. 5.3a in particular must cast doubt on the customary attribution of Walton's false relations to his familiarity with the repertoire of the English Renaissance.

Ex. 5.3a   Hindemith *Kammermusik No. 5* (op. 36 no. 4), 2nd movement

Ex. 5.3b   Hindemith *Kammermusik No. 5*, 4th movement

The fact that Hindemith's second movement begins with an imitative, *Langsam*, 9/8 melody might give grounds for proposing a further derivation, were it not for the fact that the similarity between the Walton and the beginning of Prokofiev's First Violin Concerto is even closer (Ex. 5.4).

Ex. 5.4   Prokofiev Violin Concerto No. 1, 1st movement

And Prokofiev's recapitulation (also shortened, and also introduced by some imitative double-stopping from the soloist) gives the melody of Ex. 5.4 to a solo flute, while the violin embroiders it with triplet arabesques, a procedure almost identical to Walton's. Walton, too, exchanges material between solo and orchestra; the solo's double-stops recall the preludial imitations in the strings, and the reminiscences of the principal melody are also entrusted to woodwind solos (Ex. 5.5a shows the beginning of the movement, and Ex. 5.5b the beginning of the soloist's reinterpretation of it).

Walton was to employ the same device ten years later to usher in the recapitulation in the first movement of the Violin Concerto: the solo violin just before 22 has a short cadenza based on earlier orchestral material (see [3]2), leading to the principal theme on the flute (at 22), with the earlier cello counter-melody taken over by solo violin.[13]

Kennedy has commented on the close of the Viola Concerto, where the outline of the main theme from the finale serves as an ostinato accompaniment exactly as at the close of the same Prokofiev Concerto.[14] He goes on to suggest that when Walton revised the scoring in 1961, it was not an improvement '. . . to have the harp playing the accompanying figure instead of the mixed bowed and pizzicato

Ex. 5.5a   Concerto for Viola and Orchestra, 1st movement

Ex. 5.5a   Concluded

Ex. 5.5b (End of 1st movement)

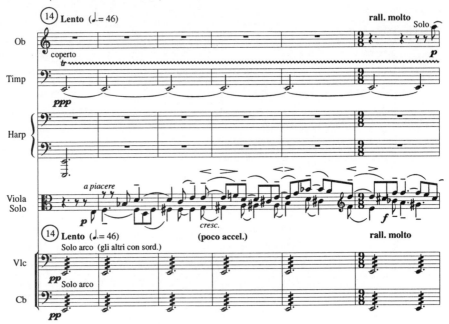

cellos of the original version'. Yet perhaps Prokofiev's texture still lingered in Walton's mind, for his amendment brings his scoring (particularly in the use of harp and bass clarinet) markedly closer to Prokofiev's (where harp and clarinet are also prominent).

But whatever the derivations from and debts to other composers that we may acknowledge in Walton, there is no mistaking his individual voice, a fact which he himself recognized when speaking of the First Symphony: 'There was a great thing about Sibelius at that time and he influenced me a lot in the symphony, although I was surprised, when I heard it the other day, how little there is actually of him – not how much'.[15] And that voice is perhaps most succinctly caught in three characteristics discerned by Kennedy: '. . . wit, spiky rhythms and a haunted melancholy lyricism'.[16] At almost any moment in his music we will find one of these three features, and they are a continuing presence in Walton's treatment of sonata form.

Sonata Forms

Sonata form has provided the backbone of nearly every large-scale instrumental work written since the latter quarter of the eighteenth century, and many smaller ones as well, not to mention innumerable vocal works, too. It has proved one of the most versatile and durable forms ever employed in western music, and composers from Haydn to Shostakovich have created their own characteristic versions of it: some, like Haydn himself, instantly recognizable by the inexhaustible invention that they bring to it, and others, like Shostakovich, equally identifiable by certain stereotypical practices. And with an enrichment unprecedented in western music of the tonal, melodic and harmonic resources that have become available to composers in the last 150 or so years, its edges have become vague, its outlines less clear than those of, say, a Schubert sonata. So it will be as well, before embarking on an investigation of Walton's indebtedness to it, to set out the basic landmarks that articulate a sonata structure. Yet even in the process of producing something as finite as a 'definition', we are in danger of diminishing the form's almost infinite malleability, and a necessarily brief sketch here must tread the fine line between on the one hand vague generalization, which in embracing too many movements would tell us little of value, and on the other hand specific prescription, which could debar pieces as diverse, but also as legitimate, as movements from a Mahler symphony or a Bartók quartet. One of the most concise and most useful outlines is to be found in the *New Grove* article, 'Sonata form':

> A typical sonata-form movement consists of a two-part tonal structure, articulated in three main sections. The first part of the structure coincides with the first section and is called the 'exposition'. The second part of the structure comprises the remaining two sections, the 'development' and the 'recapitulation'. The exposition divides into a 'first group' in the tonic and a 'second group' in another key, most often the dominant. Both first and second group may include numerous different themes . . . . The development . . . usually develops material from the exposition, as it modulates among one or more new keys. The last part of the development prepares the recapitulation. The recapitulation . . . is announced by a simultaneous 'double return', to the main theme and to the tonic. It then restates significant material from the second group, transposed to the tonic. The movement concludes either with a cadence in the tonic paralleling the end of the exposition, or with a coda following the recapitulation.[17]

Two points at once emerge from this outline: first, the dimensions of many movements in Walton's symphonies and concertos are such that any investigation of them cannot but explore their relationship to sonata form, and secondly, it at once becomes clear that if, in the symphonies, Walton relies on the more orthodox dimensions of sonata structure, in the concertos he seizes the advantage offered by the presence of the solo instrument to expand and explore its potential. Not only is the order of the movements in the two symphonies firmly based on classical practice (fast, scherzo, slow, fast in No. 1, and fast, slow, variations in No. 2), but also, alone in the orchestral works, many other traditional secondary features are retained.

Symphony No. 1

The sonata-form dimensions of the first movement of No. 1 are set out in Table 5.1 and discussed below.

Table 5.1 Symphony No.1: first movement

beginning	1st subject, B♭	
4	transition, V of V	
7	2nd subject (i), f	
10	2nd subject (ii), f	
14	end of exposition, codetta	V-I in F
^{4}18	development	The V-I in F at 14 is followed by almost 50 bars of continuous reiteration of F; it is only at ^{4}18 that Walton moves away from F into development proper
33	recapitulation, b♭	
35	2nd subject (i), b♭	
38	2nd subject (ii), b♭	Intervals changed
^{8}38	coda	

It is hardly surprising that this movement is by far the most straightforward of all Walton's orchestral sonata-form movements, since it represents his first venture into a large-scale orchestral work with neither solo instrument nor text and voices to help point the way. And it is perhaps not so surprising either to speculate that, if he wished in the Symphony to live up to his *enfant terrible* reputation, he should turn to the dimension in which he was most at home – rhythm. There can be few movements in the symphonic repertoire that are rhythmically so relentless as this one – unless it be the ensuing scherzo: only in the second part of the second subject (at 10) and briefly in the development, is there any respite from the incessant pounding. Yet the scheme outlined above, while it demonstrates respect for the traditional landmarks and keys associated with sonata form, covers many subtleties. Prominent among these is a fondness for presenting different harmonizations of themes at the same pitch: for example, the first subject, initially falling from third to tonic, reappears in the transition, but now as a ninth falling to a seventh; and the first part of the second subject is similarly presented at the same pitch in both exposition and recapitulation.[18] Over the tonic pedal, in F minor, which concludes the exposition, we have a virtual resumé of the exposition's principal themes, from the second subject (ii) at 10 (and elsewhere) to the first subject at 15^5 and the second subject (i) at ^{5}17. And although in the recapitulation there is an allusion to the second subject (ii) at 38, its principal appearance is not until after the beginning of the coda, at 40. Through and around almost every event of the movement is the figure outlining a Dorian seventh, which first appears in the horns at the very beginning, then in cellos and basses just as the first subject enters. These and some of its later manifestations are shown in Ex. 5.6.

But if the principal impression is of a movement which remains faithful to the old sonata-form dimensions – prominent subject matter, powerful drives to the end of the exposition and, even more so, into the 'double return' of the recapitulation, and

Ex. 5.6a   Symphony No. 1, 1st movement

Ex. 5.6b

Ex. 5.6c

Ex. 5.6d

Ex. 5.6e

Ex. 5.6f

Ex. 5.6g

Ex. 5.6h

clearly differentiated key-centres leading to the ultimate affirmation of the tonic – there are also signs of later adaptations of the form which will lead to radically new alignments and relationships within movements. Especially noteworthy is the compression of the recapitulation to less than half the length of the exposition, from around 250 bars to just under 110 bars, with the result that the two principal themes – first subject and second subject (i) – appear almost cheek by jowl.

The slow movement of the First Symphony seems to partake of the methods of both the Viola Concerto and its own scherzo, its *melanconia* a reaction to the preceding *malizia*. Of special significance, as we shall discover in a closer examination of the Viola Concerto, are the apparent recapitulation in the wrong key (at 92) followed by a second subject in the tonic (at 94), and a wistful reminiscence of the first subject, back in the tonic, at the end. And it is just as difficult – and just as unnecessary – as it will prove to be in the scherzo to try to predict when, or how many times, a theme will reappear. Yet it loses nothing in coherence: from the opening solo flute, wind and *divisi* strings, as bleak as anything in Shostakovich, it is underpinned by pedals and 4-bar phrases. Equally important (though not to be ignored elsewhere in the work) is the frequent conjunct movement in the bass, leading, for instance, down an octave from 86 to 89, and down almost two octaves from 92 back to the tonic at 94.

Once the first two movements were completed, there seems to have been some delay in the composition of the third – even though its principal theme had been in Walton's mind from the work's inception.[19] Angus Morrison recalled that at some time during the middle of 1933:

> he would like to write something like the slow movement of the Schubert C major string Quintet. That sort of timeless serenity was not in Willie's make-up, but the agonised bitter-sweetness of the movement as it finally emerged, certainly was . . . .[20]

Although the two movements are in many ways totally unlike, present-day views of the Schubert would incline more towards agonized bitter-sweetness than to timeless serenity: perhaps Walton was closer to his goal than Morrison realized.

Viola Concerto

The overall shape of the Viola Concerto was to serve its successors for violin and cello: an initial, lyrical slow movement, a faster scherzo and a moderately fast finale,[21] and its first movement will reveal a pattern which, with some slight variants, characterizes most of Walton's sonata structures. In fact its very beginning has a feature in common with the first three movements of the First Symphony, for they all sound like dominant preparations. An initial triad, either plain (Violin Concerto), or decorated (Cello Concerto, Second Symphony), is immediately marked down as a tonic; but a single note, or open fifth, reverberates, via Mahler's First Symphony and other landmarks of the nineteenth-century repertoire, all the way back to Beethoven's Ninth, and cannot but arouse expectation of a tonic to come.[22] Nor does increasing familiarity with these works do much to allay this false expectation.

Peter Evans[23] has indicated the most important thematic relationships and derivations in the Concerto; the structural outline of the first movement is given below. Howes[24] is both confused and confusing on its dimensions, but Tovey is clear (Table 5.2).

Table 5.2 Viola Concerto: first movement

bar 3	1st subject, a
4	2nd subject, d
5^3	development
14	recapitulation, a,
16	2nd subject, a

Source: Tovey, D. F. (1936) *Essays in Music Analysis, Vol. 3: Concertos*, London: OUP, pp. 222–3.

The far-reaching effect of this apparently arid schematic outline may best be grasped by noting from it the movement's proportions, for it emerges that the development is longer than the exposition and recapitulation combined. It becomes the core of the movement, the climax (at 12) its high point, and the recapitulation turns into an epilogue, a reminiscence, rather than the triumphant consummation of the development's tonal conflicts. At one especially significant point in the development (9) Walton presents his second subject scarcely developed at all, but very much as it had appeared in the exposition: the melody is in canon between principal and orchestral solos – viola and flute in the exposition, viola with flute, cor anglais and bassoon in the development – over a bass that almost outlines a circle of fifths. Were we examining a Haydn quartet, we would call this a false recapitulation; were it not for the key (which here is F# minor), we could take it for the recapitulation proper. But it is neither, for the development resumes almost at once (at 10). The subsequent return of the first subject and a trace of the second scarcely warrant the designation of a full-blown recapitulation.

We have, then, the following sequence of events:

1. First subject
2. Second subject
3. Development
4. Return of either first or second subject, not necessarily in the tonic
5. Further development
6. Recapitulation/coda.

This is a pattern which we will find repeated – with occasional variants – on no less than six subsequent occasions: the finale of the Viola Concerto, the third movement of the First Symphony, the first and last movements of the Violin Concerto, the first and last movements together of the Cello Concerto (a particularly ingenious version) and the first movement of the Second Symphony. In other words, in all the sonata-form related movements in the remaining concertos and Second Symphony, Walton's personal adaptation of the form is basically the same. It is summarized in Table 5.3 (including the first movement of the Viola Concerto); numbers in the top row refer to the list above.

Table 5.3 Sonata-form dimensions in the symphonies and concertos

	1	2	3	4	5	6
Viola I	beginning	4	5^3	9 (2nd)	10	14
Viola III	beginning	40^4	42^2	48^5(2nd)	51	61
Symphony 1/III	bar 3	84	α	92 (1st)	94	100
Violin I	beginning	5	9	15 (2nd, 1st)	18	22^2
Violin III	beginning;52	53^5	55	64 (2nd)	66	73
Cello I & III	beginning	3	link: 4–5	5 (1st)	6; III,14	III: 14^5
Symphony 2/I	beginning	70,92	133	β 217 [227 254 276]	305	338

α: In this movement there is scarcely any development that can be so identified: the middle section consists largely of the reiteration of a 4-bar melody (beginning at 86).
β: Here the plan is taken even further, for the recapitulation, beginning with the transition at 227, is in reverse; after two parts of the second subject at 254 and 276, there is still further development, at 305.

But although these movements are strikingly close to each other, there are nevertheless distinctions to be drawn, and a summary of these now follows. We must first, however, briefly summarize the *Sinfonia Concertante* which, although too simple to be contained in the above table, does still exhibit in embryo some of the features that were to appear more fully developed in the bigger concertos. The first movement contains no real development, but merely a nine-bar link leading from the end of the exposition back to a recapitulation; however, the recapitulation is compressed (50 bars as compared with the exposition's 93), and by presenting the first subject in 2/4 (at 17^4) rather than 6/8, Walton is able to save the 6/8 version for the coda, when it can return at 21 in its authentic version to round off the movement. The recapitulation in the finale (at 39) is more conventional, but still manages to suggest a cyclic dimension to the movement by means of the perky fanfare (at 41) with which it had begun,[25] and of course the whole work ends, as will the later concertos, with a recollection of the first movement.

Viola Concerto

We have already investigated the first movement; the development in the finale includes treatment of the second subject in an Elgarian manner[26] at 43, the first subject in canon at 44, and a broad, lyrical melody at 45^4 which makes its first appearance in the development, with one further echo later. Once again Walton here uses earlier thematic material as an ostinato accompaniment, in this case both the first subject and a fragment of transition (from 39); after the return of the second subject (at 48^5 – see 4 in Table 5.3 above), the lyrical theme reappears (from 57^6 to 60) to dominate the climax of the whole section, with yet another ostinato accompaniment, formed from the first ten notes of the first subject in augmentation.

Here too the centre of gravity of the sonata movement has shifted to the development, with the result that the joint return of the openings of both first and third movements at 61 seems like a dream, a feeling reinforced by the fact that the first movement theme is now in A major, although it is pitched a third lower than before: by analogy with the first movement it ought to be in F sharp minor, but it is instead harmonized in A. Fragments of earlier themes drift by, including the development melody (at 63³), and are gradually filtered away until all that remain are the two sixths, and we are left on the edge of their A-minor, A-major ambivalence.

Violin Concerto

There is a wonderful urgency, an immediacy almost of words, in Walton's writing for violin, which surpasses even the warmth of his viola lines. Wide-ranging, languorous melodies seem to soar to impossible yet inescapable heights, and fall only to acquire a sudden surge that propels them even higher and to even greater eloquence. Such writing pervades the Violin Concerto (the end of the first movement, for example, from 22), and appears also in the Violin Sonata (as in the passage beginning at bar 102).[27] Perhaps that is why the first subject in the Concerto consists of not one but two simultaneous lyrical melodies, as in Ex. 5.7.[28]

Ex. 5.7   Violin Concerto, 1st movement

Only rarely do they appear separately, such as in the development, metamorphosed into pointed, angular fragments (at 9 and 12), and the original version of the opening violin melody is presented only twice alone – at 10³ and, in augmentation, at ⁷17. Otherwise they are inseparable, either complete, as in the recapitulation (at 22, with roles reversed) or in the accompanied cadenza at the close of the finale (the first few notes of each for clarinet and solo cello – ³80).

The second subject, at 5, is in E flat minor (only in the two Symphonies does Walton adhere to the traditional subsidiary keys for his second subjects), and the shift to E minor at 6 is echoed in the first pages of the development, when F minor at 9 gives way to F sharp minor at 10. This movement, too, reaches its climax through developmental procedures – fragments of first and second subjects simultaneously at 20 – though the ensuing course of the recapitulation proper, at 22, is sustained a little longer than in the Viola Concerto. As in that work, the second subject is acknowledged by the merest reminiscence, and the movement closes with the first subject (both parts, at 26⁴).

Howes[29] proposes an ingenious palindromic structure for this movement, in which he discerns 'a very much modified sonata form'. He divides the movement into periods consisting of bar-lengths as follows: 44, 30, 'about 65', 65, 30, 45, with the cadenza at the central point between the two 65s. However, the bar numbers are not entirely accurate: while the second 65 (actually 64) and the second 30 (actually 33) may be allowed, the first proposed 65-bar period is in fact only 50 bars long, nor do these dimensions tally with sonata-form elements, which would divide the movement as follows:

44 + 30 bars	65 + 65 + 30 bars	45 bars
Exposition	Development	Recapitulation

Were the putative symmetry intentional, we would expect some correspondence, or compromise, with sonata elements – not as thorough as in, say, the first movement of Bartók's Fifth String Quartet (1934), but not creating the impression, as here, that if there is a palindrome, it has been casually superimposed onto the sonata.

The finale embodies some of the sharpest contrasts in any of the concertos, between on the one hand a jaunty, slightly tipsy march of a first subject (despite its prevailing 3/4 time-signature) that almost out-swaggers the hero of Stravinsky's *Soldier's Tale*, and on the other a second subject that exploits the sheer beauty of lyrical melody that at its finest only the violin can create.[30]

After a *molto animato* subsidiary theme at 52, the second subject is in E major; like the first movement of the Viola Concerto, it is again in the subdominant and, like the principal theme in the first movement of this concerto, it too has a counter-melody (solo flute), though we hear little more of this one, apart from passing references at 64 (bassoon) and in the closing cadenza (solo cello at 76). The development (from 55) largely takes on the second part of the first subject, and brings together the movement's two extremes of mood when it is transformed and augmented by the solo at 60 against the first subject's rhythm in the cellos. The second subject returns in the tonic at 64; both its opening phrase and, when violin and orchestra switch roles (at ¹65) its continuation, chasten the cocky first subject into a pensive accompaniment.

Howes[31] marks 66 as the beginning of the recapitulation, though this seems odd in view of the presence of a dominant pedal and of further development, which once more leads to the movement's climax (at 72). Over a subdominant pedal and accompanied by fragments of the first subject (the finale of the Viola Concerto again comes to mind), the solo quietly ruminates on the main theme from the beginning of the work.[32]

This concerto has inevitably invited comparisons with Elgar's Violin Concerto, principally because they share the unusual key of B minor, through which each expresses 'a peculiarly personal and introspective' mood,[33] and also because of the accompanied cadenzas towards the ends of their finales. But even though the Walton cadenza may have been suggested by the Elgar, there are a number of differences between the two. Leaving aside their length – the Elgar occupies fully half the movement, whereas Walton's is much shorter – the differences lie in their functions.

Superficially they recall earlier themes (including, in the Elgar, the second movement), but crucially, Elgar's structural argument is over by the time his cadenza is reached, whereas Walton's must double as recapitulation and reminiscence. Elgar's soloist '. . . recalls themes from earlier movements, caresses them, lingers lovingly over them and finally bids them a fond farewell'.[34] Walton's solo can afford no such indulgences, nor can his orchestra, and while both elaborate on earlier themes (we recall that Elgar's accompaniment consists almost entirely of ' "thrummed" pizz. tremolando', as he called it), they are firmly anchored to a dominant pedal, to careful barring and even suggested metronome markings. The whole work is finally brought to its goal when, at 80, the second phrase from the finale's second subject takes over from the first movement's first subject. As in the Viola Concerto, this loosening of the finale's ties with sonata form as it harks back – perhaps even *because* it harks back – to the beginning, makes it a conclusion not just to this movement but to the entire work.

Cello Concerto

A ripple of disappointment ran through the musical press when the Cello Concerto appeared in 1957: when stylistic evolution, enrichment of idiom and ever more challenging insights were the order of the day, it seemed as if Walton were standing still or, worse, going into reverse. Donald Mitchell, in an article whose very quotation marks withheld the implicit approval of its title ('The "Modernity" of William Walton'), suggested that *Troilus and Cressida* 'offered no more than a strikingly derivative romanticism coupled with revivals and reminiscences of familiar idiosyncracies that in their context seem to have lost their old pungency',[35] and then went on to condemn the Cello Concerto in the same terms, asserting that it 'appears to confirm the style that Walton assumed in "Troilus", and is to sustain, it seems'. Peter Evans, rather more gently, observed that 'in the later concertos . . . and large-scale sonata-structures . . . he is most prone to fall back on earlier solutions'.[36]

Walton was moving into the final stages of what Meinhard Saremba has proposed as the British composer's typical career:

Waltons Leben kann man durchaus als Musterschicksal eines Komponisten in Großbritannien sehen: Die Etappen der Initiation des Neulings, der Inthronisation des Erfolgreichen, der Institutionalisierung des Berühmten und des Ignorierens durch eine neue Generation stellten nicht nur bei ihm die wichtigsten Stationen dar.[37]

And it was more than ten years before a more balanced, if florid, view emerged:

> While it can be said that this late concerto is not more mature in its musical motiva-
> tion than the 1929 Viola Concerto, it can certainly be said that in the later works
> Walton digs deeper into the rich vein of his instrumental imagination to produce ore
> of a finer quality. In this respect he is very much like Brahms, whose music did not
> so much mature as become more subtly defined: in other words, more Brahmsian.[38]

And part of that finer quality lies in an even more subtle exploitation of sonata form – so subtle, in fact, that in the first movement it almost dissolves, only to be reconstituted in the finale.

The very first chord must be one of the most delicately judged that Walton ever devised: the dynamic markings are simultaneously *mf, p, pp* and *ppp*, spread across flutes, oboe and bassoon and *divisi* first and second violins, pizzicato, with four solo violas, *con sord.* and *sul tasto*, pizzicato cellos and (solo) double bass, harp and vibraphone. They announce a gently rocking C major/minor chord with added flattened sixth, which the soloist almost at once turns into a melody. Howes postulates a *quasi*-rondo structure, ABCADA = Coda,[39] with each section roughly ten bars in length (though, as with the supposed symmetry of the Violin Concerto, the crucial word is 'roughly'), yet elements of sonata form are still discernible, particularly if we take into account the passage in the finale from 14 to the end, clearly marked by Walton *a tempo di No 6 Io Mov. ma un po' più lento*. For what we find now is as shown in Table 5.4.

Table 5.4 Cello Concerto: first movement and end of finale

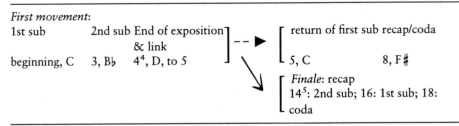

First movement:					
1st sub		2nd sub	End of exposition & link	return of first sub	recap/coda
beginning, C	3, B♭	4⁴, D, to 5		5, C	8, F♯

Finale: recap
14⁵: 2nd sub; 16: 1st sub; 18: coda

In other words, the first movement's true recapitulation occurs in the finale, with first and second subjects reversed as an acknowledgement that the passage is providing a coda to the entire work. Two further points reinforce this view: first, the thematic references back to the first movement at the end of the finale are far more extended and far more literal than in either of the other concertos (where they really are reminiscences and not restatements), and secondly, the tonal plan at the end of the first movement adumbrates that of 14 in the finale: between 6 and 8 in the first movement the key rises by a semitone (F – F#), followed by 12 bars of first subject – apparently a recapitulation, but in the wrong key, F#

rather than C, after which Walton simply sidesteps to C (at 9) for a formal close in the tonic. In the finale, the key again rises by a semitone, from B at 14 to the return of the first subject – now, as it should be, in C, at 16. Consequently, the presence of the first movement in these closing pages is so powerful that, unlike the Viola and Violin Concertos, the wistful recollection is of the finale itself (five bars at 18), rather than of the first movement. Sonata form has rarely received so ingenious a modification.

Second Symphony

The gestation periods of Walton's two Symphonies have some common features: the First was commissioned in 1932, with hopes for a first performance in 1933, though in the event it was not completed until 1935; the Second was commissioned in 1956, with similar hopes for a première the following year, but it too was delayed, this time for three years – until 1960. The delay with the Second Symphony was not, however, a compositional block, but was due to further commissions, notably the *Partita* for Orchestra, music for a television series and *Anon in Love*, a cycle of songs for Peter Pears and Julian Bream.[40] Among a number of notices surrounding its first performance, at the Edinburgh Festival on 2 September 1960, Felix Aprahamian was one of the few critics to give it a warm welcome:

> The Second Symphony has been garnered at a time when artificial husbandry is at its zenith, tonality suspect, and precious human rehearsal time too often squandered on the inhumanly conceived desiccations of an ingenious but tone-deaf *avant-garde*. In his new symphony Walton shows himself able to juggle with the fashionable *materia musica* and procedures as deftly as any of his juniors, but to more communicable and rewarding effect.[41]

Further familiarity and the passage of time have not rendered it as popular as the First, though as Kennedy has observed:

> The truth is that the Second Symphony is curiously reluctant to yield its secrets and inner meaning through a few hearings. Not that it is difficult music, but it does need concentrated and frequent listening before, suddenly, the veil parts and one is admitted to the inner circle of its highly distinctive sound-world.[42]

And Howes, too, implies as much:

> . . . what seems to escape one in this symphony is its individuality, its subtler beauties, its individual flavour.[43]

The sonata structure in this first movement is indebted both to its own predecessor and to the concertos; from the First Symphony it inherits a certain security of key-centre, particularly in that the second subjects are both in the traditional keys – B flat major and G major/minor in exposition and recapitulation respectively – and from the concertos the presentation during the development of material masquerading as recapitulation, but in fact not that at all. The structure is again more secure than the concertos, however, in that the final return to the first subject in the tonic is not in the form of a fragmentary, last-minute reminiscence, but actually invites a reading which suggests a recapitulation in reverse. Table 5.5 summarizes the form.

Table 5.5 Second Symphony – first movement

beginning	1st subject, g
bar 37	transition
bar 71	2nd subject (i), B♭
bar 92	2nd subject (ii), *Agitato*
bar 132	end of exposition, D
bar 133	development
bar 227	transition (from 42)
bar 255	2nd subject (i), G/g
bar 276	2nd subject (ii) *Agitato*
bar 305	further development
bar 338	1st subject, g
ca. bar 353	coda

If the notion of sonata form's 'double return' as proposed by Webster (see p.75) is to have any significance, the reappearance of the first subject at bar 217 must still be no other than development, since it is not in the tonic. But we are to be presented with the second subject first and, like his classical predecessors (Mozart in the first movement of his K.311 piano sonata, for instance), Walton therefore slides into his recapitulation proper via the transition, at bar 227. The recapitulation of the first subject (at 338) now acquires some of the characteristics of a coda, since it is much more static than in its original appearance – here, nearly every instrument is playing some kind of ostinato or other, closely linked to G minor. But the chords at 356 announce an imminent end to the movement, partly through their insistent rhythm and partly by recalling much the same effect from the end of the first movement of the Stravinsky Symphony in C. We shall in due course turn to a discussion of the finale to this work, which is a set of variations on a serial theme. Although the variations never lose their allegiance to tonality, some features of this first movement anticipate the serial proclivities of the finale; principal among these is the relationship between the first subject and the first element of the second subject, both of which, if we examine them in the same key (i.e., as from bars 1–2 and 255, Ex. 5.8), consist of the same prominent intervals, that is, major seventh, augmented second/minor third and semitone.[44]

Routh has pointed out not only that 'the totally chromatic first subject uses, in the course of its exposition [by bar 16], all twelve notes . . .', but also that the melody of the second subject 'is confined to six notes (B flat-A-F sharp-G-E flat-D) which are the first six of the twelve-note passacaglia theme that is to come later'.[45] His assertion that 'Notes 7–12 of the passacaglia theme of the finale direct the tonality of the second movement towards B major, which thus complements the second subject of the first movement'[46] is, however, an oversimplification, for all 12 notes are present in the first four bars of the second movement, though not in any order discernibly related to the passacaglia.

Ex. 5.8 Symphony No. 2, 1st movement

Scherzo

Most twentieth-century symphony and concerto scherzo movements retain –
even if not always in 3/4 time – a structure recognizably related to the old
|| : A : || B A^2 : ||, with the same shape for the trio, usually a relatively relaxed
interlude prior to the reprise of the scherzo without repeats. But if, as I have
suggested, Walton devised his own idiosyncratic exploitation of sonata form,
his treatment of the scherzo is even more individual. Only the Violin Concerto
retains an outline to which the traditional scherzo-trio-scherzo structure can be
readily related, though ironically it almost has the makings of two trios, which
is presumably why he found it necessary to label the real trio (at 36), lest the
tune at 31^8 be mistaken for it.

'*Portsmouth Point*', writes Michael Kennedy, 'is the prototype Walton scherzo',[47]
and it certainly rattles along without a moment's hesitation, never stumbling into
silence or pausing to reflect a moment; its mixture of irregular rhythms (more justifi-
ably described here than elsewhere as Stravinskyian) and its almost random sequence
of tunes do point the way to the later scherzos. But its mood is playful rather than
malicious, markedly English rather than Italian, and it is so indifferent to its own
whereabouts that it has to end with a pronounced deceleration, for there is precious
little else in its structure to signal that it is over. By the time of the next two scherzos,
in the Viola Concerto and First Symphony, Walton will have sacrificed none of the
energy of *Portsmouth Point*, but a pronounced return in the Concerto and a good
100 bars of dominant pedal in the Symphony will help us find our bearings.

Of the four scherzo movements in these orchestral works – the second movements in each case of the Viola Concerto, First Symphony, Violin Concerto and
Cello Concerto – it is that in the First Symphony which is the most notorious,
and which we shall first consider.

As I have already suggested, it is difficult not to conclude that in discussions of
the First Symphony, most commentators have avoided getting to grips with this
movement, even though they are largely agreed on what it is: in addition to
Howes' summary (he calls it a scherzo), we find brief and generally inconclusive
surveys in Kennedy (also scherzo), Cox (scherzo), Ballantine ('generic scherzo'),

Routh (scherzo), Avery (scherzo: he discerns 'malice incarnate', in the final five-bar silence and transformation of the initial theme), Evans (scherzo), Tierney (scherzo) and Evans (scherzo).[48]

It seems clear from the start, however, that although the movement is in E (not only Dorian, as suggested by some critics, but with marked Lydian and Phrygian emphasis, too), its structure will be more clearly explained by reference to rhythm and recurrence of themes than to tonal relationships. But the movement is still full of pitfalls, for themes and rhythms rarely have the patience to appear the same way twice. We encounter distortions of various kinds, as when 3/4 bars turn themselves into 5/4, or themes either stretch or compress themselves, or scurrying melodic activity evaporates to an eerie stillness. And this is in fact the *malizia* in the movement's title, for a musical malice refuses to deliver what we have been led to expect. We anticipate 3/4 and are given 5/4; we expect a figure to be reiterated, only to find it lurch over by one crotchet (see Ex. 5.9a); we are offered Ex. 5.9b, which later mocks itself as Ex. 5.9c.

Ex. 5.9a   Symphony No. 1, 2nd movement

Ex. 5.9b

Ex. 5.9c

We are led to assume a scherzo, and everywhere find its components warped and twisted. The inevitable questions then arise: has Walton discarded all order in favour of whim, or arbitrary fancy, as Hutchings implied in 1937? Does he drag us through the movement simply by the momentum of his unrelenting rhythms? Or do just enough remnants of the scherzo structure survive to enable us to cling onto a semblance of formal coherence? These are the issues that must be addressed in an investigation of this unique movement, and one possible structure is set out in Table 5.6.

This suggested structural outline, which, alongside some affinities with the traditional scherzo form and, in many places, secure four- or eight-bar phrasing

Table 5.6 First Symphony: scherzo

Beg.	Introduction	Sounds like a dominant preparation on E, and with modal inflection ($\flat$7), though which mode is unclear.
45	A	But it was a tonic preparation: principal theme on E; modes implied turn out to be Phrygian and Lydian.
46^4	A^2	Repeat of A on F$\sharp$ (with G$\sharp$ bass).
47	Closing section	Moves to close in E over dominant pedal. Clear cadence in E (again combining Lydian and Phrygian features) at 48.
48^5–^{1}55	B	Development & extension of A; blaring figure at 51 (Ex. 5.9b). Hovers on diminished seventh from 52–54.
55–62	B^2	Begins much as B, but with another added fragment (at 57 – Ex. 5.11, the only fragment to appear only once in the movement), and including at 59 the dancing figuration from 50. Blaring theme distorted at 60^4 (Ex. 5.9c).
62^5–^{3}64	a	If any shreds of a trio linger in this movement, they are here, despite the continuing E$\flat$ pedal, and are characterized by the initial 5/4 bar and the remnants of the theme (from 45^5).
^{2}64–^{1}66	a^2	Again the 5/4 opening bar and the figure from 45^5; a further theme added at 65.
66–67	b	A stuttering rhythm (dotted crotchet, quaver, crotchet, barline, crotchet rest, dotted crotchet, quaver, barline, crotchet, two crotchet rests, barline, three crotchets) is picked up after 67 and prepares the return to A.
68^{16}–71^8	A	Return of main theme, which stops and hovers twice; includes a distorted version of diminished seventh outline from^{7}53.
71^9–^{1}73	a^2	Defined as before by the initial 5/4 and the scherzo figure; slightly changed around 72, and includes the theme from 65.
73–76	b^2	Includes the stammering figure, the diminished seventh outline from^{7}53, and the frothy figure from 50, leading at 76 to the Lydian/Phrygian cadence from 48.
76^5–^{1}78	A	Final statement of A, interspersed (not, as Howes alleges, combined) with outbursts from Ex. 5.9b.
78	Coda	A long (close on 100 bars) dominant pedal, making much use of the stammering figures from (b).

(as in, for example, much of the passage from 57–62) may on the face of it lend a certain overall coherence. But do we hear it that way? Its relentless manic rush scarcely gives the listener a moment's respite; the very rhythm seems to pick up each fragment of theme in an almost random manner as it hurtles along, only to brandish it for an equally random time and then to toss it aside as another takes its fancy. It constantly taunts the listener with the thought that if only the red herrings could be identified and cast aside, it would be perfectly straightforward, but it never reveals where the red herrings are. There can hardly be upwards of 650 bars more continuously rapid and kaleidoscopic music in the whole symphonic repertoire, and at Walton's metronome marking of $\downarrow$. = 116 (and ignoring the 5/4 bars) it should all be over in about 5 minutes and 42 seconds.[49] As a passing comparison we might note that the first movement of Mahler's Eighth Symphony, with some 580 bars (and tempo fluctuations, to be sure, but basically *Allegro impetuoso*), is timed on Klaus Tennstedt's recording at over 24 minutes.

But the schematic outline suggested above also reveals that, with the double return of A, the movement has some distant relationship with a rondo, and this observation leads to a possible connection with another scherzo exhibiting rondo characteristics – the third movement of Elgar's Second Symphony. In fact, as Ex. 5.10 shows, the similarity between the openings of the two principal themes is striking, and it cannot but provoke a speculation as to the source of Walton's *malizia*. Kennedy[50] relates how the two composers met for the first and only time at Worcester in September, 1932. Walton was there for a performance of the Viola Concerto, and Elgar to conduct *For the Fallen*. Elgar, not at all taken with the Concerto, was heard 'deploring that such music should be thought fit for a stringed instrument', and it seems inconceivable that word of his disapproval did

Ex. 5.10a   Elgar, Symphony No. 2, 3rd movement

Ex. 5.10b   Walton, Symphony No. 1, 2nd movement

Ex. 5.10c   Elgar, Symphony No. 2, 3rd movement

not get back to the younger composer. Almost at once Walton began work on the First Symphony: 'From October (perhaps September) 1932 until March or April 1933 is a reasonable estimate for the writing of the first two movements in short score'.[51] Given the proximity of the composition to Elgar's dismissal of the Viola Concerto, the close similarity of the two scherzo themes quoted above, the pervasive use of cross-rhythms in both movements, and given the resemblance they bear to a rondo structure, it is tempting indeed to speculate that Walton's scherzo may have been intended as a mischievous parody of Elgar's, and a retort to his dismissal of the Viola Concerto.[52] There is even something distinctly Elgarian about the tune at 57 (Ex. 5.11 – it is the only passage in the movement marked *cantabile* and, as Table 5.6 shows, the only tune in the movement to be heard just once, as if its presence carried no implications for the movement's structure).

Ex. 5.11   Walton, Symphony No. 1, 2nd movement

A comparison with a later appearance of Elgar's theme (see Ex. 5.10c) makes the rhythmic likeness unavoidable. That Walton had a few years earlier been one of the signatories of the famous letter to the Press Association defending Elgar against Edward Dent's denunciation,[53] or that his admiration for Elgar included the E-flat Symphony itself, and is documented as late as 1942,[54] does not render impossible a barbed response to criticism from an older, and for him a bygone, generation.[55] Be that as it may, however, the scherzo from Walton's First Symphony is the most complex he ever wrote, beside which those in the remaining works present few problems. Let us briefly consider each in turn.

Viola Concerto

This movement, too, shares features with a rondo, as was noted by Tovey[56] and Howes,[57] although the latter prudently adds that it does not 'lend itself to confinement within a formula'. Foss picked up an important feature of the scherzos of the Viola and Violin Concertos and of the First Symphony when he observed that:

> ... apart from all interplay of varying rhythmic versions of main subjects, Walton has a habit of suddenly introducing a new rhythmic phrase, which he baldly states, and ... such phrases are nearly always in a kind of 'catch' phrase of their own .... The effect is nearly always electric, a clean statement with an unusual pulse succeeding a jumble of exciting cross-rhythms.[58]

Presumably he would designate as this movement's 'catch' phrase the *Risoluto* outburst at 22 (quoted as Ex. 5.12c), which begins the third section. The three principal themes are indicated in Ex. 5.12 a–c.

Ex. 5.12a   Viola Concerto, 2nd movement

Ex. 5.12b   Viola Concerto, 2nd movement

Ex. 5.12c   Viola Concerto, 2nd movement

Table 5.7 Viola Concerto: second movement

beginning	A	Two statements of Ex. 5.12a, one in the tonic and one (at 17^3) in the dominant, comprise the first section, which returns at its close to the tonic, E.
		An extended middle section follows, from 19–32:
$19-^522$	B	begins with Ex. 5.12a, and closes with Ex. 5.12b[59]
$22-24^7$	C	begins with Ex. 5.12c, and closes again with the fanfare.
24^7-^128	B;C	amalgamates a restatement of the two previous sections, with Ex. 5.12a (as at 19), the grouping of quavers in threes (from just before 21), Ex. 5.12c at 26 and the fanfare in D at 27.
		This leads to a dominant pedal at 28, which turns out not to prepare the principal return, but to lead to:
30–33	C	a restatement in F# of Ex. 5.12c, with the fanfare at ^{631}. Pedals on A and B lead to the return of:
33	A	in the tonic, but taking up in its second half the repeated dominant version from 18. At 36 the fanfare's function as a closing figure is verified.

Such a plan gives some idea of the succession of themes, but little impression of either the rapidity and unpredictability with which they succeed each other, or the exhilarating rhythmic contrasts and sudden shifts of emphasis that the movement seems without warning to pull out of its hat. It remains the most approachable of Walton's scherzo movements.

Violin Concerto

'Gaga' was the word used by Walton to describe the scherzo in this work: '. . . quite gaga, I may say, and of doubtful propriety after the 1st movement'.[60] And it does career around in a manner that at times can only be described as crazy, with the augmented triads which give it much of its harmonic flavour, bizarre solo harmonics alternating with pizzicato chords, not one but three raucous phrases (at 30, 31 and 35 – see Ex. 5.13c–e) of the kind noticed by Foss,[61] and despite its designation of 36 as 'Trio (canzonetta)', the movement has virtually two trios; but in the reprise it 'forgets' to restate the first one and recalls it in its closing pages, relegating the 'real' trio to a token reference. In addition, if the actual sequence of events in the scherzo of the First Symphony was constantly disconcerting, at least its lopsided melodies and overall rhythmic impetus remained generally recognizable. Here the opposite is the case, for while it is a 'reasonably regular scherzo with a trio',[62] nearly every theme, except those of the bogus trio and the trio proper, is subjected to rhythmic variation and distortion. Perhaps that is why, behind its tarantella-like frenzy, its shape is – needs to be – reasonably regular.

An introduction takes us to 28, where the principal theme appears (Ex. 5.13a), followed by the most Neapolitan theme of the movement, at 29 (Ex. 5.13b).

Ex. 5.13a   Violin Concerto, 2nd movement

Ex. 5.13b

Examples 5.13c–e show the three raucous themes and their rhythmic variants, the first of which blusters in at 30, and the second at 31. The pseudo-trio follows, sounding as if it has sauntered in from *Façade* (especially the blips for solo clarinet), but its repeat is cut short by an almost complete restatement of the scherzo, introduction and all, at a tritone's distance from its original pitch. This time it is the third raucous tune (at 35 – Ex. 5.13e) which interrupts, and the real trio follows – its two-fold *aaba* is the simplest and most guileless structure in all six works under discussion. When the scherzo resumes (at 42), this time a third below its original pitch, its own rhythm has been turned from quintuplet quavers in 2/2 to semiquavers in 4/4 (Ex. 5.13f shows the new version of the Neapolitan theme as presented by solo violin and two trumpets). More distortions of the first two raucous themes lead directly to the final statement, and reminiscences of both trios – the real and the fake – culminate in a closing adaptation of the introduction. The whole movement gives the soloist an opportunity for hair-raising virtuosity, from rapid arpeggios and spectral harmonics to languid parallel sixths, double-stopped trills and, in the trio, a stratospheric *cantabile*, again on harmonics. No wonder Heifetz was reported as being 'very crazy about it'.[63]

Ex. 5.13c   Violin Concerto, 2nd movement

Ex. 5.13d

Ex. 5.13e

Ex. 5.13f

Cello Concerto

The Viola Concerto had been almost immediately acknowledged as a landmark in the genre; Constant Lambert called it 'that least sensational yet most satisfying of all things, a finished and well-balanced work of art'.[64] And of the Violin Concerto Hubert Foss was moved to write:

> It is the real Walton – the rhythmic humanist, the genuine romantic, the man who can laugh at, even while he loves, his fellow humans. Above all, it is intensely musical, like all Walton's music: and it has the splendid quality of sounding far better than it looks.[65]

So it comes as something of a surprise to discover Walton himself writing to Gregor Piatigorsky, who had commissioned the Cello Concerto, 'I am so happy to receive your cable and . . . that you should think the whole work wonderful. It is to my mind the best of my, now three concertos'.[66] Susana Walton continues:

> [William] thought of the cello as a melancholy instrument, full of soul; accordingly he wrote a rather sad tune to the opening . . . . He certainly had a special affection for the cello concerto as it had come very spontaneously, and he felt it was the closest to his personality.

And this is indeed a more introverted concerto than its showy predecessor: if the solo part in the Violin Concerto is often a soaring *bel canto* aria, in this Concerto it is a pensive, expressive soliloquy; if the violin's scherzo is 'gaga', the cello's is impassioned, and even the electric catch-phrase which Foss observed as a characteristic of the scherzos has in this work a relatively low voltage (at 6).

We have already seen how readily Walton changed the key of the second subject in the first movement of the First Symphony, and that almost casual approach to tonality is not exceptional. Movements do conform to the most basic tonal requirements, by beginning and ending in the same key, but there are times when the reprise of an extended section will happily wander through far more keys than on its first appearance; this scherzo from the Cello Concerto demonstrates the genre.

After a five-bar orchestral introduction which hovers on the supertonic seventh chord of C# minor, the solo announces the principal theme, A (see Ex. 5.14a–d for the main themes of the movement). The rest of the movement is summarized in Table 5.8 (see page 97).

We can observe from this table that the paragraph B-C-C'-D-cadenza[67] from 5–12 is virtually repeated at 12–19, but there is no consistent treatment of pitch relationships between the original and repeated sections. This inexact treatment of pitch can also be seen in, for example, the paired statements of the figure at 51 in the First Symphony's scherzo (which are never in the same relationship to each other), and we have already encountered it in the scherzo of the Violin Concerto; we shall meet it in the finale of the present concerto, too. It is quite different in effect from the stability achieved by the restatement, in the first movement of the Second Symphony, of some 50 bars (roughly from 254–305) of recapitulation a third below the exposition pitch, that is, in the traditional relative major/tonic minor relationship.

Ex. 5.14a   Cello Concerto, 2nd movement

Ex. 5.14b

Ex. 5.14c

Ex. 5.14d

Of the remaining movements, the finale of the Second Symphony is a set of variations, and that of the Cello Concerto a *Tema ed improvvisazioni*; the finale of the First Symphony is both the most interesting and the most controversial. The delays in its composition are well known, as is the fact that (possibly against his better judgement) Walton consented to have the first three movements performed three times, in December 1934 and April 1935, before the first complete performance in November 1935.[68] This hiatus has undoubtedly made both composer and critics self-conscious about the movement: for the composer, the pressure somehow to crown the sheer physical power of the first three movements must have been considerable, and ever since its completion, critics have felt bound to ask themselves whether he succeeded. The result is that their verdicts on it, comprehensively summarized in Schaarwächter,[69] vary far more than those on any other symphony or concerto with, at two extremes, Eric Walter White and Benjamin Britten. For White, it is 'one of the boldest designs in all symphonic construction; in certain respects it deliberately challenges comparison with Beethoven's 9th',[70] while Britten condemned the entire work, writing of its 'fate-ridden "gitters", [its] pretentiousness, [its] abominable scoring'.[71] Kennedy's verdict sets out as perhaps the gentlest and yet the most guarded, for final approval seems to be withheld: 'Walton was right to balance the symphony with a Finale of lighter substance, but there was so much to balance that the Finale has to gird its loins for a culminating onslaught on our feelings.' However, he continues, 'Still, one would not have it otherwise.'[72] But David Cox *would* have it otherwise:

> The mood suggests an aspiring, rhetorical affirmation, a 'massive hope', [the expression is Elgar's] which does not quite ring true – and there is too superficial a jauntiness in the fugal section. The issues already expounded are bigger than this, and fulfilment is not found in a ceremonial *maestoso* . . . .[73]

Table 5.8 Cello Concerto: scherzo

bar 6	A	Ex. 5.14a.
2	B	Ex. 5.14b, repeated a semitone up at 2^5.
3	A	Beginning only, a semitone below original, then moves away. Leads to a brief cadenza-like passage at 4.
5	B	Minor third higher than the original, together with the repeat at the upper semitone, but with two bars omitted.
6	C	Ex. 5.14c the 'electric charge' figure: orchestra.
7	C'	Ex. 5.14d: an extension of C, now played by solo; leads to a half-close on E at 9, and to
10	D	A short, harsh figure with major seventh and trill, derived from A. Some further development of A leads to a second short cadenza at 11^9.
		Much of the previous section (5–11^9) is now repeated (at 12–18^8).
12	B	Begins at the same pitch as at 5, with alternating *poco meno mosso* and a *tempo sub*. The same two bars are omitted as before (i.e., $^{3-2}6$).
13^2	C	Now a minor third higher than before (at 6). Its two phrases are interrupted by some solo triple-stopped pizzicato chords (which previously came just before D) after which the second phrase is a major sixth higher than before; the pizzicatos are extended and lead to
14^2	C'	Now a fifth higher than before (at 7); leads to a half-close on B at 16, and to
17	D	Continues a fifth higher than before (at 10), and by way of further development of A to a longer cadenza than at 11^9 (now at 18^9).
19	B	The version from 12 (with alternating tempi), now a fifth higher, and including the repeat at the upper semitone; the two missing bars (from $^{3-2}6$) are replaced.
21	C	A tone higher than the first version (at 6, preceded by the original two bars); and a semitone distant from its second version (at 13^2). Both phrases back at the same pitch.
		They are not followed by D, but linked by a further short cadenza to
22	A	A *quasi*-return (same pitch as bar 6), with fragments of the original A leading to the supertonic seventh of C#, and hence to the final cadence.

And the word 'ceremonial' is exactly right: where movements I–III are the shared utterances of private, personal feelings, the finale never rises above the communal pomp of some grand public ceremony – an international conference, perhaps, or a coronation. If not a ceremony, then film music. For a composer who spent much of his career writing extremely successful film music, it must rank as a considerable achievement that Walton's orchestral, non-film music nearly always retains its own integrity and strength: hardly ever does it suggest the medium of film, but this movement is the exception.[74] But film music or not, there is little doubt that the movement fails to maintain the idiom of the first three. Where they are dissonant and chromatic, it is largely consonant and diatonic; where they are rich in structural detail, it is relatively straightforward; it also contains far more phrase-repetition – even the 17-bar introduction consists of two-fold statements of almost identical 8½-bar fanfares. And the *Vivacissimo* halfway is an illusion: without a score, nothing much seems to have happened, for the ♩. = circa 88 (i.e., ♪= 264) turns out to be exactly the same speed as the earlier *Brioso ed ardamente*, where ♩ = 132 also produces ♪= 264. Moreover, in places the music unmistakably hints that in seeking a satisfactory conclusion to the Symphony, Walton turned back to the final section of *Belshazzar's Feast*, and it is not difficult to detect matching passages in the two works (Table 5.9).

Table 5.9 Finale of First Symphony and final section of *Belshazzar's Feast*

Symphony I	Belshazzar's Feast	
Opening fanfares and first subject	'Then sing aloud' leading into 68	The 6–5 appoggiatura is ubiquitous in the Symphony movement, and frequent in *Belshazzar*.
107: slower-moving melody	62^9: 'While the Kings of the earth lament'	The pace broadens, but the basic tempo remains unchanged. In *Belshazzar* Walton suggests a slow 4 in a bar; in the Symphony a slower beat, even if irregular, could be superimposed.
109^2 and	57^6: 'Blow up the trumpet'; 60^6: 'sing aloud'	A 6/8 pulse cuts across a basic 3/4.
122: V of ♭VI	71: V of ♭VI (in F)	The C♯ and G♯ are pedals which return quite abruptly to the tonic (B♭ and F respectively).
124^9	56^7: 'Take a psalm'	I to V of V, 2nd inversion.

Despite the assumption of a number of critics that the finale of the Cello Concerto is nothing more than a set of variations with a different name,[75] Walton clearly intended to distinguish between the more formal, structured nature of variations and the rhapsodic, spontaneous atmosphere of improvisations (which Ottaway is one of the few critics to acknowledge).[76] Variations have a number of characteristics which we take for granted. For example, they tend to grow in complexity; each variation retains the structure of the theme; each explores one particular means of embellishing it; each, whether or not the same length as the original, adheres to its relative dimensions, and many preserve its harmonic plan. Not one of the so-called 'variations' in the finale of the Cello Concerto meets these requirements rigorously enough to merit the name (see Ex. 5.15 for the first nine bars of the theme). Thus the first improvisation – potentially the closest to a real variation – alters the relative pitches of the three principal phrases of the theme, and the part of the theme (bar 13 onwards) beginning with downward sequences is vastly expanded when nine bars from the original become 23 in the improvisation. At one of the most beautiful moments in the entire work the unison and octave orchestral accompaniment suddenly ripens into harmony (at 5^5), and from there on, both orchestra and solo linger over various fragments, as if reluctant to discard them.[77] The same processes characterize the two cello cadenzas: they each explore, with differing emphasis, features of the theme such as the *quasi*-Phrygian cadence of bars 1–2, the falling 4ths of bars 3–4, the rising semitone and 5th of 8–9, and so on. The *Allegro molto* contribution from the orchestra sets out like a variation, but again is more of a collective improvisation, spending three bars on bars 1–2 of the theme, followed by five bars on bars 3–4, and five bars on 5–6, only to begin a repeat at the tritone rather than proceeding with the same asymmetrical treatment.

It is a long-standing tradition in sets of variations that the original theme often appears at the end, serving both as a coda and as a retrospective reminder of the mutations it has undergone; but at the end of these improvisations we encounter, as we have seen, a recapitulation of first-movement material. Perhaps that is why Walton chose to write a finale which, as a series of improvisations, would present even fewer structural issues of its own than would a set of variations, and would be thus readier than even variations might have been to accept a resumption of an earlier movement. And with its falling sequential figure (at 14^{2-3}) and its placid reminder of the A♭–G relationship, that resumption could almost pass for a

Ex. 5.15 Cello Concerto, 3rd movement

further improvisation (though never as a variation), so much so that when, at 18, the falling double-stopped sixths and thirds from the end of the first movement blend into the opening of the finale theme, which in turn leads back to the closing bars of the first movement, we sense a union between two inseparable strands of one musical argument.

When we turn to the finale of the Second Symphony, the difference between improvisations and variations becomes even more apparent. Each variation invents and exploits a particular texture, five of the ten variations are the same length as the theme (14 bars),[78] and even those of differing lengths exhibit a consistency of structure and treatment which immediately marks them out as variations, not improvisations.

In two sets of variations – the finale of the Second Symphony and, ten years earlier, the second movement of the Violin Sonata – Walton made use of a twelve-tone row, though in neither did he abandon tonality. This present finale is firmly rooted in G minor, and most variations begin and end in that key as, by implication, does the row itself (see Ex. 5.16).

Ex. 5.16a   Symphony No. 2, 3rd movement

Ex. 5.16b

Like many tone-rows, it possesses a degree of symmetry, though it is not consistent, nor is it consistently exploited: Ex. 5.16a shows that while note (6) begins the second half of the row at a tritone's distance from the first half, and (7–11) are in the same relationship as (1–5), any potential overall symmetry is forestalled by the minor third from (0–1) and the semitone from (6–7). Or again, the relationship of the last three notes of the first half to the last three notes of the row is the same. A further potential symmetry is evident from Ex. 5.16b: each group of four notes consists of a triad (major or minor) plus a note at a semitone's distance from either the root or the fifth.

The row's presentation at the beginning of the movement, in stark unison and octaves, and with rasping trills on two of the notes, reawakens thoughts of *malizia*, reinforced by an affinity with the malevolent introduction to Iago's 'Credo' in Act II of Verdi's *Otello*. But the variations themselves are anything but malevolent,[79] and their exploitation of the row falls into three principal categories. First, in each of the 14-bar variations (that is, 1, 3, 4, 5 and 6) the row is treated as a *cantus firmus*, and always in its P-0 version (see Table 5.10 for the row's possible mutations).

Then in Variations 2 and 8 he exploits the chordal potential of the row, and finally in Variation 9 he does both, i.e. solo brass instruments present the row, but more as a melody than a *cantus firmus*, against a gentle wash of string chords. Variation 7 functions less as an independent variation than an introduction to Variation 8; it presents a continuous tonic pedal against which RI-10 appears as an ostinato. And Variation 10 frames the fugato, for it immediately precedes it – almost as a second statement of the row/theme – and when at bar 307 the first two trumpets begin a statement of P-7 (significantly on D, which will come back to D and the affirmation of the tonic chord, at bar 326), we hear it as a variation of Variation 10 itself. It is in the fugato that Walton departs most radically from P-0 versions of the row: statements of the prime often lead directly to their own inversions (e.g., P-0 at bar 166 leads to I-0 at bar 171,[80] and P-8 at bar 181 leads to I-8 at bar 185, and so on), and any residual respect for serialism finally disappears at bar 227 when P-9 is presented by the first trombone over a dominant pedal.

Table 5.10 Second Symphony: the finale's row

		I-0	I-3	I-7	I-8	I-2	I-11	I-6	I-5	I-9	I-10	I-4	I-1			
			INVERSION													
		↓	↓	↓	↓	↓	↓	↓	↓	↓	↓	↓	↓			
	P-0 →	G	Bb	D	Eb	A	F#	Db	C	E	F	B	Ab	←	R-0	
	P-9 →	E	G	B	C	F#	Eb	Bb	A	C#	D	G#	F	←	R-9	R
	P-5 →	C	Eb	G	Ab	D	B	F#	F	A	Bb	E	C#	←	R-5	E
P	P-4 →	B	D	F#	G	C#	A#	F	E	G#	A	D#	C	←	R-4	T
R	P-10 →	F	Ab	C	Db	G	E	B	Bb	D	D#	A	F#	←	R-10	R
I	P-1 →	Ab	Cb	Eb	E	Bb	G	D	Db	F	F#	C	A	←	R-1	O
M	P-6 →	Db	Fb	Ab	A	Eb	C	G	Gb	A#	B	F	D	←	R-6	G
E	P-7 →	D	F	A	Bb	E	C#	G#	G	B	C	F#	Eb	←	R-7	R
	P-3 →	Bb	Db	F	Gb	C	A	E	Eb	G	G#	D	B	←	R-3	A
	P-2 →	A	C	E	F	B	G#	D#	D	F#	G	C#	A#	←	R-2	D
	P-8 →	Eb	Gb	Bb	B	F	D	A	Ab	C	C#	G	E	←	R-8	E
	P-11 →	F#	A	C#	D	Ab	F	C	B	D#	E	Bb	G	←	R-11	
		↑	↑	↑	↑	↑	↑	↑	↑	↑	↑	↑	↑			
		RI-10	RI-1	RI-5	RI-6	RI-0	RI-9	RI-4	RI-3	RI-7	RI-8	RI-2	RI-11			
			RETROGRADE INVERSION													

The most eminent English composer prior to Walton whose music was firmly based in the Austro-German symphonic tradition was of course Elgar. By the time Walton was beginning to make his mark, Elgar's compositional life was virtually over, his long career distinguished by the firm establishment in the orchestral repertoire of two symphonies, two concertos, a set of variations, and an oratorio that was probably the finest in the English language since Handel. At the same time, it was clear almost from the outset that Walton did not intend to find his own personal solution to the crisis facing tonality by taking the English-ethnic route favoured by composers such as Vaughan Williams. On the other hand, his propensity for a lyricism grounded in tonality and for recognizably traditional forms, even if subject to personal adaptation, placed him in a western symphonic heritage rather than in any atonal/serial school, and even his acidulous harmony and his liking for modal inflections were potentially far less disruptive of long-established tonal relationships than the uncompromising dissonances of a Bartók. Consequently, comparisons with Elgar were almost inevitable, and were probably helped by sporadic appearances of melodies that could almost have been written by him. As early as 1936 Havergal Brian was noting that 'There is a strong resemblance between Walton and Elgar',[81] and Hugh Ottaway went much further when he found the First Symphony 'a profoundly traditional work', with a 'strenuously aspiring romantic approach . . ., to be thought of more as a successor to Elgar's symphonies than as a first cousin to Vaughan Williams's No. 4'.[82] Howes notes that Elgar and Walton wrote their share of ceremonial music;[83] they both produced patriotic music during two world wars, and certain areas of their outputs are strikingly similar – two symphonies along with concertos for stringed instruments, for example – though Elgar wrote no operas. But Walton's moods range more widely than Elgar's: there is little in his music that could be marked *nobilmente*, nor does Walton have that elusive but unmistakable English voice that immediately identifies Elgar; his is a richer, cosmopolitan amalgam of northern bluntness of expression, Russian brilliance of dissonance and rhythm, French elegance of orchestral colour, and Italian warmth of melody. He may not have 'that consoling compassion which makes Elgar's music a source of solace',[84] but he does have an infectious sense of humour, a characteristic notably lacking in Elgar. By 'a sense of humour' I mean a particular manner of treating music, not the affectionately whimsical portraits of the *Enigma Variations*, which for all their charm would mean little without foreknowledge of their prototypes. To define humour in music is to seek to pin down one of its most elusive attributes, yet among its components must be lightness of touch, a certain detachment and a readiness to substitute without warning the rhythmically predictable (what we expect) with the rhythmically incongruous (what we don't expect). The scherzo of the First Symphony takes a wicked delight in its own malice, the cocky brass cadences in the Viola Concerto (see Ex. 5.12b) are akin to the ironic, fatuous fanfare that heralds the praise of the gods in *Belshazzar's Feast*, and we have already remarked that the first, bogus, trio (itself a piece of wilful deception) in the Violin Concerto's second movement is a parody straight out of *Façade*. Although both he and Elgar are rightly commended for their orchestration, there is in Walton's scores a sharp-edged resplendence – the counterpart to his dissonance – to which Elgar's opulent and detailed textures rarely attain.

Both composers inherited the time-tested formal structures of the western European tradition; of the two, it was Walton who made the more ingenious use of them. Elgar's sonata forms, and to a considerable extent his scherzos, too, follow the pattern of Brahms, even at times having earned the epithet, 'text-book'. Walton adapted sonata form in his own way, moving its centre of gravity and the relationships of its parts, turning its recapitulation from consummation into nostalgia, but never producing anything approaching a formula; and his scherzos are predictable only in their unpredictability (none of the so-called 'scherzos' in the four works that by common consent contain one – the First Symphony and the three string concertos – is actually so designated in the scores).[85] Where the two composers are deeply related, and where their prodigious virtues lie, was perceived by Havergal Brian in the essay referred to above:

> There is a strong resemblance between Walton and Elgar. . . . It was not that Elgar invented a new system, but that he presented a contemporary idiom in his own individual way. Similarly with Walton: he has [this essay dates from 1936] all contemporary modernist tendencies at his finger-tips, and directs them to his own individual purpose.[86]

'. . . Directs them to his own individual purpose': unless we fall into the trap (which the late twentieth century has not entirely evaded) of demanding that every creative artist push back the frontiers of language, idiom, technique and structure, we cannot ask of a composer much more than that.

Notes

1. Hutchings, A. (1937) 'The Symphony and William Walton', *Musical Times*, 78, p. 212.
2. Avery, K. (1947) 'William Walton', *Music and Letters*, 28, p. 6. My italics. Avery's description of the two 3/4 bars is virtually a definition of the Baroque hemiola.
3. Tovey, D. F. (1936) *Essays in Music Analysis*, Vol. 3: Concertos, London: OUP, p. 223.
4. Howes, F. (1974) *The Music of William Walton*, 2nd ed., London: OUP, p. 31.
5. The comparison is doubly interesting because Walton uses the same chord in the same key as the opening chord from *Petrushka* and, like Stravinsky, constructs his theme from the notes of that chord – an open D-A, with added G and E (though with two extra F-sharps). His introduction also begins with the chord: perhaps he hoped that Diaghilev would suppose it an act of homage and accept the work on the spot, but it was not to be (see Morrison (1984), pp. 122–3).
6. Routh, F. (1972) 'William Walton', in *Contemporary British Music: The 25 Years from 1945 to 1970*, London: Macdonald, p. 32.
7. See also, for example, the Viola Concerto, finale, beginning at 57[6], or the Cello Concerto, Scherzo, beginning at 1. (Where Walton supplies only rehearsal numbers, bars are identified as above, i.e., 57[6] is the 6th bar of 57; [6]57 is the 6th bar before 57, etc.)
8. For an outline of the pedals which articulate the first movement, see P. Evans 'Instrumental Music I', in *The Blackwell History of Music in Britain, Volume 6: The Twentieth Century*, ed. Stephen Banfield (1995), Oxford: Blackwell, p. 210
9. Howes (1974), op. cit.
10. Ibid., p. 32. In fact they do not do so: in due course we shall note that the one interrupts the other.
11. Tovey, (1936) op cit., p. 225.
12. Skelton, G. (1975) *Paul Hindemith: The Man behind the Music*, London: Gollancz, p. 98.
13. For further probable indebtedness of Walton to Prokofiev (whose music he admired), compare the main theme from the finale of Walton's *Sinfonia Concertante* with that of the first movement of Prokofiev's Third Piano Concerto, and from Prokofiev's finale with the finale of Walton's Violin Concerto.

14. Kennedy, M. (1989) *Portrait of Walton*, Oxford: OUP, p. 51. Walton will later create much the same effect in the first movement of the Violin Concerto, at 15, where figurations from the first subject serve as accompaniment both to the second subject, and later, at [7]17, to the first subject itself in augmentation. In the finale (at 60) the first subject furnishes part of the accompaniment to an augmented version of the melody from 52, and at 73 the similarity with the Viola Concerto is even more striking, when a figure based on the first subject again serves as accompaniment to recollections of the first movement.

15. Warrack, J. (1968) 'Sir William Walton talks to John Warrack', *The Listener*, 8 August, pp. 176–8.

16. Kennedy, M. (1983) 'Walton in Perspective', *The Listener*, 11 August, p. 130. In 'William Walton's 70th Birthday', *The Listener*, 23 March 1972, pp. 394–5, E. Rubbra isolated almost exactly the same characteristics: '. . . a delicate balance in the best work between warm lyricism and explosive energy.'

17. Webster (1980) *New Grove Dictionary of Music and Musicians*, p. 497.

18. It is somewhat surprising to find that these alternative harmonizations possibly arose by accident. Ottaway explains that the key of the second subject may originally have been E (a fashionable tritone from the tonic), but Angus Morrison pointed out to Walton that the scherzo was very much E centred. 'This is the end of the exposition,' he suggested, 'so why not take it to the dominant, F?' Walton agreed, rewrote the preceding passage (though we do not know from what point) and raised what followed by a semitone (F is reached at Fig. 14). See Ottaway, H. (1973) 'Walton's First and its Composition', *Musical Times*, 114, p. 998; and Morrison, A. (1984) 'Willie: The Young Walton and his Four Masterpieces', *RCM Magazine*, 80, 3, pp. 119–27 (from a talk at the British Festival of Recorded Sound).

19. Ottaway, H. (1973) op. cit., p. 998.

20. Morrison, A. (1984), op. cit., p. 126.

21. It is worth noting, too, that even with a text (or perhaps provoked by the text), *Belshazzar's Feast* has much the same plan: the slow, mournful opening section is followed by a wild scherzo, complete with extended trio *a tempo di marcia* and full reprise. And this scherzo brims over not only with *malizia*, but with *sarcasmo, furia, disprezzo* and *pompa* as well. The jubilant text makes the finale more lively than those of the concertos, but both its contrast with the earlier movements and its relationship to them are no less marked.

22. This expectation creates a further parallel with *Belshazzar's Feast*, where the headlong open fifth which announces the second section (at 15) sounds like a dominant of G minor, and our assumption seems to be confirmed at the choir's G-minor cadence to the words 'In Babylon . . . .' But later we are obliged to make an adjustment when we learn that the whole 'scherzo' section is after all in D.

23. Evans, P. (1959) 'Sir William Walton's Manner and Mannerism', *The Listener*, 20 August, p. 209.

24. Howes, F. (1974) op. cit., pp. 80–3.

25. It is tempting to speculate, when listening to the *Sinfonia Concertante*, on the possibility that the Russian influence manifest in Walton was reciprocated as late as 1957 in Shostakovich's Second Piano Concerto. Despite the likelihood of a common ancestry in Prokofiev, features such as the brilliance of the piano writing, the rapid, high-register figuration in octaves, the melodies that constantly shift between toccata and fanfare, the end-on juxtaposition of keys a third from the tonic (compare the beginning of Walton's finale to 30 with Shostakovich's first movement from 22 to the end), the abrupt extension or compression of a bar by a beat added or lopped off, and the glitter of the orchestration, all suggest a link across 30 years between Shostakovich and Walton.

26. It is astonishing how many times, in the midst of a passage of razor-sharp Walton, a moment of pure Elgar will appear, as here, completely unannounced, and just as quickly vanish: see also, for example, the falling sevenths just before the *Allegro spiritoso* in the first movement of the *Sinfonia Concertante*.
27. Perhaps Walton was inspired by the extended range of the violin, or by its association with an Italianate melodic ardour. The same passionate lyricism informs much of the love music in *Troilus and Cressida*, in passages such as Cressida's Act II arioso, 'At the haunted end of the day'.
28. Both Howes and Kennedy quote these two melodies, and both include the same divergences from the published score in the lower part in bars 8, 13 and 14. Curiously, the version of bars 13 and 14 as shown here in Ex. 5.7 reinforces the analytical point Howes wishes to make. See Howes, F. (1974) op. cit., pp. 90, 92 and Kennedy, M. (1989) op. cit., p. 102.
29. Howes (1974), op. cit., p. 91.
30. Walton underlines the contrast with the instructions *marcato* and *flessibile* for the two themes respectively.
31. Howes (1974) op. cit., p. 99.
32. The theme is presented here in parallel 6ths, but Walton makes no attempt to recall the alluring *Seguidilla* that was the second theme in the scherzo, despite the fact that it, too, appeared almost throughout in parallel sixths; clearly his intention is to close the circle, and not to bring together disparate sections of the work.
33. Kennedy, M. (1989) *Portrait of Walton*, Oxford: OUP, p. 101.
34. Kennedy, M. (1982) *Portrait of Elgar*, revised edn, London: OUP, pp. 250–1.
35. Mitchell, D. (1957) 'The "Modernity" of William Walton', *The Listener*, 7 February, p. 245.
36. Evans, P. (1959) 'Sir William Walton's Manner and Mannerism', *The Listener*, 20 August, p. 297.
37. 'Walton's life can be seen as typifying a British composer's fate; he is not the only one to demonstrate its most important stages – the initiation of the new arrival, the enthronement of the success, the acceptance of the celebrity, and the neglect by a new generation.' Saremba, M. (1994) *Elgar, Britten & Co: Eine Geschichte der britischen Musik in Zwölf Portraits*, Zurich & St Gallen: M & T Verlag, p. 246.
38. Rubbra, E. (1972) 'William Walton's 70th Birthday', *The Listener*, 23 March, p. 395.
39. Howes, F. (1974) op. cit., pp. 102–3.
40. For a summary of these commissions, see Kennedy, M. (1989), op. cit., pp. 205–11.
41. Aprahamian, F. (1960) 'Walton and his New Symphony', *The Listener*, 25 August, p. 321.
42. Kennedy, M. (1989), op. cit., pp. 211–12.
43. Howes, F. (1974) op. cit., p. 42.
44. It is also tempting to speculate that these shapes could be unconsciously indebted to an important figure from the finale of Prokofiev's Second Violin Concerto, where at 57 the clarinets have the following arpeggio:

45. Routh, F. (1972) op. cit., pp. 34–5.
46. Ibid., p. 36.
47. Kennedy, M. (1989), op. cit., p. 41.

48. Kennedy, M. (1974) p. 83; Cox, D. (1967) 'Walton', in Simpson, R. (ed.) *The Symphony 2*, p. 192; Ballantine, C. (1983) *Twentieth Century Symphony*, London: Dennis Dobson; Routh, F. (1972), op. cit., p. 33; Avery, K. (1947) op. cit., p. 6; Evans, E. (1944) 'William Walton', *Musical Times*, 85, p. 366; Tierney, N. (1984) *William Walton – his Life and Music*, London: Robert Hale, p. 184; Evans, P. (1959) op. cit., p. 212.

49. The recordings by Charles Mackerras and Simon Rattle could hardly be closer to Walton's marking, at 5'44" and 5'50" respectively. And the first recording, made in December 1935 by Hamilton Harty and the London Symphony Orchestra, is only marginally slower, at just under 6 minutes.

50. Kennedy, M. (1989), op. cit., p. 52.

51. Ottaway, H. (1973) op. cit., p. 998.

52. Is Walton even poking fun at Elgar by making his scherzo just a notch faster? Elgar is ♩. = 108; Walton is ♩. = 116.

53. Foreman, L. (1987) *From Parry to Britten: British Music in Letters, 1900–1945*, London: Batsford, p. 147.

54. Kennedy, M. (1989), op. cit., p. 38.

55. Keith Grant, the administrator of the English Opera Group at the 1962 Aldeburgh Festival, commented some years later that he would sooner work for Britten than Walton: 'Willie Walton . . . you had to handle *very* carefully. He was very suspicious and thin-skinned, and could be difficult' (quoted in Carpenter, H. (1992), *Benjamin Britten: a Biography*, London: Faber and Faber, p. 416). It would, I think, have required quite a thick 30-year-old skin to brush off such a dismissive snub from the Master of the King's Musick.

56. Tovey, D. F. (1936) op. cit., p. 223.

57. Howes, F. (1974) op. cit., p. 83.

58. Foss, H. J. (1940) 'William Walton', *Musical Quarterly*, 26, p. 464.

59. This fanfare functions as a cadential figure, signalling the end of a section, despite Tovey's description of it as the 'main theme of the first episode' (Tovey, D. (1936) op. cit., p. 224). We note too its rhythmic similarity to Ex. 5.9b, and also the fact that both Ex. 5.12a and 12c maintain the major/minor duality of the Concerto's first movement.

60. Quoted in Kennedy (1989) op. cit., p. 99.

61. These almost uncouth interruptions recall similar occurrences from time to time in the late Beethoven quartets: see, for example, the 2/4 interpolations in the *scherzando vivace* of Op. 127.

62. Howes F. (1974) op. cit., p. 94. Merrick, F. (1941) 'Walton's Concerto for Violin and Orchestra', *Music Review*, 2, pp. 312–5 provides more detail, but his details are almost exclusively pictorial: the title of the movement, *Presto capriccioso alla napolitana*, has clearly inspired him to images of delirious Italian dancing.

63. Quoted in Tierney, N. (1984) op. cit., p. 86.

64. Lambert, C. (1936) 'Some Angles of the Compleat Walton', *Radio Times*, 7 August, p. 232.

65. Foss, H. J. (1945) 'The Music of William Walton', *The Listener*, 17 May, p. 557.

66. Walton, S. (1988) *William Walton: Behind the Façade*, Oxford: OUP, p. 162.

67. These brief, florid links for the solo instrument hark all the way back to passages such as that leading into 11 in the first movement of the Viola Concerto; but their extension in this movement is clearly intended to anticipate the much more elaborate solo improvisations of the finale.

68. Among the various pressures on Walton to sanction an incomplete performance could have been the fact that another symphony had recently been the subject of enthusiastic speculation in the musical world and of optimistic promises in the press, but had come

to nothing – Elgar's Third (Elgar had died on 23 February, 1934). Better perhaps to permit the performance of the three completed movements than to have public interest go 'off the boil' a second time.

69. Schaarwächter, J. (1995) *Die britische Sinfonie* 1914–1945, Koln: Dohr Verlag, pp. 248–9.
70. White, E. W. (1937) 'William Walton', in *Life and Letters Today*, 16, p. 114.
71. Schaarwächter, J. (1995), op. cit., p. 249.
72. Kennedy (1989), op. cit., p. 84.
73. Cox, D. (1967) op. cit., p. 193.
74. Schaarwächter reminds us that it was in Autumn, 1934, just when this finale was proving intractable, that Walton wrote his first film score – *Escape Me Never*. Schaarwächter, J. (1995), op. cit., p. 243.
75. For example Rutland, H. (1957) 'Walton's New Cello Concerto', *Musical Times*, 98, p. 70; Howes, F. (1974) op.cit., p. 106; Tierney, N. (1984) op. cit., p. 191; Kennedy, M. (1989) op. cit., p. 204.
76. Ottaway, H. (1980) 'Walton', in *The New Grove Dictionary of Music and Musicians*, Vol. 20, London: Macmillan, p. 199.
77. The final chord of this improvisation is already preparing the ground for the return of first movement material: it is almost exactly the chord with which the work began.
78. Variations 1, 3, 4, 5 and 6. Even Variation 2 is close to this length: its combined 3/4 and 2/4 bars amount to 45 beats, i.e., the equivalent of 15 3/4 bars.
79. That is, with the possible exception of Variation 4: has Walton simply given the bassoons a characteristically dotted figure, or is he – in the context of a movement which nods in the direction of serial techniques – gently poking fun at their pedantry by reminding us of Beckmesser's motif in Wagner's *Meistersinger*? That Walton knew *Die Meistersinger* can scarcely be in any doubt: the harmonic idiom of the *Spitfire Prelude and Fugue* is almost inconceivable without it.
80. In many of these cases, Walton begins the inversion of the row twice – again granting only limited respect to the strict procedures of serial technique.
81. Brian, H. (1986) *Havergal Brian on Music, Selections from his Journalism*, ed. M. MacDonald, Vol. 1: *British Music*, London: Toccata, p. 351.
82. Ottaway, H. (1970) 'Walton and his Critics', *The Listener*, 25 June, p. 869.
83. And that music is not without its striking similarities; the middle section of *Crown Imperial* is pure *Pomp and Circumstance* pastiche. See Howes (1974) op. cit., pp. 238–9.
84. Kennedy, M. (1989), op. cit., p. 280.
85. Does even the naming of a 'Trio' in the Violin Concerto necessarily commit Walton to writing a scherzo with which to frame it? We are left to infer by features such as their position, tempo and general character – but not always their form – that they are scherzos.
86. Brian, H. (1986), op. cit., p. 351.

Appendix

There follows a summary of dates of composition, first performances, etc., of the two symphonies and four concertos (for full details, see Craggs, S. R. (1977) *William Walton, A Thematic Catalogue of his Musical Works*, Oxford: OUP (2nd ed. 1990).

Sinfonia Concertante for piano and orchestra.

Composed: 1927
First performance: London, 5 January, 1928; York Bowen (piano) with the RPO, cond. Ernest Ansermet
Revised 1943; first performance: Liverpool, 9 February, 1944; Cyril Smith (piano) with the Liverpool PO, cond. Malcolm Sargent

Viola Concerto

Composed: 1928–29
First performance: London, 3 October, 1929; Paul Hindemith (viola) with the Henry Wood Symphony Orchestra, cond. Walton
Revised 1961; first performance: London, 18 January, 1962, with John Coulling (viola) and the LPO, cond. Malcolm Sargent

Symphony No. 1

Composed: 1932–35
First performance: First three movements: London, 3 December, 1934, with the LSO, cond. Hamilton Harty
Complete work: London, 6 November, 1935, BBCSO, cond. Hamilton Harty

Violin Concerto
Composed: 1938–39
First performance: Cleveland, Ohio, 7 December, 1939; Jascha Heifetz (violin), with the Cleveland Orchestra, cond. Artur Rodzinski
Revised 1943; first performance unknown

Cello Concerto

Composed: 1955–56
First performance: Boston, Mass., 25 January, 1957; Gregor Piatigorsky (cello) with the Boston Symphony Orchestra, cond. Charles Münch
Revised ending (never performed): 1974 (Kennedy (1989) pp. 198–9)

Symphony No. 2

Composed: 1958–60
First performance: Edinburgh, 2 September, 1960, with the RLPO, cond. John Pritchard

6 Film Music
Stephen Lloyd

When in the summer of 1934 Walton came to film music, he already had behind him the Viola Concerto and *Belshazzar's Feast*, and his First Symphony (in its incomplete three-movement form) was soon to explode upon the musical world. His reputation as a major voice in British music was therefore secure. The fourteen films for which he supplied a music score can be broadly placed into three groups: (1) those starring Elisabeth Bergner, (2) the war-time propaganda films, and (3) the films either directed by or associated with Laurence Olivier.

The first four of these films, from 1934 until 1938, were all made by the Hungarian director Paul Czinner (1890–1972). As a child Czinner had been a violin prodigy, but he was drawn instead to the cinema and made his first film in Vienna in 1919. He rose to prominence in 1924 with his German film *Nju*, a psychological love triangle drama that starred the actress Elisabeth Bergner (1897–1986)[1] who became his wife and who subsequently took the leading role in nearly all his films. In 1933, on the rise to power of Hitler, they both emigrated to England where Czinner directed *The Rise of Catherine the Great* (with his wife and Douglas Fairbanks, Jnr) for Alexander Korda, with the young Muir Mathieson as music director. He turned next in 1934 to *Escape Me Never*, which was based on a play by Margaret Kennedy[2] in which Elisabeth Bergner had created quite a stir when she made her London stage appearance at The Apollo the year before. The story is another love triangle centred on Gemma, the mother of an illegitimate baby, who is first looked after by and eventually marries a struggling composer (Hugh Sinclair) who becomes involved with another woman. The cast also included Griffith Jones, Penelope Dudley Ward and Leon Quartermain.

Walton became involved – for the considerable fee of £300 – at the suggestion of Dallas Bower who was Czinner's personal assistant on the film. For a first film score it is remarkably accomplished and effective. 'Much to my surprise', he later admitted, 'I soon found myself writing five to ten minutes' music a day without too much difficulty.'[3] In completing the orchestration – and possibly a little more – he had the help of the conductor and composer Hyam Greenbaum. Known to his friends as 'Bumps', he was married to the harpist Sidonie Goossens who remembers the two of them going through a number of scores in search of ideas, amongst them Sibelius's *Tempest* music.[4] 'Bumps' also conducted the studio orchestra on the soundtrack.

The most substantial part is a dreamy, idyllic pastoral sequence early on when the action is set in Venice (the 'In the Dolomites' section of the Suite).[5] This is scored with much subtlety with a battery of percussion instruments, including cowbells, glockenspiel, tubular bells and vibraphone – hardly a conventional choice. The other section of interest comes later in the film when the screen composer is concerned about the production of his ballet in London. This was filmed in December 1934 at Drury Lane with the Vic-Wells Ballet Company, with choreography by Frederick Ashton and with a young Margot Fonteyn among its number. But of the ballet itself, rather more substantial in the Suite than on film,[6] only six tiny sections are heard and seen – in rehearsal and performance – intercut with scenes of Gemma at the hospital after the death of her child. The ballet's yearning 'love theme' is also used most effectively for the title music.

Escape Me Never was first shown at the London Pavilion on 1 April 1935 and was an immediate success. *The Times* review[7] concentrated almost exclusively on Bergner and applied Zola's maxim that 'Art is Nature seen through a temperament' to her acting. 'The camera', it concluded, 'is there to photograph Miss Bergner, and that it does with discretion, skill, and discrimination.'[8] When it opened in America in May, the *New York Times* review[9] somehow managed to credit the music to the art director L. P. Williams and Wilfred Arnold. Its critic, André Sennwald, considered Bergner (who received an Academy Award nomination) 'a miracle of gossamer gracefulness and bewitching humour', but as regards the production he merely commented that the 'brain scoffs at the threadbare machinery'. The film was less successfully remade in America in 1947 with music by Erich Korngold.

Walton's next film score might well have been for an adaptation of George Bernard Shaw's *St Joan*. In November 1934 Shaw, who had a keen interest in films, had himself worked on a film script which he handed to Elisabeth Bergner to read. She had taken the lead in Max Reinhardt's acclaimed 1924 stage production in Berlin and Vienna, and Czinner planned to form a syndicate including Twentieth Century Fox and produce a film version of *St Joan*, starring his wife. However, he was concerned that the film might offend the Catholic Church, or – more seriously – that American financial backing would be withdrawn because of the risk of a Catholic boycott, and so he sought the approval of the Church. But Shaw would have no truck with any Catholic entanglements, and by the summer of 1935 as far as he was concerned the film was off.[10] Nevertheless, Miss Bergner did appear as St Joan when the play was produced at the 1938 Malvern Festival.

Instead, Walton's next film, in 1936, was his first Shakespeare score which – again at Dallas Bower's suggestion – more importantly brought him into contact with Laurence Olivier. (Although in an 80th birthday greeting Olivier remembered meeting Walton on the set of *As you like it*,[11] he seemed largely to have forgotten the name when it was suggested to him for *Henry V*[12] and

their strong friendship did not take shape until their collaboration on that film.)
Shakespeare in the cinema was then by no means entirely new. The previous
year Max Reinhardt had directed an unlikely James Cagney in *A Midsummer
Night's Dream* (with Mendelssohn's music arranged by Korngold), and earlier
still there had been Mary Pickford and Douglas Fairbanks in *The Taming of
the Shrew*. But these had been Hollywood confections. The film treatment of
As you like it had been suggested by Sir James Barrie for whose last play, *The
Boy David*, Walton had recently composed the incidental music and Elisabeth
Bergner had starred in the name part.[13] Olivier had at that time already
appeared in a handful of films, but the offer of playing Orlando to Bergner's
Rosalind gave him his first leading role, whatever doubts he had about the
filming of Shakespeare. As it turned out, he disliked working with Bergner and
Czinner. Furthermore, while Barrie himself had provided a film adaptation of
As you like it with a few discreet cuts, despite Czinner's assurances to Olivier
that the play would not be mutilated, in the end it was reduced to a running
time of 96 minutes. It was a film Olivier chose to forget.[14]

Neither Czinner nor Bergner was coming to *As you like it* for the first time:
Czinner had already directed a German version and in 1926 Bergner had appeared
in a stage production in Vienna. For this 'million dollar' film version Czinner
assembled a strong cast. Besides Bergner and Olivier there was Henry Ainley (the
exiled duke), Leon Quartermain (Jacques), Mackenzie Ward (Touchstone), Felix
Aylmer (Duke Frederick) and John Laurie (Oliver). Lazare Meerson, designer for
the influential French director René Clair, was responsible for the décor, and
Ninette de Valois was called in for the choreography.

As you like it opened at the Carlton Theatre, Haymarket, on 3 September 1936
to a mixed critical reception. Miss Bergner naturally stole the limelight, but
temperamentally she was unsuited to the part. As Roger Manvell has written in
Shakespeare and Film,[15] 'Rosalind is a forthright woman, capable, provocative
and determined beneath her surface diffidence and charm. Elisabeth Bergner's
screen character was exactly the opposite – she derived her charm from depicting
an ageless, kittenish quality in women, a kind of self-destructive femininity, half
innocent, half knowing, which inevitably led to frustrated infatuations with a
tragic outcome.' One critic complained of her 'inability to stop wriggling' while
another referred to her as 'an imp of delicate enchantment'. *The Times'* critic,[16]
ignoring the music, wrote that she 'soon overcomes the difficulty of her foreign
accent and speaks her words with charm and relish, but she underlines them, as
she underlines her conception of the character, with a restless and mannered
grace.' Regarding the scenery he commented: 'The fantastic architecture is apt to
resemble confectionery and the Forest of Arden, though photographed with an
extremely ingenious use of lighting, often looks like a wild garden temporarily
assembled at Olympia.' *Sight and Sound* described the Arden set as 'fake flora
and genuine fauna prodded in from the wings'. However, despite its defects, *The
Times'* critic considered it 'a serious attempt to reproduce one of Shakespeare's
plays in film' and concluded that it offered promise of further filmed versions.

But Graham Greene, in *The Spectator*,[17] was far more scornful. Remarking on 'the ubiquitous livestock (sheep and cows and hens and rabbits)' and 'English trees, in what is apparently late autumn, bearing clusters of white flowers', he continued: 'Horns and cuckolds have been heavily censored, the streak of poison which runs through the comedy has been squeezed carefully out between hygienic fingertips, and what is left, apart from Arden and absurd delightful artificial love, is Shakespeare at his falsest, Adam and church bells and good men's feasts and sermons in stone, all the dull didactic unconvincing images. That, I think, is the chief objection to Shakespeare on the screen . . .'. Certainly Olivier, despite his grand salary of £600 a week for about 13 weeks' filming (during the day only; he was Mercutio on stage each evening), was for a while to remain sceptical of the suitability of Shakespeare for the screen. When *As you like it* went to America in November, Frank Nugent in the *New York Times*[18] at least commented on 'an original score by William Walton [who] has given it just the proper musical accompaniment'.

One of the most interesting reviews appeared in the October 1936 issue of *World Film News and Television Progress*. Its young contributor was Benjamin Britten (at that time, for a fee of £200, writing his only score for a feature film, *Love from a Stranger*),[19] whose review is worth quoting in full:

> That the Directors of 20th Century Fox Film Corporation should have invited one of the 20th century stars of British music to write for one of its biggest productions is very creditable indeed. But the invitation seems to have exhausted their enterprise. His name, perhaps symbolically, is absent from the programme, and the opportunities he has had for writing serious film music seem negligible.
>
> There is, of course, the Grand Introduction over the credit titles – pompous and heraldic in the traditional manner. There is a Grand Oratorio Finale with full orchestra, based on Elizabethan songs, in which a bunch of Albert Hall contralti is very prominent. Both these are written with great competence, and indeed Walton is incapable of any sort of inefficiency.
>
> But apart from suitable *Waldweben* noises at the beginning of each sequence, which tactfully fade out as the action starts, that is the whole of Walton's contribution to *As you like it*.
>
> One cannot feel that the microphone has entered very deeply into Walton's scoring soul. A large orchestra in which strings are very prominent has been used, and in the accompanying pastoral music one is conscious of the energetic ranks of the London Philharmonic sweating away behind the three-ply trees.
>
> As far as he is allowed, Walton makes one or two musically apt suggestions. The introduction is very neatly dovetailed into the chicken-yard, and Leon Goossens on the oboe mixes very creditably with the Wynadottes. Also a neat and poetic use of the leitmotiv *Rosalind* is to be noted.
>
> But all the music for *As you like it* is not the advance on *Escape Me Never* which we all expected.[20]

Yet in spite of Britten's reservations it is an impressive score,[21] once again calling on a wide array of percussion including marimba and tabors (perhaps reminiscent of Elgar's *Falstaff*, a particular favourite of Walton's). The expansive title music is very Sibelian – especially in the writing for brass – closer in mood to *Festivo* than the symphonies, while the Forest of Arden, as Britten observed, seems to have called for a few Wagnerian bird-calls and *Forest Murmurs*. Allusions to Wagner were to occur in later Walton films. The Sibelius influence, a very potent one on British music in the 1930s, was hardly surprising. It had already been evident in the Symphony (as indeed it was at that time in varying degrees in the symphonies of Bax, Vaughan Williams and Moeran, either by inference through a dedication or by example through imitation), and even after a second perform-ance of Walton's still unfinished Symphony at the beginning of April 1935, *The Times'* critic could observe that 'technically the symphony derives from Sibelius in method'. The wedding hymn near the end of *As you like it* fulfils a similar joyous function as the *Agincourt Song* was later to do in *Henry V*, and the score also provided Walton with the opportunity to employ one of his favourite devices, the fanfare, of which he was to make considerable use in films and elsewhere, either as a fanfare *per se* or as an introduction to another form he was to make peculiarly his own, the march.

Much of 1937 was taken up with the composing of his Leeds Festival commis-sion, *In Honour of the City of London*, but there was also his next collaboration with Czinner, *Dreaming Lips*, of which Czinner had already made a German film with Bergner in 1932 under the title *Der traümende Mund*. This was another play adaptation, this time by Margaret Kennedy of the play *Melo* by Henry Bernstein. In it Bergner was well-suited to the neurotic, selfish Gaby who is married to a musician (Romney Brent) but falls in love with his colleague and violinist (Raymond Massey). Her plans to leave her husband are thwarted by his serious illness. In the end, worn out by nursing him, she throws herself into the Thames. Also in the cast were Joyce Bland, Sydney Fairbrother, Felix Aylmer, Fisher White, Donald Calthrop and Ronald Shiner. A key scene early in the film is part of a concert which includes the end of the Tchaikovsky Violin Concerto, an abridged first movement of the Beethoven Concerto and an arrangement for violin and orchestra of the Waltz from Tchaikovsky's *Serenade for Strings*. Antonio Brosa was the violinist on the soundtrack, with Boyd Neel visible on screen conducting the London Symphony Orchestra.[22]

The soundtrack in fact contains little of the real Walton. The title music is built largely out of a theme from the Beethoven Concerto, and the only music of interest is found in a brief passage when the husband is ill and in a dream sequence that follows. The predominance of 'serious' music prompted the *Times* critic to comment that 'the effect of an accompaniment of good music is so unexpectedly delightful that one cannot understand why so easy and profitable a resource should not be more often heard.'[23] The film opened at the London Pavilion on 2 February 1937 (a première attended by Queen Mary and the Duchess of Gloucester) and went to America in May. Frank Nugent, discussing the leading roles in the *New York Times*, wrote that 'those three are the only ones that count: those and a couple of fellows who wrote the score – Beethoven and Tchaikovsky'.[24] This film, which was a flop, could have done little to enhance Walton's reputa-tion as a composer of film-music.

A Stolen Life which followed in 1938, again directed by Czinner, was another obvious vehicle for Elisabeth Bergner, here playing twin roles in a script adapted by Margaret Kennedy from a novel by Karel Benes. The cast also included Michael Redgrave and Wilfred Lawson. This was only Redgrave's second film, although he was then little known as a film actor because his first film, Hitchcock's *The Lady Vanishes*, had not been released at the time of his being signed up by Czinner. Here he plays an explorer who meets Martina (Bergner) and they fall in love. But Martina's twin sister Sylvia steals him from her and marries him. When Sylvia is drowned on holiday, Martina takes her place without his realizing. Her deception is eventually discovered but all ends happily. *A Stolen Life* was first shown on 18 January 1939 at the Plaza Theatre, London, a charity screening that was attended by Lady Aberconway, the Christabel of the Viola Concerto's dedication.

In *A Stolen Life* Walton was able to offer a rather more substantial score, the most dramatic moment being the extensive storm sequence in which Sylvia drowns. Here Walton provides music to match the force and ferocity of Sibelius's *Tempest* Prelude. The cinema newsreel of Martina's 'husband's' successful mountaineering expedition in Tibet is accompanied by a brief extract from the *Escape Me Never* ballet with its soaring love theme. On the soundtrack the BBC Television Orchestra was conducted by Hyam Greenbaum who had been appointed its musical director when the television service started in 1936. The film was remade in 1946 with Bette Davis and music by Max Steiner.

In his autobiography, Michael Redgrave provides some insight into Czinner's working methods. Calling him 'an imperfect perfectionist', he goes on to quote Czinner's principle that:

> if you shot sufficient feet of film, some of this must be in the right direction. . . He printed all the takes, and this was usually a great many, of all the shots. By frequent close cutting and the selection of a look from one take, a line from another, and a particular, though perhaps quite irrelevant, expression from a third, a performance was very often much richer than the actor felt it to be, even in his best take.[25]

A Stolen Life was Walton's last film for Czinner. With the outbreak of war Czinner went to Hollywood. (In later years he was to turn his attention more to filming opera and ballet.) Elisabeth Bergner did some location shooting in Canada for Michael Powell's 1941 film *49th Parallel* (for which Vaughan Williams supplied the music), but when the Nazi blitz on London started, because of her German upbringing she made it clear that she had no intention of returning to London to complete the studio portions of the film and joined her husband instead. Her part was taken by Glynis Johns, whose father Mervyn Johns was at about that time starring in another Walton film, *The Next of Kin*, while with careful editing Michael Powell was still able to use some of Miss Bergner's exterior scenes.[26] In time her very personal style of acting, that lacked the sensuality of a Garbo or a Dietrich, was to appear rather dated.

After working with Paul Czinner, Walton's next director was another Hungarian, the more volatile Gabriel Pascal (1894–1954) whose reputation was made (notoriously, one might add) with his film adaptations of plays by George

Bernard Shaw. Pascal's first proper meeting with Shaw had been in 1935 when the playwright had been captivated by both Pascal's personality and the fanciful stories he told of his early years.[27] The upshot of this relationship was that Shaw gave Pascal the film rights to his plays. The first to be made by him was *Pygmalion*, in 1938, with Leslie Howard and Wendy Hiller. (There had already been German and Dutch film versions of *Pygmalion* that were not to Shaw's taste, which prompted him to produce his own film script.) Pascal then approached Walton with the offer of 550 guineas if he would write the music. But Walton was already too occupied with the violin concerto for which he had been commissioned by the British Council for the New York World Fair in October 1939. He had repeatedly to turn down an insistent Pascal who even tempted him with an offer of further films. In the end Honegger provided the film score.

Pygmalion proved a great success, owing in no small measure to the excellent direction of Antony Asquith (together with Leslie Howard), and in 1939 Shaw agreed to Pascal proceeding with a film of his 'parable', *Major Barbara*. Cusins, a university professor, falls in love with a Salvation Army preacher (Wendy Hiller) whose father, Undershaft (Robert Morley), is an armaments millionaire. Shaw, who had been unhappy with Leslie Howard's casting as Higgins in *Pygmalion*, objected to him as the love-struck Cusins and the part eventually went to Rex Harrison (who was later to become the definitive Higgins in *My Fair Lady*, Lerner and Loewe's musical adaptation of *Pygmalion*). The cast also included Emlyn Williams, Sybil Thorndike, Deborah Kerr, Donald Calthrop, Penelope Dudley Ward and Robert Newton (whose Bill Walker is almost a trial run for his Sykes in David Lean's 1948 *Oliver Twist*). The costumes were designed by Cecil Beaton. Location shooting began in May 1940 on the Dartington Hall estate in Devon, with some scenes later shot in London and Sheffield. This time Walton was able to accept Pascal's offer and he worked on the score during 1940 and 1941.

For at least one of the earlier films he had had assistance with the orchestration from Hyam Greenbaum who, since the outbreak of war, had been evacuated to Bristol as conductor now of the BBC Variety Orchestra. His early death in May 1942 brought to an end the chance of any further collaboration. But in November 1940 for *Major Barbara* Walton now had the help of Roy Douglas who had already had experience of working with film composers. (He orchestrated all Richard Addinsell's music for *Dangerous Moonlight*, released in 1941, with its highly popular *Warsaw Concerto*.) He was also to help with some of the orchestration for *The Next of Kin* and *Went the Day Well?*, generally the shorter sections for which Walton jotted down the music on two or three staves for Douglas to orchestrate either according to his directions or as seemed appropriate to his style. In due course Roy Douglas became much involved in preparing for publication many of Walton's scores up to the opera *Troilus and Cressida*, in much the same way as he was on a larger scale to assist Vaughan Williams.

In 1945 Penguin Books published Shaw's screen version of *Major Barbara*, this representing his idealized script which is slightly longer than Pascal's final version and which diverges in some instances from what eventually emerged on celluloid. In a prefatory note Shaw writes that:

> the verses written to fit Rossini's once famous quartet from his *Moses in Egypt* were reset by Mr William Walton for Mr Pascal's film; but I retain my first suggestion partly to explain the constrained versification imposed by Rossini's music; partly because I must not infringe Mr Walton's copyright (Rossini's is extinct); and perhaps mainly because I feel sure that Undershaft was as old-fashioned in his musical taste as he was ultra-modern in his industrial management.

This refers to the scene embodying Shaw's vision of a socialist post-war reconstruction. In Undershaft's Utopian world the employees' social and cultural welfare is well catered for, and Shaw has even foreseen the use of video. 'We have the best orchestras in the world, and the best conductors, and the best singers. We pay them handsomely for one performance, which we televise and record so that we can reproduce it as often as we like.' Shaw was not always, it seems, the most realistic of screen writers for in that particular scene he not only asks for the Rossini extract to be viewed on a television set but he specifies that it is to be conducted by none other than Toscanini. As an announcer proclaims: 'For Rossini at his greatest today there is only one conductor: Arturo Toscanini.' And at this point, according to the script, 'Toscanini enters, baton in hand, and takes his place at the conductor's desk . . . and the quartet and chorus from Rossini's *Moses in Egypt* follows, accompanied by a Wagnerian orchestra.' In the film a compromise clearly had to be made. In place of a performance viewed on a television screen, the strains of Rossini are heard coming from a church. Whatever words are sung they are fairly indistinguishable.

The seven-and-a-half minute sequence of music that includes this scene is of particular interest. Beginning in Undershaft's steel works, the percussive effects accompanying the steel production (cymbal rolls for the showers of sparks, etc.) strive for a realism not unlike those in Mossolov's *The Factory* (or *Iron Foundry*), and if the continuation, with its nervous energy, is a close prototype for the 'Battle in the Air' section in *The Battle of Britain* film, there is a double irony. Not only was Undershaft manufacturing the weapons of war but the actual filming was done at the time when the Nazi bombing of England had begun. Look-outs were stationed on the studio roof at Denham to keep watch for approaching enemy aircraft so that everyone could if necessary be evacuated to concrete cellars beneath the sound stage.

Shaw, former music critic, was at times present on the set and even suggested to Walton that at one point he added 'the effect of a single trombone sounding G flat quite quietly after the others have stopped, Undershaft pretending to play it. It ought to have the effect of a question mark'.[28] This suggestion was adopted – moderated to E flat – in the Albert Hall scene.

Walton's film score is a fine one, with some affecting love-music, even if his treatment of *Onward Christian Soldiers* in the title music is rather reminiscent of Bliss's *Checkmate* (1937). But the film as a whole, even in its final cut to a running time of 121 minutes, is not entirely satisfactory. Pascal's desire this time to take overall control of direction resulted in a film that, despite some fine acting and occasional moments of cinematic interest, is over-wordy, laboured and tedious on repeated viewings. Wendy Hiller said of it 'I saw the finished film once only – I wept with disappointment.'[29] The film overran both its schedule and its budget. Shaw's close involvement, with many rewritings, cuts and transpositions, could not have helped. *Major Barbara* was premièred in Nassau in the presence of the Duke and Duchess of Windsor on 20 March 1941, and it opened in London at the Odeon, Leicester Square on 7 April. In a preview, the *Times* critic thought it

> a freakish film, a mistaken film, but a film with honesty of purpose and some highly amusing moments. . . . It takes [Shaw's characters] out of the confines of intellectual comedy, away from the convention of dialectic cut and thrust, and turns them loose into the vague fluid world of cinematic pseudo-realism where their gestures lose that artificial precision in argument and timing which makes them a delight on the stage. . . .[30]

Like his fellow Hungarian, Alexander Korda, Pascal had both a love for the epic and a passion for cinematic detail, both expensive tastes, but his extravagance was to be his undoing in his next Shaw film, *Caesar and Cleopatra* (1945), which earned a reputation as the most expensive failure in British film history and almost terminated Pascal's film career (though he did go on to film Shaw's *Androcles and the Lion* in 1952). Arthur Bliss, who in 1934 had been asked by H. G. Wells to collaborate with him by writing the score for Korda's film *Things to Come*, was similarly invited by Shaw to provide the music for *Caesar and Cleopatra*. He actually started work on it but after meeting Pascal in person he withdrew from the project. 'One look at him made it self-evident that he would never be a sympathetic collaborator', Bliss later wrote in his autobiography.[31] Pascal turned instead to Georges Auric, Walton's film music by that time being allied to Shakespearean rather than Shavian scripts.

With the outbreak of World War Two, as Walton said himself, the problem had been, 'What could I usefully do? I tried driving an ambulance . . . and after I'd run it into the ditch several times they said perhaps you'd better not drive an ambulance, so as I'd written music for films before . . . I was put to work.'[32] Recognizing the enormous potential of film for war-time propaganda, a film division of the Ministry of Information was created by absorbing the GPO Film Unit, famous in pre-war days for its innovative documentaries, which became the Crown Film Unit. A large number of documentary-style films were produced with scores from such established composers as Constant Lambert, Arnold Bax, Ralph Vaughan Williams, Walter Leigh, Richard Addinsell and William Alwyn. The Forces also created their own film units, largely to make instructional films. Walton himself was exempted from military service and became loosely attached to the Ministry of Information on the condition that he wrote music for films 'of national importance'. (In 1944 Sir Osbert Sitwell raised the question of the conscription of artists in his anti-war tract *A Letter to my son* which was vigorously contested by the critic James Agate. Even George Orwell weighed into the debate, with Agate at least conceding that 'a wise government will not put a bayonet into the hands of a William Walton, a Constant Lambert, a Clifford Curzon, a Noël Coward, a John Gielgud or a Tommy Trinder'.)[33] None of the films Walton worked on quite falls into the category of pure documentary but each could nevertheless be said to be of national importance for its underlying message or its effectiveness as a morale booster. Certainly the sentiments of *Major Barbara* could hardly be farther from those of three of the next four films he worked on. *The Next of Kin*, *The Foreman went to France* and *Went the Day Well?*, all produced at the Ealing Studios, are essentially propaganda films that were designed, as Charles Barr so aptly put it in his history of the studios,[34] to warn against complacency and amateurishness, a lesson which was seen to be learnt at bitter cost.

The first two of these films overlapped in production. *The Foreman went to France*, with a narrative by J. B. Priestley and directed by Charles Frend (film editor for *Major Barbara*), was based on the true experience of a certain Melbourne Johns. The foreman of an ammunition factory (Clifford Evans) takes it upon himself, when his superiors seem unconcerned, to go to France to retrieve important machinery before it falls into enemy hands. Set during the period of the fall of France, it deals with fifth columnists, one a French mayor (Robert Morley) and another passing as an English officer (John Williams). It also points an accusing finger at the British obsession with red tape. Constance Cummings plays an American girl involved in the rescue operation while Tommy Trinder (in his first straight role) and Gordon Jackson provide the true British elements of humour and adventurous spirit, with the British soldier emerging, as the *Times* critic put it, as 'something of a natural philosopher and humourist'.[35] Walton provided a thoroughly efficient score, with a memorable fanfare-heralded march for the opening and closing titles and a striking passage depicting the refugees fleeing from the German advance. It is perhaps difficult now to appreciate the effect that films such as this had on war-time audiences, but there is no escaping their message and the underlying emotions. Even the French captain's closing words – 'We shall owe everything to your country, monsieur, when France lives again – one day' – can bring a lump to the throat half a century on. *The Foreman went to France* was first shown on Sunday 12 April at the London Pavilion. Previewing it two days earlier, *The Times* called it 'an outstanding British film'. Other propaganda films showing in London at that time were Harold French's *The Day will dawn* and Michael Powell's *One of our aircraft is missing*. Even in wartime Walton's humour shines through two short sections of the score that are headed *La Ravelese* (with a suggestion of *La Valse*) and *Moto Poulencuo*.

The other film being made at about the same time as *The Foreman went to France* was *The Next of Kin*, written and directed by Thorold Dickinson[36] who was specially seconded from the Army for the purpose. (He went on to direct *Men of Two Worlds* in 1945, with a score by Bliss.) It began as a War Office commission and, although little financial support was forthcoming, it was taken up by Ealing Studios and given feature-length treatment. It teaches most effectively the lesson of 'careless talk' in wartime, and at first its showing was restricted to compulsory audiences of service men and women. Churchill was worried about certain aspects of the film and delayed its general release until some of the violence had been toned down. But as the *Times* critic put it so succinctly:

> It is difficult to understand why there should ever have been any discussions as to whether *The Next of Kin* should not be shown to the public, [a] film . . . intended to jolt the public into an awareness of the danger of careless talk. A word by an infatuated officer to a striptease dancer with an unfortunate taste for cocaine is the first link in a chain of events which leads to so many unnecessary casualties. . . . The Germans are ready to meet an attack which was to have been a surprise. The operation is successful, but the cost is high.

The Cornish town of Mevagissey served as the French port on which the attack is made. *The Next of Kin* opened at the London Pavilion on 15 May 1942 where it took over from *The Foreman went to France*. The cast included Mervyn Johns, Stephen Murray, Basil Sydney, Naunton Wayne, Nova Pilbeam, Jack Hawkins and Thora Hird. An hour-long radio adaptation of the film, made by Cecil McGivern and including Nova Pilbeam, Stephen Murray and members of the BBC Drama Repertory Company, was broadcast on the Home Service on 6 July 1942 and part of the music from the film soundtrack was used.

Walton worked on *The Next of Kin* in December 1941 and once again he turned in an effective score, with a military quick march for title music that quickly dissolves in a typical cinematic cliché into a fragment of *La Marseillaise*, informing the audience that the opening scene is set in France. There is a lively 'striptease dance' and some passionate string writing for two lovers who meet on the cliff and in a bookshop (ironically the same bookshop from which a German spy is operating). Here Walton was not adverse to a little 'borrowing'. At least one of the two foxtrots used in the factory dance scene (that form part of Christopher Palmer's suite *A Wartime Sketchbook*[38]) is certainly not Walton's: the second half of the sequence makes use of Noel Gay and Frank Eyton's *All over the place* which had recently appeared, in its vocal version sung by Tommy Trinder, in another Ealing film, *Sailors Three* (1940). Like anyone, Walton was capable subconsciously of absorbing existing tunes. Dallas Bower remembers Walton playing him a dance tune he had composed for the film that turned out to resemble rather too closely a contemporary number known as *Spain*. Bower and Walton's close friend, the composer and for a while jazz-band leader Spike Hughes, had to persuade him to reject it from the film. In a similar fashion the first of the two foxtrots in *The Next of Kin* bears some resemblance to *Weary Traveller* from Spike Hughes' innovatory jazz ballet *High Yellow* of 1932, perhaps a fair exchange as Hughes' 1938 television operetta *Cinderella* had apparently contained Walton references, chiefly to the symphony.[39]

For his next film, *The First of the Few*, made at Denham, Walton produced one of his most memorable scores. After both starring in and directing *Pimpernel Smith*, a patriotic war-time update of the Scarlet Pimpernel theme (with music by John Greenwood), Leslie Howard performed the same dual role in this semi-fictional biography of Reginald J. Mitchell (1895–1937), the designer of the

Spitfire. Like *The Foreman went to France* and *Went the Day Well?*, this is a story told in flashback. At the height of the Battle of Britain, Crisp (David Niven), a former Schneider Trophy pilot now an RAF station commander, tells Mitchell's life story to a group of young pilots. As in *The Foreman went to France* its story has an underlying theme of one man's struggle against blinkered 'official' attitudes. Just as Melbourne Johns goes it alone when he cannot convince his superiors of the urgency of recovering vital machinery before it falls into enemy hands, so Mitchell first faces opposition to his revolutionary designs and then has to convince government officials of the urgency of arming in the air in the face of the Nazi threat. His late nights working on the Spitfire design take a heavy toll of his health, and the most memorable lines are when Vickers-Supermarine give the go-ahead to a prototype, telling him: 'This plane of yours, you've got to get it ready in 12 months because that's all the time we are giving you', to which Mitchell grimly replies: 'It'll be ready in 8 months – because that is all the time I can give you.' The stirring prelude, with its characteristic fanfare opening, is one of Walton's finest marches (and given a splendid performance on the soundtrack with Muir Mathieson conducting the LSO). This leads straight into a tense, agitated prologue, with the European political situation outlined by a sequence of newsreels and, with the threat of the Nazi advance, the music making oblique references to the descent into the Nibelheim (without anvils) from *Das Rheingold* and the Immolation Scene from *Götterdämmerung*, the latter recognizable from its bold descending brass figure. After the prologue, music is used sparingly but to great effect. Interestingly, the Battle of Britain sequence towards the end has no music soundtrack, unlike the parallel sequence in the much later film of that name. Together with the title music, the other important episodes are the poignant, lyrical theme with violin solo representing the dying Mitchell and the fugue depicting the Spitfire's factory production (to which piano brings an added piquancy on the soundtrack). Having found a fugue a part solution to his problems with the Symphony in 1935, Walton makes equally effective use of one at the key moment here in the film. (These three sections were later skilfully united to form the *'Spitfire' Prelude and Fugue*, the first piece of Walton music to make the jump from the screen to the concert hall.) *The First of the Few* was first shown on 20 August 1942 at the Leicester Square Cinema and has since become the most durable of Walton's 'official' war-time films.

The last of these essentially war-time propaganda films was *Went the Day Well?*, made at Ealing in the spring of 1942. Walton was working on the score in the summer, with Roy Douglas's assistance for some of the orchestration, and the film was shown on Sunday 1 November 1942 at the London Pavilion where it faced competition with Noël Coward's *In which we serve* which was showing at two London cinemas. If careless talk was the watchword in *The Next of Kin*, then complacency and misplaced trust are the messages here. Based on a story by Graham Greene, it concerns the sleepy English village of Bramley which is invaded by German parachutists passing themselves off as Royal Engineers. The squire of the village (Leslie Banks) turns out to be a quisling and the villagers, at first locked up in the church, eventually defeat the enemy in a battle at the manor house. Excellent direction by the Brazilian Alberto Cavalcanti, a former producer in the GPO Film Unit, makes this a taut, realistic action thriller, no film for the faint-hearted. Also in the cast were Basil Sydney, Valerie Taylor, Marie Lohr, Elizabeth Allan, Thora Hird, Mervyn Johns, Frank Lawton, David Farrar and C. V. France. Fanfare and march provide the robust title music. Elsewhere music, chiefly militaristic, is used even more sparingly than in *The First of the Few*, with a sinister snatch of march depicting the bogus English soldiers. Roy Douglas recalled that the inspiration for the theme of the opening march came from trying to fit the film's title to music.[40] The march returns for the end titles to provide a moving conclusion. Again, one can only wonder at the disturbing impact this film had on war-time audiences.

Up to this point Walton's work for films were all thoroughly professional jobs which, with the one exception of *The First of the Few*, had little to commend them outside the cinema. Had others taken on these scores, who can say if those films would have been any less successful? But his next three commissions, the Olivier/Shakespeare scores for *Henry V*, *Hamlet* and *Richard III*, place him at the pinnacle of film composers with three of the finest scores ever written, scores that are an integral part of the films, each one matching to perfection every action, mood and breath. *Henry V*, the first and in many ways the finest film of the three, was first shown on 22 November 1944 at the Carlton, London in aid of the benevolent funds of the Airborne Forces and Commandos, to whom the film was dedicated. It proved a great success. Its origins, however, go back a few years.

Dallas Bower, who had been an associate producer of the 1936 *As you like it* film, had in 1938, as a pioneer television producer, prepared a script of *Henry V* for BBC Television. But with the outbreak of war, television closed down. When Bower became Supervisor of Film Production for the Ministry of Information, he adapted his script for film, but the MoI was only interested in short propaganda films of a documentary nature. So Bower sold his script to Filippo Del Giudice (1892–1961), an Italian lawyer and refugee who had become managing director of Two Cities Films Ltd (and who, incidentally, had appeared in *The First of the Few*, playing an Italian). Asked if he had anyone in mind for the role of Henry, Bower immediately suggested Olivier, a view with which Del Giudice concurred.[41] On 19 April 1942 Olivier took part in a 75-minute radio version of *Henry V*, produced and adapted by Howard Rose. Four days later he was declaiming an extract in a St George's Day 'Battle for Freedom' presentation at the Royal Albert Hall, the closing half-hour of which was broadcast. But Olivier, after his experience of *As you like it*, was not easily persuaded unless he could have complete control over the film which, to Bower's disappointment, meant the overall direction. This he was granted, and although he did not use Bower's script, he nevertheless took him on as associate producer. Walton was the obvious choice of composer, again on Bower's recommendation. The three had worked together in October 1942 on the radio production of *Christopher Columbus* for which Louis MacNeice had written the play to mark the 450th anniversary of Columbus's discovery of the New World. Olivier had taken the leading role, Bower was the producer, and Walton had provided the substantial score of incidental music.

Christopher Columbus had been inspired by the broadcast ten months earlier of a radio adaptation of *Alexander Nevsky*, based on Eisenstein's 1938 film. Written by Louis MacNeice, it used Prokofiev's score. Sir Adrian Boult conducted the BBC Symphony Orchestra and Chorus, Robert Donat took the name part, and the producer was Dallas Bower.[42] The dramatic centrepiece to *Alexander Nevsky* was the Battle on the Ice, and whether or not its visual impact in the Eisenstein film as well as Prokofiev's music had influenced Walton, it has a worthy counterpart in the Agincourt battle scene in *Henry V*. Even Olivier admitted that sequence was 'littered with petty larcenies from our Master of All, Eisenstein'.[43]

Henry V was a Two Cities film (as *Hamlet* was also to be), and Del Giudice's financial and distribution link with J. Arthur Rank ensured the essential backing, even when the final cost, at £475 000, had exceeded the original planned budget of £300 000. Meanwhile Bower's friendship with John Betjeman, then Press Attaché in Dublin, facilitated the filming of the Agincourt battle scene in neutral Ireland, while his contacts in the MoI enabled Olivier to obtain the release of several key actors from their war-time duties to appear in *Henry V*. The large cast included Robert Newton (Pistol), Leslie Banks (Chorus), Esmond Knight (Fluellen), Renée Asherson (Katharine), George Robey (Falstaff), Harcourt Williams (King Charles VI), Max Adrian (Dauphin), Felix Aylmer (Archbishop of Canterbury), Robert Helpmann (Bishop of Ely), Griffith Jones (Earl of Salisbury), John Laurie (English Captain), Russell Thorndike (Duke of Bourbon) and Ernest Thesiger (French Ambassador).

To add the necessary sense of period to *Henry V*, Walton drew on several sources. Tunes from the Fitzwilliam Virginal Book were skilfully reworked for the opening Globe Theatre scene and for the death of Falstaff where he appropriately turned an old drinking song into an affecting passacaglia. He dipped into Canteloube's *Chants d'Auvergne* for scenes at the French court; part of the fifteenth-century French tune 'Réveillez-vous, Piccars' was used as a call-to-arms in the Agincourt battle scene, while the English carol 'Our King went forth to Normandy', known as the *Agincourt Song*, brought a suitably joyous choral climax. These last two tunes came at the suggestion of Vaughan Williams who had used them in his 1933 overture for brass band, *Henry the Fifth*. Some other suggestions were not taken up. 'Larry knew exactly what he liked and what he wanted', Walton once said.[44] 'For instance, he'd say: "Now, this is a beautiful tune I've thought of . . . dee da de de da dum . . ."' To which he replied, 'Yes, a lovely tune, but it's out of *Meistersinger*.' There was even the suggestion of writing the music for the battle scene first and then shooting it to the music, but this approach was wisely not adopted. (In fact a 'guide-track' was recorded on piano by Roy Douglas but never used.)

Right from the film's beginning, as the fluttering flute figure depicts the tumbling Globe playbill, one is aware of an extraordinarily skilful marriage of sound and vision. Even when Henry has raised his troops (and the film's audience) to a fever pitch of excitement in the Siege of Harfleur and St Crispian's Day speeches, Walton matches the mood to perfection with orchestral outbursts that are no less exciting and which carry the action onwards on a tide of emotion. Olivier was highly appreciative of the music Walton wrote for him (giving him the final full-screen credit), and this he openly acknowledged:

> I've always said that if it weren't for the music I don't think *Henry V* would have been a success. That is perfectly sincere, and in case you don't think it is perfectly sincere I will tell you that after he had seen a run-through of the film, naked and innocent of all sound – there was no music, no sound effects as well, he thought to himself, 'Well, I had better do something about this . . .', and when I thanked him for the music afterwards he said, 'Well, my boy', as he always did, 'I am very glad you showed it to me because I must tell you I did think it was terribly dull without the music'! He had really saved it and he knew that he had saved it too. If ever music was essential and helpful, it was there.[45]

Del Giudice was behind their next film, *Hamlet*, begun in 1947 and first shown at the Odeon, Leicester Square in May the following year.[46] This proved an even more immediate commercial success, even though because of its very nature it does not have quite the visual spectacle of *Henry V*, especially when it was shot in black and white. Olivier's talk of wanting to shoot it as a series of engravings was only a cover for certain problems he was having. As he later admitted, he was 'in the middle of a bitter row with Technicolor'.[47] (He had had problems of a different nature with the Technicolor process when making *Henry V*, both in the lighting and the colour printing.) But this gave him the chance to make use of deep-focus photography with dramatic effect. More controversial were the interchanging of certain scenes and the textual cuts, of which the most apparent, for reason of length, was dispensing with Rosencrantz and Guildenstern. Olivier (now Sir Laurence) took with him many of the technicians who had worked on *Henry V*, and the cast included Jean Simmons (Ophelia), Basil Sydney (Claudius), Eileen Herlie (Gertrude), Norman Wooland (Horatio), Felix Aylmer (Polonius), John Laurie (Francesco), Esmond Knight (Bernardo), Anthony Quayle (Marcello), Terence Morgan (Laertes), Peter Cushing (Osric) and Stanley Holloway (Gravedigger).

Walton's score for *Hamlet* is every bit the equal of that for *Henry V*. The full tragic import of the plot is graphically portrayed in a prelude of tremendous power.[48] Other memorable moments are the orchestral build-up to the 'To be or not to be' soliloquy, the scenes with Ophelia (the music to which Muir Mathieson later extracted to form 'a poem for orchestra, *Hamlet and Ophelia*'), and the Mousetrap play sequence. (The brief pirate sea battle even uses a fugue not unlike the one in *The First of the Few*.) One noticeable feature of the score is Walton's use of *leitmotiv*, particularly in the development of the Ophelia motif, with the funereal repetition of its opening phrase at her drowning, and its transformation near the end at Laertes' death. In his article on Film Music in *Grove V*, Hans Keller commented on its skilful use in the Mousetrap scene:

A score in which the Leitmotiv technique is handled with unfailing and original mastery is Walton's *Hamlet* ... Even the best Hollywood composer would just automatically have reused the music from the early backflash showing Claudius's murder, for underlining the corresponding 'murder' in the players' performance: the typical leitmotivic tautology which, among other misuses, has brought the difficult technique into such discredit among sensitive observers. Walton, however, utilises the backflash material in his interpretation of Claudius's reactions to the poisoning of the actor-king, thus impressing upon us, more vividly than the picture itself could possibly do, that the king (Claudius) is overwhelmed by the thought of his own deed.[49]

Extracts from the film soundtrack, on which Muir Mathieson conducted the Philharmonia Orchestra, were very soon released on record (at the time 78 rpm discs). In 1963 Mathieson adapted the music used for the opening titles for concert use as the Funeral March.

The filming of the last of the trilogy, *Richard III* (in Technicolor and VistaVision), came at the request of Alexander Korda[50] (in fact one of his last films). As on both previous occasions, Olivier starred and directed (not out of choice but because all the directors he approached were unavailable at the time). He assembled another fine cast that included Claire Bloom (Anne), Ralph Richardson (Buckingham), John Gielgud (Clarence), Cedric Hardwicke (King Edward IV), Stanley Baker (Richmond), Alec Clunes (Hastings) and Andrew Cruickshank (Brackenbury), as well as three who appeared in all three Shakespeare films: Esmond Knight (Ratcliffe), John Laurie (Lovel) and Russell Thorndike (Priest). (In all three films as well Alan Dent had been the text editor and Roger Furse the designer.) *Richard III* had its first showing at the Leicester Square Theatre on 13 December 1955. Bosworth Field was transported to Spain with Spanish extras for the battle scene, and once again there were substantial changes to the text, with whole scenes dispensed with and, instead of opening with the familiar 'Now is the winter of our discontent', the coronation of Edward IV from *Henry VI Part III* was inserted before that soliloquy both to provide an historical framework to the complex political situation and to focus on the film's central image: the crown.

Walton's score for *Richard III* may not be quite the match for either *Henry V* or *Hamlet*, yet the film's murderous plot did not call for the same orchestral brilliance or dramatic effect. Here again Walton made use of leitmotiv. The title music (without the opening fanfare that was later added for the concert Prelude) sets off with a bustling figure that leads into a noble Elgarian melody (close relative of the trio in the coronation march *Orb and Sceptre*), these two themes being used in the night-time fanfares before the battle scene to represent respectively the armies of Richard and Henry, Earl of Richmond. Another, poignant theme serves for the unfortunate Queen Anne. When on the death of Edward IV one of the young princes is taken to sanctuary, Walton makes ironic reference to the *Coventry Carol* (a reminder of the slaughter of the innocents by Herod the Great). Something too of that *Presto, con malizia* spirit from the First Symphony re-emerged later

during the recording sessions for *Richard III*. After *Hamlet*, Olivier had apparently asked Walton for 'less austere' music, and Muir Mathieson was amused
to find the direction *con prosciutto, agnello e confitura di fragioli* (with ham,
lamb and strawberry jam) written on the score.[51] As the film conductor Ernest
Irving once remarked: 'Walton's sardonic humour and virtuosity in colourful
orchestration [are] assets of the utmost value. He possesses a polite imperturb-
ability which stands him in good stead when faced with unexpected requirements from the directors.'[52]

The music for the three Shakespearean films has become widely known through
various concert suites and extracts, the films themselves are commercially available on video, and they have been discussed extensively elsewhere.[53] But Walton's
own commentary on the role of the film composer and his approach to these films
is worth quoting:

> Writing music for the screen is undoubtedly a specialised job. To begin with, the
> composer is rightly disciplined in his work by the time factor. For example, in
> *Hamlet* (as in all other films) my first contact with the production was the arrival of
> the script. This meant that I could obtain at least some idea of the treatment envis-
> aged by the producer-director, in translating this monumental work into celluloid.
> An occasional visit to the film set also gave me some impressions of how the project
> was coming along.
>
> The real work, however, begins when the picture is complete – complete, that is,
> in what is called the rough cut. It is only at this stage that the full atmosphere and
> dramatic impact of the screen play can be seen. However much a composer may
> examine the scenario, he can never grasp all those little individual touches which a
> director adds while he is shooting the picture. Then, again, there is this time busi-
> ness. After I have seen the film with the director and music director, the editor passes
> me a typewritten sheet giving the exact timings of each section of the film to which
> music will be fitted. For example, a sequence may call for 1 minute 23 seconds of
> music; 1 minute 24 seconds is too long, and 1 minute 22 seconds is too short. This
> means that a composer must, right from the start, adjust his approach to the composi-
> tion. In writing for the concert hall, he can work out his ideas to suit himself. His
> symphony may run for 20, 30, or 50 minutes. Not so in films. The form and content
> of the music is governed absolutely by the exacting requirements of the pictures on
> the screen.
>
> There seems to be an idea among film people that a composer can turn out pages
> and pages of fully orchestrated manuscript just on the spur of the moment. The sort
> of things that happen is that the unfortunate writer comes to the studio, is shown
> the film, finds that there is a total of 50 minutes of music required, and some bright
> spark in the music office says, 'That's lovely. We can book the orchestra in two
> weeks' time, and get the whole thing in the bag.' Frankly, two weeks is no earthly
> use for 50 minutes' music, as anyone who has attempted full scale composition will
> know. I think that composers as a whole should decry this bad aspect of film-
> making and see if some arrangement cannot be made whereby the composer is
> guaranteed a certain reasonable time in which to deliver his score, and I myself
> always insist on this.
>
> In the case of *Hamlet*, I received every consideration from Laurence Olivier, and
> the film unit, in that the music recording dates were spread over a month, thus giving
> ample time to consider the results of each of the recording days' work, and allowing

time for discussion before proceeding to the next music section. The closest collaboration was maintained between Olivier and myself, and some of my musical ideas were evolved from suggestions from him.

The value to a film of its musical score rests chiefly in the creation of mood, atmosphere, and the sense of period. When the enormous task of re-imagining a Shakespearean drama in terms of the screen has been achieved, these three qualities, which must be common to all film music, appear in high relief.

In the case of 'mood' I would quote as an example the incidental musical effects in Hamlet's soliloquies which varied their orchestral colour according to the shifts of his thought. For 'atmosphere' take the music of rejoicing after the victory of Agincourt in *Henry V*, which also illustrates the power to evoke a sense of historical period in a special way, for the contemporary Agincourt hymn which has been handed down to us was adapted to my purpose. Indeed the atmosphere of human feeling and the evocation of a past time are often combined, or made to blend from one to the other without any abruptness of transition. At the entry of the players in *Hamlet* I took the chance to suggest the musical idiom of the time by using a small sub-section of the orchestra (two violas, cello, oboe, cor anglais, bassoon, harpsichord) and then proceeded to make my comment on the action in my own personal idiom.

In a film the visual effect is of course predominant, and the music subserves the visual sequences, providing a subtle form of punctuation – lines can seem to have been given the emphasis of italics, exclamation marks added to details of stage 'business', phrases of the action broken into paragraphs, and the turning of the page at a crossfade or cut can be helped by music's power to summarise the immediate past or heighten expectation of what is to come. The analogy with printer's typography is useful, but beyond this, music offers orchestral 'colour' to the mind's ear in such a way that at every stage it confirms and reinforces the colour on the screen which is engaging the eye.

The composer in the cinema is the servant of the eye, in the Opera House he is of course the dominating partner. There everyone, beginning with the librettist, must serve him and the needs of the ear. In the film world, however, from the first stage called the 'rough-cut' where the composer first sees the visual images that his work must reinforce, an opera composer finds his controlling position usurped. He works in the service of a director. Since proportion is as important in music as in any other of the arts, the film composer, no longer his own master, is to a great extent at the mercy of his director.

A close and delicate collaboration is essential for the film must be served, but music must not be asked to do what it should not or cannot. After a while the composer who stays the pace acquires what has been called 'the stopwatch mentality', a quality which I have heard deplored; but I am quite certain the habit, a particularly strict form of self-discipline, does a composer far more good than harm when he is working on his own for his own ends. Within or outside the cinema every second counts.

A film composer must have confidence in his director or collaboration will break down. In my three major Shakespearean films I have been particularly blessed in working with a director who knew precisely what he wanted at any given point not only in quantity but in kind. Laurence Olivier understands the composer's problems. He has a genius for thinking up ways of adding to them, or increasing those that already exist, but he never demands the impossible, and his challenges have invariably led me to be grateful in the end. In the deployment of his visual resources he is himself a dramatist and though a composer's task is never anything but difficult, the confidence inspired by such a director has certainly made things far easier than they might have been.

If the musical aspect of the battle sequences in *Henry V* and *Richard III*, for instance, is considered helpful to the general effect, that is due to an unusually complex and close collaboration of sound and screen from one bar or visual movement to the next, the outcome of much patience and exercise of technique certainly, but above all, I think, the fruit of mutual confidence and esteem.[54]

There was another Olivier film project that did not materialize. Even before *Richard III* had been screened, he was touring Scotland for suitable locations for a film of *Macbeth*. But Korda's death in January 1956 effectively ended hopes for that project, even though two years later Olivier wrote to Eugene Goossens, who was looking for some film work to boost his income: 'If Macbeth comes off, as I desperately hope it will, I have already committed myself to William Walton, who, as you know, did the music for my three other Shakespeare films.'[55]

After a 14-year break from the film world, by the time Walton was commissioned to write what was to be his penultimate film score, for Guy Hamilton and Harry Saltzman's *The Battle of Britain*, attitudes towards the use of music in films had shifted. Commercial and financial considerations, rather than artistic ones, now seemed to dominate the industry. Just as Bernard Herrmann's score for Alfred Hitchcock's 1966 *Torn Curtain* had been rejected because the studio wanted a catchy title song that would sell thousands of records,[56] so three years later Walton's *Battle of Britain* score, in part orchestrated with the assistance of Malcolm Arnold,[57] was rejected by United Artists largely because there was not enough music to fill a planned LP.[58] To conclude this sorry story of shame and disgrace, without informing Walton (whose name was apparently not known to those in charge of the film's distribution), United Artists then approached another film composer, Ron Goodwin, to supply a score. The result was a forgettable bag of film-score clichés. It was only at the insistence of Olivier (who was one of the star-studded cast) that one section of Walton's score, the 'Battle in the Air',[59] was retained. These five minutes mark a return to vintage Walton and they form the core of an otherwise routine film that was first shown in London on 15 September 1969. Only later was the remainder of the score retrieved from United Artists and a suite made by Colin Matthews. What then emerged was that it also included one of Walton's most glorious marches, a march in fact to out-Walton any that he had written before. (Although its première had been announced for the Last Night of the Proms, two days before the film's opening, in the event it was not played.[60]) In the trio of the March (and elsewhere in the score) there are pointed references to Siegfried's horn call, another of Walton's Wagnerian allusions.

His last score for the cinema was for a film of the National Theatre's production of Chekhov's *Three Sisters*. As it was both directed by and starred Olivier, it seemed only natural that Walton should be turned to for the music. But, while serving its purpose well enough, the score is musically disappointing. The opening titles oddly announce: 'Main musical themes arranged and composed by Sir William Walton O.M.' with 'other arrangements by Derek Hudson and Gary Hughes'. But the 'themes' of the three sections of music turn out to be almost exclusively treatments of the Russian National Anthem, Mendelssohn's *Song without Words* Op. 19 No. 1 (a snatch of which is played by one of the characters in an early scene) and, in a dream sequence, a waltz that Walton had first composed for his short 1935 ballet, *The First Shoot*. After the first showing of *Three Sisters* in August 1970 in Venice where it had been chosen to represent Britain at the Venice Festival, it came to London in November. With a cast that also included Joan Plowright, Alan Bates, Derek Jacobi, Louise Purnell, Jeanne Watts, Sheila Reid and Ronald Pickup, it preserves Olivier's Old Vic production and his own performance as the old doctor Chebutikin, but it is too stagey to be seen as anything other than a filmed version of a stage production.

The *Battle of Britain* score had seen the last flourish of that immediately recognizable Walton style. For someone who had cornered the market in ceremonial marches it was a style readily imitated. For London Television's *South Bank Show* tribute to Olivier on his 75th birthday, Stephen Oliver provided a brilliant score that was Waltonian to its core. When permission was refused to use the Prelude to *Richard III* for the title music to the BBC TV Falklands war drama *Tumbledown*, Richard Hartley turned in a very effective pastiche (or near copy) of the Prelude, and in the title music for the 1969 film *Mosquito Squadron* Frank Cordell inserted a march that might have been chippings from the Walton work bench.

This was not quite the end to Walton's involvement in films. In 1981 ITV's *South Bank Show* presented Tony Palmer's long and probing profile of Walton, then approaching 80, calling it (after *Troilus and Cressida*) *At the Haunted End of the Day*. While Walton himself was the chief contributor, there was also a notable contribution from Olivier. That same year Tony Palmer also produced his epic twelve-hour television serialization, *Wagner*. Richard Burton played the composer. Olivier and his two fellow theatrical knights, Gielgud and Richardson, were wily courtiers. But as the King and Queen of Bavaria were none other than William[61] and Susana Walton. What more stately climax could there be to a distinguished life in films?

Notes

1. Her year of birth as given in the *Macmillan International Film Encyclopaedia*, edited by Ephraim Katz, 1994, which gives her nationality as Polish. Other sources differ: *Who Was Who?* gives 1900 and states that she was Austrian by birth, while further references even give 1898.
2. Margaret Kennedy was more widely known for her novel, *The Constant Nymph*, which was dramatized and produced by Basil Dean in 1926 with incidental music by Eugene Goossens. Elisabeth Bergner starred in its Berlin production. It was filmed twice by Dean, in 1928 (silent version) and 1933 (with a revised Goossens score), and later in Hollywood in 1943 (with a score by Korngold). *Escape Me Never* was a sequel to *The Constant Nymph*.
3. *Sunday Telegraph*, 25 March 1962.
4. In conversation with the author, 2 February 1997.

5. Three-movement suite arranged by Christopher Palmer and recorded on Chandos CHAN 8870.
6. Eric Fenby, much of whose score for Alfred Hitchcock's 1939 film *Jamaica Inn* was not used, has written that 'Willie Walton was most sympathetic and told me he had had a complete ballet cut in a film with Elisabeth Bergner' (letter to the author, 1986).
7. 2 April 1935.
8. The film's editor was David Lean who also worked on *As You Like It, Dreaming Lips* and *Major Barbara*.
9. 24 May 1935.
10. Holroyd, M. (1991) *Bernard Shaw Vol III (1918–1950): The Lure of Fantasy*, London: Chatto & Windus, pp. 381–2.
11. Kennedy, M. (1990) *Portrait of Walton*, Oxford: OUP, p. 91.
12. Walton, S. (1989) *William Walton: Behind the Façade*, Oxford: OUP, p. 94.
13. First performed at the King's Theatre, Edinburgh, on 21 November 1936 (after a lengthy postponement owing to Miss Bergner's illness), transferring to His Majesty's Theatre, London on 14 December 1936.
14. In his autobiography, *Confessions of an Actor* (Weidenfeld & Nicolson 1982, Orion 1994), Olivier does not mention *As you like it*.
15. Manvell, R. (1971) *Shakespeare and Film*, London: Dent, p. 31.
16. 4 September 1936.
17. In Anthony Holden (1989) *Olivier*, Harmondsworth: Sphere Books Ltd., p. 118.
18. 6 November 1936.
19. Based on a short story, *Philomel Cottage*, by Agatha Christie.
20. Mitchell, D. and Reed, P. (1991) (eds) *Letters from a Life: Selected Letters and Diaries of Benjamin Britten, Vol. 1, 1923–39*, London: Faber & Faber, pp. 419–20.
21. Two different suites of music from *As you like it* have been arranged by Carl Davis and Christopher Palmer respectively.
22. Boyd Neel gave an account of the problems in synchronising the action with the music in *My Orchestras and Other Adventures: The Memoirs of Boyd Neel*, University of Toronto 1985, pp. 98–100.
23. 3 February 1937.
24. 20 May 1937.
25. Redgrave, M. (1983) *In My Mind's Eye: An Autobiography*, London: Weidenfeld and Nicolson, p. 126.
26. Powell, M. (1986) *A Life in Movies: An Autobiography*, London: Mandarin, p. 377; although in the finished film there are only one or two brief scenes of hers that may have been retained.
27. Kenneth Clark, in *The Other Half: A Self-Portrait*, Hamish Hamilton, 1977, pp. 37–41, has described Pascal as a likeable but 'perfectly shameless' man, 'a sort of Baron Munchausen, who never opened his mouth without telling some obviously untrue story'.
28. Holroyd, M. (1991), op. cit., p. 477.
29. Holroyd, M. (1991), op. cit., p. 437.
30. 2 April 1941.
31. Bliss, A. (1970) *As I Remember*, London: Faber & Faber, p. 168.
32. In Tony Palmer's film profile, *At the Haunted End of the Day*, ITV, 19 April 1981.
33. Orwell, S. and Angus, I. (1970) *The Collected Essays, Journalism and Letters of George Orwell: Vol. 3: As I Please (1943–5)*, Harmondsworth: Penguin Books, pp. 296–8.
34. Charles Barr, *Ealing Studios*, Studio Vista, revised 1993.
35. 10 April 1942.
36. In a letter, dated 7 December 1972, to Stewart Craggs (to whom I am indebted for

the information), Thorold Dickinson wrote: 'I was naturally delighted when Walton agreed to do the score, and though to him our approach had to be more "music hall" than "opera house" (to reach the widest audience), he disciplined himself and delivered a score that was an object lesson in dignified and appropriate propaganda. Except for a fox trot he had to write which was neither good Walton nor good dance music. I have worked with some superb composers in my time, and I regard Walton as outstandingly professional in coping with the maddening demands of timing and emphasis that a film score demands'.

37. 14 May 1942.
38. An eight-movement suite comprised of extracts from *The Foreman went to France*, *The Next of Kin*, *Went the Day Well?* and *The Battle of Britain*, recorded on Chandos CHAN 8870.
39. Dallas Bower, the producer of *Cinderella* for TV, in conversation with the author, 18 February 1997.
40. Conversation with the author, Tunbridge Wells, 23 July 1996.
41. Del Giudice and Olivier first met on the opening night of *In which we serve*, a Rank/Two Cities film. After his break with Rank, Del Giudice set up Pilgrim Pictures in 1947. But a combination of financial difficulties and ill-health caused him to fold the company two years later. He went to the United States before retiring to Italy in 1952 where he entered a Benedictine monastery. He died in 1961.
42. Broadcast on 8 December 1941. For a second broadcast, on 26 April 1942, Nevsky was played by Michael Redgrave and Clarence Raybould conducted.
43. Olivier, L. (1982), op. cit., p. 209.
44. In Tony Palmer's TV profile.
45. In a BBC Radio 3 memorial tribute, 'Portrait of Walton', presented by John Amis, 4 June 1977, re-broadcast 20 July 1983.
46. In 1946 there had been tentative plans to film *King Lear* with Olivier, but nothing came of the project.
47. Interview with Melvyn Bragg in London Television's *South Bank Show* two-part tribute to Olivier on his 75th birthday.
48. Oddly enough, the soundtrack starts with the sound of the orchestra tuning before launching into the Prelude.
49. *Grove's Dictionary of Music and Musicians* (1954), Fifth Edition, London: Macmillan, Vol. 3, p. 100.
50. Korda had earlier persuaded John Barrymore to star in a film version of *Hamlet*. Barrymore insisted on wearing the original black costume he had worn in his youth to play the Prince (he played it in London in 1926), but he became so depressed when he found it no longer fitted him that he journeyed to India in search of Ayurveda, the ancient healing art, and the film was never made. Korda was so disappointed that he was unwilling to discuss *Hamlet* again, even when ten years later the question of producing Olivier's film arose. (Michael Korda (1979), *Charmed Lives: A Family Romance*, London: Allen Lane, pp. 124–5.)
51. Muir Mathieson, BBC Radio 3, 19 November 1969, quoted in Holden (1989) *Olivier*, op. cit., p. 345.
52. In 'Film Music', a talk given to the Royal Musical Association on 9 March 1950.
53. See the bibliography of each film score in Stewart Craggs (1990) *William Walton: A Catalogue*, Oxford: Clarendon Press.
54. James L. Limbacher (1974) *Film Music: from Violin to Video*, NJ: Scarecrow Press, pp. 128–31.
55. Carole Rosen (1993) *The Goossens: A Musical Century*, London: André Deutsch, p. 378.
56. Donald Spoto (1983) *The Life of Alfred Hitchcock*, London: Collins, p. 491.

57. Some sections of the score were even expanded and rescored by Arnold, including the last third of the *Battle in the Air*. See *The Music of Malcolm Arnold: A Catalogue*, compiled by Alan Poulton (1986), London: Faber Music p. 156.
58. The story is told in greater detail in Kennedy, M. (1990) *Portrait of* Walton, op. cit., pp. 237–40.
59. Conducted on the film soundtrack by Malcolm Arnold.
60. The Suite, including the March, was first performed on 10 May 1985 at Bristol, Carl Davis conducting the Bournemouth Symphony Orchestra.
61. I am grateful to Stewart Craggs for pointing out that Walton made an earlier film appearance, in *The Next of Kin*, in which he is seen as an officer in one of the army briefing scenes.

7 'All the things that might have been'[1]: *Christopher Columbus*

Zelda Lawrence-Curran

Christopher Columbus would certainly be a candidate if awards were to be given for the least discussed Walton score. Despite the vast amount of correspondence relating to the original 1942 radio play production, now stored in the BBC Written Archives, few critics or writers on music have given the work more than a passing mention. I suspect this apparent neglect is, in the main, due to the lack of performance of the play which is both long (over two hours), requires large resources and is subject specific, there being only a few dates in the calendar to which the topic of the discovery of America could be relevant.[2]

The first 'might have been' centres around the fact that it is astonishing that Walton contributed to the project at all. Given that he was a notoriously slow composer, the beginning of 1942 must have been something of a nightmare for him in terms of work schedule: having just managed to compose the incidental music for Gielgud's production of *Macbeth* in time for the first performance in Manchester on 16 January 1942, two film scores were planned for the immediate future. The first of these, a score for the J. B. Priestley script *A Foreman Went to France,* was sufficiently advanced for Walton to commence writing the music towards the end of January and the second, for Leslie Howard's *The First of the Few,* he envisaged beginning around the middle of March. The substantial score for the latter is well-known, in the form of the *Spitfire Prelude and Fugue,* and although there is evidence to suggest Walton did not take *A Foreman Went to France* very seriously,[3] in actuality he produced music of similar scope and stature. A third film script, this time Graham Greene's *Went the Day Well?* inspired another weighty score during September and October 1942. Thus in January 1942, when first asked to compose music for a radio play on the subject of Christopher Columbus, the script to be by Louis MacNeice, Walton did not feel he could physically manage to do so, despite the fact that 'the full resources of the Music Department will be available including, of course, the Chorus and

Orchestra A'[4] and that Olivier was to play the title role. Replying to Dallas Bower in a letter dated 27 January 1942 he wrote:

> ... This is most irritating – there is nothing I should like better to accept. ... Unless you can get the Corp. to postpone the date to mid-May instead of mid-March, I don't see how I can do it .... In fact I don't see how else you can do it, as there are precious few composers about nowadays. I don't suppose it would be possible to get Alan Rawsthorne out of the Army again ... Benjamin Britten is by way of returning ... but I gather he joins the RAF music dept. on landing. Who else is there except the old gang of V.W., J. Ireland, A. Bax ...

Dallas Bower obviously thought the play could be delayed as only three days later, Walton wrote to him again:

> ... Thank you for the sketch of C.C. I'm a bit terrified of accepting it, since you know what films are like and I'm worried that the Howard film won't be over in time to give this the music it deserves ... For the music will have to be good and one can't rely on a quick film extemporisation technique for it, so it will need more time, trouble and care. ...

Bower's willingness to delay the proposed production was probably as much prompted by MacNeice's intended treatment of the script as Walton's work commitments. Bower and MacNeice had collaborated previously on *Alexander Nevsky*, a radio play based on the pre-War Eisenstein film epic. This creation had formed part of the BBC's attempt to alter attitudes towards Russia, following the German invasion of that country in June 1941, and it was envisaged that *Christopher Columbus* would similarly promote America, Britain's latest ally after the Japanese attack on Pearl Harbor. In essence the project was an elaborate piece of propaganda. *Alexander Nevsky* had taken as its model a film of Titanic proportions and the new work was to be based on Samuel Eliot Morison's biography *Admiral of the Ocean Sea*, a similarly colossal parent. As a result MacNeice envisaged creating a formidable heroic narrative and from his point of view any extra time afforded by Walton's scheduling would be welcome.

As Walton had envisaged, *The First of the Few* took longer to complete than originally projected and owing to illness he did not start composing the music for *Christopher Columbus* until July 1942; by that time it had been decided that the new work would be broadcast on 12 October, the exact anniversary of Columbus's discovery of the New World. As Bower had promised, the music was to be performed by the BBC Symphony Orchestra and a BBC Chorus expanded by 30 extra singers, the conductor being Sir Adrian Boult. However, even with such an experienced body of musicians the production was not without difficulties: on 2 October Bower wrote to Walton 'Adrian is a little fussed at the complicated nature of the whole undertaking'. This is not really surprising: the most serious problem to beset the initial production of *Christopher Columbus* was that Walton was not the only overworked musician; in a 1992 interview with Carol Rosen on BBC Radio 3, Dallas Bower recalled:

> The schedules in those days were simply terrifying, beyond belief. For instance, the orchestra had had the night before a public performance – this was the night before our first rehearsal and evening performance of *Columbus* the following day – the

orchestra had played Elgar 2 and the new piece. . . . Now, as if that weren't enough, they had to repeat this at eight the following morning for the World Service and I said to Alan [Rawsthorne] 'Well, I'm terrified, Alan' and he said 'For God's sake come and sit with me'. I said 'Of course I will, because they are coming to *me* after they've done a repeat of this concert and they're going to do Walton'; not a note of which any of them had even seen and nor had Adrian. . . . We had no dramas of any appreciable kind other . . . than the fact we had this awful pressure on the orchestra. I think that the orchestra did have then some kind of break as far as I know. . . .

Possibly the most well known 'might have been' regarding this production of the radio play centred around the casting. As aforementioned, Olivier was to play the title role; in that there was little difficulty, indeed, he and Walton had already worked on the 1936 film of *As You Like It*. Rather, the problem lay with who was to take the part of Columbus's mistress, Beatriz. The obvious choice was Vivien Leigh, but Dallas Bower had been advised by the Casting Office at Broadcasting House that under the terms of her contract with David Selznick there was no question of Leigh's taking part and as a consequence Margaret Rawlings was to play Beatriz. Dallas Bower later commented:

> . . . to my astonishment Larry telephoned me and said 'Look, you don't mind if I bring Vivien, do you?' so I said 'Well, of course not. . .' and so she came and she sat with me and Suffield in the control box. . . . She suddenly turned to me during one of the breaks in the rehearsal and said 'You know, dear, I can't think why you didn't offer me this part'. . . . Suffield and I were totally speechless, I mean, we had to stop the rehearsal. She was allowed under her Selznick contract to do broadcasting. I was seriously misdirected by the Casting Office . . . very seriously misdirected indeed. Poor Margaret Rawlings was very put out – who played very well . . . she gave an excellent performance – but she didn't expect to find Vivien Leigh breathing down her neck which is what it really amounted to. . . .[5]

In addition to these difficulties as the broadcast date approached there was also a problem with the composer himself. Unsurprisingly, given his work schedule, Walton had already been ill once in 1942 and on 12 October was in North Wales, 'taking a rest', to quote Michael Kennedy.[6] However, Bower said 'I think he wasn't very well and he couldn't get to Bedford. . .rather upset Adrian in fact. . . .'[7] Thus, the composer missed the first performance of *Christopher Columbus*, although he had managed to hear some of it via a radio, with appalling reception. Fortunately the performance had been recorded (using the – for 1942 – new technology of the Philips-Hill process) and Bower was able to play it back to Walton: 'he said in rather a typically Waltonian way "Not too bad, really". . . .'[8]

Christopher Columbus was not just 'not too bad' it 'created a sensation in artistic circles on both sides of the Atlantic',[9] a fact on which Bower also commented and which forms yet another 'might have been':

> . . . it was in fact quite astonishing in as much as you might suppose it could have been a frightful shambles: well, it wasn't. . . .'[10]

The production in 1942 seems to have excited universal commendation. I would suggest that, even to the more cynical present-day ears, the work retains much of its power: an effect which could not have been achieved had something within the central themes of *Christopher Columbus* not operated on both MacNeice and Walton: what were the attitudes of the creators of this artistic event?

As both the composer and the poet are no longer with us, any statements regarding their creative motivation and attitudes to the work (apart from their own recorded comments) must be largely speculation: in effect informed 'might have beens'. Of the two artists MacNeice is the more open in this instance and indeed, generally. In an Appendix to the printed text of *Christopher Columbus*, which was published in March 1944, he wrote

> . . . Construction and 'over-all' unity being in a radio play of primary importance, a heroic subject such as the discovery of America, required an epic rather than a psychological treatment. The later career of Columbus, though vastly interesting from a biographical angle, would by transferring interest from the *muthos* to the character . . . have broken the programme in two, confused the listener and given him possibly a feeling of anti-climax. This programme, moreover, was intended to celebrate the 450th anniversary of the discovery of America; in writing an anniversary programme for the Battle of Waterloo I would not include that picture from 1833 of Wellington in Apsley House – the duchess lying dead inside while the mob is breaking the windows. Similarly, with *Alexander Nevsky*, neither Eisenstein's film nor radio adaptation of it was bothered by the fact that Nevsky spent his later years appeasing the Tartars.

On paper at least, MacNeice was therefore concerned with structure and action, echoing the *TLS* reviewer of his 1937 play *Out of the Picture* who recognized the poet's affinity with Wystan Auden's opinion on the matter: 'Drama is not suited to the analysis of character, which is the province of the novel.'[11] Personally, MacNeice did not have a great deal of time for psychology following an unfortunate experience with an analyst immediately before his first marriage. It is also important to remember the context in which *Christopher Columbus* was written. The play is essentially about a hero; during World War II heroes were a considerably more attractive proposition for subject matter than they are in the present day, when the emphasis has shifted towards a more psychological treatment. Furthermore, the whole object of the exercise was to applaud America and portraying Columbus as a champion of virtue was one of the most effective ways to achieve this. Today we take a more equivocal view of his character.

However, although he approached *Christopher Columbus* in a deliberately objective manner, I would argue that MacNeice could not escape his own psychological reactions to some of the issues raised by the subject matter; in the same way that he chose to bestow an epigraph from Euripides' *Hippolytus* (which Professor Jon Stallworthy translates as 'We are manifestly all obsessively in love with this thing that glitters on the earth')[12] on his collection *The Earth Compels* (1938). The title role in *Christopher Columbus* is that of an enlightened 'man of destiny' achieving his goal against all the manifold prejudice surrounding him: an enduring male fantasy which I suspect would have exerted an intense pull on a man of MacNeice's temperament and hearty sexual tendencies. MacNeice liked heroes in any form; he would travel a considerable distance to watch his favourite sports players, was nurtured on the Celtic heroic tales and Classics at Oxford.

Jon Stallworthy comments on this aspect of MacNeice's personality in discussing his visit to America in 1939:

> Much as MacNeice loved well-lit cities and the hum of the hive, nothing so quickened his imagination as lonely journeys in the darkness and silence beyond: 'it is easy', he wrote in the Introduction to *Varieties of Parable*, 'to identify with St Brandon and the others in the adventures on the western sea. . . . Such a voyage, like any form of quest, has an immemorial place in legend.' In March 1939, he had himself embarked in search of legend: 'America . . . for people in the British Isles is a legend', especially, he might have added, for Irishmen brought up within sight of the Atlantic. He was disappointed, however, by both the *Queen Mary* and the Atlantic. The ship seemed like a hotel. . . . Since he could not stand, like St Brandon or Odysseus, the a plunging prow gazing, salt-lashed, into the eye of the storm, he spent his time at the Tourist Bar observing his fellow passengers. . . .'[13]

Thus, although MacNeice intended *Christopher Columbus* to be concerned primarily with action, the most striking aspects of the radio-play for present-day listeners are those which involve the psychology of the main character and that non-cognitively, these aspects found their way into the script through MacNeice's personal response to the essential themes of the play.

There is little doubt that Walton, like MacNeice, was a robustly sexual person and, I suspect, as susceptible to the same 'male triggers' as the poet. However, he was rarely explicit with regard to his creative processes; he lacked MacNeice's candour and Celtic roots and thus there is little physical evidence to suggest the ideas presented in *Christopher Columbus* created straightforward analogues in his emotions. Indeed, on paper rather the reverse is true; in a letter written to Dallas Bower in March 1942 Walton made the following comments:

> . . . Actually from my point of view, I can't treat C.C. in any way different from a rather superior film. That is, that the music is entirely occasional and is of no use other than what it is meant for and one won't be able to get a suite out of it. Which is just as it should be, otherwise it would probably not fulfil its purpose. . . . Film music is not good film music if it can be used for any other purpose. . . . The music should never be heard without the film. . . .

Thus, the auspices were not good for his being touched by any deeper feelings when composing the score for *Christopher Columbus*; Walton was notoriously dismissive of his film music, the simple explanation being he could not give something which was written so quickly as much credence as a work of 'absolute' music which involved considerably more toil.[14] Taking Walton's statements at face value, using his 'facility v. creativity' argument it is also possible to assert that, even if his music to *Christopher Columbus* stemmed from the former, the fact that it was not subjected to the more cold-blooded, craftsman-like, processes necessary to turn it into 'creativity' must surely mean that the result must originate in a more crude emotional response; effectively it represents 'the truth' regarding his response to the script. However, I am not entirely convinced that Walton thought so little of this music. On listening to the score, it is obvious that something within the story stimulated him; not only is the work too substantial to have been turned out casually, I believe the craftsmanship upon which he placed so high a value was also engaged.

It is impossible for us to know definitely that Walton responded to a heroic theme in quite the same way as did Louis MacNeice: there is no record of him discussing the subject. Indeed, I believe he reacted in a manner quite different from that of MacNeice in that he was a fundamentally more pragmatic person than the poet. However, on studying his total oeuvre, it is obvious that he consistently wrote music for heroic subjects even if he merely made use of his 'facility' to do so: the most obvious parallel being with *Henry V* which Walton began writing in May 1943. On examining the scores, there are several analogies, especially between the section in *Christopher Columbus* where land is first sighted (Ex. 7.1) and the commencement of the *Charge and Battle* sequence in the later work (Ex. 7.2). This similarity is not at all surprising; in many ways the sections fulfil the same function within their respective plays. Both are set at dawn, both are 'preparatory' in the sense that they are followed by more primary action. Furthermore, as far as the leading characters are concerned, they preface their ultimate achievements; the discovery of land in the earlier work and the triumph of Agincourt in the latter. However, there is a further similarity between this section of *Christopher Columbus* and *Henry V*. The 'speaking chorus' passage climaxes in a *Te Deum Laudamus* but before the latter is begun the orchestral writing leading to the climax is strikingly similar to that accompanying the opening sequence of *Henry V* where wordless chorus and orchestra blend to state the 'Henry' theme:[15] the motif which is used to represent the heroic king throughout the film score. Although the opening of *Henry V* has less in common with this section of *Christopher Columbus* than *Charge and Battle*, there are some parallels. The later work opens with a panoramic view of London (in model form) and gradually moves up the Thames to settle on the Globe Theatre. The effect of this section of *Christopher Columbus* is somewhat similar; the actual finding of land after a long and tedious voyage concentrates one's attention on that land with greater intensity. Furthermore, in stating the 'Henry' motif whilst hovering over London Walton links the King with the country: Henry *is* England. Similarly, Columbus exists only insofar as he is the discoverer of the New World; he owns no allegiance to any country other than that of his discovering, confirmed in the line 'My country . . . is the future. . . .'.

Thus I would argue that, although Walton was not such a devotee of heroes as was MacNeice, there was something within the concept of heroic behaviour which inspired him to write music which is apt and valuable in both the pragmatic and psychological senses. However, *Christopher Columbus* would not be a satisfying creation if it relied merely upon the 'overcoming-hero' theme, however influential; in certain aspects of their lives MacNeice and Walton shared experiences which produced similar responses to the subject matter.

Jon Stallworthy makes innumerable references to the allure which the concept of 'the West' (in this case the west of Ireland) had on Louis MacNeice. However, as is the case with most desires, once he achieved his wish of going there for

Ex. 7.1   *Christopher Columbus*

Ex. 7.1 Concluded

Ex. 7.2　*Henry V*, 3rd movement, 'Charge and Battle'

Ex. 7.2 Concluded

various reasons he found the actuality rather unsatisfying: as a result his longing for the actual 'West' was transmuted into that for a fictional 'legendary West' which could never be fulfilled. In a similar way to his fondness for heroes, MacNeice loved quests; by their very nature these appear more enticing if they remain unfinished. In terms of his poetry this yearning manifested itself in morbid passages – the clichéd 'Celtic melancholy' or *hiraeth* – also exemplified in some of the works of Dylan Thomas; in this sense the former's *Autumn Journal* and the latter's *Poem in October* seem to suggest express aspects of the same experience.

Walton, again, was less forthcoming (honest?) than MacNeice about his emotions but the same sense of wistful melancholia finds a musical voice in many of his works; a fact acknowledged by Michael Kennedy:

> . . . But something deeper than the obvious emotion throbs beneath the surface of all his music – anger, pain, frustration, a sense of loss, one cannot be sure exactly what it is, but one senses it and it is disturbing and often uncomfortable. . . .[16]

In Walton's case I have found nothing to suggest that 'the West' had any influence whatsoever on his emotions: however, there is much to imply that for him 'the South' inspired a similar fascination to MacNeice's enchantment with the former destination. Walton's initial move south was from Oldham to Oxford: his desire to stay at the latter is what initially set him on the road to composition.[17] His association with the Sitwell's had taken him further, with consequences of similar magnitude: in 1920 he went with them to Italy. Lady Walton comments:

> . . . His own family had never been abroad and he liked retelling what this journey had been like. How uncomfortable trains were in those days when there were no sleepers. . . . How it had poured with rain all the way through France up to Modane, making him think 'Great God! Oldham again'. Then the train went into a tunnel, and when it came out on the Italian side they found the most marvellous sun. He never recovered from this moment of revelation, the shock of seeing so much brilliant light. . . .[18]

In Tony Palmer's 1981 film biography *At the Haunted End of the Day* even at the distance of some 60 years one can feel the thrill that moment held for Walton: 'there it was, ablaze with sunlight. I've never forgotten it, *a new world*' [my italics]. He had earlier acknowledged the experience '. . . changed my whole attitude about life and music'.[19] This would appear to suggest that both composer and poet would identify strongly with Columbus's mission as, put simply, both had personal experiences of wanting to be somewhere other than where they were. However, this statement needs qualifying as I do not believe this desire operated in the same way on each character and, as such, the effects hold implications for their reaction to *Christopher Columbus*. MacNeice's 'West' appears to be an escape from and an antidote to what he disliked about Ulster. Similarly, Walton viewed Oldham with distaste and first Oxford, then London, and finally Italy, 'the South', provided his escape from it. However, whereas MacNeice seems to have acknowledged that his relationship with Ulster was love-hate and, despite his revulsion for certain aspects of his early life there, he could not escape its lure or deny its influence upon him, Walton rarely spoke about Oldham and when he did he found little positive to say. MacNeice appears to have been continually searching for and never reaching his Utopia whilst Walton's escape from Oldham appears total and without nostalgia. In this sense MacNeice would have experienced the greater affinity with Columbus's character; he would have perceived the hopelessness of evading his obsession, whereas Walton would have taken a more pragmatic view.

However, if Walton did not identify with Columbus's inability to escape from his absorption with a place, he would have been very familiar with the feelings resulting from a sense of mission or inevitability concerning one's direction in life. Susana Walton writes:

> . . . I'm sure that this lack of a proper education sharpened William's awareness of his special talents. Since childhood he had been uncommonly lucky, a special person: he had been able to sing before he could read: he had been accepted at Oxford against all the odds. He felt impelled to write music, and found he could do so. But this knowledge that his destiny was to make good use of his special talent placed him under a terrible obligation. As I later learned from experience, his life was to be a constant struggle. . . .[20]

Similarly Louis MacNeice acknowledged a certain sense of isolation. Jon Stallworthy describes MacNeice thinking his way into the minds of his schoolfellows; he felt they could not have attempted to reciprocate that experience. As regards this thread of affinity I believe the most powerful trigger in the script may be found at the point just before Columbus finds land; indeed, this passage represents the climax of the play as a whole in the way that Columbus's triumphal entrance into Barcelona does not. Furthermore, this passage appears to encapsulate the impetus behind the play in addition to forming the climax; a man driven by his own destiny. At this stage in the action the character has the following lines:

> 'Where shall wisdom be found and where is the abode of understanding?
> God makes the weight for his winds and he weighteth the waters by
>   measure'
> They knew that I was to come.
> Isaiah and Esdras and Job and John the Divine –
> They knew that I was to come.
> And the Roman poet, Seneca, knew it too –
> . . . venient annis
> Saecula seris quibus oceanus
> Vincula rerum laxit . . .
> 'The time will come in a late
> Century when the sea
> Will loose the knots of fate
> And the earth will be opened up
> And the rolled map unfurled
> And a new sailor sail
> To uncover a new world.'
> 'The time will come . . .' The time has come already

Given the emphasis placed upon this section one would expect the accompanying music to be similarly symbolic. Structurally the words fall into two parts; the opening to *rerum laxit* and the more dynamic 'The time will come . . .' to 'The time has come already' and similarly the music (designated *Night Music* in the score) is divided in two. Example 7.3 is the opening of this piece, a classic Walton 'suspense' section which mirrors the 'preparative' nature of the words. Example 7.4 represents a section of the first movement of Symphony No. 1 which fulfils the same function: it gathers the tension built up over the preceding, more active, section and holds it over in preparation for the subsequent intensification of activity. In addition there are affinities with bars immediately before the initial entry of the baritone soloist in *Belshazzar's Feast* (Ex. 7.5); an essentially preparative section for a build-up of tension over the following bars which too have elements of priest-like prophecy. Lastly, the similarity between this section and that written to accompany the movement of refugees in *The Foreman Went to France* is too close to be a mere coincidence (Ex. 7.6). As aforementioned, the second portion of 'night music' is a more dynamic method of increasing tension, reflecting the corresponding tightening of the written action to the climax 'The time has come already' (Ex. 7.7). Again the obvious relationship is with Symphony No. 1 (Ex. 7.8), as is the abrupt alteration of style between the two sections, which accentuates the change in pace of the words and intensifies the drama of 'The time will come. . . .'

Given Walton's personal sense of destiny it is not surprising that the music for this section echoes his most significant works: in effect he identifies himself musically with the character's awareness of his fate. Furthermore, both *Belshazzar's Feast* and Symphony No. 1 are 'heroic' works in the Beethovian manner; reflecting the tone of the play. The affinities with *Refugees* are more subtle: despite being a 'man of destiny' Columbus is essentially a solitary figure, cut off from the allegiances of normal men; articulated in the play through his denial of any country but that of the future. Therefore, Walton emphasizes musically the duality of the path Columbus is compelled to tread, both heroic and tragic: a subtlety which doubtless would have been achieved if he had merely been making use of his 'facilitative' powers.

However, as aforementioned, Louis MacNeice conceived *Christopher Columbus* as an action-drama and, as such, a recurrent theme of the play is the effect that Columbus's power, derived from his sense of his own destiny, had on those around him. Columbus is portrayed as a solitary authoritarian figure; a 'voice crying in the wilderness' who adheres to his course in the certain knowledge of his own worth and of his eventual vindication. One suspects that this presentation of stubborn righteousness would have come very easily to MacNeice as it formed one facet of his father's character. MacNeice's relationship with his father Bishop John MacNeice was not always happy (especially during his time at Marlborough), largely because he could not share his parent's religious beliefs: the situation was not helped by the distress Bishop MacNeice felt regarding the breakdown of Louis' first marriage and subsequent divorce, even though the latter had not played the instigative part. The Bishop was a man of principle in the best sense of the word and on several occasions risked his own position for the sake

Ex. 7.3   *Christopher Columbus*, 'The time will come . . .'

Ex. 7.3 Concluded

Ex. 7.4   Walton Symphony No. 1, 1st movement

Ex. 7.5   Walton, *Belshazzar's Feast*

Ex. 7.5 Concluded

of 'doing the right thing', notably when he stood out against the Government over the arrangements for Carson's funeral and tomb. Louis could admire this integrity and, despite their problems, felt consummate respect for his father. After the latter's death Louis' process of grieving, his sense of 'what might have been', was protracted and his catharsis achieved largely through poetry.

Walton's relationship with his father is not as well documented. However, based on the evidence we have, it seemed less than happy and there is little to suggest that Walton afforded his parent the degree of respect which characterized Louis MacNeice's dealings with his father. Charles Walton was an accomplished bass-baritone, a fact William acknowledged and for which he could admire his father; Susana Walton recalls 'William would often remark that his father was a very good singer and, had he been alive after broadcasting started, he would have been very well known indeed. . .'.[21] However, to quote Susana Walton again, Walton's father 'was very severe, had a violent temper and was a keen disciplinarian'; not attributes calculated to endear him to his children. Singing success was not forthcoming and his musical activities were confined to annual recitals and filling the posts of organist and choirmaster in the local church.

Ex. 7.6   *The Foreman Went to France*

Ex. 7.7   *Christopher Columbus*, 'The time will come . . .'

Ex. 7.7   Concluded

Ex. 7.8   Walton: Symphony No. 1

Ex. 7.8   Continued

Ex. 7.8 Concluded

Noel Walton, William's older brother, wrote 'our attendance at Service and Rehearsals was indeed compulsory'[22] and William did not enjoy this regime: when he made a mistake his father rapped him on the knuckles with his ring 'and it hurt'.[23] Furthermore, Charles Walton seems to have attempted to curb William:

> . . . Because his father couldn't afford to send the second son to the local grammar school, William was sent to a board school. . .and William found it very rough. He resented having the girls separated from the boys by an iron grille. He thought his father had decided to bring him down a peg or two . . . .[24]

It appears that neither of his parents realized Walton's musical ability; indeed Charles Walton, possibly embittered by his own lack of success, was determined that his children should not be musicians. Noel Walton believed

> the only reason my parents sent Willie to Oxford was the opportunity to give him a superior education at a comparatively low price . . . it is my definite opinion that my parents were unaware of Willie's musical talent. . . .

As Charles Walton had spent the money intended for his wife and son's train fare to Oxford in the pub the previous evening, William had almost missed his audition at Christ Church. Given these circumstances, it is not surprising that when William was accepted at Christ Church and moved to Oxford, all his letters home are addressed merely to his mother whom Susana Walton acknowledges 'adored William'. The only mention of his father in these letters occurs when Dean Strong was to write to William's parents regarding his becoming an undergraduate; '. . . Mind Dad replies in the affirmative immediately . . .'[25] a comment not brimming with filial affection.

It appears, therefore, that both poet and composer would have had experience of the sort of severity that imbues the character of Columbus within the radio play. However, as with their attitudes to their respective 'escapes', it appears that their experiences affected them in different ways. MacNeice, as observed above, seemed to be continually searching for his Utopia; similarly there is much evidence to suggest he never fully resigned himself to his emotional distance from his father, at least whilst the latter was still alive. It is significant that in the play, on Columbus achieving his aim, the erstwhile broadminded hero becomes as bigoted as those against whom he has fought so long: in his conversation with his notary, who suggests the possibility of the existence of another mainland between Europe and Asia, he states '. . . we are now on the fringe of Asia . . . I know so. . .you are my notary, you are not a cosmographer. I tell you, signor, what we have done is to find the Western passage to Asia. This island on which we stand is off the shore of Asia . . .'. Thus it transpires that MacNeice's hero has feet of clay; similarly his absolute respect for his father's admirable qualities was tempered by his knowledge of the consequences of these qualities with regard to family life.

In comparison Walton seems to have discarded entirely any adverse experiences with his parents. One has to search long and hard before uncovering any references to them and I have yet to discover any comments regarding the death of his father in 1924. This is in contrast to MacNeice's recurrent references to his parents, whether obvious or oblique. In fairness to both poet and composer, it is possible that the loss of Walton's father was ameliorated by his relationship with his mother who outlived her husband by some 30 years, whereas MacNeice's mother died tragically during his childhood, an event which affected him deeply and further distanced him from his father. The music Walton wrote for *Christopher Columbus,* having a flawed titular hero, bears a marked resemblance to that which he produced for *Henry V* where the hero, although severe, is classically impeccable (at least as far as the part of his life which the play covers is concerned). The fact that he was able to do so says much about his attitude to adverse events in reality and heroes in fiction: although he could easily relate to the sort of severity displayed by the characters of both Columbus and Henry V through his relationship with his father, he was able to discard these experiences as regards his own life. Thus, in this aspect of the lives of both poet and composer as well as in their 'escapes', there is a strong suggestion that fundamentally Walton was the more pragmatic of the two.

However, there is another aspect of *Christopher Columbus* which appears to display a greater degree of unanimity between the poet and composer: the character of and music created for Columbus's mistress Beatriz. In examining this element of the action, the attitude of Walton and MacNeice to the various women in their lives, and indeed women generally, suggests that it played a critical part in their response to Beatriz. It is undeniable that both artists liked women: Walton's susceptibility had caused various degrees of trouble with the Sitwells when he was under their patronage and MacNeice's liaisons scatter the pages of Jon Stallworthy's biography. Therefore, one would expect Beatriz to be treated sympathetically rather than with condemnation for her undeniably licentious behaviour, and indeed this is the case.

MacNeice portrayed Beatriz as a strong, honourable character; weak only with regard to Columbus (another enduring male fantasy), and faithful without hope of such faith being rewarded. However, he did not make the mistake of creating a one-dimensional 'angel of goodness': Beatriz is irredeemably stubborn and therefore throughout the play her hopes and desires are on a collision course with those of Columbus, the personification of obstinacy, creating the requisite dramatic tension between their characters. In this, I would argue, lies the key to MacNeice's acknowledged or unconscious model for Beatriz.

As MacNeice had married Hedli Anderson only a few months before the first performance of *Christopher Columbus* she would form the obvious model for the character of Columbus's mistress. However, although Hedli did on occasions behave as illogically as Beatriz, there is a strong case for Eleanor Clark being MacNeice's real inspiration: this lady had held the poet's amorous attention, virtually unchallenged, since he first met her in America in 1939 until 1942; she was his principal reason for his return to that country in 1940. However, there is one important difference between this relationship and the majority of MacNeice's encounters: it remained strictly non-sexual.[26] This was quite a feat, bearing in mind that most other women with whom MacNeice had had relationships had surrendered to his charm with almost unseemly haste; it says a great deal for Eleanor's obstinacy. When MacNeice finally acknowledged that, for him, the 'real' relationship was not going to happen it affected his attitude to America itself; he wrote of 'a sudden revulsion from America on my part'.[27] Thus MacNeice had fresh and painful experience of contumacious behaviour very much like that of Beatriz in the radio play: a parallel far too appropriate to be merely coincidence. Had Eleanor Clark capitulated, it is anybody's guess how the character of Beatriz might have been: perhaps she may have been as transparent as the secondary 'lower-class' Spaniards on the quayside. It is doubtful whether she would have elicited such poignancy as she did in the event.

However, MacNeice's response to Beatriz suggests a more complex situation than a simple representation of his frustration at Eleanor Clark's lack of complicity with his desires. It is true that Beatriz is portrayed as stubborn and illogical but she is more than that: her character yields to that of Columbus and it is she, not Columbus, who is left to long for what might have been. Maybe in this aspect of his portrayal of Columbus's mistress there is both an element of MacNeice fulfilling his personal fantasies with regard to Eleanor Clark as well as an element of catharsis. Furthermore, in her yearning for Columbus, Beatriz expresses MacNeice's own longing, but she is the passive element whilst Columbus represents the active; the opposite of the situation where the would-be active MacNeice was forced to accept Eleanor's decision. In a final twist, Beatriz retreats from telling Columbus about his child: she withholds something which would contribute to his possible future happiness and thus effects a passive revenge. Possibly this expresses certain of MacNeice's feelings over the deterioration of his relationship with Eleanor but whereas Beatriz actively conceals the truth from Columbus, MacNeice, from his point of view, was prevented from attempting to be completely happy: it is he who was left with feelings of what might have been. His 'revenge' on Eleanor can be said to be passive also; effectively Eleanor deprived herself of the happiness which MacNeice was convinced a sexual relationship would create. Thus, the character of Beatriz in *Christopher Columbus* may be said to be a fusion of aspects of both Clark and MacNeice as they were perceived by the latter.

In comparison to MacNeice, Walton's personal life in the period immediately before the composition of *Christopher Columbus* had been considerably more settled. Since 1935 he had been involved in a passionate relationship with Alice Wimborne whose influence on him from that point until her death in 1948 must not be underestimated. Roy Douglas, writing to Michael Kennedy on 1 September 1987, recalled:

> I . . . was well aware of her discriminating and helpful criticisms of William's music. For instance, after dinner William would often go away and write some film music and then bring it to play to Lady W. and myself and I have known her to say: 'That's not really good enough, William, you can write a better tune that that.' And he would meekly go back to the music room and do so . . . she frequently expressed acute and valuable opinions. I am also strongly of the opinion that she had a very good influence on his character. . . .

Walton himself acknowledged Alice Wimborne's influence: on his marriage to Susana William had told his new wife 'she [Alice] had been the most important woman in his life, and that, as with me, he had known on their first encounter that he had met the right person with whom to share his life.'[28] Therefore, prima facie it seems unlikely that Walton approached the composition of music for the character of Beatriz with the degree of emotional turmoil that MacNeice experienced in dealing with her literary depiction. However, that is not to say that everything was entirely blissful in the Walton household: Alice Wimborne was 22 older than Walton, rich, elegant and, to quote Neil Tierney 'one of Peter Quennell's grand society chatelaines'.[29] Furthermore, Walton's relationship with Alice had commenced whilst her husband was still alive (which, however, superficially at least seems not to have distressed any of the parties). A more crucial difficulty was that, on being widowed, Alice had wanted to marry Walton. To quote Lady Walton, '. . . William told me he could not allow her to do so. After a lifetime of being the exquisite Lady Wimborne, he could not allow her to become Mrs Walton. . . .'[30] Walton's scruples thus prevented him from legitimizing his relationship in much the same way as Columbus's obsession precluded his relationship with Beatriz.

Furthermore, Walton was no stranger to the distress occasioned by an unhappy relationship: there is much evidence to suggest that the breakdown of intimacy with his companion immediately before Alice Wimborne, Countess Imma von Doernberg, affected him deeply. Much of the problems in completing his First Symphony over 1934–5 seem to stem from the collapse of that relationship and the composition was thought by many at the time to be his manner of dealing with the pain he felt over its disintegration. Furthermore, it appears that this symphony had the power to rekindle those feelings: Gerald Jackson, writing in 1968, described Walton conducting it during the war:

> Throughout his face was marked by intense suffering. . . . My impression was, and remains, that the composer must have endured a considerable amount of spiritual turmoil during its composition and this he re-lived. . . .[31]

Certain similarities between Walton's first symphony and the score for *Christopher Columbus* have already been noted and it is not at all surprising, given the above, that the music used to depict Beatriz throughout the play (heard in its entirety in *Beatriz's Song)* inhabits the same emotional sphere as the symphony's slow movement. However, there is a precursor of *Beatriz's Song* even further back in Walton's past: his early work *The Lyke Wake Song* for soprano (treble) and piano. The text, by A. C. Swinburne, is revealing of Walton's schoolboy taste for the morbid, an inclination which affected him to a greater or lesser degree throughout his life:

> Fair of face, full of pride
> Sit ye down by a dead man's side
> Ye sang songs a' the day
> Sit down at night in the red worm's way.

Proud ye were a' day long
Ye'll be but lean at evensong.
Ye had gowd kells on your hair
Nay man kens what ye were.

Ye set store by the silken stuff
Now the grave is clean enough.
Ye set scorn by the rubis ring
Now the worm is a soft sweet thing.

Fine gold and a blithe fair face
Ye are come to a grimly place.
Gold hair and a glad grey een
Nae man kens if ye had been.

It is questionable whether Walton would have recognized the resonance between 'Fair of face, full of pride, sit ye down by a dead man's side' and Beatriz's situation (Columbus being a 'dead man' as far as the opinions of most of the other characters in the play are concerned). Perhaps he responded to Beatriz's allusion to her 'shameful' condition in carrying Columbus's illegitimate child: 'A lady like me has no right to be alive . . .' and subconsciously connected it to his earlier work. Certainly the music he created for Beatriz has more than echoes of his response to Swinburne's poem: Ex. 7.9 shows the opening of *A Lyke Wake Song* and Ex. 7.10 that of *Beatriz's Song*; both have the same drooping melodic line and chordal accompaniment, the harmony rendered more piquant by the addition of sevenths and ninths. Furthermore, as is the case with Columbus's most striking speech mentioned above, *Beatriz's Song* may in some ways be viewed as the precursor to music Walton wrote for *Henry V*, in particular (and most appropriately with regard to Beatriz) *Touch her soft lips and part* (Ex. 7.11) and *Death of Falstaff* (Ex. 7.12).

Thus there are many indications that MacNeice approached Beatriz with a heart not entirely salved by his recent marriage and in many ways his treatment of her character contributed to the healing process. Walton too, I would suggest, could relate both to the concepts of parting and death and to the impossibility of creating a conventional relationship out of one which was, out of necessity, unorthodox. Both poet and composer associated well with women. These attitudes must have had a bearing on their treatment of Beatriz and collectively they contributed to the creation of a character more human than Columbus, with whom both artists had more sympathy. Despite Beatriz's weakness the listener is compelled to respect her but it is a different sort of respect from that engendered by Columbus himself: it is imbued with love rather than with awe and in this I would argue strongly for Beatriz being the greater character of the two both in terms of music and literature: however much we can admire heroes, we love those who are weak like ourselves and in this respect Walton and MacNeice were not so fundamentally different from other, less creative, people.

The final common thread linking MacNeice and Walton in the creation of *Christopher Columbus* is their attitude to religion. As aforementioned, MacNeice's

Ex. 7.9 *A Lyke Wake Song* (Swinburne)

Fair of face, full of pride, Sit ye down by a

dead man's side ye— sang songs a' the day: Sit down at

night in the red worm's way Proud ye were a' day long:

Ye'll be but lean at ev - en - song. Ye had gowd bells on your

Ex. 7.10   'Beatriz's Song'

Ex. 7.11 *Henry V*, 'Touch her soft lips and part'

father was a clergyman and therefore he was surrounded by Christianity throughout his formative years. Perhaps as a reaction against his father's piety, MacNeice was a total atheist during the earlier part of his life; towards its end his views became more ambivalent. Speaking about his poem *Autumn Sequel* he commented:

> . . . if I were asked whether this were a Christian poem, I should not know what to reply. All I know is that I have been saturated from my childhood in Christian symbolism and that some of these symbols seem to me still most valid. . . .[32]

At the start of *Christopher Columbus* it is made plain that the major impetus behind Columbus's desire to travel to the unknown West is evangelism; to convert the '. . . seven thousand islands that have never heard of Christ . . .',[33] to quote the Prior of La Rabida. His motivation is portrayed at this stage as being entirely altruistic and the religious theme is dwelt upon at some length, particularly with regard to Columbus's dealings with Queen Isabella. Indeed, the comparatively rational Beatriz reprimands Columbus, reminding him that 'no one has more faith, or vision, than Isabella'.

However the stated principal motive for Columbus's mission might have appeared in the late fifteenth century, it is hard to imagine that even the relatively non-cynical and devout listeners of the early 1940s could have taken it at face value, especially an outright atheist such as MacNeice. Thus it is not surprising that cracks begin to appear in this edifice of piety at a relatively early stage in his

Ex. 7.12   Passacaglia – *Death of Falstaff*

script – significantly, not created in an obvious fashion, but rather suggested obliquely through the behaviour of the characters themselves. The Queen's confessor, the Most Reverend Ernando de Talavera, 'a saintly character' to quote Isabella, is portrayed as a pompous, narrow-minded bigot, bound up in his own importance. Temporal rivalry is suggested in Columbus's meeting with Cardinal Mendoza: 'Talavera is the Queen's confessor, she pays great attention to all that he says. It is a pity you have set him against you . . . Talavera is powerful: so am I. Senor Columbus, I will arrange you an audience with the Queen. . . .'

It is not long before one of the 'real' (at least, I suspect, for MacNeice and certainly for the majority of modern day listeners) motives for the quest surfaces: immediately prior to Columbus's first audience with Queen Isabella, the Marquesa de Moya hints at the possible riches to be found in new lands. From that point on the emphasis begins to shift from evangelism to the acquisition of wealth, culminating in the triumphal procession of the explorer through Barcelona where the majority of the dramatic attention focuses on the possessions he has acquired, not the potential number of souls he has saved. Money and power tend to be linked and MacNeice stresses the latter as the other convincing motive for Columbus's journey. Initially this is achieved through the same means as the exposure of material gain as a motivator; much is made of the ironic fact that those with power – who, as spiritual leaders should give their help to Columbus – in reality actively oppose his evangelical mission. In my opinion, MacNeice's personal feelings regarding Columbus's obsession are most openly revealed in the passage where Columbus appears before the Royal Commission for the second time. Columbus makes quite outrageous demands with regard to his share of possible rewards accruing from any discoveries: from this point onwards even the most naive listener can no longer believe the conversion of heathen races is uppermost in his mind.

MacNeice had plenty of encounters with secular ambition clothed in religious dress: he had grown up in Northern Ireland and unfortunately in this he could be said to share some experience with the modern-day listener. Similarly, there is evidence that Walton had some experience of inter-religious strife: Susana Walton comments:

> . . . After much pleading, I was taken to Oldham, in the industrial north-west of England, to meet William's family. On the journey north William told me how strong anti-papist feeling remained in parts of England, and that his mother would naturally worry as I was a Roman Catholic and we had married in a Catholic Church . . . It was a tricky encounter . . . his mother's only question to me was, 'Has the Pope got him?'. . . .[34]

However, this aspect of his northern upbringing seems not to have made much of an impact on Walton; probably because there is little to suggest he was greatly interested in religion. Although he was obliged to sing at services, firstly in his father's choir and then in that of Christ Church, Oxford, this probably had more of an adverse effect on any pious tendencies than the opposite. He refused to keep the Bible Thomas Strong, Dean of Christ Church, gave him on his confirmation and his later comments regarding his *Missa Brevis* (1965–6) say much about his attitude when a choral scholar:

> I'm also on to the Missa Brevissima. I doubt if there will be more than 8 to 10 minutes of it. Remembering the boredom I suffered as a dear little choirboy, I've made it as brevissima as poss. It should be v. popular among Communion takers. But how uninspiring the words!. . . .[35]

In an earlier letter to Malcolm Arnold, dated 20 February 1965, Walton had also mentioned the *Missa Brevis,* consoling the other composer with the comment 'But don't think I've got religious mania!'.

Thus, there is much to suggest that Walton was simply indifferent to religious matters, not a strident atheist and later agnostic in the manner of MacNeice. Like other similarities of experience between poet and composer noted above, Walton probably did not give religious matters much thought once he had left Christ Church whereas MacNeice seems to have been unable to discard the impressions his encounters had left upon him. Their respective attitudes are revealed in

Christopher Columbus: the questions of faith and evangelism are continually worried in the script but, beyond a few instances of plainchant, there is no 'religious' music.

However, although I do not believe Walton was a particularly religious man, he did care deeply about his music and strove to produce the best he could. His craftsmanship in this respect is overtly displayed in his choice of plainchant for *Christopher Columbus*. In the early 1940s 'early' music was not understood or studied to the extent that it is in the 1990s and on this basis, and given the fact that the music he was writing was for a radio play, it would have been conceivable for Walton to have merely made up some vocal lines that sounded similar to plainchant to create necessary atmosphere when required. However, the plainchant used is largely authentic (only one or two notes have been altered) and, more significantly, Walton selected specific chants broadly relevant to the themes within the radio play. One of Columbus's most emphasized lines is 'I am Christopher, the bearer of Christ. . .I am the last apostle. . .'. Surely it is more than a coincidence that the plainchant used to represent the community at La Rabida is that used on the feast day of the Apostles; one can only conclude that Walton responded to Columbus's speech and reiterated the point musically. Similarly, the *Exsurge Domine* used in the play immediately before Columbus sets sail usually forms part of the service during Lent: musically Walton draws parallels between Columbus's long journey in an oceanic desert and Our Lord's 40 days in the wilderness. Consequently, despite my conviction that Walton did not respond particularly strongly to the religious perspective in the radio play, like MacNeice he could not escape his Christian upbringing and drew on the tradition to enrich his contribution to the project.

Thus, it appears that in some respects there were similarities between Walton and MacNeice; that MacNeice's experiences may have encouraged him to produce a script with which Walton was able to identify and thus produce music of integrity and power of which he need not have been dismissive. Although poet and composer reacted to and against their experiences in a different manner, the implications of both their pasts influenced the creation of *Christopher Columbus* and led to its present incarnation.

But apart from his involvement with MacNeice, Walton also incorporates intra-musical allusions in his score for the play and these are also significant when considering this composition. Firstly, and perhaps most notably, the play is set largely in Spain and one would expect at least a suggestion of Spanish music to create the appropriate atmosphere. Both MacNeice and Walton had been to Spain (the former in 1936 and 1939, the latter in 1925) and the composer was not the sort of person to avoid exposure to local colour whilst on holiday; to quote Susana Walton, 'William loved going to *everything*'.[36] In this light, it is surprising that there is not a more overtly Spanish quality to the score: apart from the triplet ornamentations (perhaps intended as a cliché whenever the intention is to suggest Spain) any 'Spanish' feel, with one notable exception discussed below, would appear to stem from allusions to Ravel's idiom. Although it is true to say that

Ravel was half Spanish and produced many works in a Hispanic vein, he is nevertheless one step further away from truly indigenous music and prima facie it is most peculiar that this is the case. Indeed, there is a strong case for French influences predominating in the music Walton produced for *Christopher Columbus*: the most obvious being the 'sea' portions of the score which are vaguely reminiscent of *La Mer*; although in fairness to Walton, in 1942 anybody writing music on a sea theme would find it difficult to resist the influence of that work. Furthermore, there are other hints of France within the score: the section entitled *Court Music (Sarabande)* (Ex. 7.13) is exquisite and undeniably redolent of the Fauré *Pavane*; it is a mystery why this has been omitted from the *Christopher Columbus Suite* as it deserves to be as well known.[37] Finally, the background music to the scene on the quay immediately prior to Columbus's departure (Ex. 7.14), based on a previous number, *Woman's Song,* is very similar to Walton's use of Canteloube's *Bailero* in *Henry V:* I do not believe this can be attributed entirely to coincidence.

A notable exception to the largely French-filtered 'Spanish' effects is *The Marquesa's Song* for soprano with guitar accompaniment (Ex. 7.15). This song occurs at the point in the action where Columbus argues with Queen Isabella: the lyric is based around the image of the Spanish fighting the Moors at Granada and thus mirrors Columbus pitting his 'faith' against Isabella's 'unbelief'. The undeniably Hispanic taste of this number is probably the reason why it is less popular than *Beatriz's Song*: as a result of its Spanish references it is more firmly anchored to the play than the latter and therefore runs the risk of appearing ridiculous if taken out of context. It was deliberately written to provide a number for Hedli Anderson, an accomplished performer who was more than capable of giving it an 'authentic' feel: therefore Walton had more scope to create a more virtuosic piece than *Beatriz's Song* which was originally intended for an actress to perform. Similarities can be drawn between *The Marquesa's Song* and Manuel de Falla's extremely popular *El Paño Moruno* (Ex. 7.16) (published in 1923 as part of *Siete Canciones Populares Españolas*), even though the former is for different accompanying instrumentation. As aforementioned, Walton was a keen concert-goer and this song was popular during his 'Sitwell' period when he appears to have gone to a great many performances: he developed the habit of studying other composers' works at Oxford and retained it throughout his life. Given this circumstantial evidence it is more than likely that Walton was familiar with the Falla song and unconsciously used it as a model for his own.

Walton could produce respectable Spanish pastiche if he chose to: that is obvious from *The Marquesa's Song* and notably certain sections of *Façade*. On examining the background to the radio play I suspect the reason why he did not use more overtly Hispanic elements in *Christopher Columbus* is because it was primarily a propaganda exercise: its purpose was to honour America, not Spain, and thus on artistic grounds Walton probably deemed it sufficient to add a few splashes of a generally 'foreign' nature rather than weight the score with more specific cultural references. Furthermore, a propaganda play written by an Irishman with music by an Englishman, designed to show regard to America with the action

Ex. 7.13   Court Music (Sarabande)

Ex. 7.14   *Christopher Columbus*, Act II (Cue 24)

being set largely in Spain, could not have included more homogeneous allusions to authentic Spanish music without appearing ridiculously artificial. The polyglot nature of the problems were similar to those Walton encountered in a chronological sense with regard to *Henry V* where he had to create viable twentieth-century music for a play written in the sixteenth century on a fifteenth-century theme.

There is one section of the *Christopher Columbus* score which is subject to neither French or Spanish influence, nor does it very much resemble mainstream European music: the *Indian Chorus* sung by natives on Columbus's discovery of San Salvador (Ex. 7.17). Given the care, noted above, with which Walton selected his plainchant in order that it would reflect the action of the play, the basis of this number also is likely to be an authentic indigenous song; Walton visited America in 1939 and it is not inconceivable that he could have heard examples of native music at that time. It was not in Walton's character merely to invent 'native' music; when composing the *Johannesburg Festival Overture* in 1956 he requested that the African Music Society forward recordings of African music and he

Ex. 7.14   Concluded

included African melodies in the work. Furthermore, the structure of the *Indian Chorus* is based around a 'call and response' pattern typical of much ethnic music and quite unlike Walton's usual idiom. *Indian Chorus* is almost unique in Walton's output; its closest relative perhaps being the *Striptease* music written for the film *The Next of Kin* (1941), especially in its use of primitive rhythm. If anything, this latter piece proves Walton's ability to create viable pastiche as it is perfectly suitable exotic nightclub music. (I believe that the climax of *Striptease* quotes that of Constant Lambert's *Rio Grande* at an accelerated pace; this further confirms my view that *Indian Chorus* is not merely a product of Walton's imagination but a synthesis of an outside influence.)

There is possibly a reference to another work within the score of *Christopher Columbus* which shows Walton's consummate sensitivity and sense of craftsmanship in welding his music to the script. The concluding passage in the score is a triumphal number for chorus and orchestra, very much in the vein of the closing

Ex. 7.15 'Marquesa's Song' from *Christopher Columbus*

section of *Belshazzar's Feast*. The final phrase for chorus (Ex. 7.18) can be compared with Hindemith's *Mathis der Maler*. The use of this quotation is peculiarly apt: the titular heroes of both works suffer humiliation and hostility for doing what they believe to be right; both are compelled by a sense of social responsibility and both as a result are effectively isolated from those around them. Furthermore, on Hindemith's part *Mathis der Maler* was unashamedly autobiographical, and represented his stance against the German National Socialist government. It was therefore eminently appropriate to quote this piece in a work of wartime propaganda. Furthermore, Hindemith was a friend of Walton's; he had premièred the latter's Viola Concerto when Tertis had refused the engagement. Could it be that Walton was affirming his friendship and admiration for Hindemith, achieving his propaganda brief and making a musical point about the nature of *Christopher Columbus* all at once; a typically economical gesture?

Whether or not Walton may have been unconsciously influenced, or may have deliberately quoted, other composers, *Christopher Columbus* is quintessentially Walton and as such it needs to be placed within the context of his other works. There are various parallels with his earlier compositions, notably *Belshazzar's Feast* and the First Symphony, but *Columbus* also held implications for later works. I have drawn some analogies between it and *Henry V* and possibly the most tantalizing 'might have been' lies in considering how *Henry V* might have

Ex. 7.16   Siete Canciones populares Españolas (Manuel de Falla)

Ex. 7.16 Concluded

Ex. 7.17   *Christopher Columbus*, Act II (Cue 34A)

Ex. 7.18   *Christopher Columbus*, 'Glory to God'

taken shape had not *Christopher Columbus* been its successful precursor. However, the two pieces are so close chronologically that there is a case for considering them together. Michael Kennedy certainly hints at this in that he heads a chapter of his Walton biography *Columbus and Henry V*; this being the case it becomes necessary to consider Walton's post-War works in the light of the developments within *Christopher Columbus* and its success.

There is a strong argument for stating that *Christopher Columbus* in some ways anticipates Walton's later, more neglected, period, especially in terms of choral style, one particular example being the 'chanting chorus' *miserere* section of the *Gloria* (Ex. 7.19). This appears to owe something to the use of a *sprechstimme*-like technique for the Voices of Doubt and Hope in the earlier work. Paradoxically, in that the use of precise rhythmic speech over music in *Christopher Columbus* echoes *Façade*, *Columbus* can also be said to form a link with Walton's earlier work. It is possible to trace the development of his use of spoken or chanted words through 1922 to 1942 to 1960 in these three works: *Façade* is a celebration of the intrinsic sound of words as distinct from their meanings; in this composition speech becomes part of the musical texture. *Christopher Columbus*

Ex. 7.19   'Miserere' from the *Gloria*

shows a more 'traditional' interpretation in that the words are more important than the orchestral backdrop which accompanies them. *Gloria* fuses these two ideas, the words being chanted at pitch to form part of an accompaniment to solo lines above. Furthermore, the Voices of Doubt and Hope are portrayed as 'leaders', followed by more subordinate choral sections. The idea of such alternation of textures is a consistent feature in Walton's *oeuvre* and one which appears to stem ultimately from his experience of responses in daily services at Christ Church. The most obvious use of the leader-chorus motif is in the middle section of the opening of *Belshazzar's Feast,* from the entry of the baritone soloist, but it is also prevalent in *Gloria* (1960), particularly in the section quoted in Ex. 7.19, and more generally in the *Coronation Te Deum* (1953). Most significantly, given Walton's aforementioned recognition of Columbus's identification of himself with the Apostles, *The Twelve* (1964–5) also shows this tendency particularly at the opening and the section immediately following the soprano soloists.

There is a secondary development of the leader-chorus principle: the alternation of different pitches and textures in the chorus. This feature is also found in *Belshazzar's Feast,* the *Coronation Te Deum, Gloria, The Twelve* and, unsurprisingly, in *Christopher Columbus.* In the latter work the obvious use is in the pointed contrast between the male chorus following the Voice of Doubt and its female counterpart associated with the Voice of Hope. However, it also permeates the two primary chorus sections (found at the fall of Granada and Columbus's procession to Barcelona) in terms of alternation between male and female chorus. Through this feature, *Christopher Columbus* is linked not only to Walton's large- and medium-scale choral works but to his choral miniatures and late liturgical pieces such as *Jubilate Deo* (1971–2) and *Magnificat and Nunc Dimittis* (1974). Again, this feature of Walton's style probably stems from his early experiences; in this instance from the alternation of *decani* and *cantoris* in the sacred music he would have sung at Christ Church.

The script which MacNeice produced for *Christopher Columbus* calls for a certain number of fanfares in the music score. In this respect it is possible to view *Columbus* as a link in the development of Walton's style. The somewhat drawn out fanfare at the opening of *Long Steel Grass (Façade)* by 1931 had contracted to a more spare, dramatic style at the commencement of *Belshazzar's Feast.* The fanfare which opens the 'praise' section of the latter work indicates a still dramatic, more elaborate but nevertheless sectionally distinct style which may also be heard at work in Symphony No. 1, notably in the fourth movement. The principal fanfare Walton wrote for his score *The First of the Few* (later formed into *The Spitfire Prelude and Fugue*) would seem to indicate the beginnings of a change of approach: the opening flourishes are integrated into the ensuing music in a more cohesive manner and this is the stage to which the opening of *Christopher Columbus* belongs. Intriguingly, in this sense the opening of *Henry V*[38] is something of a hybrid: after the initial flute lead-in the orchestra announces what appears to be a second-phase integrated fanfare which, however, reverts to a more *Belshazzar's Feast*-style spare enunciation for horns, trumpets and side drum.

However, the composer uses a format for the integrated fanfare which he favoured for later works such as the *Gloria* and *The Twelve* (Ex. 7.20a–c). In most of Walton's post-War works his fanfares or flourishes tend to be integrated into the major thrust of the music in a more synthesized fashion than in the works before the War where the break between sections is more obvious. The opening of *Christopher Columbus* is indicative of the transition phase of this evolution: the listener is aware that the opening is a preliminary flourish but there is a 'soft' link between it and the ensuing section; the shift from one to the other is blurred, although less fluid than those found in later works.

Leaving aside fanfare as an indication of Walton's stylistic development, it is also used in *Christopher Columbus* as an indication of the fortunes of the hero and is therefore as example of Walton reacting to the text. For example, after Columbus's failure at the first Royal Commission, the male chorus 'No, never again' is based around the 'Talavera' fanfare. Much is made in the play of the contrast between Talavera's public image of a godly man and his internal, prejudiced temperament. Talavera's fanfare is echoed at this point; perhaps a deliberate attempt by Walton to indicate musically that Columbus's arch-enemy (and thus parochialism), had triumphed over Columbus and liberality. In contrast, when Columbus lands on San Salvador 'his' fanfare echoes that of the Duke of Medina Celi. The latter character is portrayed in the play as a man of adventure and action and one who not only believed in Columbus's mission but who sheltered him for two years. Thus Walton not only links Columbus with Medina Celi's character but indicates their purpose has triumphed over that of doubt and passivity. In some senses I feel this integrated use of fanfare may be seen also as a stylistic development in text setting from, for example, the somewhat obvious trumpet flourishes above the text 'blow the trumpet in the new moon' in *Belshazzar's Feast*.

Although there is clear evidence that *Christopher Columbus* forms a significant transitionary point in the development of some of Walton's characteristic compositional traits, I would not wish to overstress the case. It was an outstanding success at its première but that opinion needs to be qualified, given that we live in a much more cynical age than that of 1942. Michael Kennedy makes the following observation:

> ... The play itself is characteristic of radio-drama of the day, ambitious, high-flown, sometimes banal (as in the Portland Place Mummerset speech of the lower-class Spaniards), yet with a loftiness of aim that compels admiration. Like the adaptation of *The Pilgrim's Progress* in 1942, for which Vaughan Williams wrote the music, and *The Rescue* (1943) and *The Dark Tower* (1946) which had marvellous Britten scores, *Columbus* represents BBC radio-drama at its serious best. ... [39]

Whatever the stature of *Christopher Columbus* as regards radio-drama, few would make a convincing case for it being great literature. Walton himself made no claims for the music and, unusually, also cast doubt on the quality of the text – when it was suggested that some of the songs from the score might be published he wrote:

Ex. 7.20a   Walton, *Gloria*

Ex. 7.20b   Walton, *Gloria*

Ex. 7.20c   Walton, *The Twelve* (Auden)

. . .One must draw a line somewhere about the horrors of one's past being allowed to be dragged up and I am for a complete ban on those songs even to destruction of the MSS. I'm not at all sure that MacNeice wouldn't feel the same about the lyrics!. . . .[40]

In an earlier letter to Alan Frank, he had made the comment '. . . About Chr. Columb. I can't believe that there is anything worth resuscitating from that vast and boring score. I don't remember a thing. . . .'

But Walton's comments in this context need not be taken too seriously: he was notoriously dismissive of his film music and he regarded *Christopher Columbus* in the same light. Furthermore, he was extremely sensitive to the then widely-held belief that his music had deteriorated after the War and his reluctance to expose the music from the play to a wider audience may have been a reaction to that: to publish something he felt to be 'inferior' would be inviting more opprobrium from an already critical audience. Finally it 'might have been' that he recognized that *Columbus* as a radio play is fundamentally a product of the War years and felt it would do the music no favours to be taken out of context, heroic topics having reached just about the nadir of popularity at the time he wrote.

I believe Walton was mistaken in his assessment of the music for *Christopher Columbus*: it is obvious on first listening to the score that although the work may be 'vast' it is quintessential Walton and certainly not 'boring'. However, neither is it his First Symphony or *Troilus and Cressida*; the play does not have their universality of appeal. It was written in a specific manner for a specific purpose at a specific time and therefore I would suggest cannot be applied out of context with equal certainty of victory. However, putting the play as a whole aside, much of the music is extremely valuable and the aforementioned *Christopher Columbus Suite* distils only a proportion of it. In this chapter I have tried to identify some of the 'might have beens' that surround this work; a modern-day 'might have been' centres around all the music that was not included in the suite; perhaps this also forms a 'might be' for the future.

Notes

1. A quotation from *Christopher Columbus*, the full line being:

    > *All the things that might have been. . .*
    > *When we cross the Western Sea*
    > *All those things shall be. . .*

2. To date, the play has been performed only three times: the original production in 1942, re-broadcast in 1973, and a new production in 1992.
3. In a letter to Roy Douglas dated 25 January 1942 he wrote:

    > . . . Tomorrow I start on Cavalcanti's film at Ealing, a rather boring one to fill in the time until the Howard film which I saw yesterday and is very good. That shouldn't be ready until the middle of March. However, you never know. . . .'

    Furthermore, two of the items for the film are entitled *Moto Poulencuo* and *La Ravelse*, designations I would suggest are not purely in response to the largely French setting.
4. Letter from Dallas Bower, the original producer of *Christopher Columbus*, to William Walton, 26 January 1942.
5. Ibid.
6. Kennedy, M. (1989) *Portrait of Walton*, Oxford: Oxford University Press, p. 119.
7. Ibid.
8. Ibid.
9. Asa Briggs (1970) *The History of Broadcasting in the United Kingdom*, Vol. 3, London: OUP.
10. Ibid.
11. *Times Literary Supplement*, 24 July 1937.
12. Jon Stallworthy (1995) *Louis MacNeice*, London: Faber.
13. Ibid.
14. In an article in *BBC Music Weekly* dated 28 March 1982 he made the following comment: '. . .Creativity and facility aren't quite the same thing. When it's creating something like a symphony, it's not like writing film music. One can probably write two hours of film music in a couple of weeks and it'll take you a couple of years to write half an hour of a symphony. . . .'
15. This chorus section is not included in the Muir Mathieson *Suite from 'Henry V'* (1963) but may be found in both Sir Malcolm Sargent's similarly titled arrangement of 1945 and Christopher Palmer's *Henry V: A Musical Scenario* (1990).
16. Ibid.
17. '. . . William remembered Oxford as the most beautiful place he had ever seen; Christ Church itself, the quadrangle, and Tom Tower were his lovely new world. To avoid having to return to Oldham when his voice broke, he decided to make himself interesting in the only way he knew, so he set pen to paper and started to write music. . .' Susana Walton (1988) *William Walton: Behind the Façade*, Oxford: Oxford University Press, p. 43.

18. Ibid.
19. Anson, H. (1949) *T B Strong: Bishop, Musician, Dean, Vice-Chancellor*, SPCK.
20. Ibid.
21. Ibid.
22. Letter to Hugh Ottaway, dated 11 April 1970.
23. Recalled by William Walton in Tony Palmer's film *At the Haunted End of the Day*, (1981).
24. Susana Walton, ibid.
25. Letter dated 16 July 1918.
26. This is not for want of trying on MacNeice's part as it was Eleanor who resisted any opportunity to consummate the relationship; indeed MacNeice described her as 'sexually inhibited and to some extent self-deceiving' in his letter to her dated 21 May 1940. In a later letter (19 November 1940) he wrote '. . .you don't appear to need the sort of intimate relationship which I need so badly. I have tried to softpedal the sex business but the more I softpedal it, the more it obsesses me. . .The only way I can stop sex interfering with my work. . .is to have a sex life and I certainly shall have one when I go back [to England] . . .I don't suppose that will affect my (deeper) feelings to you at all. . . .'
27. Letter to Eleanor Clark, 19 January 1942.
28. Susana Walton, ibid., p. 32.
29. Neil Tierney (1984) *William Walton*, London: Hale, p. 77.
30. Susana Walton, ibid.
31. Gerald Jackson (1968) *First Flute*, London: J. M. Dent & Sons.
32. MacNeice, speaking in a broadcast on 1 August 1954.
33. MacNeice, *Christopher Columbus – a radio play* (1944), London: Faber & Faber.
34. Susana Walton, ibid, p. 40.
35. Letter to Alan Frank, head of Oxford University Press Music Department, 17 March 1965.
36. Susana Walton, ibid.
37. Suite arranged by Christopher Palmer. The *Sarabande* was not included in the 1942 performance due to lack of time. It was, however, restored in 1992.
38. I refer here to the first section of the Muir Matheson *Suite from 'Henry V'*.
39. Michael Kennedy (1989) *Portrait of Walton*, OUP: Oxford, p. 120. Brief brass fanfares (for single trumpet or horn) were written for each of the following and prefaced their appearance in the play: Talavera; Duke of Medina-Sidonia; Duke of Medina-Celi; Cardinal Mendoza. No brass bands were involved.
40. Letter to Alan Frank, dated 12 January 1967. Walton later allowed publication of *Beatriz's Song* in 1974.

8 'A lost Child': A Study of the Genesis of *Troilus and Cressida*

Scott Price

For many of William Walton's admirers *Troilus and Cressida* was long overdue. As early as 1936, in concluding an analysis of Walton's Viola Concerto (1929), Donald Tovey, with characteristic perspicacity, remarked that 'Walton's dramatic power has asserted itself in oratorio; but its unobtrusive presence in this thoughtful piece of purely instrumental music is more significant than any success in an oratorio on the subject of Belshazzar's feast'. It was, Tovey concluded, 'obvious he ought to write an opera'.[1] That it was to take some 20 years before the opera Tovey felt so inevitable was to actually reach the stage is a phenomenon attributable to several factors. Not least amongst these factors was the absence of a permanent professional opera company in London during the 1930s: Walton was, in the words of Michael Kennedy, 'a wily, hard-headed northern businessman',[2] unlikely to undertake the time-consuming task of composing an opera with neither a commission nor guarantee of performance. By the mid-1940s, however, the attitude of London's musical establishment towards opera had considerably altered. Perhaps the single most important development was the re-opening of the Royal Opera House, Covent Garden, in 1946, and the establishment therein of a full-time opera company. Lord Keynes, then chairman of the Arts Council of Great Britain, established what became the Covent Garden Opera Trust and, at the suggestion of Constant Lambert, invited William Walton to contribute.[3] The Trust outlined a set of proposals for the promotion of English opera:

> The repertoire should be as catholic as possible, and contemporary opera should not be allowed to suffer the neglect it has in the past. Particular regard should be reserved for opera by our own composers ... to find their works fobbed off with, at most, half a dozen performances was not exactly encouraging to composers.[4]

Such sentiments can only have been extremely heartening to Walton and a spur to his operatic aspirations.

But the immediate catalyst that stimulated Walton's interest in opera composition was, as had often been the case before, the success of a work by a

182

contemporary: Benjamin Britten's *Peter Grimes* (1945).[5] Two weeks after attending the premiere of *Grimes* (7 June 1945), Walton wrote to Britten, praising his 'extraordinary achievement'. 'This is just what English opera wants and it will, I hope, put the whole thing on its feet . . . not that you will find many other composers, if any, emulating your success.' These sentiments were no doubt genuine. But Walton was careful to conceal the resentment he was increasingly coming to feel over Britten's glowing critical acclaim and considerable public popularity. During the 1930s, the *enfant terrible* of *Façade* (1921–3) had matured into England's leading composer, with each new work awaited 'in the certainty of getting something of permanent value'.[6] During the war years, however, Walton's energies had been directed towards the Ministry of Information's propaganda films, and he had produced no major work for the concert-hall since the Violin Concerto of 1938. During the same period, Britten had created a string of masterpieces, including *Les Illuminations* (1940), the *Sinfonia da Requiem* (1942), and the *Serenade* (1943), culminating in the opera *Peter Grimes*. With this work 'at one stroke Britten had acquired world-wide fame as an opera composer and it became a matter of general concern to know what he was going to write next'.[7] This acclaim was achieved in part at Walton's expense; if Walton was to reclaim the limelight from his younger adversary it was apparent that this would have to be achieved on Britten's own territory, namely the opera house.

Walton had firmly decided upon composing an opera by, at the latest, the winter of 1946. Writing to his parents, on 12 January 1947, the poet Dylan Thomas enquired, 'Did I tell you about the opera-libretto I have been asked to write? A full-length grand opera for William Walton . . . I want to set the opera in a near-docks area. . . . If this ever comes to anything it will be the biggest operatic event of the century'.[8] Nothing ever did come of it. The artist Michael Aryton (who was to have designed the opera) told Thomas's biographer that the poet quickly lost interest in the project, eventually contributing merely a postcard, on which was written: 'With a sound like thunder-claps, The little mouse comes out, perhaps'.[9] What was required was the stimulus and commitment that a specific commission would produce: this was to be provided by the British Broadcasting Corporation. On 8 February 1947, Victor Hely-Hutchinson, the BBC's Director of Music, wrote to Walton:

> The BBC has decided to commission an opera and would like you to compose it. I do not know how you are placed as regards time, but I very much hope you will be interested in the idea.[10]

The opera was to be composed in the following 18 months, with the first performance being not staged but in the studio and broadcast on the Third Programme, for a fee of £500: Walton accepted.

Attention now turned to the question of who might act as librettist. According to Walton's biographer, Michael Kennedy, it was the BBC in the person of Stanford Robinson (Head of BBC Opera) who suggested that Christopher Hassall be approached.[11] No surviving correspondence between the BBC and Walton recommends the appointment of Hassall, but in a letter to the critic and composer

Cecil Gray, written sometime in the winter of 1947, Walton explained how 'the BBC has commissioned me to write an opera . . . and recommended Christopher Hassall whom you may know to go into the question of the libretto'.[12] Following the first performance of the opera in 1954, Walton wrote to Stanford Robinson stating, 'I don't forget it was you who brought Christopher and I together'.[13] However, a letter from the BBC to Walton, dated 24 March 1947, by which point Hassall had already been appointed librettist, explains that 'special terms will have to be arranged for this [payment of the librettist] *when the librettist is decided upon*' [my italics], suggesting perhaps that the BBC had not in fact played any role in acquiring Hassall's assistance. When writing the letter to his friend Cecil Gray quoted above, Walton may well have been choosing his words carefully, as Gray had most enthusiastically discussed an operatic project with Walton as early as 1941, to no avail.[14] Greatly disappointed that his enthusiasm had not been shared by his potential collaborator, Gray might well have been offended, as were all three of the Sitwells, by not having been asked to provide the libretto. And Walton's letter to Stanford Robinson is perhaps merely a figurative reference to the opera having been initially commissioned by Robinson and the BBC, thus ensuring Walton's interest did not dissipate at the first sign of difficulty. It would seem more likely that Hassall's involvement was achieved at the suggestion of Walton's companion at this time, Alice Wimborne, and brought about through her friend, Edward Marsh, a patron of Hassall's.[15] Wimborne is known to have long been an admirer of Hassall's poetry: in a letter to Edward Marsh, dated 13 October 1936, Wimborne described Hassall as 'the only one of the younger poets'.[16] The critic Gillian Widdicombe, who spent many hours with Walton during the 1970s with a view to writing his biography, was in no doubt that 'Lady Wimborne suggested the poet Christopher Hassall, for whom she had the highest regard'.[17]

It was certainly Lady Wimborne who arranged Walton's first meeting with Hassall, which took place sometime in February or March 1947. Christopher Hassall was, at first sight, perhaps a strange choice for librettist, as he had no previous operatic experience; he had, however, worked for Ivor Novello, producing the lyrics for several of his romantic musicals.[18] At this first meeting Hassall appears to have suggested four possible operatic subjects although *Troilus and Cressida* was not amongst them. On 31 March, Walton wrote to 'Dr Charles [*sic*] Hassall', stating 'I look forward to receiving the librettos when they are ready'. Within a week Hassall provided highly detailed synopses of the four subjects then under consideration: *Volpone* (based on Ben Jonson's play of 1605–6), *Byron*, *Anthony and Cleopatra* (based on Shakespeare), and *Duke Melveric*. 'I hope the four that you now have in your hands are enough to clarify your ideas about the various themes concerned', Hassall wrote in his accompanying letter, 'I'm most anxious to hear your new idea'. What this new idea was is unclear, though it could quite possibly have in fact been *Troilus and Cressida*. Alan Frank, then head of Oxford University Press Music Department (Walton's publishers), recalled that Thomas Beecham had suggested Shakespeare's *Troilus and Cressida* as a possible operatic subject in the 1930s; it may also not be without significance that *Troilus* was amongst the favourite Shakespeare plays of Walton's closest friend during these years, Constant Lambert.[19] Hassall later insisted, however, that it was he who had come up with the idea of *Troilus*. Discussion with Walton as to the kind of heroine the composer wished to portray, 'happened to recall to my mind a description of a woman's character that I had read some years before in a work of literary criticism'.[20] The book of criticism was C. S. Lewis's classic study of medieval literature *The Allegory of Love* (1936), and the vivid depiction contained therein of Chaucer's Cryseide and her 'ruling passion': 'it is fear – fear of loneliness, of old age, of death, of love, and of hostility'.[21] Regardless of whose idea it was, Walton was clearly immediately struck by the subject, informing Hassall that 'Troilus has definite possibilities', just prior to his leaving for Prague in May 1947.[22]

On his return Walton, accompanied by Lady Wimborne, met again with Hassall to discuss the merits of the various subjects under consideration, which by this point also included *Queen Jocasta* (based on Jean Cocteau's *The Infernal Machine* of 1934), *The Woman of Andros* (based on a novel of 1930 by Thornton Wilder), and *Hassan* (based on a play of 1922 by James Elroy Flecker). Lady Wimborne wrote to Hassall the day after this meeting (15 June) urging him not to be discouraged by Walton's 'procrastination'. 'The difficulty', she wrote, 'is to find the perfect subject . . . the story or plot must be so easy and clear and flowing and scenic. Troilus and C. has got that. And it's got, as we agree, the Manon lady he so obviously prefers to the Juliets!'

Following these discussions, Hassall produced a detailed synopsis of the favoured subject, *Troilus and Cressida*. From the first, the opera was conceived in three acts: the first and third acts are divided into two separate scenes ('Act I Scene i – Before the Temple of Pallas, Scene ii – The Garden of Pandarus: Act III Scene i – Outside the Pavilion of Calchas in the Greek Encampment, Scene ii – The Great Terrace of Priam's Palace'); the second act is in one short scene ('A Sumptuous bed-chamber in Pandarus' House'). The action is set in Homeric Troy near the end of the Greek siege, although Hassall made the curious suggestion that 'the play could be shifted into a Christian setting by making the temple of Pallas a Cathedral, Calchas a cardinal, and the place some French city besieged by the English in the 15th century . . . the characters would then be Sir Pandarus, etc'.[23] Act I Scene i of this first-draft synopsis contains all of the essential action that was eventually to make up the opera's entire first act; Calkas' false proclamation, the intrusion of Antenor, the first meeting of Troilus and Cressida, Pandarus's first entry and the formulation of the plan to win Cressida for Troilus, and finally, the defection of Calkas to the Greeks. All of this Hassall derived from Geoffrey Chaucer's epic poem *Troilus and Criseyde* (c.1385). The desertion of Calkas, which in Chaucer's text occurs prior to the opening of the poem, is introduced into the action, and combined with the religious ceremony, which provides the occasion of Troilus and Cressida's first encounter.[24] Hassall informed Walton that he had introduced Calkas's desertion (and also Antenor's departure for battle) because 'in drama so vital an ingredient of the plot should be shown and not merely narrated'. For the substance of the opening scene, Hassall invented Calkas's false prophecy and the people's angry reaction to this, thus making the desertion of Calkas all the more plausible.

For the action of Act I Scene ii, Act II, and Act III Scene i, Hassall turned from Chaucer's working of the *Troilus and Cressida* legend to that of Shakespeare. Act I Scene ii where, with the assistance of Pandarus, Troilus wins Cressida's affections, was derived from Act II Scene ii of Shakespeare's play; Act II of the synopsis combined Shakespeare's Act IV Scenes ii and iii, showing the eponymous lovers' declaration of love, followed by the entry of Diomede and the claiming of Cressida in exchange for the captured Antenor (in an altered form this was eventually to become the opera's Act II Scene ii); finally, the opening scene of Hassall's Act III was based largely upon Act V Scene ii of Shakespeare's play, where Troilus, having come to rescue Cressida from the Greek encampment, oversees her give herself to Diomede, she having resigned all hope of ever again being with Troilus. One important innovation Hassall brought to this scene, however, was the invention of the character Evadne, Cressida's waiting-lady.[25] In order that Cressida be spared as little of the responsibility for her falseness as possible it was necessary that she in some way be deceived. This role she fulfilled, as it was Evadne who burns Troilus's letters from Troy, thus leading Cressida to believe she has been deserted.

It is curious that so much of the initial conception of the opera's plot should have been derived from Shakespeare, as both Hassall and Walton later came to hold Shakespeare's working of the legend in low regard, and to deny the play any role in the shaping of the opera. 'There is nothing of Shakespeare in the libretto', Hassall was to later write, 'beyond a similarity of situation here and there inevitable in two works derived from the same source'.[26] Certainly, Shakespeare's portrayal of Cressida as little more than a whore can have held no appeal to Walton, who was determined from the outset to portray his heroine sympathetically; the plight of the lovers was in any case only half the story for Shakespeare who was equally interested in the political implications of the Trojan Wars: Walton was certain that he had no wish to emulate the huge proportions of Berlioz's *Les Troyens*. Another reason for making light of the debt owed to Shakespeare's play, however, may have been Walton's desire to avoid comparison with the decidedly colloquial Shakespearean operas of the pre-war years, such as Holst's *At the Boar's Head* (1924) and Vaughan Williams's *Sir John in Love* (1929). *Troilus and Cressida*, it was hoped, would be an international success (as *Peter Grimes* had been before it): association with the home-spun, rather amateurish efforts of the previous generation were to be avoided at all cost.[27]

Neither Shakespeare nor Chaucer, however, provided a suitable, operatic conclusion to their tales. According to legend, Cressida, soon abandoned by Diomede, sinks by degree to the level of a common drab. Hassall had therefore to contrive a new denouement. The first of numerous suggested alternatives is to be found as Act III Scene ii of the first synopsis. At the Great Terrace of Priam's

Palace, Priam sits enthroned, surrounded by his courtiers. Cassandra (Cressida's sister) prophesies that the war against the Greeks should be conceded, an opinion that Pandarus alone is in agreement with. Calkas enters and challenges Troy's greatest warrior to fight with Diomede, who accompanies him. Diomede is sporting Cressida's love token (a crimson scarf), which she had earlier given to Troilus. Impetuously, Troilus attacks Diomede, and is slain. Cressida, who has also accompanied her father to Troy, laments over Troilus's body and denies her love for Diomede. Declared 'False Cressida' by all present, she dies in shame and despair. With the lovers' bodies centre-stage, Cassandra again steps forward to foretell the imminent fall of Troy, as the curtain falls. Comparison of this synopsis with the final form of Act III reveals how little of this scenario was to remain unaltered (see Appendix). Neither King Priam nor Cassandra were ever to make it to the stage. Priam is still mentioned in comparatively late drafts of the opera's finale; Cassandra was quickly consigned to the wings, however, pronounced 'musically a luxury that a librettist cannot afford'.[28] Hassall appears to have regretted the need to excise Cassandra, as he liked her 'quality of grave superstition, her ill-diving nature'. These qualities, and specifically Cassandra's 'constant consciousness of the presence of the gods', Hassall later worked into the role of Cressida.[29]

But such alterations were to come later. Walton received this synopsis early in July 1947 accompanied by the following:

> I think this new version is full enough to help you decide whether we should take it a stage further. I'm always ready to hunt up more ideas. If you like this one I shall be pleased because it is entirely my own play as opposed to a version of someone else's novel and because I agree that it's the best of the lot so far.

The composer replied in excited fashion on 15 July. 'T & C is excellent. I've been reading it on and off all day & find little to suggest which might be an improvement, & I think the time has come when the actual text might be got under way.' This letter ended with some advice: 'Remember that only about one third of the words is necessary for a libretto to what there would be if it was a play.' From the first, Walton was under no illusions as to the inexperience of his collaborator.

Walton and Hassall continued to discuss and alter the opera's synopsis throughout the summer months of 1947. It was at some point during this period that the structure of Acts I and II were revised, bringing them considerably closer to their final shape. 'It occurred to me', Hassall wrote to the composer (probably at some point in August), 'that a great deal must have happened during the first interval for the lovers to have reached going-to-bed terms. . . . In Chaucer there is material for a short Act 2, sc i – if we wanted it.' Hassall was referring to a passage contained in Book Three of Chaucer's poem.[30] Cressida is caught at Pandarus's house by a storm; Pandarus summons Troilus, whilst concocting a story that the Trojan is racked with jealousy; Troilus, playing along with Pandarus's deceit, successfully woos Cressida, whilst Pandarus, as the storm dies away, excuses himself on the pretence of fetching a cushion. Walton approved of this idea, and the second act was duly split into two scenes, with the second scene now presenting all the action of the original Act II. Both scenes would employ the same set, Hassall explained, and would be divided merely by the fall of the curtain.

But Walton had other ideas. Rather than the storm dwindling away, the composer suggested that, as the lovers are united, it should swell, allowing him to compose a 'short orchestral interlude (descriptive!)', depicting the raging weather conditions and also the storms of passion taking place behind the lowered curtain. This first reference to what became known as the 'Pornographic interlude' is contained in a detailed synopsis that Walton himself appears to have produced sometime late in the summer of 1947. In the light of Hassall's recommendations, Act II is neatly divided into two scenes, separated by the interlude; as a result of this alteration, Act I is now in a single scene (much of the action of Act I Scene ii, which contained the lovers' first efforts at courtship, had been included in the new Act II Scene i). Walton provided two possible alternative synopses for the opening Act. Cautious perhaps of appearing to impeach upon his librettist's territory, the first version followed closely the synopsis that Hassall had himself drawn up earlier in the year. As a possible alternative, however, Walton suggested a number of revisions to the Act's basic structure. Hassall had been keen to stress that the meeting of Troilus and Cressida before the Temple in Act I should be their very first meeting; Troilus was to mistake Cressida for a member of the unruly crowd, begin to reproach her, and then be overcome by her beauty. Alternatively, Walton suggested that, prior to Cressida's appearance, Antenor should tease his friend Troilus about his love for Cressida; Troilus, left alone, should then sing of his love for Cressida, at which point she emerges from the temple, and there follows 'a rather tentative love scene (more Chaucerian)'. Hassall appears to have been convinced that it would be more effective to show the lovers' first actual encounter and not merely their first conversation. But the synopsis was revised in line with Walton's wishes nonetheless. This was not to be the last time that Hassall's opinion was to count for little.

The plot of Acts I and II had, therefore, reached a form very close to that of the finished work. Act III, however, was to be the source of great difficulties; Hassall was barely indulging in hyperbole when he later described how 'revisions lay as thick as the seven layers of Troy'. The essential difficulty was explained by Hassall in a letter he wrote to the actor Laurence Olivier in 1953, barely a year prior to the opera's first performance, at which time the libretto of the third act still lay in shambles. 'The problem arises from three things', Hassall explained:

> First, we must build up sympathy for Cressida to the end, and so far from cheapening her, she must grow into a tragic, or at least intensely poignant, figure. Two, she is universally known as 'False Cressida', and it is important not to whitewash her legend, as it is vital to give her tragic dignity. Three, the existing end of her legendary story is essentially unoperatic, so a change is necessary anyway; but any departure from the customary must be of a kind in keeping with the first two of these points.

Walton does not appear at this stage to have been convinced by Hassall's second point in the above quotation. In his draft synopsis, the composer suggested that

Diomede should force himself upon Cressida, and that Troilus, watching from a distance, should misinterpret what he witnesses; Cressida's downfall would therefore be even more tragic due to her innocence. But Hassall recognized the folly of this idea. 'C[ressida]: need not have actually and already become Dio[mede]'s lover, but she must, I feel have given up Troilus for lost, & shown a genuine interest, however slight, in Diomede's blandishments.' He concluded: 'I have grown far too fond of Cressida to do her reputation any damage! I shall not jeopardize your sympathy for her.' Hassall was clearly more keenly aware than Walton of the difficulties involved in portraying sympathetically a character universally infamous for her infidelity.

For the remainder of 1947, Walton was occupied in the composition of music for Laurence Olivier's film, *Hamlet*. Meanwhile, Hassall set about the task of turning the synopsis into a libretto. Act I was completed first. 'I've made T[roilus] an aspiring, active personage', he informed Walton, 'Cressida, a subtler person, and not without a quiet sense of humour'. Much of the dialogue contained in this first draft was to survive unscathed into the libretto's final form; what is perhaps most surprising, however, is the absence of any extended passages for the principal characters. Neither Troilus's aria 'Is Cressida a slave?', nor Cressida's 'Slowly it all comes back' are present, whilst Cressida's arioso 'Morning and evening' is merely hinted at. By 15 December 1947, the two remaining acts were also completed; Hassall wrote that he was 'very pleased with the way it has turned out'. Walton's letters from these months do not survive, but he was clearly sufficiently impressed to consider starting work immediately ('Should you wish to postpone the sonata and work on "Cressida" you can count on me to be on tap', Hassall informed him.).[31] *The Times* of 29 January 1948 announced that Walton had been commissioned by the BBC to write an opera, the subject of which would be *Troilus and Cressida*. This apparent optimism is not entirely reflected in the surviving correspondence between Christopher Hassall and Alice Wimborne dating from this time, however. 'We must remember I think', Wimborne wrote to Hassall on 23 February, 'that we are still of very enquiring mind as to the bare subject of Troilus & C'; on 13 March she wrote 'You know that I am not entirely happy about it'. Lady Wimborne's chief concern was the difficulty presented by a drama set in Classical times yet with characters motivated by Medieval Courtly ethics; if the Ancients had no scruples about openly courting one another, then what is the justification for the go-between, Pandarus. It may well have been at her suggestion that the libretto was sent to the distinguished music critic of *The Sunday Times*, Ernest Newman, for his opinion, sometime around March 1948.

Whilst all involved awaited Newman's verdict, Hassall wrote again to Walton, with the news that he had had a 'brain-wave'. Hassall had discussed the libretto with his friend, the Oxford academic Nevil Coghill, a leading authority on medieval literature.[32] Coghill had suggested that the opera's conclusion should be based on the Scottish poet Henryson's continuation of the tale in his poem *The Testament of Cresseid* (1532). As a result, Hassall had drawn up an alternative synopsis for Act III Scene ii. The scene is set before the walls of Troy, several

months after Cressida's first moment of indiscretion; Cressida has since been
spurned by Diomede and become, along with her father Calkas, a diseased beggar;
Troilus and Pandarus are standing before the gates to Troy when a group of
beggars including Cressida and Calkas approach them and ask for help; neither
lover recognizing one another, Troilus throws to the mob a ring given to him by
Cressida at their last meeting, and returns into Troy; Calkas recognizes the ring
and sends after Troilus, only to be told that he has died of a broken heart; on
hearing this news, Cressida also dies; Calkas, standing before the gates of Troy,
repeats the oracle with which he opened the opera, but with the last phrase
portentously altered from 'Go Parley with the Greeks' to 'Go Parley with the
Gods', at which point the curtain falls. This solution, Hassall felt, would be 'more
interesting, more unexpected and more affecting': it also had the undoubted
advantage of eliminating the superfluous characters of Priam and Cassandra,
whilst allowing Walton to repeat the opening music over the final moments.
Walton's reaction to this idea does not survive although it can be safely assumed
to have not been favourable, as nothing more is heard of the alternative.[33] The
notion of Cressida descending to the level of a leprous prostitute can have held
little appeal to Walton. Neither could the idea of Calkas stealing the final curtain
have been especially attractive to a composer intent on avoiding the political
machinations of Homer's legend.[34]

Ernest Newman's report on the libretto finally arrived on 18 April 1948. It
was far from entirely complimentary. 'As a piece of dramatic construction
it's admirable', Newman wrote; but, he thought, 'there are far too many long
words *for music*', a criticism that Alice Wimborne had already made. Newman
continued:

> In the second place, I don't think C. H[assall] has always, or even often, realised the
> difference between verbal speech and musical speech . . . Here is a minor example.
> In the first act Antenor makes a casual reference to 'the widow Cressida', whereupon
> Troilus, left alone, ejaculates 'Is her name Cressid[a]? Is that her name?'. That is
> excellent in poetry, but, I venture to think, wrong in music, where the order should
> surely be 'Is that her name? Cressida?'. For the cry of 'Cressida' is the highlight, and
> it should be held in reserve to the last. The dactylic word, with its natural fall of
> pitch through the three syllables is positively made for music . . .

These were extremely astute observations, and Hassall took back the libretto,
revising it thoroughly during the summer of 1948. The longer sentences were
shortened, and where the language was felt to be overly poetical, it was simplified.[35] Newman assisted him in this task, and continued to take a paternal interest
in the opera's development during the subsequent years.

Over the following eighteen months events in William Walton's personal life
were to largely override his operatic aspirations. Firstly, on 19 April 1948, Alice
Wimborne died after suffering a protracted, painful illness. Wimborne had been
intimately involved in the development of the libretto, and following her death,
at least according to Widdicombe, 'Walton had no heart for the opera'.[36] Nonetheless, the composer wrote to Christopher Hassall on 19 August, inquiring 'How

are you and how is T & C?' Walton was about to embark for Argentina 'and I am wondering if it would be possible for you to let me have a copy of the revised version for me to study on the voyage?' Hassall duly provided Walton with the new libretto and copies of his correspondence with Newman in which the revisions were discussed. 'I shall certainly have something to get my teeth into on the voyage', Walton wrote on 31 August. The trip to Argentina was to have monumental consequences for Walton, as it was here that he was to meet and marry Susana Gil Passo with whom he was to spend the rest of his life. On their return to England, in February 1948, Walton completed his Violin Sonata, and also took the decision that he wished to spend at least six months of every year in the south of Italy. In October 1949, settled into his new home on the Island of Ischia in the Bay of Naples, Walton was at last able to begin the composition of *Troilus and Cressida*: more than two and a half years had passed since the BBC had commissioned the work.

'For one reason & another I have got going on Act II', Walton wrote to Hassall on 20 November 1949, '& I've now got as far as I can without consulting you about some changes.' The composer had evidently been making swift progress, having completed in less than a month some 28 pages of short score.[37] At this point, however, what was perhaps the most fundamental weakness of the libretto was revealed. 'As the script stands', Walton informed his librettist, 'there is no chance for any of the principal parts to get going, or the music either . . . the only people who have anything to sing are the most unimportant people: i.e. the women! with "Put off the serpent girdle"'.[38] To overcome this difficulty, Walton suggested several additions to the remainder of Act II Scene i; a recitative and aria for Cressida in which she, 'lets the audience into the secret of her growing love for Tro[ilus]'; also 'an aria for Pand[arus]: [which] should contain reference to Tro[ilus]'s supposed jealousy feelings, about 2 mins'; and finally, 'a love duet developed from "Oh Strange new love"? in verse – rhyming probably'. Hassall replied on 30 November, not surprised that Walton should feel the need for such changes. 'It was only to be expected', he wrote 'that once you began properly to delve beneath the surface of the thing you'd find yourself having far more *positive* ideas than hitherto'. Enclosed along with this letter was Cressida's new recitative ('How can I sleep') and aria ('At the haunted end') which were to be inserted immediately prior to the point where Cressida, left alone, is about to retire to bed. This first draft was not to Walton's liking, however, being not long enough, and overly poetic.[39] 'It is not direct enough', the composer informed Hassall. He then went on to suggest what he wanted:

> Cress: should be angry with herself for falling for T: & perhaps full of presentiments – but she can't help herself. This should come out in the recit (about 45") & might run something like this. 'How can I sleep? I could not keep my head on that silly game for thinking of him. Troilus who now ever fills my thoughts, blast him. Why must I fall for him I thought never to love again' etc.

The composer suggested that Hassall might fashion his text along the lines of examples in Verdi: 'I think Cress: aria "At the haunted end" should correspond to the tenor recit and aria "Celeste Aida" in length – about 2'45" – this will give you a model to work on.' On several other occasions, Walton pointed out prototype forms, always from Italian opera and primarily Verdi, which Hassall could employ as models. Walton wished to compose an opera firmly in the romantic tradition: to achieve this, he would require a text similar in form to those of his musical antecedents.[40]

Hassall sent a further revision, which he described as 'fraught with unsatisfied longing', on 16 December. On Christmas Day Walton replied, stating that the revision was 'a great improvement and I am forthwith proceeding with it'. The second extension that Walton had requested, however, (the aria for Pandarus regarding Troilus's jealousy) was not to the composer's liking. Walton again suggested what he wanted: 'P's aria should be on the subject of "Jealousy" per se . . . you know the kind of thing. "Jealousy, that all consuming fire that gnaws at the vitals etc. etc".' In the libretto's first draft, a trio followed at this point; Troilus, on entering Cressida's bed-chamber, would deny Pandarus's story; Cressida would chastise Troilus for his lack of faith, whilst Pandarus happily philosophized about his antics. Walton feared that a formal ensemble might be dramatically inappropriate, and proposed instead that Troilus (unseen by Pandarus and Cressida) and Cressida should interject over Pandarus's new 'jealousy' aria:

> Cres. can make appropriate interjections. 'What does this mean? Is he out of his senses?' etc. About halfway through the aria T[roilus]. opens the door and concealed by it adds his interjections.[41] 'He's gone mad'. 'I must stop him' 'he'll ruin everything' etc. Then T. should burst in. 'Cress. forgive me – your uncle is trying to stir up trouble between us. . .' Then let P. explain 'I made it all up – it was just a little stratagem of mine to bring two lovers together'.

Hassall's first revision did not follow Walton's specifications closely enough and the composer requested another; the second working was far closer to Walton's doggerel verses and this the composer did eventually set though not without, as he put it, 'taking a few liberties with the text'.[42]

Writing again on 16 January 1950, Walton now turned his attentions to the opening of the first act. In the summer of 1947, the composer had envisaged that the opera would open with a short ('2 mins') prelude, possibly employing the chorus heard behind the lowered curtain. But Walton now intended that the curtain should rise immediately, revealing 'the priests intoning a prayer (a new one about eight lines) behind the scene, as from the temple'.[43] As in Act II Scene i, the absence of extended passages for the principals was a difficulty. 'We must somehow manage to get T[roilus] something to sing – an aria like C[ressida]'s in Sc i Act II' Walton wrote, stressing 'the better the poem the better the music'. The composer suggested a place in the libretto which might be suitably expanded to include such an aria.[44] His attentions then turned to the end of the opera:

> Instead of C[ressida] killing herself as she is about to plunge the dagger into her midriff, Diomede (who I should like to think of as being on horseback) seizes her wrist & carries her off with the cry of 'To the whore-house with you my girl'!

General confusion, Antenor puts his sword through Calchas – cry of 'To battle' & quick Curtain.

Hassall considered this 'drastic suggestion' a worthwhile alternative. 'The big advantage lies in the fact that Cressida, as a legendary figure, obviously met the very fate you suggest', he replied on 21 January, 'it is also slightly less conventional than a suicide'.

By the middle of February 1950, Walton had completed Cressida's aria 'At the haunted end' ('it has turned out fairly well – if sailing a bit near the wind!') and Pandarus's jealousy sequence ('it is not very satisfactory but I think we'll get it right if we work at it a bit'[45]). The next task was the composition of Troilus and Cressida's love-duet ('Oh strange new love'). After making some exploratory efforts, however, Walton decided to postpone this task, admitting to Hassall that he was 'finding love music very difficult to get any originality into – Wagner, Verdi, Puccini, Strauss always popping their heads around the corner'. Instead, attention was turned to Act I. Whilst Troilus's new aria ('Is Cressida a slave?') was satisfactory, 'C[ressida]'s position is bad still, consisting as it does of some 15 or 16 short fragmentary sentences with which little can be done musically speaking'. Surely Cressida might be given more to say at the first meeting with Troilus, Walton enquired? Hassall felt this alteration would be inappropriate. 'Cressida, at this first encounter, should be withdrawn and unforthcoming' he wrote (27 February) and he suggested three alternative positions where Cressida's role might be happily extended. One of these suggestions was 'a dramatic monologue . . . immediately after Calchas has torn himself away from her arms [to defect to the Greeks]'. This was to eventually become Cressida's 'Slowly it all comes back'. But Walton's wishes were to prevail over Cressida's text in her initial meeting with Troilus. By 14 March, Hassall had considerably extended her role in this scene: 'in fact it is now "her" scene', he informed his collaborator.

Meanwhile, Walton was progressing, though not without difficulty, with the opera's opening; Hassall was required to revise the chorus's text a number of times before the composer was satisfied.[46] For Calkas' lengthy monologue ('Launching at the dead at night', where Calkas attempts to convince the gathered Trojan crowds that they must surrender to the Greeks) Walton had rather an unusual idea. 'This [the monologue] I contemplate having spoken against a background of percussion . . . rather in the manner of "Façade" but on a grander scale' he informed his librettist on 22 February. 'Consequently I feel it should be rewritten so that it is in a strict rhythm. Perhaps rhyming – or would hexameters be better to give it a formal & classical touch?' A spoken monologue in hexameters accompanied by percussion Hassall thought 'a grand idea', and immediately worked Calkas's speech into hexameters, marking clearly the scansion (as Walton had requested, 'or else I am sure to get it wrong'). By the time the revision arrived in Ischia, however, Walton had changed his mind about the monologue being spoken. The false declaration of the Oracle was to be spoken from within the temple immediately following Calkas's speech, and Walton was afraid that for Calkas also to speak might detract from the effectiveness of the Oracle. The passage remained in hexameters, however, when Walton finally came to set it (which he did with the use of full orchestra and not merely percussion).

Despite these aforementioned difficulties with the libretto, Walton was clearly pleased with the work's progress. On 1 March, he wrote to Steuart Wilson, BBC Director of Music, informing him that 'I shall be pleased if I get it [the opera] finished in sketch by this time next year [1951]. I aim for a Cov. Gar. performance about June '52'.[47] Soon after this, however, Walton was visited by his friend Walter Legge who, according to Susana Walton, 'tore *Troilus's* libretto to pieces . . . [Walton] was devastated, and took weeks to recover and to be able to work again'.[48] With his confidence severely shaken, Walton searched for a further outside opinion, this time the conductor, Ernest Irving.[49] Irving was not entirely impressed by the libretto either, stating that 'it seems to me that your difficulties are largely caused by flaws of construction'. In Greek drama, Irving stressed, the gods were of greatest importance, followed by the war, and finally the lovers. 'But we must not lose sight of the fact that this is a story of medieval origin and character which the author has set in Troy' Hassall countered; 'the gods are, therefore, of less, and the lovers of more, importance than they would be in a Greek drama proper'. With this observation Walton was in firm agreement: the composer, momentarily at least, was reassured.

Having worked relentlessly at *Troilus and Cressida* since October 1949, Walton appears to have paused for breath over the summer of 1950, and there is a considerable gap in his correspondence with Christopher Hassall.[50] Work began again in earnest in the winter of 1950, and when the composer finally wrote to his librettist, on 10 February 1951, he was able to report that Act I was 'now well on its way & I hope to complete it by the middle of next month or so'. The meeting with Hassall in London in the previous June had evidently been most fruitful, with many of the libretto problems being ironed out. One difficulty remained, however, in the form of Troilus's opening aria, 'Child of the wine-dark wave', which the composer described as 'a major disaster'. 'I'm quite unable to cope with "Child of the grey sea wave [*sic*]". It evokes the worst type of music from me, real neo-Novelloismo . . . it is the regularity the *tum*-tum tum *tum* tum *tum*.' Walton's reference to 'neo-Novelloismo' was thoughtless. Hassall, a personal friend of Ivor Novello, was in no sense embarrassed by having acted as his librettist. His response barely concealed his indignation. 'I'm *so* sorry you've had such trouble – due to me – I can only say that at least the passages in question aren't in fact Novelloistic, though they may not be good enough.' Walton quickly apologized for his tactless remark: 'I meant it to refer to the music not the verse.'[51]

For the moment, at least, this unfortunate disagreement was forgotten, and Hassall travelled to Ischia in April 1951, staying for several weeks, during which time the remaining difficulties over the libretto of Act I would appear to have been solved. By the time Walton returned to London at the end of June, this Act was all but complete in short score. Interviewed in *The Times* (30 August 1951), he rather mischievously announced that, 'the first two acts were already in the last stages of completion . . . the opera would be finished by the end of April next year [1952]'.

Returning to Ischia in November 1951, Walton began work again by revising the completed section of Act II Scene i. The love-duet between Troilus and Cressida (which Walton had put off composing in the previous year by turning his attentions to Act I) could be avoided no longer. 'I am at the moment at a complete standstill & see no signs of a move', Walton informed Hassall on 21 December, 'in fact the most important scene in the opera is non-existent'. The difficulties, Walton was sure, again lay with the libretto: 'I believe the crux is in the para. "If one last doubt!". It is too flat and English . . . if I were in his [Troilus] position I should be more inclined to be more impassioned & insistent & not so self excusing. . .'.[52] A copy, revised along the lines of Walton's suggestions, was sent to the composer, but he was still not satisfied. 'I should like more about her [Cressida's] fears as I propose to use a cross-reference or if you like motive, the bit in Act I when Cress says "I'm afraid".' Walton had been intent from the first to emphasis the role Cressida's fears play in her downfall and attached to them an oscillating semitonal motive. Whilst Hassall had in all probability discussed it with him, Walton had not in fact yet read C. S. Lewis's description of Cressida and her 'ruling passion'; a copy of *The Allegory of Love* was sent out to the composer in March 1952, which Walton described as 'extremely interesting especially on Cressida's fears'.[53] Hassall introduced the lines 'Now nothing stands between us, Nothing but your fears!' and the passage was duly set with extensive use of the 'fear' motive.

With Troilus's declaration of love settled, attention now turned to the love-duet itself. In the first draft, the duet was conceived in four verses: the first and last spoke of the earthly lovers, whilst the central two praised the gods.[54] Surprisingly, perhaps, it was the middle two stanzas that Walton felt comfortable with, though he did not think them long enough. 'I'm sure it's too short' he wrote on 6 March 1952,'for instance from "Kind are" to "my lover" will take only about 30 secs – so two more verses would bring it to about the required length'. Two more verses were provided, which Walton duly set 'with a bit of chivying here and there'; the composer had in fact entirely rewritten (or 'transformed' as Walton put it) one of the new verses, though he reassured his librettist that 'you can easily rewrite when you are here if you think it necessary. I think it rather a good piece of WaltonHassallese!' Hassall did in fact rewrite Walton's text, producing new words to fit the already-composed music. Both composer and librettist evidently found this a satisfactory method of working, and an increasing amount of the score was fashioned in this manner. Having expanded the tribute to the gods, Walton now felt that the outer verses ('Oh strange new love') were extraneous. 'As C behaves quite contrarily in the last scene of Act III it might be as well to cut it', Walton told Hassall on 29 March.

Perhaps the single most important passage of the correspondence from these months, however, was contained in a letter Walton wrote to Hassall on 29 December 1951, in which the composer outlined for the first time material that was eventually to form the opera's ending. Although Cassandra and her lament were already excised, the remainder of Act III Scene ii stood very much as it had done in 1947. Within this framework, Walton suggested the following:

> After D[iomede] says 'Shame on Argos', Cress realising what is in store for her hysterically appeals to each in turn, Pandarus to help her, Diomede to forgive her, and to Priam to pardon her, all in vain. In fact an ensemble with chorus and everyone and finally Calkas giving her the dagger. Then she can bellow 'Open the gates' etc., collapse and immediate curtain. . . .

It was far from immediately obvious that this constituted the best conclusion to the opera, and both Hassall and Walton continued to devise alternatives.

Whilst the text for the love-duet was revised, the composer worked at Act II Scene ii. By 29 December 1951, Walton had sketched in detail Diomede's entrance with the news that Cressida must be exchanged for the captured Antenor. The remainder of the scene, and in particular the quartet that Hassall intended should form the climax of the act, was not to the composer's liking. An ensemble, Walton feared, might be 'too static & spoil the impetus for the curtain'.[55] Alternatively, he suggested that an extended scene of farewell between Troilus and Cressida might form a more effective conclusion to the Act. Hassall was intent that the ensemble be retained, however, and the composer, for the moment at least, agreed to 'leave the question of the quartet in abeyance'. The close of the second act, along with the Orchestral Interlude that was to divide the two scenes, therefore, remained to be completed, as Walton now turned his attentions to Act III.

The opening of the final act was to be yet another source of disagreement between composer and librettist. Since 1947, Hassall had revised his original synopsis and the third act now began with Diomede threatening Calkas with dire consequences unless Cressida responded to his advances. But Walton was not impressed. 'Three and a half pages of dialogue set in recitative or dramatic recitative are going to be stiff both for the audience and for the unfortunate composer', he explained to Hassall, and suggested that the original opening be reinstated, portraying the night-watchmen expressing their longing for Greece. Concerned, as always, that Cressida should win our sympathies, Walton also suggested the introduction of 'a scene between Calk[as] and Cress[ida]. He urging her to yield to D[iomede] & urging the advantages & in what precarious position they'll be if she dozent [*sic*]'. The original opening was duly reinstated, the exchanges between Diomede and Calkas were cut, and Hassall drafted a scene between Cressida and her father (including a long monologue for Calkas, in which he urges his daughter to yield to Diomede).

Christopher Hassall again travelled to Ischia early in May 1952 and worked alongside Walton for some two weeks. After he had returned to London, Walton wrote, describing how the opening of Act III had been realized. Walton had envisaged that the act would open with a chorus of Greek soldiers lamenting their homelands, 'a good old sentimental nostalgic yearning one with lots of all's welling from the watchmen echoing backstage . . .'(2 February 1952). By 10 June, however, this had altered: 'I've cut the soldier's song in the distance completely, substituting 3 All Wells with fanfares getting further and further off.' The Chorus of soldiers was to have anticipated the sentiments of Cressida's monologue 'No answering sign' (where Cressida sings of her longing for Troilus); continuity of atmosphere was now achieved by opening the Act with the melody to which Cressida later sings her monologue (played on a solo cor anglais), over which the soldier's 'All's Well' sounds.

Walton's letter of 10 June contains the first reference to a figure who was to play an important and sometimes contentious role in the shaping of the remainder of the opera: W.H. Auden. Along with his companion, Chester Kallman, Auden had spent the summer months on Ischia since 1948.[56] Over dinner, Auden offered to give his opinions on Hassall's text and prompted, no doubt, by his persistent lack of confidence in the libretto (and his librettist) Walton agreed:[57] 'It will be interesting to get an outside opinion' he reassured Hassall.[58] Some two weeks later, Walton wrote once more to Hassall, reporting that he had 'played through T & C & had a long talk with him about it'. Auden had been 'genuinely enthusiastic about the music', but had made a number of 'minor' but 'important' criticisms of the libretto.

Auden's criticisms were perhaps not as minor as Walton suggested, as they addressed the overall tone and style of certain passages and individual characters. In particular, Auden disliked Hassall's portrayal of Pandarus, feeling that his text should be 'more in line with the rest'; the opening of Act II, a scene dominated by Pandarus, the poet criticized for being 'too modern, small & fashionable'. He disliked the quartet in Act II Scene ii and also the very end of this act where, with Cressida having been removed to Troy, Antenor (for whom she has been exchanged) is reunited with a distraught Troilus; 'any business after her [Cressida's] exit [would] be anti-climactic'. Walton was particularly struck by Auden's suggestion that Act III open with a scene revealing Calkas 'either bribing or threatening' Evadne to intercept Troilus's letters to Cressida. 'It is to say the least a bit of a bore to have to start the [third] act all over again', Walton wrote, 'but I think it may be worth it as the opening anyhow is not entirely satisfactory'. In conclusion the composer added 'we needn't necessarily agree on all his criticism and suggestions but on the whole I'm of the opinion that they are good'.

Replying immediately (7 July) Hassall stated that he was 'delighted with your letter containing Wystan A's comments': the tone of his response was considerably firmer than any of his previous letters, however, and Hassall countered many of Auden's criticisms with persuasive argument. The character Pandarus was deliberately different in style from the others, Hassall wrote, as, 'one cannot have a uniform style in a play, as in a poem'. As for the opening of Act II, 'I see every reason for the "small and fashionable" atmosphere, and none against it', he countered, 'it all seems to me consistent and dramatically of *great* value in the light of what has gone before and what is to follow'. Conceding that Antenor's entry would be an anticlimax, Hassall was still determined to retain the quartet: 'I admit it's undramatic, but I still think this is a spot where the drama can afford to be suspended.' And he was adamant that there should be no scene between

Calkas and Evadne, informing the audience that Troilus's letters were to be intercepted. The audience must 'share in C[ressida]'s suspense and longing for news and begin to wonder what will happen'. Hassall, clearly not entirely happy that Walton had sought yet another outside opinion, rather pointedly reminded the composer not to forget that Auden 'had to make snap decisions and judgements concerning points to which I have devoted leisurely hours of thought'. Walton conceded this fact, and the openings of both Acts I and II were to remain as they stood. The quartet in Act II Scene i was cut, however; this act was now to end, as Walton had wished, with Troilus and Cressida's farewells. But having removed this ensemble, on the grounds that it was 'undramatic' and would 'spoil the impetus for the final curtain', Hassall must have been frustrated and perplexed to learn that, at Auden's suggestion, Walton now wished to include, near the end of the third act, 'a grand quintet'. And in light of this development, the composer now wished to revise further the last moments of the opera:

> the curtain should come much quicker after that [Troilus's death] and it should come thus: Diomede says at the moment 'as for C[ressida], she has her uses'. I propose he should say to the soldiers 'Take her – she's all yours' or something like that and the curtain comes down as they are about to pounce on her. Perhaps a bit brutal but it makes it more dramatic and less Isolde-ish. . . .

Hassall may well have wondered whether he, W.H. Auden, or indeed Walton himself, was now writing *Troilus and Cressida*'s libretto.

* * *

As had been the pattern in previous years, the composition of *Troilus* was largely suspended during the summer months, whilst Walton returned to England. Resumption of work was delayed by the coronation of Elizabeth II (which took place on 2 June 1953), for which Walton was asked to provide a substantial amount of music.[59] Discussion of the third act of the opera continued around these tasks. At some point during this hiatus the composer had evidently decided that the final act should not be in two separate scenes, with different settings and a time lapse of several weeks between them, but in one continuous scene. Walton's reasoning that inspired this alteration does not appear in any of the correspondence, but Hassall was evidently in agreement. On 26 November 1952, however, the librettist wrote to Walton explaining a difficulty this new structure brought about. 'Since it is all in one scene', Hassall wrote, 'there's no chance for C[ressida] to be *physically* unfaithful to T[roilus]'. To overcome this problem, the librettist suggested that, at the climax of her love scene with Diomede, Cressida should 'positively throw herself at D[iomede], yielding herself to his embraces with an almost sensual abandon'. With this idea, the composer strongly agreed, elaborating (on 4 February 1953), 'she should positively let rip with all her pent up sex which she has been accumulating in the past weeks so there is no doubt in the minds of the audience that she intends to be unfaithful'. Since having this thought in November, Hassall had held further discussions with Ernest Newman, who felt the alteration to be 'a grave mistake'; Cressida should yield with 'dumb resignation. The circumstances are too much for her'. But his opinion was disregarded, and in the final libretto Cressida gives herself wholeheartedly to Diomede.[60] Whilst these discussions continued Walton busied himself orchestrating those passages that he had completed. By 22 February he was able to report that he had scored the whole of Act II Scene i (but had not 'taken the plunge yet into the interlude') whilst the opening of Act III was also orchestrated as far as it was composed, and by 5 May a considerable portion of Act I was complete in full score. At the same time as he was scoring, Walton was also revising the music: after orchestrating the opening of Act I, he reported that he had 'managed to knock off nearly 3 mins . . . it's meant a lot of rewriting – however all an improvement'. Walton was greatly concerned with the length of each act ('no one except me seems to realise how long a minute is and of what vital importance it is not to have too many of them!' he wrote). Even the composer's earliest synopses had been marked with detailed projected timings. Having expanded the text at numerous junctures, allowing the insertion of extended passages, there was now the need to shorten some of the sections of dialogue. To Hassall's considerable exasperation, Walton only infrequently consulted his collaborator whilst carrying out this task.

Writing on 5 May, Walton stated that he planned 'to finish the scoring of Act I & II before we come back here [Ischia] at the end of Sept'. The summer of 1953 entailed both the coronation and Walton's first tour of the United States of America as a conductor of his own works, and he did not write again to Hassall until 8 December 1953. The orchestration of Act I was now completed but the composer was still 'immersed in Act II, which I fear will take me to the end of June'. This letter is of interest in that it was to precipitate tense exchanges between composer and librettist. Walton had discussed the opera further with Auden, and explained to Hassall how 'the enclosed turned up just before he [Auden] left'. The 'enclosed' was a fully texted ending to the opera, written, it would appear by both Auden and Chester Kallman;[61] beginning at the point where Diomede enters proclaiming Cressida his queen, the text builds to a sextet (involving Troilus, Cressida, Pandarus, Calkas, Diomede and Evadne) following which Troilus is slain by Diomede and Cressida is imprisoned. 'Whether we decide to have a sextet or not, I'm not at all sure, but if we do, this is a model of how it should be worked out' Walton wrote. Also included with this letter was a denouement for the opera written by Walton himself. This was written along the lines of Walton's 'brutal' suggestion of the previous year; after Troilus is slain by Diomede, Evadne kills herself and Cressida is given to the soldiers to do with what they will.

Hassall's usual prompt reply was not forthcoming. On 30 December Walton sent a postcard saying 'I hope you received my letter safely', and some ten days later he wrote again, at more length, perhaps fearing that Hassall had been offended by Auden's intrusion: 'I'm not absolutely sold on Wystan's quintet, in fact it may be quite out of keeping with the construction of the rest of the opera', he backtracked. The long-awaited reply finally came on 12 January 1954. Listing the letter's contents, Hassall wrote, 'the above all explain themselves and leave no controversial stone unturned, so I'll say nothing more about them here'. Despite this measured and controlled tone, his resentment at Auden's intervention, and more especially Walton's tactless handling of the matter, did surface: 'When Auden's text arrived I nearly sent you a wire – "Auden's text excellent, am sending it to Alan [Frank (Walton's publisher)] to set".' But, Hassall felt, Auden's text was far from excellent, and with uncharacteristic force he laid out in considerable detail his objections. Both alternative final curtains were dismissed. 'The idea of Eva[dne] killing herself and Cress being dragged away to the stews' he felt, 'is one of those alternatives to the conventional or obvious that is grossly inferior to the thing it seeks to improve on'. This development would give Evadne an 'advantage' over Cressida, Hassall wrote: 'if anyone dies it must Cres . . . and if *she* dies Eva must *not*. The end must be a sudden tidal wave of concern and compassion for *Cres*. alone.' Nor did Hassall agree with the content of Auden's sextet, in particular Troilus's description of Cressida as 'False! Faithless! And unclean!':

> [Auden] makes Dio's and Tro's attitude to Cres identical at the end. This isn't right. Dio's rejects her utterly [*sic*]: but in Tro there is enough lingering regret and nostalgia and affection in spite of everything.

With this letter, Hassall enclosed his own reworking of the finale of Act III. This further draft absorbed two points made by Walton's version that the librettist felt to be most valid. Firstly, that Diomede and Cressida should enter the final scene together, not separately as had previously been the case; Hassall still thought that Troilus and Cressida should have a final moment of blissful reunion (a suggestion of Newman's) and this was achieved through Diomede's wearing Cressida's love-token not on his helmet but on his arm, covered by a cloak. Troilus would not challenge Diomede, therefore, until the latter threw off his cloak thus revealing the token. Secondly, Walton had suggested that Troilus's death would result in 'a big relaxation of tension', and therefore must occur as near as possible to the final curtain; once Troilus was slain the action would need to be swift-moving. Immediately following the proposed ensemble, Diomede calls Cressida a 'whore', arousing Troilus into attacking him; Diomede is quickly unarmed but as Troilus steps in for the kill he is surrounded by Greek soldiers and himself mortally wounded (that Troilus should die in a circle of Greek spears was an idea of Laurence Olivier's); Troilus is led off by the Greek soldiers whilst Cressida discovers his abandoned dagger; taking this dagger as a sign, she prays to the gods and to Troilus for forgiveness, and then, despite Evadne's pleas that Cressida kill her, she kills herself.

The composer swiftly replied to Hassall, apologizing for his thoughtlessness in sending Auden's typescript without sufficient explanation. The sextet was to be regarded as nothing more than a guide, he insisted, and Auden had 'never meant that I should set it & I never for an instant thought of doing [so]'. This may or may not have been true, but secretly Walton was rather pleased by the turn of events, reporting to his publisher, Alan Frank, on 16 January how, 'Chris H[assall] has sent me the new version of Act III. The Auden intervention seems to have put him on his mettle & he has produced something better than either A's solution or the previous version.' But not even this draft was to prove entirely satisfactory and there were still to be a substantial number of further alterations over the following months.

During this delay, Walton had busily set about finishing Act II, which by 25 March was finally completed, including the long-feared orchestral interlude that divides the act's two scenes. 'The interlude gave me a good deal of bother & is I fear not very good', he informed Alan Frank on 19 February; around the same time Walton explained to Hassall how the interlude 'suffers as I always told you from lack of thematic material attached to T & C'.[62] But the way was now finally clear to complete Act III. A date for the opening night was firmly fixed (3 December 1954), and casting discussions form increasingly frequent excursions in Walton and Hassall's correspondence. Walton was fearful that the opera would not be ready ('a terrifying thought') and was generally pessimistic about the work: 'at the moment', he told Hassall on 28 March, 'I'm full of gloomy prognostications'.

Nonetheless, progress continued. On 4 April, Walton informed Alan Frank:

> At the moment of writing I've completed about 15 mins of Act III which only means 5 or 6 pages of score and am about to begin on the crucial and very difficult love scene between Cress: and Dio: . . . there are three crucial spots in this act – the love scene I'm about to embark on, what I hope will be the celebrated sextet & the last page or two . . .

Changes to the text of Diomede and Cressida's love-scene had already been requested. On 11 March Walton wrote, doubting that Diomede's role was correctly characterized: 'Isn't it wrong for him to weaken & put it [Cressida's decision] off 'till [*sic*] tomorrow when he should not be taking "no" for an answer, in fact he should be getting more and more that he wants her and the bloody scarf right here and now?' The composer's chief concern, however, was that Diomede, in spite of his dramatic importance, possessed no prolonged passages of text and was 'not getting much of a show vocally speaking'. Despite the opening of the act having been entirely revised, with extended passages for Cressida ('No answering sign' and her prayer 'You gods, you deathless gods') and Calkas (his long monologue 'Cressid, daughter, why so heavy hearted') having been inserted, Walton had been unable to set any of these solos in a more heightened musical style than what he termed 'dramatic recitative'. The love-scene between Diomede and Cressida merely continued this predicament: 'aria is called for here, immediate and pressing', Walton explained on 17 March. An aria for Diomede was provided but, as was often the case where several versions of the same section existed, Walton cobbled his text together from various different sources. By 8 April this difficult passage was completed, though, as with Troilus and Cressida's love-duet the text would 'remain fluid till [*sic*] you [Hassall] arrive and see what it's like'.

Hassall duly travelled to Ischia for the final time early in May 1954, for what was to be an extremely fruitful period of collaboration. Over these two weeks, the conclusion to the opera was finally settled. Over the hotly debated issue of when and to whom Evadne would confess her guilt, Hassall's views were to finally hold sway; after Cressida has yielded to Diomede, Evadne, unobserved, was to burn Troilus's letters in the brazier. She would not now clutter the opera's final moments and risk detracting from the plight of Cressida;[63] instead she would confess her guilt, to Calkas alone, as part of the entirely original sextet that Hassall drew up to take the place of Auden's.[64] A crucial alteration was made to the manner of Troilus's death; in all previous drafts, he had either been slain by the sword of Diomede, or by the spears of Diomede's soldiers: in this final working, however, Troilus, about to kill Diomede, is stabbed from behind by Calkas.[65] Thus a final twist to the tale was achieved, and Calkas (who was in danger of appearing more victim than villain) is finally revealed as beyond doubt a dastardly traitor.

Another important innovation surrounded the re-entry of Diomede and the manner in which he was to discover Troilus and learn of Cressida's falseness. Rather than Diomede and Cressida entering together, with Diomede rather melodramatically concealing the love-token beneath his cloak, Cressida was now to enter alone, adorned in bridal costume; a final duet of reunion between Troilus and Cressida was excised at Walton's request, as he felt that the end of the opera should be 'action without much interruption'.[66] In the opera's final form, this reunion is prevented by the sounding of trumpets and the entry of the chorus proclaiming Cressida 'Bride of Calydon and Argos'. Walton set about composing this passage, which he labelled 'pomposo', following Hassall's return to London. On 18 June the composer sought confirmation of this revision:

> Let me just get this right about 'pomposo'. I imagine it thus. Tpts & Chorus more or less together 'Hail-Argos' backstage. Then Tro:[ilus] What is this (sudden?) uproar? These voices? What are they calling? The orch. in front then takes up whatever tum-ta-tum God gives me during which Cress, sings It's too late. . . .

The passage was eventually realized along these lines, though not without the usual difficulties. In particular, Walton struggled to provide music for the chorus's entry; what was needed 'was one of those elastic bits of music (I've no ideas at the moment) which may be played slower without ill effect if 10 secs or so more is required'. This link was eventually filled with what Walton described as 'a ceremonial march (rather protestant & abbeyish)'.[67]

By 22 August, Walton was able to report that 'the 6tet is more or less satisfactory & will doubtless improve when I score it'. The ensemble had evidently not been overly troublesome: the final moments were proving more difficult, however, and in particular Cressida's final aria. This passage had been extended, with a prayer for forgiveness, 'Turn, Troilus, turn' (initially conceived by Hassall as an alternative to the sextet but now included alongside it), having been attached to the original, frantic lines 'At last a message!', as Cressida discovers a dagger and decides that she must kill herself. As a way out of the deadlock Walton found himself in when he came to set this passage, Hassall had suggested that the prayer might come before and not after 'At last a message!'. Walton reconsidered the issue and in his letter of 22 August explained that:

> Having looked into the question of whether 'At last' should go before 'Turn Tro' I think it better as it stands originally. The transition from the hysteria . . . to the more or less detached calm of 'Turn Tro' without anything in between is too sudden.

Concerned as always with the practical aspects of staging the work, Walton had been worried that Cressida would be required to sing her final aria whilst concealing a heavy dagger. But, he had realized, 'It is really finding the sword that gives her a way out & makes her take this attitude [the calm repose of the prayer]. Without finding the sword she wouldn't embark on 'Turn Tro' because she has no means of killing herself'.[68] This problem solved, Walton then described how he envisaged the final moments of the opera:

> The end will I think have to be vaguely similar to the end of Act II 'And by this, I'm still your Cress' [Cressida's final line: actually 'And by this sign'] being identical almost with Tro's last words in Act II & therefore being almost obliged to use the old T & C theme. I think it highly dangerous to resurrect the 2nd most awful piece in the work at the last moment when I hope everyone will temporarily have forgotten it!

'The second most awful piece in the work' is a reference to the Orchestral Interlude from Act II, where the 'Troilus and Cressida' theme, employed to form the final moments of both Acts II and III, is heard for the first time.[69] 'The last bit is proving a bit tiresome', Walton wrote on 7 September, 'it's not that it's really difficult but that I'm ever so slightly exhausted'. Two days later, Walton scribbled Hassall a short note: 'Dear C. Thank you for everything. I'm finished. Next please.' More than seven and a half years had passed since the BBC had commissioned an opera from William Walton, and since he, Alice Wimborne and Christopher Hassall had first discussed the subject of *Troilus and Cressida*. To the manuscript score, dated 13 September 1954, Walton added the dedication 'To my wife'.

Notes

1. Tovey, D. 91936) *Essays in Musical Analysis, iii: Concertos*, London: OUP, pp. 220–6.
2. Kennedy, M. (1989) *Portrait of Walton*, Oxford: OUP, p. 287.
3. Besides Walton, the Trust was made up of Kenneth Clark, Edward Dent, Leslie Boosey, Ralph Hawkes, Samuel Courtauld, Stanley Marchant and Steuart Wilson.
4. Walton, S. (1988) *William Walton: Behind the Façade*, Oxford: OUP, p. 134.
5. Several of Walton's major works came about through his desire to emulate, and top, the success of others, most famously *Belshazzar's Feast* (1931) which was written in an attempt to outdo the acclaim awarded Constant Lambert's *The Rio Grande* (1928).
6. Hutchings, A. (1937) 'The Symphony and William Walton', *Musical Times*, 78, p. 215.
7. White, E. W. (1983) *A History of English Opera*, London: Faber & Faber, p. 413.

8. Ferris, P. (1977) *Dylan Thomas*, London: Hodder & Stoughton, p. 615.
9. Ibid., p. 218.
10. BBC Written Archives.
11. Kennedy, M. (1989), op. cit., p. 136.
12. Tierney, N. (1984) *William Walton: His Life and Music*, London: Hale, p. 130.
13. Letter dated 21 January 1955, held at BBC Written Archives.
14. The opera was to have been entitled *Gesualdo*. Although he wrote no music, Walton did make several suggestions for alterations to the libretto. Gray was convinced that the subject matter was 'ideally suited to William Walton' (Gray (1948) *Musical Chairs*, p. 243).
15. Marsh, editor of the anthology *Georgian Poetry*, was a well-known patron of the arts. Hassall was to write his biography later.
16. OUP Archives.
17. Widdicombe, G. (1977) Sleeve notes to *Troilus and Cressida*, EMI SLS BC 997.
18. Peter Pears, describing the difficulties that Britten had in selecting librettists emphasized that, in the 1950s, 'No one in England knew much about writing libretti' (Alexander (1986) 'The Process of Composition of the Libretto of Britten's *Gloriana*', *Music and Letters*, 67, pp. 147–58).
19. '*Troilus and Cressida* is as marvellous as *All's Well That Ends Well* is boring', Lambert wrote in 1948 (Shead (1973), *Constant Lambert*, London: Simon Publications, p. 144.
20. Hassall, C. (1954a) 'And Now – Walton's First Opera', *Music and Musicians*, 3, p. 12.
21. Lewis, C. S. (1958) *The Allegory of Love: A Study in Medieval Tradition*, 2nd ed., Oxford: OUP, p. 185.
22. Walton went to Prague, accompanied by Alan Bush and Gerald Abraham, to represent British music at the Prague Festival.
23. The spelling of the name 'Calchas' was altered midway through the opera's composition to 'Calkas', the form in which it appears in Greek legend. For the sake of consistency, the Ancient Greek form is used throughout this essay, other than in quotations, where the original orthography, if different, is preserved.
24. Book One, Stanzas 10–11 of Chaucer's poem describe Calchas's desertion (Warrington (1974), p. 5), whilst Book One, Stanza 24 provided the initial idea for the opera's opening scene (Warrington (1974), op. cit., p. 9).
25. The name Evadne may possibly have been an allusion to the Christian name of Hassall's wife, Evelyn.
26. Hassall, C. (1954b) *Troilus and Cressida: Opera in Three Acts*, Oxford: OUP, p. 5.
27. The cosmopolitan nature of the opera's source was emphasized by Hassall in the preface to the libretto, where he described how 'the opera owes the broad outline of its action to Boccaccio' (1954b, p. 3). Chaucer had, of course, based his poem on the fourteenth-century Italian poet's *Il Filostrato*.
28. Hassall, C. (1954a), op. cit., p. 12.
29. Cressida's text is riddled with references to the gods and their powers. In Act I, at her first meeting with Troilus, she ominously declares 'We must not meet again. The gods are frowning', whilst in Act III, having received no word from Troilus, she exclaims 'You gods, you deathless gods, What have I done to deserve your harsh displeasure?'.
30. Warrington, J. (ed.) (1974) *Troilus and Criseyde* by Geoffrey Chaucer, London: Dent, pp. 140–58.
31. Walton was in the middle of composing a Violin Sonata for Yehudi Menuhin. This was in fact completed before work began on the opera.
32. Coghill was Merton Professor of English Literature from 1956–67. In late 1949, a translation by Coghill of Chaucer's poem was broadcast on The Third Programme. Transcripts of these broadcasts were sent to Walton at Ischia, accompanied by notes

Hassall produced as a guide, as the composer does not appear to have been able to face (or understand) Chaucer's original text. Hassall informed Coghill that Walton had found reading the translations 'most useful'.

33. A trace of Henryson's ending to the legend is to be found in the opera's conclusion. Following the death of Troilus, Diomede declares that Cressida will remain in the Greek camp ('As for that whore, and her comely graces, she shall remain with *us*. She has her uses.'). Cressida clearly faces the fate that Henryson outlines, but mercifully she is able to kill herself, thus cheating her captors.

34. Walton evidently felt that there were too many political complications as there were, as when he revised the opera for the 1976 revival, the composer greatly shortened the role of Calkas, the chief representative of the political element of the opera's plot.

35. Not untypical of the style of the first draft of the libretto was the following sentence: 'There stand the satyr-faced plump urns that spill superfluous oleander for the sparrow rooting for grubs among festoons of flowers.' Not surprisingly, perhaps, this line was cut.

36. Widdicombe, G. (1977) 'Troilus revisited', *Music and Musicians*, 25, p. 5.

37. Act II, Rehearsal Figures 1–22.

38. 'Put off the serpent girdle', a song sung by Cressida's waiting ladies as she is prepared for bed.

39. Hassall's first draft read:

How can I sleep? Dazzled, afraid,
My thoughts keep returning,
ever, ever one way;
like moths to a candle:
The flame is Troilus!

In the light of Walton's advice, it was revised as follows:

How can I sleep? All thro' that stupid game
the table swam before me.
I could think of nothing, nothing but Troilus.
Must I again endure this wild unrest?. . .

40. Following the opera's first performance, the aspect of the work that dominated its critical reception was this reliance upon standard operatic procedures and forms. Peter Heyworth, for example, felt that 'an attempt to work on an imposing scale lured the composer into borrowing too many *grandes toilettes* for the occasion'(Kennedy (1989) op. cit., p. 202).

41. Hassall originally intended that Troilus, who was to be party to Pandarus's trickery, should enter by a secret door concealed in the scenery. Walton dismissed this notion on the grounds that it was 'too conspiratorial'.

42. Even at this early stage Walton frequently appears to have rewritten lines of text that he did not feel were appropriate. At the point where Troilus bursts into the bed-chamber Hassall originally had the character exclaim 'Cressida, be comforted'; Walton did not feel this 'emphatic enough' and added his own line, 'Enough of this damnable lying' (for this passage in its finished form see Hassall (1954) op. cit., pp. 40–1).

43. The idea of opening the opera with a prelude was later suggested by others (among them Walter Legge and the composer and pianist Franz Reisenstein) but Walton, having abandoned the notion, was not to change his mind.

44. This is the first reference to what was eventually to become 'Is Cressida a slave?', Troilus's main aria of Act I.

45. Walton was never to be entirely satisfied with this section, which he described as 'a routine piece of composition'. The composer did not feel it was dramatically effective either: it was amongst the very first passages to be cut from the score for the 1963 revival.

46. Walton suggested that Hassall employ 'Dio, fulgar' from Verdi's *Otello* as a model on which to base the chorus verses.

47. On 2 February 1950, Stanford Robinson, Head of BBC Opera, had suggested that the opera's first performance should take place not in the studio but in the concert hall. Replying on 1 March, Walton dismissed this idea: 'For one thing I don't think it would stand the cold hard light of a concert performance, & it may, with luck, just get away with it on the stage.' Certain members of the BBC's staff, already unhappy that Walton had failed to comply with the time-limit of the commission, were concerned by Walton's apparent disregard for the conditions of the commision. The BBC Written Archives contain a memo in an unidentified hand stating that, 'We must remind W W that a BBC performance must come before a Covent Garden one!' In the October of 1950, R. J. F. Howgill, a senior member of the BBC's music department, met with Walton to discuss the relationship of the BBC to the opera. Howgill reported (18 October) that Walton, 'now finds that it [*Troilus and Cressida*] is turning out to be so essentially a stage work that he is anxious that it should not have its first performance as a studio opera . . . he is willing to forego the commission'. The commission was paid, however, thus ensuring that the BBC's name was linked to the work. Walton was paid in two instalments of £250, on 21 September 1953 and in October 1954. Hassall received 175 guineas for his contribution to the work.

48. Legge's opinion was of particular importance to Walton, as he was composing the role of Cressida with Legge's wife, the German soprano Elisabeth Schwarzkopf in mind; as well as dominating his wife's career, Legge was also Head of EMI Records, whom Walton hoped might record the work once it was completed. Schwarzkopf was never to sing the role on stage (though she did record certain passages of the opera, with Walton conducting, in 1955). In his memoirs, Legge was to describe the opera's text as 'Ivor Novelloish' in reference to Hassall's previous collaboration with the popular composer (Schwarzkopf, E. (1982) *On And Off the Record: A Memoir of Walter Legge*, London: Faber & Faber, p. 143).

49. Walton had worked with Irving on several theatre projects during the war, including, in 1941, *Macbeth* (for which Walton provided incidental music) and the ballet *The Quest* (1943).

50. Amongst other things, Walton spent the summer months of 1950 revising the Overture, *Scapino* (1940) (see Craggs, S. (1990) *William Walton: A Catalogue*, Oxford: OUP, p. 80).

51. Walton became quite fond of this particular joke, frequently employing it to disparage his librettist's contribution. Hassall's papers (now housed in Cambridge University Library) contain a letter Walton wrote to Hassall in 1963, apologizing for having referred in an interview with Arthur Jacobs to the 'ghost of Ivor Novello' having 'guided his fingers'. Thirteen years after Hassall's death, Walton stated that 'I think his [Hassall's] style had been ruined by Ivor Novello' (interviewed by Alan Blyth in *The Times*, 12 November 1976). According to Susana Walton, 'he [Walton] came to believe that Ivor Novello had taken possession of Christopher's soul' (Walton, S. (1988), op. cit., p. 135).

52. Hassall's original suggestion read:

> If one last doubt, one lurking fear remains
> Banish it, Cressida. Put your trust in me.
> I was his victim too. He summon'd me;
> I obeyed, just for one glimpse of you.
> How could I stay away? Be comforted . . .

53. It is tempting to suggest that Walton's interest in Cressida's fears stemmed from his own emotional insecurities. The image of Walton as a man haunted by the fear of

rejection and loneliness has been put forward, most notably in Tony Palmer's television documentary on Walton made in 1981 entitled *At the Haunted End of the Day* (the title is of course derived from Cressida's main aria of Act II). Quite how much, if any, insight into Walton's psyche the choice of *Troilus and Cressida* reveals is obviously difficult to gauge. It is perhaps not so much the case that Cressida's emotions are a unconscious reflection of the composer's psychological makeup, but rather that Walton's biographical persona has unwittingly absorbed the characteristics of his heroine.

54. Hassall's first draft began as follows:

> O strange, new love,
> You parted the storm like a curtain.
> I was alone and afraid,
> Come put your arms, like the walls of a city,
> Strong around me.
>
> Kind are the gods,
> Or our joys have silenced over Olympus.
> Their threats are over.
> They have pass'd us by.
> Far away on their shining journey
> They frown no longer . . .

55. Walton's doubts reflect his thorough working knowledge of operatic convention: Abbate has described how 'Wagner knew well enough that denouements should never be arrested by epic exposition; in opera, especially, swift pacing for endings is critical' (Abbate, C. (1991) *Unsung Voices*, Princeton, NJ: Princeton University Press, p. 239).

56. Auden described the island as 'one of the loveliest spots on earth' (Carpenter, H. (1981) *W. H. Auden: A Biography*, London: Allen & Unwin, p. 357).

57. Auden was an experienced librettist, of course, having collaborated with Britten on *Paul Bunyan* (1939) and with Stravinsky on *The Rake's Progress* (1949).

58. Around this time, Walton wrote to Roy Douglas that he was 'still having libretto trouble with Act III but Auden . . . is having a go at it so I'm hoping it may turn out not to be quite so awful in the end' (Kennedy, (1989) op. cit., p. 161).

59. For the service Walton provided a Te Deum and the march, *Orb and Sceptre*. These were composed between November 1952 and February 1953. A further slight delay ensued when Walton was asked to contribute to *Variations on an Elizabethan Theme 'Sellinger's Round'* for the Aldeburgh Festival of 1953 (see Craggs (1990), op. cit., p. 116).

60. At this point in the published text Cressida exclaims:

> No more, my heart have done with waiting.
> Take it. [the scarf]
> Take all you ask of me,
> and let it be for ever.

61. The involvement of Chester Kallman in this draft has previously gone unnoticed. Auden and Kallman frequently collaborated when writing texts for the stage, most famously for Stravinsky's *The Rake's Progress*. That Kallman played a part in the draft conclusion of *Troilus and Cressida* is evidenced in several sources; 'both he [Auden] and Chester [Kallman] had separately reached the conclusion that a Quintet or Sextet or some such concerted piece was needed', Walton informed Hassall (undated letter, written at some point in January 1954), whilst Hassall, having drawn up a revised version of the opera's conclusion in the light of Auden and Kallman's contribution, remarked how he had 'borrowed a phrase or two of Chester's which I liked'. (In the Auden/Kallman draft Diomede exclaims 'How comes it, Troilus, you wander here?' to which Troilus answers 'Trojan and Greek in time of truce are free'. In

Hassall's revised libretto Diomede asks 'How comes it you wander about our camp at will?' to which Troilus responds 'Trojan and Greek in time of truce are friends'. Both lines survived to the libretto's final form, though Walton recast Troilus's line, giving it to Pandarus.) Edward Mendelson (Auden's literary executor) has provided details of a draft copy of Auden's sextet, found posthumously amongst his papers. At the foot of this draft, Auden has written 'Then Chester's MSS'. Mendelson suggests that 'Chester' 'is presumably a slip of the pen for "Christopher" [Hassall]' (Mendelson (1993) *W. H. Auden and Chester Kallman. Libretti and other dramatic writings by W. H. Auden 1939–1973*, London: Faber and Faber, pp. 503–6). It would appear more likely that both Kallman and Auden were involved in composing this alternative denouement, and that Auden may have, in fact, supplied only the sextet.

62. In this same letter, Walton vividly described the intended effect of the interlude: 'Its form is like this: 48 sec. storm to where the gauze comes down, 40 sec. fumbling and then back to the "storm" for 40 sec. and the "effing" and storm work up to a climax for another 40 sec. (in fact, if without offence I may say so, they come together) followed by 45 sec. dawn . . .'.

63. Walton had hinted at this possibility in a letter of 21 January 1954: 'Evadne is a bloody bore & I don't see the absolute necessity of her treachery being brought to Cres's notice.'

64. Hassall's sextet is a virtuoso piece of writing, rather pointedly outdoing Auden's ensemble. Where Auden had written only four, eight-line verses (Evadne, Calkas and Pandarus were to sing the same words), Hassall provided individual stanzas, of ten lines, for each of the six characters. Hassall followed Auden's example in employing the same rhyme-scheme in each stanza, but skilfully used the same rhyme-sounds as well, a not inconsiderable feat.

65. It is perhaps surprising that Walton, intent on avoiding comparison with Wagner, was not concerned by the similarity of Troilus's death with that of the death of Siegfried at the hand of Hagen.

66. A final reunion for the two lovers had been a suggestion of Ernest Newman's. Walton had become slightly wary of Newman's opinions, as he wrote to Hassall in January 1954: 'though while trusting dear Ernest N's judgement to a large extent, one mustn't forget that he can't but help seeing things through rose Wagnered spectacles'. Amongst other things, Newman advised that Troilus must die on stage (and not be carried off to Troy) and that Cressida should sing her final lament over his body. Walton was determined that similarity with *Tristan and Isolde* be avoided 'at all costs'. It must have been frustrating for the composer to discover the opinion of Frank Howes, who, in what remains the standard survey of Walton's music, states 'The comparison that forces itself upon me is *Tristan and Isolde*' (Howes (1965) *The Music of William Walton*, Oxford: OUP, p. 191).

67. It is interesting to note that Walton had resorted to the writing of a march-like passage when 'stuck' during the composition of *Belshazzar's Feast*. Kennedy has described the music heard at the entry of Diomede and the chorus as 'a sad let-down at a crucial point' (Kennedy (1989), op. cit., p. 192).

68. In order to lessen the (perhaps comical) difficulty of Cressida attempting to conceal a weapon whilst she sings, Walton suggested that the soldiers who come to apprehend her should enter only once the aria was completed. This was adopted.

69. The worst piece in the work, Walton felt, was Troilus's Act I aria 'Child of the wine-dark wave', which he described as his 'most sensitive point' (letter of 9 March 1954). The composer need not have worried over the interlude, which was generally regarded as the high point of the entire opera: Kennedy has described 'Child of the wine-dark wave' as 'feeble' however (1989, op. cit., p. 192).

9   The Recorded Works
Lyndon Jenkins

As the twentieth century progressed it became quite the accepted thing for composers to produce a comprehensive recording of their musical *oeuvres*. But Edward Elgar was the first in any country, and while others followed – Rachmaninov in the USA, for instance, and later Stravinsky – so far as England is concerned, William Walton was the second.

In coming to the gramophone, of course, his and Elgar's situations were quite dissimilar. Elgar was nearing 60 when he began recording his works, Walton a mere 27. At Elgar's earliest sessions, in 1914, the gramophone was still widely regarded as something of a toy, the acoustic process of recording almost primitive: a ludicrously reduced orchestra and music that more often than not had to be severely truncated to fit the length of shellac sides lasting only a few minutes was the order of the day. At least by the time Walton stepped into a recording studio for the first time in 1929 electrical recording spared him some of that. The other significant difference between them was that Elgar was already long established as the pre-eminent interpreter of his own music, while Walton had no track record at all; in fact when he made his début as a conductor, directing the première of *Façade* in 1922, the music was making its début too. Facing a hostile critical reception, a bemused audience and rebellious players – 'Has any clarinet player ever done you an injury?' he was asked by his clarinettist Paul Draper – that early *Façade* must have been a baptism of fire, but it doubtless stood him in good stead in learning how to deal with players. At the first performance Edith Sitwell alone declaimed her poems to Walton's instrumental accompaniments, but when a young man named Constant Lambert (1905–51) came on the scene he was soon taking part as well. Lambert was an exact contemporary of Walton and the pair quickly became friends, so it was natural that when *Façade* was put down for recording in 1929 Lambert should join Edith Sitwell in the studio. In Walton's opinion Lambert was one of the best of all the reciters of *Façade*, and it is not difficult to see why. Even in an essentially rhythmic number such as the *Polka* there is a natural musical quality to Lambert's speech.

Despite having made successful recording and conducting débuts Walton was not immediately taken up as a conductor of his own music, although he did take charge of the first performance of his Viola Concerto in 1929. Afterwards, most of the premières of the major works were taken by other batons and are worth detailing for the cosmopolitan balance they disclose: while *Belshazzar's Feast* and the two symphonies remained firmly in the hands of Malcolm Sargent (1895–1967), Hamilton Harty (1879–1941) and John Pritchard (1921–1989) respectively, the first (1928) version of the *Sinfonia Concertante* for orchestra with piano obbligato went to Ernest Ansermet, the Violin Concerto to Artur Rodzinski, and the Cello Concerto to Charles Munch.

After the 1929 *Façade* recording the next gramophone opportunity did not present itself to Walton until 1936 when EMI's recording impresario Walter Legge (1906–79) invited him to record *Façade* in its purely orchestral arrangement. This was a great success: working with the crack players of the London Philharmonic Orchestra, founded four years earlier by Sir Thomas Beecham (1879–1961), Walton obtained playing that was smart and polished to an enviable degree. Among many outstanding touches Léon Goossens's oboe playing in the *Popular Song* is inimitable. A small anomaly may strike the listener familiar with the dates and contents of the two orchestral *Façade* suites published in 1926 and 1938 respectively. The first consists of five movements and the second (introduced in New York in 1938 by John Barbirolli (1899–1970), then the conductor of the Philharmonic-Symphony Orchestra) of a further six; yet despite No. 2 not being published until 1938 most of it was evidently written earlier, because Walton had added four of its movements to the first Suite's five in his 1936 recording. Completion followed, for the gramophone at least, when the two missing numbers from Suite No. 2, *Noche espagñole* and *Old Sir Faulk*, were added in 1938 as a coupling for *Siesta*. As before Walton conducted the LPO, with Legge as producer, so that when all the *Façade* pieces were collected together for their first reissue in 1986 (with *Noche espagñole* and *Old Sir Faulk* restored to their rightful places) the sound quality from separate sessions two years apart was found to match perfectly satisfactorily.

The delightfully romantic miniature *Siesta* dates from 1926 and is important, aside from its intrinsic merit, as being one of the few works that Walton himself introduced, at an Aeolian Hall concert in London that same year. 'A charming piece!', its composer remarked upon hearing a recording of it many years later. He claimed then that he had almost forgotten it but, upon renewing its aquaintance, decided to revise it and it found a place in his last recording sessions in 1970.

At the end of 1936 the BBC offered Walton a commission to write a ceremonial march for the coronation on 12 May 1937 of King George VI and Queen Elizabeth. Perhaps the triumphal music in *Belshazzar's Feast* opened their minds to the thought that Walton might be the natural successor to Elgar (who had died in 1934) as a composer of ceremonial marches. Walton duly obliged with *Crown Imperial*, which was recorded – with a fine display of financial acumen – one month before the coronation so that the record could go on sale immediately afterwards. Walton was not asked to conduct, though this was understandable:

the BBC had commissioned the piece and naturally they wanted their own Symphony Orchestra to play it under their director of music, Adrian Boult.

In 1937 Walton was invited by Decca Records Ltd to record his Viola Concerto for them. Decca was at that time a small company, hardly the equal of HMV or Columbia, but under its energetic chairman Edward Lewis had achieved a considerable coup the previous year by rushing out a recording of Sir Hamilton Harty and the London Symphony Orchestra in Walton's First Symphony within a few weeks of its première. It is clear now that Edward Lewis actually paid the costs of this recording (about £650) out of his own pocket. The symphony had become all the rage, partly because it had had a somewhat bumpy gestation. When in 1933, with most of the music written, Walton found his creative powers hanging fire, the LSO and Harty obligingly postponed the advertised première for a whole season. But when nothing had changed as the new date approached they determined to play what there was and, on 3 December 1934, they did. Completion of the symphony followed the next year and the work was heard in its final form on 6 November 1935. Harty now conducted the BBC Symphony Orchestra, but the LSO was not to be out-manoeuvred and, with the support of Edward Lewis and Decca, quickly announced that they were going to record it with Harty on 10 and 11 December 1935.

Despite appalling playing and recording conditions in an unheated, rarely-used warehouse in Thames Street above London's Cannon Street Station – reached via a graveyard and then up endless flights of rickety stairs – Harty and the LSO produced a performance which, in Constant Lambert's words, '[had] all the vitality' one expects from this orchestra and conductor in collaboration'.[1] Hubert Foss, head of the Oxford University Press Music Department and Walton's publisher and friend, effectively acted as producer during the two days. Just one of his problems was avoiding the train whistles from the Underground finding their way onto the records. Although Walton was present it was Foss who had to deal directly with Harty on all matters affecting the recording, as a laconic sentence in a letter at the time reveals: 'I had to have a few words (which Willie meant but would not say) with Harty . . . [who] . . . became like a lamb after losing his temper.'[2]

In an article in the February 1953 issue of *The Gramophone* Foss, inexplicably trying to convey the impression that he had merely happened to be present at the sessions, recalled how 'the trials and tribulations of those grim hours were lightened by the visits of distinguished guests who dropped in unheralded – Constant Lambert, Alan Rawsthorne, Spike Hughes and others . . .'. One of the 'lightened' moments must have been the sight and sound of those present in the recording room singing what Walton termed 'the bawdy words' of *Colonel Bogey* to the Symphony's finale. Walton himself had made the discovery that they fitted the music and consequently led the unusual 'première' which, apparently, bewildered and shocked the recording staff by its frivolity.

Decca's enterprise was well rewarded: within six weeks of the Symphony's issue they had sold 400 sets of the six records, including a remarkable 87 during

Christmas week. It was an astute piece of business, and now the company was keen to capitalize on its success with another Walton work. As soloist for the Viola Concerto they proposed Paul Hindemith, who had premièred the work under Walton's baton in 1929. Walton was grateful to Hindemith, who had stepped into the breach when Lionel Tertis (1876–1975) had unexpectedly turned the Concerto down, but this did not blind him to shortcomings in Hindemith's playing: 'His technique was marvellous', he said, 'but he was rough. No nonsense about it: he just stood up and played.' Tertis was critical too: 'The notes were all there, but the tone was cold and unpleasing.' He thought the instrument Hindemith played was partly responsible: 'It didn't deserve to be called a viola', he said, 'it was far too small.' Tertis had quickly realized his error in rejecting the Concerto and became one of its greatest advocates, although he never really grew to love it. He was more in love with the viola, to which he had devoted his life in furthering the cause of what had long been regarded as the 'cinderella' of the orchestra. Realizing that the instrument had practically no repertoire of its own he launched a tireless campaign among composers for solo pieces and was rewarded by a number of works from Vaughan Williams, Holst, Bax and others: several bore dedications to him and many he introduced.

Quite why Tertis rejected Walton's concerto (which Beecham had suggested as a vehicle for him) has never been fully explained, although he claimed at the time to be out of sympathy with Walton's style. Whatever it was, his conversion was rapid: he played it for the first time less than a year after the première and, by the time of Decca's recording initiative, had become closely identified with it. All this makes it more surprising than ever that it was Hindemith that Decca wanted to record the work; not only Tertis, but the young William Primrose (1904–82) had played the Concerto in London the previous year, so he was another possibility. In the event none of them played for the recording: Frederick Riddle, principal viola of the London Symphony Orchestra which Walton was to conduct at the sessions, carried it off with great success.

With the Viola Concerto safely on disc for Decca, Walton returned to EMI and his allegiance to that company remained constant throughout the next 30 years. He and Walter Legge celebrated their new partnership by recording music that Walton had selected from various passages of J. S. Bach and clothed in modern orchestral dress for the ballet *The Wise Virgins*. After the ballet's première at Sadler's Wells under Constant Lambert in April 1940 Walton had made a concert suite of six of the nine movements. This gave EMI the opportunity of a 'novelty' (which gramophone companies always relish) and Walter Legge hurried the composer and the Sadler's Wells Orchestra into a recording studio to make sure of it for his own company. By this time, he and Walton knew each other well. Legge saw the point of Walton's scores as clearly as anybody, and was determined to persevere with the concept of Walton directing recordings of his own music.

The outbreak of war in 1939 meant Legge abandoning large-scale recording in London, so instead he struck up fruitful associations with the City of Birmingham and Liverpool Philharmonic orchestras as well as the Hallé in Manchester.

Constant Lambert, Malcolm Sargent, Leslie Heward and Warwick Braithwaite undertook often hazardous wartime journeys to these orchestras to keep the HMV and Columbia catalogues stocked with new recordings. When Birmingham was dropped after being blitzed Legge centred himself upon Manchester and the Hallé, despite the changes that were imminent there: indeed when Walton made his record of the *'Spitfire' Prelude and Fugue* with the Hallé, Barbirolli had only recently arrived from the USA to begin his famous rebuilding of the Orchestra. Walton unexpectedly became involved in a piece of gramophone history, because his disc was actually the last the 'old' Hallé made, on 24 June 1943: three days later the Orchestra gave its final concert, under Malcolm Sargent, and then overnight half the players left to return to the BBC's Northern Orchestra. But during the previous four weeks Barbirolli had been busy auditioning new players to fill the anticipated gaps, and the 'new' 70-strong Hallé assembled for its first rehearsal the very next morning after the Sargent concert.

The name of Constant Lambert, one of the greatest of Walton's musical contemporaries, has already been mentioned: a fine conductor as well as composer, he was very active in the recording studio at this time for Walter Legge on his own account in a whole range of music from Auber overtures to Tchaikovsky symphonies. However, after the 1936 *Façade* session, whenever Walton works were scheduled for recording Legge tried to arrange sessions with Lambert present as well. Possibly he felt that Walton would benefit from somebody of greater experience having charge of the orchestra first; perhaps Lambert even rehearsed the Walton pieces in readiness for the composer to take over. *Siesta* and the two *Façade* movements in 1938 were the first products of these dual sessions (at which Lambert conducted Delius's *On hearing the First Cuckoo in Spring*) while the *'Spitfire' Prelude and Fugue* came at the end of a session at which Lambert completed his Columbia recording of Borodin's Second Symphony. Lambert himself made only one recording of Walton's music: in 1950 Legge invited him to replace the composer's – by then elderly-sounding – 1936 version of the *Façade* orchestral suites. This Lambert did, quite brilliantly, but it was his last recording: he died the following year at the age of only 46.

The last joint Walton–Lambert session had taken place in 1945. Walter Legge had assembled 24 strings as the basis of what was to become the Philharmonia Orchestra, and he was trying them out in the studio under conductors such as Lambert and Walter Susskind. The music, the 'Two Pieces for Strings' from *Henry V*, was needed to provide the sixth side 'fill-up' to the *Sinfonia Concertante* set which Walton had already made for HMV with Phyllis Sellick and the City of Birmingham Orchestra. Since it was Miss Sellick's husband, Cyril Smith, who had given the first performance of the *Sinfonia Concertante* in its newly revised form in Liverpool in February 1944 under Sargent, it would have seemed logical that he should also have done the recording; but a letter from Legge to the CBO setting up the Walton session showed that it was his intention all along that Smith's wife should make the records. No doubt this was another of those occasions when the demarcation lines between the two EMI labels, HMV and

Columbia, needed to be respected: Walton was (up to then) an HMV artist, Smith's records appeared on the Columbia label.

Legge would surely have appreciated Constant Lambert's help at the two Sunday sessions in Liverpool in January 1943 at which the prodigious feat (for those days) of recording *Belshazzar's Feast* was undertaken. According to a local newspaper report, it took ten hours. Instead he recruited another conductor, also a composer and friend of Walton's as well as being intimately acquainted with his music, to help on the technical side. This was Ernest Irving (1877–1953), whose experience with the baton in theatre pits and film and recording studios was legendary. At one point in the recording he detected a rise in pitch and insisted that the passage be repeated; no more satisfied with the repetition he asked for a second retake, but when singers and instrumentalists united in an even louder groan than had greeted his first request he let it go. Later he had the finished records tested with a tuning fork, and was vindicated: the passage was a quarter of a tone above pitch.

The first of the two recording sessions was preceded by a concert performance on the previous afternoon in Liverpool. Walton conducted a programme entirely of his own music including, in addition to *Belshazzar's Feast*, the *'Spitfire' Prelude and Fugue* (first performance) and the Violin Concerto with the orchestra's leader Henry Holst as soloist. This was arranged by the Liverpool Philharmonic Society in conjunction with the British Council who were also the sponsors of the records. Walton must have been delighted to find that the Liverpool Philharmonic of that period included, besides Holst, such celebrated players as David Wise, Herbert Downes and Anthony Pini as the other string principals, and Reginald Kell and John Alexandra among the woodwind. These were a few of a select group of players who had moved to Liverpool in 1942 after finding themselves high and dry when the BBC disbanded the Salon Orchestra which it had formed at the outbreak of war specially for broadcasting purposes.

The name of Rex Mortimer from the illustrious northern brass family among the extra contingents brought in for *Belshazzar's Feast* recalls the famous story that it was Beecham, as conductor-in-chief of the Leeds Festival, who advised Walton to 'throw in a couple of brass bands' when they discussed the production of the new work at a meeting in Leeds early in 1931 prior to its first performance there that year under Malcolm Sargent. There are various versions of this story, but its main thrust is now more or less discredited, even if it did originate with Walton. What is difficult to believe is that Beecham was at all interested in the precise scoring of *Belshazzar's Feast*. He was not even going to conduct it, having his hands full of scores which were much more to his liking such as Handel's *Solomon* and Delius's *A Mass of Life* besides Berlioz's *Grande Messe des Morts*. More likely, the presence in the Leeds programme of the Berlioz, which is scored for a great deal of extra brass, held the key to the whole incident: the additional forces were available anyway. For all we know the idea might have been Walton's own, and he subsequently thought it might be amusing to lend Beecham's name to it: Walton could dissemble with the best. But however the idea arose, the brass bands went in. The première was a famous triumph, especially for Malcolm Sargent, who was credited with bringing off a tremendous feat of choral conducting. Only Walton was dissatisfied: he thought the performance lasted ten minutes longer than he had wanted, though it is difficult to believe that so great a disparity in timing could occur in a work lasting only 35 minutes.

The mention of Sargent's name raises the question of why *he* did not conduct the *Belshazzar's Feast* recording for EMI. After all, he had had an outstanding triumph with it at Leeds. For sheer excitement that première still ranks among the great nights of British music: principally Walton's doing, of course, but there is little doubt that Sargent's choral skill and flair in bringing off that first of hundreds of performances he was to give which raised the roof in dozens of English and foreign concert-halls helped put *Belshazzar's Feast* firmly on the musical map. From that moment it was 'a Sargent score' and he remained faithful to it throughout his long career; he conducted it on tours to Australia in 1938 and 1939, and later in Brussels, Vienna and Boston as well as regularly at the London Promenade Concerts. Moreover, the choral and orchestral forces taking part in the recording, the Liverpool Philharmonic Orchestra and the Huddersfield Choral Society, were 'his' at that time, and so it would have seemed both natural and commercially sensible that Sargent, well established as England's greatest choral director and with an enormous popular following among the record-buying public, should have conducted.

Probably it was Walter Legge who stuck out for Walton, perhaps citing the greater authority that the composer's name would lend to a British Council-sponsored recording. Perhaps, too, only Walton had the time to give to the project: he was able to spend a fortnight preparing everybody in the run-up to the recording whereas Sargent was a notoriously busy man. It was not long since his commitments had forced him to cut in half a recording session he was doing for Legge with the Hallé, leaving the orchestra's leader to conduct the rest; Legge would not have liked that, particularly as it meant he had to omit any mention of a conductor from the record labels, thereby losing the commercial advantage of Sargent's name. Legge and Sargent were, in any case, uneasy bedfellows: in 1937 Legge had reviewed Sargent's conducting of the première of *In Honour of the City of London* most unfavourably against a subsequent Walton perform-ance: Walton's account, he wrote, 'at once showed up the shortcomings of the first performance and the intrinsic worth which the first performance partly obscured'.[3] In 1945 Legge recorded Elgar's *The Dream of Gerontius* with Sargent, but after that they did not work together again in the recording studio for many years, and then only over a 'starry' concerto collaboration in 1958; and even though Sargent made records with Legge's Philharmonia Orchestra from 1947 onwards, he invariably had another producer. Legge's decision probably arose out of a combination of all these things, together with his growing conviction that Walton was a first-rate conductor of his own music; while he was available and they got on well, no doubt Legge planned to continue to use him.

In 1953 an attempt was made to transfer Walton's pioneering recording of

Belshazzar's Feast from 78s to LP, but it was a failure: 'a mere adumbration of the original' was how the 1955 *Record Guide* quite rightly described it. Time has shown, however, that it was not the tape made from the 78s that was below standard because, in 1992, the same tape was used with highly satisfactory results as the basis of the issue of the performance on CD: rather, it was the process of making the LP disc from the tape that was at fault. The same thing was to happen in the case of Walton's performance of his First Symphony (see below). The preservation of Walton's 1943 recording of *Belshazzar's Feast*, quite apart from its outstanding musical merit, is also important in that it gives us the original score. In 1948 he rethought some vocal passages in the final chorus, and adjusted the orchestration both there and elsewhere. Subsequently he was to extend and rescore the concluding bars of the work, filling out the final chord with the organ. These definitive thoughts were first heard on disc when Sargent finally made his own recording of *Belshazzar's Feast* in 1958.

After the war Walton recorded almost exclusively with Legge's new Philharmonia Orchestra, and between 1945–1963 undertook an extended survey of his music in the ever-improving sound that marked the various periods. Legge's enthusiasm for the music remained constant. Though not notably a film man, he even arranged for Walton to make a studio recording of excerpts from the score he had composed for the soundtrack of Henry V (first screened at London's Carlton Cinema in 1944). On these records Laurence Olivier spoke some of the lines of other characters as well as those of King Henry, and the whole sequence originally fitted onto eight 78rpm sides. When these were prepared later for microgroove issue, they proved too long for a single LP side, and about seven minutes of music was cut from the beginning and end of the sequence. In EMI's 'Walton Edition' (1994) these passages were restored for the first time since the 78s were in circulation.

Earlier the same year (1946) Walton made his second recording of his Viola Concerto, this time with William Primrose as soloist. Like Lionel Tertis, Primrose was originally a violinist but he found himself drawn to the viola partly through Tertis's pioneering work on its behalf; according to Tertis it was after a performance of Mozart's *Sinfonia Concertante K364* in which the 24-year-old Glaswegian played violin to Tertis's viola that Primrose made the break. Primrose became a staunch champion of Walton's Concerto: he introduced it in the USA and, as well as his 1946 version with the composer, recorded it again later with Sargent. In both these versions the revised scoring which Walton had made by 1936 can be heard. In 1961 he made an extensive further revision of the orchestration but left the solo part unaltered, 'save for an odd 8ve here and there – mostly culled from W.P.'s performance'.

It was William Primrose who in 1936 suggested Walton's name to Jascha Heifetz, who was looking to commission a violin concerto. Walton jumped at the chance, knowing instinctively that the association with Heifetz's name would be invaluable, and that it would guarantee a recording of the concerto when it was written. He was right: very soon the first performance was being sought by the

British Council for inclusion in one of the concerts connected with the World Trades Fair in New York in 1939. But that première never took place. The British Council, with a supreme lack of understanding of world-famous violinists' engagement diaries, left it too late to secure Heifetz for the date of the concert. The next plan was for a first performance in Boston with Walton conducting the Boston Symphony Orchestra, but the outbreak of war in September 1939 prevented Walton from travelling and eventually conducting the Concerto. Although Walton was correct in forecasting a quick recording, any hopes he might have had of conducting it himself were again frustrated. While he was trapped in England it was recorded in Cincinnati in February 1941, with Eugene Goossens conducting. It was not until 1950 that Walton had his own chance at the work with Heifetz, on one of the latter's visits to England. They played it together at the Royal Festival Hall on 9 June prior to recording it over two days, later in the month. Walton had revised the Concerto's orchestration in 1943, so that a comparison between his and Heifetz's version with Goossens is highly instructive: in effect, the second version amounts to a complete rescoring. Walton said at the time that he had started out to do 'a little patching here and there', but found it was not a satisfactory way of doing it . . . 'so more or less I started from the beginning . . .'.

With the introduction of tape recording in 1948 heralding the arrival of the long-playing record, Legge knew that some of Walton's large-scale works such as the First Symphony had become a more realistic proposition for the gramophone. Even though Harty's old recording was still available he was especially anxious to attempt the Symphony with the composer conducting and, in October 1951, they set to work. In the event a disappointing tape-to-disc transfer, not uncommon in those days, resulted in poor sound on the finished record and it was only when EMI returned to the original tapes when preparing an 80th birthday tribute of Walton's recordings in 1982 that it was fully appreciated what a fine performance he had secured on that occasion. At the same sessions he conducted his *Scapino* overture, though this was only ever issued in 78rpm form and became a rare and most collectable item among Walton enthusiasts. *Scapino* had been commissioned by the Chicago Symphony Orchestra to commemorate the 50th anniversary of its founding in 1891. Walton was the only British composer among ten who were invited to contribute new works. Dedicated to the Orchestra and its conductor Frederick Stock, the Overture was given its first performance by them in April 1941. They subsequently made a record of it which is once again of particular interest because it presents the original score. When Walton revised *Scapino* in 1950 the new première was secured by Legge for a Philharmonia concert in London in November 1950 when the conductor was, unusually, Wilhelm Furtwängler.

Next on disc from Walton came a miscellany of shorter pieces, notably his newest march, *Orb and Sceptre*, composed for the coronation in 1953 of Queen Elizabeth II. Displaying the same sound commercial sense as his 1937 predecessors, Legge arranged for Walton to record this several months before the royal event so that the music could be released on its own on a single 78rpm disc without delay. On its subsequent LP issue it was joined by the earlier coronation march *Crown Imperial, Portsmouth Point* and 'Sheep may safely graze' from *The Wise Virgins*, by then a popular favourite and recorded by other conductors besides Walton.

More recordings followed at regular intervals. The ever-popular orchestral suites from *Façade* were begun in April 1955, though not completed until 1957 when they were launched with the bonus of Walton's latest *pièce d'occasion*, the scintillating *Johannesburg Festival Overture*. This exhilarating piece was the result of another commission, this time from the City of Johannesburg which was planning a music festival to mark its 70th anniversary in 1956. Sargent introduced it there with the South African Broadcasting Company's Symphony Orchestra. It is typical of Walton in his most unbuttoned mood: 'slightly crazy, hilarious and vulgar', was his own highly apt description. Indeed it is in many ways a pity that such a delightful *jeu d'esprit* is saddled with a title which surely mitigates against more frequent performance. Walton's recording was the first work of his to be issued in stereo.

Meanwhile in 1954 *Troilus and Cressida* had been premièred at Covent Garden, again under Sargent. It brought in its wake something of a cooling in the relationship between Walton and Walter Legge from which it perhaps never quite recovered. This arose because even in the earliest stages of its composition Legge had been severely critical of some aspects of the opera, and then his wife, Elisabeth Schwarzkopf, declined to sing the role of Cressida which Walton had composed with her voice in mind. She never sang it on the stage. Perhaps partly as a peace offering, in 1955 Legge invited Walton to record some scenes from the opera with Schwarzkopf singing. The result was a uniquely valuable historic document, not only for Schwarzkopf (and for Richard Lewis, the original Troilus) but because it contained some passages that Walton later cut from his score. Always the inveterate reviser, he first pruned each Act between the première and some performances which followed the next year under Reginald Goodall. Subsequently he shortened the work by another eight minutes for its first Covent Garden revival in 1963, and by a further 30 for the next revival, which was not until 1976; by this time he had also transposed the role of Cressida down so that Janet Baker could sing it. The contrast between what is heard in these 1955 excerpts and EMI's complete recording compiled from several performances at Covent Garden in 1976 is, therefore, quite marked, not only textually but in timbre.

It would seem possible that the recording of the *Troilus* excerpts mended bridges between Walton and Legge because, later in 1955 and obviously at Legge's instigation, Walton made arrangements of 'God save the Queen' and 'The Star Spangled Banner' specially for a tour of the USA which the Philharmonia Orchestra was making under Herbert von Karajan. (The previous year Karajan had played the First Symphony in Rome: Walton's frustration that nobody had let him know so that he could have heard it may be imagined.) Not content with the anthem arrangements Legge also got Walton to write a *bon voyage* message for the tour.

The language is uncharacteristically flowery for Walton, and one cannot help suspecting the hand of Legge in the drafting:

> The collaboration of the Philharmonia Orchestra of London and Austrian Herbert von Karajan has written a new and revolutionary chapter in the history of European music-making. From Shakespeare onwards Britain's supreme achievements in the arts have been the fruits of cross-fertilization of our nation's qualities with the finest flowers of the Continent. To my friend Herbert von Karajan and each individual member of the Philharmonia Orchestra I send my best wishes for every one of the concerts they play together in America.[4]

Two more composers contributed messages, Britten and Sibelius. They too might strike one as unusual for this particular task until one realizes that Karajan and the Philharmonia had recently produced recordings of their works: Legge was perhaps calling in his favours! As for the anthem arrangements, after the tour Legge had the orchestra under George Weldon record 'God Save The Queen', together with another arrangement Walton had made of it for Covent Garden's use on the opening night of Britten's new opera *Gloriana* in June 1953. But the record was never issued.

Only two more Walton–Legge collaborations now remained, the first at least marred by further controversy. In her biography of her husband, Lady Walton recalls how, during the preparations for the stereo remake of *Belshazzar's Feast* in 1959, Legge suddenly made the astonishing suggestion that the Philharmonia chorus-master, Wilhelm Pitz, should actually conduct the recording, Walton's name nevertheless to appear on the record label. It is most probable that this idea arose out of a moment during rehearsals when Walton was absent, listening to a play-back in the control room. In the hall Pitz seized the opportunity to go over some passages with the choir and Walton, returning to the recording floor, was so impressed by the results that he remarked disarmingly to the singers: 'Why can't you do it like that for me?' But if Legge saw the chance to seize an initiative, the composer would have none of it, quietly but firmly rejecting the suggestion. Lady Walton says that Legge took his revenge by withholding the composer's fee for the recording, but he may also have expressed his displeasure by absenting himself from the remaining sessions; certainly one of his assistants completed *Belshazzar's Feast*, while the recording sheets do not show a producer's name at all against *Partita for Orchestra*, recorded at the same time.

In 1960 there was disappointment for Walton when EMI decided not to record his Second Symphony. The première at that year's Edinburgh Festival by the Royal Liverpool Philharmonic Orchestra under John Pritchard had been greeted coolly by the critics and EMI wanted to wait until the work was better known. But the next year the Symphony was taken up in America by George Szell and the Cleveland Orchestra so successfully that Walton felt himself completely vindicated. These forces went on to make a magnificent recording of the work. When Walton heard it he was overjoyed, writing to Szell:

> Words fail me! It is a quite fantastic and stupendous performance from every point of view. Firstly it is absolutely right musically speaking, and the virtuosity of the

performance is quite staggering, especially the Fugato: but everything is phrased and balanced in an unbelievable way for which I must congratulate you and your magnificent orchestra. . . .

Walton had every reason to be grateful to Szell, who had performed his First Symphony as far back as 1938 when he was with the Scottish Orchestra and had not lost sight of his music in the years since. Then in 1956 Szell's orchestra in Cleveland had invited him to be one of the composers (again he was the only Englishman) to write a work for its Fortieth Anniversary Season in 1957–8. He responded with the *Partita for Orchestra*, which Szell duly introduced and subsequently recorded. Prior to the first performance the *Cleveland Plain Dealer* newspaper tried to get Walton to write them a note on the new piece. Although his response began a trifle unpromisingly, in the end it could be said that his succinct summary told them all they needed to know:

> Two major difficulties confront me in responding to your kind invitation to contribute a few words about my new Partita for Orchestra. Firstly, I am a writer of notes and (to my regret) not of prose. Secondly, it is surely easier to write about a piece of creative work if there is something problematical about it . . . Unfortunately, from this point of view, my Partita poses no problems, has no ulterior motive or meaning behind it, and makes no attempt to ponder the imponderables. I have written it in the hope that it may be enjoyed straight off. . . .

Szell and the Clevelanders maintained their enthusiasm for Walton's music, quickly taking up (and again recording) the *Variations on a theme of Hindemith* within a few weeks of the first performance which Walton conducted in London in March 1963. Walton heard them play the work in Amsterdam, afterwards writing to his publisher: 'It was stupendous. After rehearsing it he [Szell] turned to me and asked me for any comments. How can one comment on a performance which is flawless in every aspect?'

1964 saw what proved to be Walton and Legge's final sessions together. This time the music was from the film scores, most of which had been composed in the decade after 1935. At times they had been his financial saviour – never in his life, he said, had he seen such a large sum as the £300 he was paid for one of his early film scores. Legge was right to encourage its revival: Walton's film music is of a very high quality, and it would have been a great pity had it been allowed to be forgotten, especially since a fine piece such as *Spitfire Prelude and Fugue* (which so thrilled wartime cinemagoers) has subsequently proved to be capable of holding its own in the concert hall. Also included at this time was the Funeral March from *Hamlet*, the Prelude and Suite from *Richard III* and the Suite from *Henry V* in the arrangements by the conductor Muir Mathieson (1911–75).

So closed a chapter in Walton's life that had run uninterrupted for nearly 30 years. By the time they recorded the film music together Legge had already resigned from EMI and in March 1964 he astounded the musical world by announcing the disbanding of the Philharmonia Orchestra. Happily, the orchestra declined to be broken up, and successfully reappeared under the title New Philharmonia: with them but with a new producer, Ronald Kinloch Anderson,

Walton made one more recording when, in 1968, he conducted his Viola Concerto for another EMI artist of long standing, Yehudi Menuhin. This was issued with the Violin Concerto, again played by Menuhin, but recorded a year later. (Both recordings used the revised orchestrations.)

In the Violin Concerto recording Walton conducted the LSO, an orchestra which he had been gradually getting to know more intimately during the previous few years, along with André Previn who had become its principal conductor in 1968. When Walton heard in 1966 that Previn was intending to record his First Symphony he wrote to his publisher: 'I'm not sure I know who he is! Ought I to?' Previn quickly became one of his staunchest champions. Meanwhile, also in 1966, EMI decided to record the Symphony under Malcolm Sargent, which resulted in both his and Previn's recordings being published together in January 1967. Walton was photographed attending the Sargent sessions and wrote a few lines of commendation for reproduction on the record-sleeve: 'Dear Malcolm, Thank you, the orchestra and all concerned for a truly magnificent recording of my First Symphony.' Afterwards he maintained defensively that he had been 'let in for doing the blurb thro' circumstances and could hardly refuse': he regretted it more than ever when he heard the two records because he thought Previn's the better of the two.

Subsequently he was to be seen at Previn's Decca recording sessions and in 1971 travelled with him and the LSO to Russia where some performances of his Symphony were outstandingly successful. During the next few years Previn went on to record the Second Symphony, Violin Concerto, *Improvisations on an Impromptu of Benjamin Britten*, *Orb and Sceptre*, *Scapino* and *Portsmouth Point* as well as premièring the *Varii Capricci*, Walton's rescoring for full orchestra of his Five Guitar Bagatelles (1976). But the biggest scheme of all involving Previn ended in disappointment when he was prevented by illness from conducting the 1976 revival at Covent Garden of *Troilus and Cressida*: Lawrence Foster took over and a recording was subsequently issued of a performance compiled from several evenings' tapings.

1968 marked, albeit briefly, Walton's return to the Decca Company, firstly with some passages from *Troilus and Cressida* as part of a Covent Garden anniversary retrospective. These were Cressida's 'How can I sleep?' featuring Marie Collier, who had sung the role in 1963, and the ensuing scene where Pandarus gleefully announces to her Troilus's 'unexpected' arrival in his house. Peter Pears, who had been the original Pandarus in 1954 but through being contracted to Decca could not take part in the Schwarzkopf–Walton excerpts recording, repeated the role he had created. When EMI prepared their Walton-conducted excerpts for CD issue in 1994, however, permission was obtained to incorporate Pears's contribution in them; not only that, the passage was joined up in such a way that it extended EMI's 'How Can I Sleep?' sung by Schwarzkopf. Collier's few lines in the scene with Pears sound perfectly realistic in their new setting; interestingly, one hears Pears describe to her Troilus's love-stricken state with the words 'On jealousy's hot grid he roasts alive': this was later altered to 'On desire's hot grid . . .' –

Walton always had a good sense of the erotic. The next year Walton recorded, again for Decca, the complete 1951 version of *Façade* with members of the London Sinfonietta. Peggy Ashcroft and Paul Scofield were the reciters, though their contributions were added some time after Walton recorded the music and, perhaps because of it, the result was not a success.

Finally, over three days in April 1970 with either the LSO or the LPO, he recorded several of his shorter pieces for the Lyrita label. There were some pleasant surprises because, in among remakes of works he had recorded before – *Scapino*, *Portsmouth Point*, *Siesta* and the *Sinfonia Concertante* – there was one piece he had never conducted for the gramophone, *Capriccio Burlesco*, and two scores that had never appeared on disc before from anyone. *Music for Children* was his own orchestration of a handful of pieces composed in 1940 for two pianos. When recorded in May that year by Ilona Kabos and Louis Kentner (with Walton present) the two 78s joined that select group of titles whose recorded performance also constituted the music's première. (As mentioned earlier, the two coronation marches were other Waltonian contributions to this unusual *genre*.) Walton's orchestration of *Music for Children* was introduced by Basil Cameron and the LPO at a Prom in 1941 but had hardly been heard since. The other work, the ballet *The Quest*, was even less well known, never having been revived since its staging at Sadler's Wells under Constant Lambert in April 1943. In 1961 Walton and the conductor Vilem Tausky collaborated over a suite of four movements drawn from the complete score, which Tausky introduced in the same year. It was that suite that Walton now recorded. When first issued the seven Lyrita titles were awkwardly spread over three LPs, only one of them devoted solely to Walton, but in 1994 all seven were happily united on one CD.

So ended Walton's long association with the making of gramophone records. The break was in many ways unnecessary, as there was still a great deal more he could have given. He was not yet 70, relatively young by conducting standards, and while he was in general impressed and pleased by the recordings Previn was making there is always an extra element of authority when a composer is involved. Without question, all Walton's recordings bear testimony to what an eloquent interpreter he was of his own music. He always maintained that he did not enjoy conducting, though he never had any doubts about his effectiveness with the baton: 'I think I did and certainly could conduct my own music better than most conductors', he said in 1976, instancing *Portsmouth Point* '[which] was neglected because of conductors not being able to conduct it. So I had to conduct it myself because it was to me child's play . . .'. Moreover, he was always popular with orchestral players, who appreciated his laid-back style with no hint of pose. During rehearsals with the Hallé Orchestra for the British première of his *Partita for Orchestra* in 1960 he stopped at one point, saying: 'Pay no attention to me, I've got out . . . I'm only an *amateur* conductor, you know.' Players everywhere appreciated that sort of thing, and there is no reason to think that his relationships with the orchestras he conducted were ever other than completely harmonious.

The other vitally important development in his life, in the way that it affected his career as a composer-conductor, was his association with Walter Legge. There is no doubt that Legge was genuinely keen on Walton's music but it was his position at EMI which enabled him to provide Walton with the kind of patronage that every composer dreams of but few attain. To what extent Legge was motivated by the desire to challenge the other leading composer of the day, Britten, whose works were being captured contemporaneously by the Decca Record Company, can only be conjectured upon. Walton's colleagues must have looked on with envy if not bitterness; and Legge was nothing if not thorough. Between 1936 and 1964 he saw to it that nearly all the major Walton works were placed on disc, and in practically every case his personal reputation and enormous abilities as one of the world's leading recording producers lent its distinction to the finished result. It was really only in one important instance that he appeared to fail Walton: over EMI's decision not to record the Second Symphony he apparently could not (or would not) interfere.

Legge's importance is thrown into further relief by noting how Walton's position changed after Legge left EMI in 1964. Walton did not become involved in more EMI recordings until 1968/9, and then only to conduct the Concertos for Menuhin, a disc that was surely soloist-led. In the interim, recordings of his First Symphony (with Sargent) and the opera *The Bear* were made, the latter within a few weeks of its première at Aldeburgh in June 1967. While one can understand that the cast and conductor involved in *The Bear* should remain undisturbed from the first performance (even if the composer's participation would have lent the record extra authenticity) it would have seemed eminently sensible for Walton to conduct his Symphony. His recording of 1951, with its unsatisfactory reproduction, had long since disappeared and had in any case been only in monaural sound. The obvious man to make its stereo replacement would seem to have been Walton, who would have been reunited with the orchestra, the (New) Philharmonia, which he knew, and which knew him, best. Perhaps it should be said that he could not have conducted it *at that moment* because he was undergoing treatment for cancer, and it may have been his record company's anxiety to rival the RCA version by André Previn that proved too strong for them to wait.

It might also be thought strange that no attempt was made by EMI to arrange its own recording of Walton's Cello Concerto when it was new. It was RCA which moved quickly to capture the original performers (Gregor Piatigorsky, Charles Munch and the Boston Symphony Orchestra) shortly after the première on 25 January 1957 but, notwithstanding that, an alternative bearing Walton's own imprimatur would surely have had commercial appeal. Paul Tortelier might have been the man to do it: he did make a fine version of it, though not with Walton and not until 1973. By that time André Previn had joined the roster of EMI artists and was recording Walton's music with the LSO. Walton's time as composer-conductor had evidently passed.

With hindsight it is difficult not to feel that when Legge disappeared from the scene Walton's 'special relationship' with EMI went with him. Doubly fortunate, then, that Legge's patronage, if not quite encompassing everything, proved to be so wide-ranging. Whether without his personal enthusiasm for the music and the undoubted influence he had at EMI the company would have afforded Walton so benevolent an arrangement we shall never know. But it did all happen and at this distance the pattern of Walton's career as a composer-conductor is easier to distinguish. In his early days he was forced to take charge of his own music simply because its rhythmic twists and turns proved so unsettling to other conductors; to him they were second nature. Then during the Thirties he came of age as a conductor, and in the post-war period, encouraged by Walter Legge, he emerged as his music's leading interpreter, an impression nourished by the regular appearance of his own recordings. In this respect there is a distinct parallel with Elgar, who had a similar champion in Fred Gaisberg, one of Legge's EMI predecessors; and, just as in the older composer's case, the existence of Walton's equally definitive recordings shows that we have every reason to be grateful that events developed as they did.

Notes

1. Constant Lambert writing in *The Sunday Referee*, 10 November 1935, p. 20.
2. Hubert Foss cited in Michael Kennedy (1989), *Portrait of Walton*, Oxford: OUP, p. 85.
3. From a review of the first London performance of *In honour of the City of London* in *The Manchester Guardian*, 2 December 1937.
4. Quoted by Walton from G. Widdicombe, sleeve notes for the 1982 EMI recording 'Walton conducts Walton'.

Appendix

There follows a complete list of Walton's recordings of his own works.

Notes:

1. EMI SLS5246 is a four-LP set 'Walton conducts Walton' issued in 1985.
2. EMI CHS5 65003 2 is a four-CD set 'The Walton Edition' issued in 1994.
3. Recording locations are in London except where stated otherwise.

Façade, an Entertainment
11 items. Edith Sitwell, Constant Lambert (reciters), Instrumental Ensemble. 'Black Mrs Behemoth', 'Jodelling Song', 'Long Steel Grass', 'A man from a Far Countree' (Sitwell); 'Polka', 'Foxtrot' ('Old Sir Faulk'), 'Tango-Pasodoble', 'Scotch Rhapsody', 'Tarantella', 'Valse', 'Popular Song' (Lambert). Recorded Chenil Galleries, 28 November 1929. Decca T124–5 [later K991–2] (78rpm), ECM834 (33rpm), OUP110 (45rpm) [part of de luxe edition of score of *Façade*].

Complete 1951 version. Peggy Ashcroft, Paul Scofield (reciters), London Sinfonietta. Recorded Decca Studio No.3, Broadhurst Gardens, 5–7 May 1969 (music recorded first, voices added later). Argo ZRG649 (33rpm).

Façade, Suites Nos 1 and 2
London Philharmonic Orchestra. Recorded No.1 Studio, Abbey Road, 5 March 1936. ('Noche espagnole'* and 'Old Sir Faulk'* recorded 25 October 1938.) HMV C2836-7, *C3042 (78rpm), EMI ED29 0715 1 (33rpm), CDH7 63381 2 (CD).

Philharmonia Orchestra. Kingsway Hall, 20 April 1955 and 26 March 1957. Columbia 33C1054 (33rpm), EMI HQM1006 (33rpm), SLS5246 (33rpm), CHS5 65003 2 (CD).

Belshazzar's Feast
Dennis Noble (baritone), Huddersfield Choral Society, Liverpool Philharmonic Orchestra. Recorded Philharmonic Hall, Liverpool, 3 and 10 January 1943. HMV C3330-4 [Auto C7572-6] (78rpm), ALP1089 (33rpm), EMI ED29 0715 1 (33rpm), CDH7 63381 2 (CD).

Donald Bell (baritone), Philharmonia Chorus, Philharmonia Orchestra. Recorded Kingsway Hall, 2-5 February 1959. Columbia 33CX1679 (33rpm), SAX2319 (33rpm), EMI SXLP 30236 (33rpm), SLS 5246 (33rpm), CHS 5 65003 2 (CD).

Troilus and Cressida, Opera in three Acts
[Excerpts] Act 1: 'Is Cressida a slave?', 'Slowly it all comes back'. Act 2: 'How can I sleep?', 'If one last doubt remains', 'Now close your arms', Interlude, 'From isle to isle chill waters'. Act 3: 'All's well!', 'Diomede! . . . Father!'. Elisabeth Schwarzkopf (soprano), Richard Lewis (tenor), Monica Sinclair (contralto), Philharmonia Orchestra. Recorded Kingsway Hall, 18-20 April and 16 May 1955. Columbia 33CX1313 (33rpm), World Record Club OH217 (33rpm), EMI CDM7 64199 2 (CD).

[Excerpts] Act 2: 'How can I sleep?'. . ., 'Is anyone there?'.* Marie Collier (soprano), Peter Pears (tenor), Orchestra of the Royal Opera House, Covent Garden. Recorded Kingsway Hall, 26-27 February 1968 [as part of Royal Opera House Anniversary Album]. SET392-3 (33rpm), *EMI CDM7 64199 2 (CD).

Symphony No.1 in B flat minor
Philharmonia Orchestra. Recorded Kingsway Hall, 17-19 October 1951. HMV ALP1027 (33rpm), EMI SLS5246 (33rpm), CHS5 65003 2 (CD).

Portsmouth Point, Overture
Philharmonia Orchestra. Recorded Kingsway Hall, 21 March 1953. Columbia 33C1016 (33rpm), SEL1506 and SEG8217 (45rpm), EMI HQM1006 (33rpm), SLS5246 (33rpm), CHS5 65003 2 (CD).

London Philharmonic Orchestra. Recorded Walthamstow Assembly Hall, 15 April 1970. Lyrita SRCS47 (33rpm), SRCD224 (CD).

Scapino, Comedy Overture
Philharmonia Orchestra. Recorded Kingsway Hall, 19 October 1951. HMV DB21499 (78rpm), EMI ED29 0715 1 (33rpm), CDH7 63381 2 (CD).

Johannesburg Festival Overture
Philharmonia Orchestra. Recorded Kingsway Hall, 26 March 1957. Columbia 33C1054 (33rpm), EMI HQM1006 (33rpm), SLS5246 (33rpm), CHS5 65003 2 (CD).

Crown Imperial, Coronation March (1937)
Philharmonia Orchestra. Recorded Kingsway Hall, 18 March 1953. Columbia 33C1016 (33rpm), SEL1504 (45rpm), EMI HQM1006, (33rpm), SLS5246 (33rpm), CHS5 65003 2 (CD).

Orb and Sceptre, Coronation March (1953)
Philharmonia Orchestra. Recorded Kingsway Hall, 18 March 1953. Columbia LX1583 (78rpm), 33C1016 (33rpm), SEL1504 (45rpm), EMI HQM1006 (33rpm), SLS5246 (33rpm), CHS5 65003 2 (CD).

Partita for Orchestra
Philharmonia Orchestra. Recorded Kingsway Hall, 6 and 16 February 1959. Columbia 33CX1679 (33rpm), SAX2319 (33rpm), EMI SXLP30236 (33rpm), SLS5246 (33rpm), CHS5 65003 2 (CD).

Capriccio Burlesco
London Symphony Orchestra. Recorded Walthamstow Assembly Hall, 13 April 1970. Lyrita SRCS49 (33rpm), SRCD224 (CD).

Siesta
London Philharmonic Orchestra. Recorded No.1 Studio, Abbey Road, 25 October 1938. HMV C3042 (78rpm), EMI ED29 0715 1 (33rpm), CDH7 63381 (CD).
London Philharmonic Orchestra. Recorded Walthamstow Assembly Hall, 15 April 1970. Lyrita SRCS47 (33rpm), SRCD224 (CD).

The Wise Virgins, ballet suite
Sadler's Wells Orchestra. Recorded No.1 Studio, Abbey Road, 24 July and 8 August 1940. HMV C3178-9 (78rpm), EMI CHS5 65003 2 (CD). 'Sheep may safely graze' *only*, HMV B9380 (78rpm).

Sheep may safely graze from 'The Wise Virgins'
Philharmonia Orchestra. Recorded Kingsway Hall, 21 March 1953. Columbia 33C1016 (33rpm), SEL1504 (45rpm), EMI CHS5 65003 2 (CD).

The Quest, ballet suite arr. Vilem Tausky
London Symphony Orchestra. Recorded Walthamstow Assembly Hall, 14 April 1970. Lyrita SRCS49 (33rpm), SRCD224 (CD).

Music for Children
London Philharmonic Orchestra. Recorded Walthamstow Assembly Hall, 15 April 1970. Lyrita SRCS50 (33rpm), SRCD224 (CD).

Sinfonia Concertante for orchestra with piano obbligato
Phyllis Sellick (piano), City of Birmingham Orchestra. Recorded Town Hall, Dudley, 8 August 1945. HMV C3478-80 [auto C7635-7] (78rpm), World Record Club SH128 (33rpm), EMI EH29 1276 1 (33rpm), CDH7 63828 2 (CD).

Peter Katin (piano), London Symphony Orchestra. Recorded Walthamstow Assembly Hall, 14 April 1970. Lyrita SRCS47 (33rpm), SRCD224 (CD).

Viola Concerto
Frederick Riddle (viola), London Symphony Orchestra. Recorded Decca Studios, Thames Street. Decca AX199-201 (78rpm), Dutton Laboratories CDAX8003 (CD).

William Primrose (viola), Philharmonia Orchestra. Recorded No.1 Studio, Abbey Road, 22–23 July 1946. HMV DB6309–11 [auto DB9036–8] (78rpm), Imprimatur IMP6 (33rpm), EMI EH29 1276 1 (33rpm), CDH7 63828 2 (CD).

Yehudi Menuhin (viola), New Philharmonia Orchestra. Recorded No.1 Studio, Abbey Road, 9–11 October 1968. HMV ASD2542 (33rpm), EMI CHS5 65003 2 (CD).

Violin Concerto
Jascha Heifetz (violin), Philharmonia Orchestra. Recorded No.1 Studio, Abbey Road, 26–27 June 1950. HMV DB21257–9 [Auto DB9611–3] (78rpm), BLP1047 (33rpm), RCA DM1511 (78rpm), LM1121 (33rpm), LM2740 (33rpm), LVT1033 (33rpm), LSB4102 (33rpm), GD87966 (CD), BMG 09026 617542 (CD).

Yehudi Menuhin (violin), London Symphony Orchestra. Recorded No.1 Studio, Abbey Road, 12–15 July 1969. HMV ASD2542 (33rpm), EMI CHS5 65003 2 (CD).

Henry V, scenes from the film
Laurence Olivier, Chorus and Philharmonia Orchestra. Recorded No.1 Studio, Abbey Road, 27–28 August and 12–13 October 1946 [extra session 13 November 1946 conductor Roy Douglas]. HMV C3583–6 [Auto C7678–81] (78rpm), ALP1375 (33rpm), RCA RB16144 (33rpm), LSB4104 (33rpm), EMI CHS5 65003 2 (CD).

Henry V, Two Pieces for Strings (Passacaglia, 'The Death of Falstaff'; 'Touch her soft lips and part')
Philharmonia String Orchestra. Recorded No.1 Studio, Abbey Road, 12 October 1945. HMV C3480 (78rpm), EMI ED 29 0715 1 (33rpm), CDH7 63381 2 (CD).

Henry V, Suite arr. Muir Mathieson
Philharmonia Orchestra. Recorded No.1 Studio, Abbey Road, 15 October 1963. Columbia 33CX1883 (33rpm), SAX2527 (33rpm), World Record Club T656 (33rpm), ST656 (33rpm), EMI SXLP30139 (33rpm), SLS5246 (33rpm), CHS5 65003 (CD).

Hamlet, Funeral March arr. Muir Mathieson
Philharmonia Orchestra. Recorded No.1 Studio, Abbey Road, 15 October 1963. Columbia 33CX1883 (33rpm), SAX2527 (33rpm), World Record Club T656 (33rpm), ST656 (33rpm), EMI SXLP30139 (33rpm), SLS5246 (33rpm), CHS5 65003 2 (CD).

Richard III, Prelude and A Shakespeare Suite arr. Muir Mathieson
Philharmonia Orchestra. Recorded No.1 Studio, Abbey Road, 15 and 16 October 1963. Columbia 33CX1883 (33rpm), SAX2527 (33rpm), World Record Club T656 (33rpm), ST656 (33rpm), EMI SXLP30139 (33rpm), [Prelude *only*] SLS5246 (33rpm), CHS5 65003 2 (CD).

Spitfire Prelude and Fugue
Hallé Orchestra. Recorded Houldsworth Hall, Manchester, 24 June 1943. HMV C3359 (78rpm), 7P312 (45rpm), EMI ED 29 0715 1 (33rpm), CDH7 63381 2 (CD).

Philharmonia Orchestra. Recorded No.1 Studio, Abbey Road, 16 October 1963. EMI SXLP30139 (33rpm), SLS5246 (33rpm), CHS5 65003 2 (CD).

10 Walton's Words

Lewis Foreman

Sir William Walton wrote some of his most personal and effective music under the stimulus of words and yet, at a first glance, his relationship to English literature does not reflect the close sympathy of many of his composer contemporaries in the UK, and the received assessment is that most of his greatest works were all instrumental. However, on examination, this proves to be a somewhat superficial judgement, for in his treatment of words Walton actually achieved something quite individual, perhaps best illustrated in his Shakespearean film scores.

Walton composed incidental music for three plays, for one BBC feature and for no less than 14 films. There were six works for chorus and orchestra and eight unaccompanied choral works; but there were only nine pieces for solo voice, excluding *Façade*, which in a sense is really instrumental chamber music. There were also his operas, the three act grand opera *Troilus and Cressida*, and 'an extravaganza in one act', *The Bear*.

So, as we consider the case of William Walton, a composer who spent his most impressionable years living with the Sitwells, one of the most celebrated literary families of the early twentieth century, we find a man who exhibited little conventional sympathy for poetry, nor, apparently, did he acquire any deep literary culture. Yet from a 1990s perspective, many of his most successful scores drew on English literary sources whether poetry, plays or the King James Bible.

Walton's first exposure to literary sensibilities came when he wrote the music for Edith Sitwell's *Façade* poems at the age of nineteen. Edith Sitwell at that date was nearly 35. What can their relationship have been like, or rather, how did Walton see her? His reaction was surely one of a teenager being given the opportunity by his much older sister of letting his hair down. His response was instinctive, and it may well be that his reaction was so spontaneous because he did not carry with him the baggage of 500 years of 'Eng. Lit.' He did not know what he should and should not do, he just reacted instinctively. As his wife Susanna much later wrote: 'despite William's apparent lack of appreciation of words or poetry, the music he produced for the *Façade* poems turned out to be brilliant'.[1] She went on: 'The Sitwells were deeply involved in William's early music-making, starting with *Façade,* which amused and impressed them. Even if William had little appreciation of poetry, he certainly had managed to produce what Sachie termed "a terrific noise".'[2]

228

One must remember that *Façade* was intended to be performed behind a drop curtain, hiding the performers, and that the speakers had to present their stylized rhythmic delivery of the words through the sengerphone, a megaphone. In fact there were three different curtain designs over the period of *Façade's* evolution. Unable to afford an artist of the stature of Picasso, the Sitwells had first chosen Frank Dobson whose studio was near the Sitwells' London house at Carlyle Square. Later came a design by the Italian Gino Severini and in 1942 a design by John Piper which has become widely known since he also produced a lithograph of it. This has become one of his most characteristic and evocative images.

In one of his volumes of autobiography, Osbert Sitwell recounted the gestation and evolution of *Façade*. He remembered

> the rather long sessions, lasting for two or three hours, which my sister and the composer used to have, when together they read the words, she going over them again and again, while he marked and accented them for his own guidance, to show where the precise stress and emphasis fell, the exact inflection or deflection.[3]

There came a time in the 1950s and 60s when a young, later generation of music critics felt that Walton had betrayed the modernist ethic. A eloquent statement of this view dates from 1957:

> *Façade*, let it be said here, was the most misleading of false starts. Walton's subsequent career has exposed the work as an irrelevance, significant in the present context only for its competence and as a sign of his ambivalent attitude to modernity: for *Façade* was a satire on that very theme. That Walton, in Dr Adorno's 'heroic' days of modern music, was disposed, as it were, to play the fool - with some charm, perhaps – is a measure of his immaturity in 1923 and, at the same time, an indication of the insecurity of his position as a budding composer. *Façade,* while leading the critics and the public by the nose, left every major aesthetic question unanswered.[4]

In its day, *Façade* was surely intended by the Sitwells to be at the forefront of modernism, even if there was an element of fooling in Walton's response to Edith Sitwell's self-regarding avant-gardism. Once they had made the essential leap forward of inventing the genre it must have been comparatively easy for so talented a young man as Walton to busk accompaniments to as many of Edith's poems as she cared to give him. Much later Walton found composition difficult; here he seems to have been fluent and inventive without any oppressive thoughts of a reputation to live up to.

Façade was first presented privately in 1922, and then given publicly the following year, an event that has been flagged as a celebrated scandal. But it seems likely that the sensation was rather more a wished for event by the Sitwells, than one with any reality. The pianist Angus Morrison was there and remembered that 'everyone was perfectly good-mannered and no one objected violently at all'.[5] John Pearson described it as 'central to the whole mythology of the Sitwells'.[6]

In fact, of course, as Michael Kennedy has reminded us,[7] the evolution of *Façade* was an ongoing one, and early performances actually consisted of different numbers. Of the 18 items given at Carlyle Square only six survived into the final version published in 1951, and the first public performance, at the Aeolian Hall in June 1923, heard 28 numbers, ten of which had been written since those first private performances. In fact it seems probable that at the Aeolian Hall, on a warm summer's day, with a less than full audience, the first public performance was not well done and fell flat on its face. The Sitwells were saved by a fairly hostile press, from which it was possible to construct, in retrospect, a French-style *scandale*. Walton was so diffident about the whole thing he planned to rescue five numbers as *Bucolic Comedies*, though the score is now lost. However, we know that in this work the words suddenly loomed larger, and the soloist was to *sing*. Three of them ultimately saw light of day as the Three Songs first performed by Dora Stevens and her husband, Walton's publisher Hubert Foss, at the Wigmore Hall in October 1932. In fact they appear not to have got *Façade* itself right until a revised (and shorter) verson appeared at the New Chenil Galleries in April 1926.

'Façade gave Walton a sense of adulthood in the Sitwell family. But what all the Sitwells later preferred to ignore or dismiss was the extent to which Walton continued to work on the music, using it as an interminable student exercise', wrote Gillian Widdicombe.[8] Yet, in 1923 Walton's real musical interest was with a more rigorous and solemn new music, preparing his distinctly European string quartet, redolent of early Bartok and of the Second Viennese School, for the ISCM Festival in Salzburg, where he attracted the attention of Berg who took him to meet Schöenberg. This was certainly not a young composer whose musical develop-ment was intimately associated with word-setting. It is worth remembering Stephen Banfield's aside concerning *Façade* that 'there are surprising moments of expressionism, though the recent publication of some of the earliest numbers suggests that these were played down as the work grew'.[9]

By 1928 *Façade* was candidate for the ISCM festival in Siena where it really did prompt a scandal. The composer Frank Bridge was there and he remarked in a letter to his patron Elizabeth Sprague Coolidge: 'My own personal feelings happen to coincide with many of the foreigners in thinking this is concerned with a high class cabaret and not much – if anything – to do with music itself.'[10] He went on: 'Listening one heard no words and so one concentrated on the small orch[estra], which seemed to be performing stray items by the best jazz compos-ers.' Spike Hughes was also there and in one of his volumes of autobiography he recounts what the – afterwards – celebrated fuss was about:

> Very shortly afterwards, however, came the Tarantella. The enthusiastic audience of a little time before now became the angry mob, infuriated by this irreverent parody of a national dance. There were shouts and cat-calls, hats and shoes thrown at the stage and the kind of uproar which only the Latins know how to create. It was a puzzling *volte face*.[11]

Façade was recorded in 1929 with the words spoken by Edith Sitwell and Constant Lambert and with Walton himself conducting.[12] By this time the ballet suite (i.e. Suite No. l) had appeared, underlining its essentially instrumental divertissement character, and was first performed as 'symphonic interludes'. These were commis-sioned by Diaghilev for performance between ballets. Even as early as 1919 the names of British composers as varied as Bax, Berners, Goossens, and Howells could be seen in the list,[13] probably commissioned through the good offices of the all-seeing critic Edwin Evans. Doubtless it was Evans who arranged for Walton's music, now recast for the orchestra, to be heard in the same programme as Berners' ballet *The Triumph of Neptune*, on 3 December 1926. Roy Fuller remembers hearing it at a Hallé Concert in 1930 conducted by Walton: 'tall, pallid and awkward, carrying his left arm as in an invisible sling'.[14]

The appearance of the ballet score resulted in the original version being forgotten as a frequently heard concert work. Ultimately it was revived in June 1942 at a Boosey & Hawkes concert at the Aeolian Hall where for the first time the connection with Schöenberg was made in public for it partnered Schöenberg's *Pierrot Lunaire* ('Three times seven poems') and Walton's score time was billed as 'seven times three poems'.

Yet the origins of *Façade* were instrumental – the precedent had been *Parade* (Walton saw it in 1919) with décor by Picasso and music by Erik Satie – the impetus coming from Osbert and Sacheverell rather than Walton or the Sitwells' sister. Of course that is Osbert Sitwell talking again, for the principal fact we remember about Satie's avant-garde ballet is its drop curtain by Picasso, scenario by Cocteau and the fuss it created. Walton himself felt his source was probably the Stravinsky of *L'Histoire du Soldat*.

The National Portrait Gallery's Sitwell exhibition in 1994/95 underlined how successful the three had been in making their own world an influential facet of the Twenties, at least in retrospect.

> Theoretically their aims were most ambitious: to achieve a fusion of poetry and music and get through for once to 'that unattainable land which, in the finest songs, always lies looming mysteriously beyond, a land full of meanings and nuances, analogies and images'. More to the point, much of the Sitwells' own sense of fantasy and 'fun' was wonderfully preserved within the poems and the music, as was something of their attitude to life – magical, witty and stylish to an extraordinary degree. Walton's music matched the mood and rhythms of the poetry so perfectly that one feels that only a composer who was virtually a member of the family could have managed it.[15]

Perhaps Sacheverell Sitwell should have the last word, writing in April 1971:

> I would not say that W T W, to call him by his initials, was a fervent lover of poetry, but he was attuned to them and had, when directed to them, an instinctive understanding. This can be the only explanation of the extraordinary conveyancing into another medium of the ideas and images expressed in the poems.[16]

He added:

> I remember Constant Lambert who helped Walton as copyist for the 1926 performance being dazzled and amazed at the speed and unerring understanding of the settings . . . Of course there is the one peculiarity in this very special genre, that is they are neither songs, nor recitations. They are accented and rhythmic readings to a foreground of music.

*   *   *

The inner world of many British composers can be illuminated by their reaction to a wide conspectus of English literature, or at least literature in English, as set to music throughout their lives. When assembled in a chronological sequence, such a collection becomes a fascinating anthology in its own right, demonstrated only too vividly by Boris Ford's sequence of poetry set by Benjamin Britten.[17] In the case of another composer, Gerald Finzi, the extent of his poetry library warranted a specially designed room at the University of Reading Library, and is another example of how the wide span of English literature intimately informed the music of a characteristically English composer in the first half of the century. Elgar, too, was very widely read, set a variety of poets, and being a self-educated man liked to parade his learning on occasion, as is seen in his contributions to the *TLS* after his wife's death.[18]

The wonderful effect of startling juxtapositions of texts by writers of genius in the choral works of composers such as Vaughan Williams and Bliss, appears to underline that to be a successful British composer one must have a close familiarity with the breadth and depth of English literature. And not only English, for it is actually literature, particularly poetry, in English with which we are concerned. This familiarity must extend to the American poet Walt Whitman and the English translations (by Shigeyoshi Obata, Arthur Waley and Witter Bynner) of Chinese poets that became so fashionable just after the First World War.

Walton's earliest surviving works give every indication of a mainstream interest in the heritage of English literature. His earliest – one that is both published and recorded – *A Litany*, sets words by the Spenserian poet Phineas Fletcher (1582–1650), sometime rector of Hilgay in Norfolk. Walton composed his setting in 1916 when at 14 he was a pupil of Dr Henry Ley, organist of Christ Church, Oxford. Soon after, he set Shakespeare's *Tell Me Where is Fancy Bred?* Later came the songs *The Winds* (words by Swinburne) and *The Passionate Shepherd* (Marlowe), followed by the 'pedagogic overture' *Dr Syntax*, after William Combe's verses written to evoke the grotesque adventures recorded in Thomas Rowlandson's celebrated suite of etchings. But in the case of Walton this recourse to bookish sources was not to last.

The early 1920s were a turning point in British music and certainly the role given to vocal music – particularly choral music – was lessened with the demise of the Festival Movement in many centres. Only Norwich, Leeds and the Three Choirs really survived the war. The vogue was for the ballet and the composers it inspired. The new music was largely orchestral: Holst's *The Planets*, Vaughan Williams's *London* and *Pastoral* Symphonies, Bax's tone poems and first symphony, Bliss's *A Colour* Symphony. There was also that genre in which composers treated voices instrumentally, perhaps reflecting Ravel's usage in *Daphnis and Chloë*. Evocative examples can be found in the works of these and other composers. One of the most striking of the new pieces to appear immediately after the war was Gustav Holst's choral work *The Hymn of Jesus*, full of choral tricks and using choral speech as well as music.

In the Victorian oratorio tradition texts were taken either from the Bible or written in quasi-biblical language by clerics or music critics of the day. The choice of familiar and less well-known poetry was first made by Parry who trawled the length and breadth of English literature for his 12 sets of English Lyrics and who looked to Milton for some of his greatest choral successes (*Blest Pair of Sirens*, 1887 and *L'Allegro ed Il Penseroso*, 1890) and Dunbar (*An Ode on the Nativity*, 1912). He found original and lasting tunes for some of the most familiar words in the language, in John of Gaunt's celebrated words from Shakespeare's *Richard II*, 'This royal Throne of Kings, This sceptred isle', in his *England*, and Blake's *Jerusalem*. Stanford, too, found the contemporary narrative ballad a suitable genre for popular choral works that would be sung throughout the land, and achieved his greatest success when he produced his choral ballad *The Revenge*, in 1886, setting familiar words by the Poet Laureate, Alfred Lord Tennyson. Stanford had set out, ten years earlier, looking to the German philosopher Klopstock for the words of his *The Resurrection*. This was the source that Mahler would turn to in 1894 for the choral finale of his Second Symphony. For the rest of his life Stanford ranged over the span of English literature returning to Tennyson four more times for extended works for chorus and orchestra.

The American Walt Whitman's realism, and his democracy, appealed to a wide range of progressive artists in England at the turn of the century. 'Whitman tackled the themes of love and death in an affirmatory manner, with plenty of apostrophes to the "Soul", a convenient new name for God, that satisfied both Christian and agnostic.'[19] Stephen Banfield in this analysis proposes a bridge between Whitman and that other charismatic late nineteenth-century writer of philosophical verse, Friedrich Nietzsche, remarking 'Whitman could be an Englishman's Nietzsche'. Stanford set Whitman in 1884 (in the *Elegiac Ode*) and subsequent composers as different as Delius and Vaughan Williams quarried *Leaves of Grass* for some of their best works. Delius, of course, also set Nietzsche in his masterpiece *A Mass of Life*. The crucial difference between these composers and, later, Walton, was that, by and large, all these earlier composers were writing philosophical works; the words mattered to them. Walton was surely only ever painting vivid pictures, even when it was on an epic canvas.

The tradition of assembling thematic anthologies of literature in English from several poets and writers – often interspersed with words from The King James Bible – was possibly first invented by Walford Davies, but was really a phenomenon of the 1930s and was notably a creation of Sir Arthur Bliss in his *Pastoral: Lie Strewn the White Flocks* of 1928 (including words by Ben Jonson, John Fletcher, Robert Nichols and Theocritus), followed two years later by *Morning Heroes*, his tribute to his brother and comrades who fell in the Great War. *Morning Heroes*, a particularly rewarding example, includes passages from *The Iliad*, from Whitman, the Chinese Poet Li Tai Po (in an English translation published in 1923) and the two war poets Wilfred Owen and Robert Nichols, the latter a friend of Bliss. Bliss wrote of his *Pastoral*, 'I began to collect a short anthology of poems which should depict a Sicilian day from dawn to evening.' He explained:

> This was the first occasion on which I employed the device of the anthology for constructing a musical work. I found it very attractive to choose verse from quite different epochs, each poem having the same general subject as its theme. However widely separated the centuries music has the mysterious power of linking them together.[20]

The anthology approach was reinforced by Vaughan Williams, first in his *Dona Nobis Pacem* which mixed biblical words with Whitman's poetry and a parliamentary speech by John Bright, and later in that most unexpected success RVW's *Thanksgiving for Victory* (now called *A Song of Thanksgiving*) in which his choice of words encompasses Shakespeare, the Old Testament and Kipling. Later Britten used a particularly varied collection to great effect in his *A Spring Symphony*. There were many other composers who assembled a text in this way, and almost always this recourse to the riches of English literature signalled a work with philosophical rather than purely musical intent.

Walton never essayed a choral work on this basis, but in the early 1960s, when he came to write his song cycles *Anon in Love* and *Songs for the Lord Mayor's Table*, Christopher Hassall, the librettist of his opera *Troilus and Cressida*, prepared suitable anthologies for him. At this time Hassall (who died in 1963) enjoyed a brief but very active vogue, and prepared similar collections for a variety of composers, of which probably the best remembered may be the later choral works, *The Beatitudes* and *Mary of Magdala* (Bliss).

'The idea of the composer of *Façade* metamorphosed into a Three Choirs Festival composer was piquant – and mistaken' wrote Martin Cooper.[21] In fact nothing could have been less like a Victorian biblical oratorio than Walton's choral work *Belshazzar's Feast*. 'The captive Hebrews are here represented as an oriental tribe no less savage than their captors' continued Cooper.

> In his setting of Psalm 137 ('By the waters of Babylon') Walton does not balk at the cry for vengeance and gives full dramatic expression to 'Happy shall he be that taketh thy children and dasheth them against a stone'. The barbarity of the feast itself and the character of the Babylonian gods are vividly expressed in glittering music which stands nearer to Rimsky-Korsakov than to Parry, and the Hebrew chorus of rejoicing over Belshazzar's death has the character of an orgiastic ritual dance. With *Belshazzar's Feast* Walton not only conquered a new public. He set a new standard of dramatic writing for choral music in this country and went far towards abolishing the artificial distinction between 'sacred' and 'secular music'.

It is difficult now to understand the reasoning behind the banning of *Belshazzar* for 25 years from the Three Choirs, apparently for its mention of eunuchs and concubines,[22] for it was not heard there until 1957 (when it was still regarded in some circles as a dangerous modern work, but by then real modernity had far less red blood in its dodecaphonic veins).

Allying a dramatic libretto with brilliant use of both chorus and orchestra produced a masterpiece. Walton had showed his flair for rhythm in *Façade*. But it was a considerable step from that to *Belshazzar*, a work requiring a virtuoso manipulation of words in complex and difficult textures. By then Walton's reputation was largely made by four purely orchestral works, but it was crowned by *Belshazzar's Feast*.

Belshazzar originated in 1929 with a BBC commission for a small-scale choral work, but Walton found that the material quickly outgrew his original conception. We should not overlook the essential part played by Osbert Sitwell in this success, for in working the biblical words into a compact and vividly contrasted libretto, he encapsulated the dramatic images of the story in a form which allowed Walton's emergent genius a canvas on which it could work. The poetic anthology approach tended to encourage composers to produce extended works; in contrast when Walton came to write *Belshazzar's Feast*, Osbert Sitwell pared away all unnecessary padding. Again Walton was in debt to the Sitwells for presenting him with a text which allowed his genius to spark. It gave every opportunity for evocative description and Walton was able to produce a masterpiece, stamping his personality on his material in distinctive fashion.

Indeed, Walton's tight control of his material is underlined by his remark that he regarded the work less as an oratorio than a three-movement choral symphony. It is notable that in this vocal work the principal innovations were the use of a variety of extras in the orchestra, including the high E flat clarinet, the alto saxophone (so evocative when underlining words like 'concubine' and 'silver') and the pagan depths added by the lower notes of the piano used orchestrally (later to be such a striking feature of Prokofiev's film music for *Alexander Nevsky*). The percussion section, when it was new, was also thought very exotic, including woodblock, slapstick and anvil. Finally two brass groups were placed antiphonally on the platform to underline what his publisher Hubert Foss called the 'vulgar splendour' of the triumphal passages. Beecham's celebrated caustic remark on hearing of the score, 'why not throw in a couple of brass bands as well?', was nearer the mark than he realized.

The final section is a mighty hymn of praise, truly joyful in mood. However, there is a limit to the amount of triumphal din that can be assimilated at one sitting. In his finale Walton interpolates a remarkable and heartfelt interlude in which he suddenly extends his vision, lamenting the fate of Babylon in surprisingly tender terms. In a review in the early 1960s, David Drew was critical of Walton's lack of identification with the words, finding in it a:

> crippling failure of dramatic sensibility. Oratorio is by definition a moral institution, and the text of Belshazzar lays claim to that definition; but the music does not support it. After the 'Mene, mene, tekel upharsin' episode and the slaying of Belshazzar, the chorus hymn the God of Jacob in precisely the same musical terms as they had earlier hymned the God of Gold and Silver. Instead of a Peripeteia which would make a moral point, there is a crude return to the status quo. Babylon does not fall: it triumphs. . . . The chief virtue of Belshazzar is its conviction: it may offend, but it is seldom dull.[23]

This is a view with which few would now identify, but it does underline Walton's lack of personal involvement with the meaning of the words. What he wants is a vehicle for orchestral drama even if it is actually presented by a choral texture.

Yet occasionally, for example as when he presents the heartfelt setting of the words 'By the Waters of Babylon, There we sat down, Yea we wept', he touches a deeper vein. No sooner have the unaccompanied men's voices in dissonant choral writing introduced Isaiah's prophecy, when a rising figure in the lower strings emphasizes the mood of resignation, and the women's voices join, still largely unaccompanied. This breaks quickly into fast music, driven by a repeated brass figure. Now the opening string idea becomes an accompaniment as the baritone expresses the Israelite's longing for home: 'How can I forget thee O Jerusalem.' A great choral outburst returns us to the lamenting of 'By the waters', now with a tolling orchestral accompaniment. Again, fast music returns as the chorus with renewed fervour sing 'O daughter of Babylon' and the driving rhythm of the earlier fast passage reappears. The first section now closes with the lamenting voices and the opening rising string figure.

We do not have to discuss the whole work in this vein. This brief summary shows how Walton, through generating endless contrast and variety, and a fleet-footed treatment, quickly develops his narrative in what was then a totally new way. And in some ways it gives the lie to the charge that Walton had no sensitivity for words. Yet, before the sound cinema, this was a more cinematic technique, one more concerned with vivid changes of mood, which might or might not be deeply felt by the composer, than with expressing verbal resonances, however freshly caught. But in the descriptive passages he is of course pre-eminent.

Yet the return to the Bible for his text is to appreciate the essential drama of that collection of stories. 'In some respects, for all its surface modernity, *Belshaz-zar's Feast* does not so drastically challenge the traditional concept of oratorio as did *The Dream of Gerontius*, where Elgar did for oratorio what Wagner had done for opera' wrote Ernest Bradbury.

> Sir Osbert Sitwell showed a sound instinct when he returned – against the general trend of modern oratorio – to a full-blooded biblical text in furnishing Walton with his libretto. Our Victorian forefathers would hardly have understood Walton's musical treatment of the words; but they would have understood the words themselves, qua oratorio, better than those employed by Elgar, and they would have responded instinctively. None the less, Walton breaks new ground since he has modern resources – and a modern technique – at his command.[24]

Hugh Ottaway refuted this line, finding

> Belshazzar's Feast is primarily concerned, not with the liberation of Oratorio or of subject peoples, but with the maximum exploitation of every opportunity found in the text: in these (opportunistic) terms, the God of Gold fares as well as the God of Jacob, and perhaps better, for Walton's sense of radiance and ecstasy is at once involved.[25]

To this extent Belshazzar is typical of Walton's approach to every text with which he was associated.

*   *   *

Walton's three celebrated Laurence Olivier Shakespeare films, *Henry V, Hamlet* and *Richard III*, have tended to turn our attention from the other music he wrote for the drama. His incidental music for the theatre, largely written in the 1930s, his earlier films and his music for the radio, notably his celebrated score for Louis MacNeice's *Christopher Columbus* in 1942, were for many years pretty well forgotten.

Walton composed incidental music for only three stage plays, Lytton Strachey's tragic melodrama *The Son of Heaven* in 1925, J. M. Barrie's *The Boy David* in 1936 and Shakespeare's *Macbeth* in 1942. There is a long and honourable heritage of composing extended, even symphonic, orchestral scores for the London stage. Certainly the nineteenth-century tradition, which lasted from the 1860s through to the 1930s, saw extended scores contributed by composers as diverse as Sullivan, Mackenzie, Parry, Stanford and Edward German, all of whose theatre music helped establish their reputations; then to Bliss, Bantock, Norman O'Neill, and in the 1930s Benjamin Britten. During the first world war Elgar's music for the children's play *Starlight Express*, and afterwards Delius's extended score for *Hassan* both underlined the escapism of the theatre, but were central in evoking the other worlds of the playwright's imagination.

This music tended to consist of overtures, preludes and entr'actes of one sort or another, with songs or in some cases choral numbers. Delius, in *Hassan*, possibly took the medium furthest towards the melodrama in the twentieth century, in having music to be played underneath speech. It set the agenda for the sound film when it emerged in the 1930s. It was probably Bliss in his celebrated score for *The Tempest* who, in 1921, introduced a note of modernism into the music for the London stage, with a spectacular storm in a rhythm that would have been not unrecognized by Gustav Holst in warlike mood!

Walton's first music for a play, *The Son of Heaven*, appears not to have survived: all we know is that he conducted and his 20-year-old friend Constant Lambert played the tympani. Possibly these two young iconoclasts contemplated scandalizing the rich patrons of the theatre with their music: scandalizing one's elders is one of the satisfactions of youth, which Walton knew all about. However, we have firmer evidence concerning Walton's two later theatrical productions; for both, Walton's music was played in the theatre from recordings which have survived.

By the time Walton came to write music for J. M. Barrie's 1936 West End play *The Boy David*, he had fairly recently composed the music for his second film, *As You Like It*. This film score had a notably dramatic opening prelude that establishes Walton's personality in a striking way, and set his agenda for later ceremonial music as well as his films. The play, like the film, featured Elisabeth Bergner, though cast as the boy David, and she would appear in other films with Walton music before the second world war.

Barrie's play is in three acts, the first two presenting, in a continuous narrative, the familiar Old Testament story of David. In the third act we have six visions of what is to come. The play ends as it began with David guarding his sheep, though now he has his trophy of Goliath's mighty spear as a symbol of the future. All the music comes from Act II and listening to the three surviving 10" 78rpm sides of the production recording of Walton's music for *The Boy David*, we find two sections for orchestra and one for solo harp. They are marked 'Cue 21–22', 'Cue 22A' and 'Cue 29'. The last two are marked 'Act II scene 1'. The cue numbers appear not to establish the sequence of the music in the play. Reference to the published text[26] does not give a clear indication where the first orchestral passage appears. It includes a middle section of typical Waltonian scherzando music, which frankly could have come from almost any of his works. The scherzando music is framed by marching funereal chords over which a plaintive flute sings forlornly. This could well find a place in Saul's first exchange with David, or David before he kills Goliath.

We can be more specific about the second orchestral cue, a wild dance over an exotic ostinato. This is almost certainly the music accompanying the stage instruction at the end of Act II Sc. 2 after Goliath has been killed: 'With barbaric dancing and wild shouts Israelites pour on to the scene',[27] though at the beginning of the next scene there is also a brief instruction: 'There is music and singing in barbaric joy and leaping over an Israelite victory'.[28]

Finally the harp solo at the end of the second act. The harp is played by David in the tent of Goliath – David's booty – during his dialogue with Saul after the death of his giant adversary. The King, while recognizing David's claim to the throne, debates whether to kill him. David has no fear of Saul and plays his harp. Saul tells him it is he, David, he is to kill. David continues playing. Saul throws his javelin into the tent: silence. But David survives and Saul is a broken man, immediately overcome by remorse (has he killed the Lord's anointed?). David continues playing, now with one hand.

> Then, with great courage and determination, he draws quite close and plays his harp strongly – confidently, but never taking his eyes off Saul. . . . here is great danger in his expression when he recognises David crouched, playing at his feet – smiling – radiantly happy. Then all tension leaves Saul and he is merely listening to the music like one very far away.'[29]

The harp piece has a duration of 1 minute 54 seconds, and with its folksong-like single line, gradually elaborated, the tune repeated again and again, it would make an attractive concert encore, but it is in no way typical of its composer.

The most striking aspect of *Boy David* is how *cinematic* is the treatment, intended to set a mood under or between passages of dialogue. The shifting restless scherzando music is an example of 'standard Walton'. But of course that is unjust, because almost everything Walton does is informed by his commanding sense of occasion.

If we follow that with the similar contemporary private recording of the music for the John Gielgud, Gwen Ffrangçon-Davies' *Macbeth*, we have a more fragmentary score, though more music survives. The *Macbeth* music was recorded privately by HMV for use during the performances which were in Manchester and London. These are very much music for the business of theatre, though again one has the overwhelming impression of a film score *manqué*. Walton was little concerned with words, much involved with setting scenes and making the drama work.

When he wrote the music for *Macbeth*, Walton was writing in the middle of a succession of film jobs. In 1942 we have *The Next of Kin*, the music for the radio play *Christopher Columbus*, then *The Foreman Went to France* and *The First of the Few*. Next came *Macbeth*, followed by *Went the Day Well?* Not a bad achievement for one year in the middle of the war, and a tribute to what immutable deadlines can do for a man. From the musical point of view, to all intents and purposes it seems that the *Macbeth* music could well have been for another film.

For his Chandos CD series[30] the late Christopher Palmer pieced together a Fanfare and March from *Macbeth*. This assembled various versions of the banquet music, to which Walton gave a Scottish feel with a bagpipe effect, and a trio taken from what Palmer calls 'the Funeral March of the eight Kings'. In fact, the score consists largely of fanfares, transitions, ghosts and murders – and witches' music. Walton's atmospheric music for the first appearance of the witches is quite extended, ending with a movement low in the strings that looks forward to *Hamlet*, and distant trumpets over a soft tremolando, redolent of the still-to-come night before the battle in *Henry V*. This is a texture repeatedly evoked in Walton's score. He signs his personality with few notes and the fanfares may be identified as Walton after only a note or two. There is also an exotic dance, several times heard, and although not particularly characteristic of the composer it again arguably looks forward to *Henry V*. There is one particularly powerful passage in *Macbeth* which does not recur elsewhere in his music. It involves a gently tolling bell over slowly oscillating chords, again counterpointing with distant muted trumpets; the result creating a magnificent effect in the theatre.

Again Walton had created a genre of incidental music which needed the expansiveness and contrast of the film to give him the ideal canvas on which to develop his art. In *Macbeth* he is little concerned with specific words. This is a technique that he later brought to perfection in the music he wrote for the films *Henry V* and *Hamlet*. But when, in *Henry V*, 'entertaining conjecture of a time', we hear the distant trumpets echoing so evocatively through the night as the king moves quietly round his men, we remember that he had already tested the effect in *Macbeth*. And when, still in *Henry V*, they come to the Battle of Agincourt, it is the earlier score for *Much Ado* he revisits. There is a fascinating aside to be made here. In July 1935 the opera *Iernin* by the 21-year-old Cornish composer George Lloyd was seen in London. Walton is reported to have attended and been condescending in his assessment. Yet the pacing of Walton's Battle of Agincourt music is clearly pre-echoed in George Lloyd's third act. In truth Walton was a magpie, able to put his personal stamp on any material.

Walton himself summarized the role of his music. 'The music subserves the visual sequences,' he wrote, 'providing a subtle form of punctuation . . . phases of the action broken into paragraphs . . . and the turning of the page at a crossfade or cut can be helped by music's power to summarize the immediate past or heighten expectation of what is to come.'[31] It is not that Walton was unsympathetic to words, but that his reaction took a particular form: in essence he wrote melodramas with music. When one hears 'Kiss my soft lips and part' or the passacaglia on the death of Falstaff, we find ourselves in the grip of a master of atmosphere. As Susana Walton pointed out '. . . nobody believed in *Henry V* . . . when [Olivier] first heard the passacaglia for the death of Falstaff . . . he suddenly realized he had a great film on his hands because he found the music so moving and so exactly right'.[32]

*   *   *

Although between the two world wars works calling for speaker with large-scale forces, such as Bliss's *Morning Heroes* and Honegger's *King David* and *St Joan at the Stake*, created a new interest in melodrama, it was the cinema and then the BBC features department with their use of specially commissioned music that newly minted this old form.

At the end of the nineteenth century there had been an interest in the melodrama (recitation with piano or orchestra), which in the UK had focused on Frederick Corder and the Royal Academy of Music. It was Sir Alexander Mackenzie, Principal of the RAM for many years, who asked for accompanied recitation in his choral work *The Dream of Jubal* (he called it 'a poem with music') in 1889. Probably the two best-known works for speaker and accompaniment are Grieg's *Bergljot* (with piano or orchestra) dating from 1871 and Richard Strauss's *Enoch Arden* (with piano) of 1897. Delius, when a student at the Leipzig Conservatoire in the late 1880s (where he met Grieg) produced a particularly striking example in his melodrama *Paa Vidderne*, and its revival in the 1980s in both Norwegian and English, setting Ibsen on a large scale, gives us an unexpectedly vivid piece and a window on audience sympathies in the late nineteenth century.

The melodrama with orchestra, in the form of the sentimental or humorous monologue, was also a feature of the music hall and the dividing line between this popular medium and the aspirations of the concert repertoire can be somewhat hazy. There was quite a school of such compositions in central Europe centred on the Czech composers Fibich[33] and Ostrcil. Interest in recitation and melodrama was promoted in the UK by Frederick Corder, Professor of composition at the Royal Academy of Music, who contributed to a very extensive book[34] on it published at the turn of the century. This included many extracts for verse reading and recitation. Corder also encouraged his pupils to write such works, and those who complied included his son Paul Corder, and Arnold Bax. The recent revival, by Pamela Hunter, of the surprisingly effective melodramas of Stanley Hawley[35] illustrates the genre at its best, though it is unlikely that Walton could have heard them before *Façade*. Almost certainly the best-known examples were the three wartime works that Elgar produced for emotional and nationalist concerts during the first world war. All of them set words by the now-forgotten Belgian poet Emil Cammaerts. The first *Carillon*, setting topical and emotional words about the 'rape' of Belgium, generated an enormous following in its day. When Elgar attempted a sequel with *Le Drapeau Belge*, he attracted a smaller audience. Between them the second recitation, *Une Voix dans le Désert*, was more reflective and can still be found to be touching today. It included the poignant soprano song 'When spring comes round again', which begins to touch wider sensibilities than its somewhat crude companions. Did Walton, perhaps, hear one of these – very probably in his early or middle teens – and could *Façade* have been his rejection of such heavily pointed art?

This interest in melodrama was not confined to the UK. It was at the same time that *sprechtstimme* was first proposed in the works of the second Viennese school as a method of highlighting sensibility in a vocal work. When Schoenberg's *Pierrot Lunaire* was first announced, Walton immediately took an interest and almost certainly had a score before he could have heard the music. He had no living tradition of Schöenberg's music, indeed no aural tradition, for it was not heard in London until November 1923, but when he came to write *Façade* he could experiment in using the voice in new ways and without having to worry about the meaning of the words.

Walton was first closely associated with Laurence Olivier when he wrote the music for Louis MacNeice's radio play (pageant would be a better word) *Christopher Columbus,* with Olivier as Columbus. This was produced by Dallas Bower who, eighteen months later when working on the film *Henry V*, would press Olivier to ask Walton to compose the music. *Columbus* was 'a most prestigious affair when broadcast in 1942 . . . for it represented a page of BBC history' remarked Gillian Widdicombe on the rebroadcast of the BBC Archive recording of that performance in April 1973.[36] She later noted how MacNeice's musical cues sometimes 'sound awkward, or contrived. Perhaps he did not realise how effectively Walton's music could sew atmosphere and scenes together'.

'A small minority of radio-dramatic programmes, of which *Christopher Columbus* is one, were conceived from the start as joint literary and musical works . . . the music, though much more conspicuous, must still be strictly functional, subordinated to the dramatic purpose of the whole.' Thus wrote Louis MacNeice in his introduction to the published text of *Christopher Columbus*[37], though in an appendix to that volume[38] he added:

> *Christopher Columbus* is an untypical radio play (by which I mean play written specifically for radio) because it is so long and because it involved so much music, and particularly vocal music. . . . as an example of its importance, I can point out that the whole of Columbus's triumphant procession from Seville to Barcelona had processional music in the background; this meant that the running commentaries in verse during these sequences were delivered, over the music, with much the same tempo and punch that characterise a real running commentary delivered over the noise of a crowd on a sportsground. William Walton's music, I should add, served its purpose admirably; i.e. it was structural.

This was a time when the BBC Features Department was active with ambitious radio plays and features with music and they quickly accumulated a considerable repertoire so powerful in its style and assumptions that it was not many years before it stimulated a backlash, and with the eventual abolition of 'Features', for years many felt it to be an outmoded and stilted genre. It was, nevertheless, a significant commissioner of music and Walton's contribution was a notable one. In their day such works certainly had a powerful impact, and during and soon after the war, before the invention of the Third Programme, they achieved a wide audience. Another pre-eminent example from the mid-war period was Edward Sackville-West's *The Rescue* with a notable score by Benjamin Britten.[39] In its author's 'Preamble' to his published text[40] he writes: 'As my friend and colleague, Louis MacNeice, has pointed out . . . a considerable degree of stylisation is necessary in radio-drama.'[40]

But Sackville-West subtitles his play 'a melodrama for broadcasting', and from the outset it was envisaged that music and speech had an equal contribution to make to the success of the enterprise. In a footnote Sackville-West differentiates between *The Rescue* as 'essentially operatic' and *Columbus*: 'a kind of pageant in the production of which the music played a subsidiary role'.[41] Yet it is Walton's triumph that he succeeds in contributing music that determines in a significant way the final effect of the production. Without Walton's score the pace and impact of *Columbus* would have been largely lost. (Even more so, of course, in *The Rescue*, where without the music the whole enterprise could have been in doubt.) For the BBC's 1988 production of *The Rescue*, the music and speech were recorded separately and only married together later at the editing desk. While recording the play, the director, the late Ian Cotterell, suddenly announced over the talkback: 'My God! It's beginning to sound like a Third Programme play!'

In fact Walton's scene painting, particularly in passages of ceremonial or crowd scenes, works excitingly well – a sure harbinger of what was to follow in *Henry V*. Walton's music is used to change scenes, such as in Act II where he characterizes the contrast between the crowds blessing the voyage in plainsong, while at sea the sailors sing 'We're bound upon a wild goosechase'. With solos he is successful but perhaps less memorable. There are three touching soprano songs, the principal one of which, Beatriz's Romanza 'When will he return?', is particularly notable. When in the *Gloria* the tenor soloist sings 'They sailed away to the West', the music exhibits a typical Waltonian rhythmic drive familiar from his orchestral music, but nevertheless fully effective, and to reappear in his opera

Troilus and Cressida. Why did Walton tend to have recourse to such formulae when confronted with words? Was it merely an intrinsic characteristic of his style or did it signify any failing on his part when moving away from instrumental writing?

During the Service of Thanksgiving for the Life and Work of Sir William Walton, held at Westminster Abbey on 20 July 1983, a frail Sir Laurence Olivier ascended the pulpit and launched into a speech from *Henry V* to the packed congregation, suddenly appearing to throw off infirmity in the vigour of his rendition. He was celebrating a partnership in the cinema that had lasted almost 50 years. Olivier had first encountered Walton in *As You Like It* in 1936, though it was *Henry V* in 1944 before Olivier's regard for Walton the film composer was truly cemented.

Walton wrote the music for 14 films, and in the mid-1930s the cinema suddenly provided him with a financial stability he had previously found elusive. This was the time when the commissioning of film scores from leading composers (in the UK Bliss's *Things to Come*, while not the first, was certainly the best known) generated a distinctive new repertoire. Generally, however, film music was not highly regarded by serious musicians, Walton himself turning down the – then enormous – offer of £1650 to write the music for Shaw's *Pygmalion* in 1938 because he was working on his Violin Concerto. He remarked: 'It all boils down to this: whether I'm to become a film composer or a real composer'. On another occasion, indicating his opposition to his film music being played in a concert, he said: 'Film music is not good film music if it can be used for any other purpose.' Rarely can a great artist have been more wrong in his judgement.

Walton wrote the music for *As You Like It*, starring Laurence Olivier and Elisabeth Bergner, in 1936, only his second film. The score was forgotten until revived in 1986, when the expansive title music revealed the ceremonial Walton emerging newly minted by the catalyst of Sibelius from the world of his own first symphony. In this play, of course, Shakespeare supplied several well-known lyrics, of which 'Under the Greenwood Tree', is probably the best known, but although Walton set it, it was not used in the film. A perfectly respectable setting, it lacks the memorability of the orchestral set pieces. Nevertheless it was published in 1937 in versions for solo voice and piano and in a version for unison voices in the *Oxford Choral Songs* series.

During the war Walton wrote a succession of film scores and by the time he worked with Olivier again on a film, another seven had been completed. The wartime scores included *The First of the Few*, from which 'The Spitfire' Prelude and Fugue, taken from an extended flying sequence in the film, quickly became a concert favourite, first performed in January 1943. As Angus Calder, historian of the Blitz, remarked, 'the war years produced notable music, some of it propagandist . . . but this did not have to be specific about current realities'.[42] In 1943 *Henry V* was to be an icon of British victory in France: a reminder that we had successfully invaded France once before and could do it again. It was conceived and shot before Operation Overlord became a reality in the summer of 1944, and first seen when the return to Europe was still in progress, and when the outcome was by no means assured. Many of those associated with the making of *Henry V* were unconvinced of the likelihood of its success. In fact, Olivier's vision was articulated by Walton's music to a remarkable extent, Olivier confessing 'for me the music actually made the film'. It was surely the contribution made by Walton's music which caused the audience at the first showing to stand and applaud after the Battle of Agincourt.[43]

Walton's title music establishes the role of music at the outset. Rarely have the credits for a film been so bound up with the music that accompanied them, the camera panning across a model of London based on Visscher's celebrated engraving. It arrives at the Globe Playhouse as a handbill for the Theatre, flutters to the screen accompanied by flute roulades, and the fanfares announce the Chorus's opening speech. Particularly at the beginning the music is not continuous but underlines various episodes. In the interlude, 'At the Boar's Head', the opening knockabout between Nym, Pistol and Bardolph quickly changes to Walton's touching slow music (based on the traditional tune 'Watkins Ale') for the death of Falstaff, interpolating King Hal's repudiation of the old man from *Henry IV, Part Two*.[44] Such moments were clearly capable of a life separate from the film, but it took longer for the possibility of a suite of orchestral extracts to be considered viable. This was due mostly to Walton's attitude to film music, but it also derived from his close identification with the words, words and music creating an unforgettable melodrama which makes them hard to separate once the connection has been made. So close was this that when the music appeared on records, on eight 78 sides,[45] it became an equal vehicle for Olivier (who played all the parts himself in the recording) and Walton, now in a true symbiotic relationship.

One of the most famous moments, finding Olivier in much-parodied melodramatic mood, is the scene before Harfleur. Here the music is essential to build the mood if Olivier is not to appear ridiculous. Walton introduces Henry's celebrated speech 'Once more unto the breach' with vivid scherzando music evoking great tumult, and follows it with triumphal bombast, providing the perfect frame for Olivier's taste for *rodomontade*. The quiet scenes are some of the most musically successful in creating atmosphere, the night watch scene before the battle ('Now entertain conjecture of a time') thus becoming the pivotal point of the film, its wonderful atmosphere almost totally created by Walton.

Yet Walton's best-known film music remains that underpinning action, rather than that associated with words. Probably the two most widely acclaimed examples are the 'Spitfire Fugue' from the film *The First of the Few*, and that for the Battle of Agincourt, the latter underpinning a wide tracking shot which is given character and credence by Walton's music.

Hamlet followed four years later and was shot in black and white at a time when colour was the vogue. Capitalizing on the success of *Henry V*, the Olivier–Walton combination now created considerable anticipation on the part of film-goers and music-lovers alike. The title music, with its vision of the mist crowned, sea-skirted castle of Elsinore, gives us a ghostly preview of the final dénouement, underlined by Walton's passionate funeral march. Fanfares announce the opening scene in the Castle (the first has been the ghost's initial visitation on the battlements). Hamlet is sitting apart self-communing. Less than a month after his father's death his mother married his uncle who is now king ('the funeral bak'd meats / Did coldly furnish forth the marriage tables'). The music underpinning Hamlet's soliloquy 'O! that this too too solid flesh would melt, / Thaw and resolve itself into a dew', with its brooding contrapuntal textures, enhances the mood and the words in a true melodramatic partnership.

Walton himself illustrated how he approached Hamlet's soliloquies, remarking 'the incidental musical effects . . . varied their orchestral colour according the shifts of his thought'.[46] An example of this and one of the high points in the film is the question: 'To be or not to be', perhaps the most famous speech of any playwright. This is preceded by dramatic music as the camera races up a spiral staircase, open on one side, underlined by the rising tumult of the music. As he delivers the speech, Olivier is shot from below, the music closely integrated into and reflecting the varied moods of the words.

Muir Mathieson, who conducted the music on the *Hamlet* soundtrack, chose the players' scene to 'illustrate the extraordinary ingenuity Walton brings into his screen writing'.[47]

> The arrival of the Court is heralded by trumpet calls and a superb march theme which appears to keep step with the retinue as they take their places around the King's dais. Then the players make their entry, accompanied by a small group of musicians. For this, Walton hints at the idiom of the period, and uses an orchestra of two violas, cello, oboe, cor anglais, bassoon and harpsichord. He opens with a sarabande, music in slow three-in-a-measure dance time often encountered in seventeenth- and eighteenth-century music, and follows this with a slow sinister passage for the entry of the poisoner.
>
> As the camera moves round to show the reactions of the audience, and particularly of the King, the stage music dissolves into the Players theme, which is taken up by the full symphony orchestra, as the dramatic undercurrent of the scene, and the tension of the Court, rises.
>
> The camera, from its circular tracking orbit, returns to the Players, and the music reverts to the quiet accompaniment of the play. The actor-king has been poisoned; the King can no longer stand the strain. ('The play's the thing, Wherein to catch the conscience of the King.') The full power of the orchestra rises in a tremendous chord, as the King roars out, 'Give me some light'.
>
> William Walton's score was a constant delight to record, being so perfect in detail and sure in its dramatic conception. It will prove the perfect complement to a great subject.[48]

Hamlet has already encountered the ghost of his murdered father, the deep pulsating effect produced by Walton suggesting a heartbeat, or perhaps Hamlet's own heart beating in apprehension of what is to come. Probably the best music from this film is the funeral march. Composers as varied as Berlioz and Shostakovich have written gripping funeral marches for *Hamlet*, but Walton's is possibly the best of them all. It rounds the film with a remarkably stirring yet utterly appropriate mood.

Seven years passed between *Hamlet* and *Richard III*, by which time the music for the earlier Shakespearean films had become established. So had Walton's coronation marches, including *Orb and Sceptre*, the march for the 1953 Coronation. The film is launched with title music which consists of one of his most memorable marches. Setting the scene and creating the mood, it immediately joined the canon of his popular works. Yet overall the musical contribution is somewhat plainer than in the two previous films. For the only time in any of these films the complete soundtrack was issued on LPs,[49] and thus it is possible to assess the function of the music without visual distractions. The opening Coronation music and the following scene has plenty of music, but it is stage business music, and is not related to the words. This throws the following scenes, without music, into sharp relief. The tone is set by possibly the best known speech in this play, 'Now is the winter of my discontent', which on screen is to all intents and purposes without music.

There are several striking orchestral sequences but they are far less integrated into the fabric of the film than before. When the young Prince Edward is brought to a snow-covered London to be crowned, Walton produces a child-like scherzo, almost a miniature Russian sleigh ride. Really the only time Walton approached the intensity of the earlier scores comes with the murder of the two young princes in the tower, for which, as in his two heartfelt interludes in *Henry V*, he only uses string orchestra.

Richard, horseless on Bosworth field, is killed with melodramatic death throes and an expressive wisp of cello solo. Then with his body dangling across a horse, the music becomes a funereal cortège which gradually transforms into a great royal march for the close. Only as the camera pans skyward for the end credits does Walton fully elaborate his march, which now assumes a longer perspective, not a march for Richard but for 500 years of English history.

*   *   *

Any discussion of Walton's approach to words must consider his operas, *Troilus and Cressida* and *The Bear*, sharply contrasted in scale and treatment, the one setting a literate and poetic (perhaps over-poetic) libretto, the other approaching doggerel in the song texts.

Like *Belshazzar*, Walton was first prompted to write his opera *Troilus and Cressida* by a commission from the BBC. And like *Belshazzar* he failed to deliver because the project outgrew its original conception which had been for an opera for broadcasting. It was Alice Wimborne who suggested the poet Christopher Hassall as librettist and 'she led their combined search for the subject'.[50] The composition spread over several years and the romantic story, started by Walton's companion 30 years his senior, was in the end stimulated and finished after he married Susana Gil, 25 years his junior. It was not completed until 1954 and first performed at the Royal Opera House Covent Garden on 3 December that year.

Walton wanted to write a big traditional romantic opera. He largely succeeded, though without consistent strikingly memorable invention, and this was the reason for some adverse criticism. Because Walton was living in Ischia while composing much of the music and Hassall was living in London, an extensive correspondence survives documenting in some detail the evolution of the libretto. This is discussed in length in Chapter 8, but it is certainly worth picking up one or two points of detail here. Christopher Hassall wrote 'In the last analysis a composer of opera is his own dramatist, so it is vital at every stage for each collaborator to know precisely what the other is doing and why'.[51]

Walton wanted 'a tidy love story with political motivations; he did not want epic proportions' reported his intending biographer Gillian Widdicombe.[52] Walton had very specific ideas of what he wanted, derived from the operas of Verdi and Puccini, in fact *bel canto* in English. Writing to Hassall in January 1952 about the love duet he asked his librettist for words 'so impassioned as to set fire to the typewriter', adding 'we must make the love scene the best and highwater mark not only of the act but the whole op.'[53] In fact in the end the climax of the love duet was an orchestral interlude, 'and the ecstasy of Troilus and Cressida's lovemaking is juxtaposed with the violent foreboding of the storm outside'.[54] Significantly in spite of the importance which Walton attached to the duet it is the powerful impact of the orchestral interlude that one tends to remember. Walton himself referred to it as 'pornographic' in its evocation of the lovers' consummation of their passion against the storm which breaks outside.

Hassall had never written an opera before and tended to be flowery and poetic, rather in the vein of the then in-vogue playwright Christopher Fry. But Walton had been schooled in the disciplined aesthetic of the Sitwells and he was aware of the danger of prolixity. He knew what an audience would stand for on the stage and what it would not. At one point Walton wrote to his collaborator complaining that 'three and a half pages of dialogue set in recitative or dramatic recitative are going to be stiff both for the audience and the unfortunate composer'.[55] Later, reviewing the first performance, Eric Blom would refer to 'recitative that is very far from dry and never unvocally declamatory'.[56]

Walton had before him the example of the successful operas of Britten and the personal voice of Vaughan Williams, the latter in his recent *Pilgrim's Progress*. Both these composers were the product of a long experience of vocal writing (decades in Vaughan Williams' case). Walton did not have that personal resource in writing for the voice, but he had developed with Hassall a viable drama but only intermittently to be articulated with striking and memorable invention. Yet 40 years on, on the stage at Covent Garden in January 1995, the Opera North production came over as a memorable and colourful evening, the choral writing and the orchestra being particularly characteristic of the composer.

To what extent is any failing of the opera owing to the libretto *per se* – the actual words set – and to what extent is its success due to the structure of the libretto? Certainly there are passages where there are too many words. Walton was alive to the potential problems, as his correspondence with Hassall makes clear. Hassall had previously provided Ivor Novello with lyrics and it must have been difficult for him not to repeat that approach for Walton's opera. One may best judge their success from the historical recording of extracts with Elisabeth Schwarzkopf as Cressida and Peter Pears as Pandarus.[57] The work was written with Schwarzkopf's voice in mind though she never sang it on the stage. Here we have all the plums one after another and it is certainly enjoyable and effective music, but surely nowhere does it achieve the memorability to make it a concert favourite. There are no popular encores (even Samuel Barber's similarly unsuccessful *Anthony and Cleopatra* produced two). To the extent that Walton was potentially capable of such a coup, he failed. Yet in his characters he had some successes, in particular the slightly camp figure of Pandarus, who in the hands of Peter Pears was remarkably successful. A fragment of Pears' characterization is transferred to CD, but the first performance of the opera in 1954 was broadcast, with Pears in the role, and survives on tape.

In fact the early performances at Covent Garden were a considerable popular success. 'The first performance of Sir William Walton's *Troilus and Cressida* last night was the proudest hour for British music since the premiere of Benjamin Britten's *Peter Grimes* nine years ago' wrote the *Daily Express* critic. 'For four years the 52-year-old composer and his librettist, Christopher Hassall, laboured to create an opera worthy of the national opera house. The acclaim of the celebrity-studded first night audience told them that they had succeeded.' He concluded, 'I consider *Troilus and Cressida* a musical landmark because it returns British opera to a healthy course. It was not composed for a small band of intellectuals. It is an opera *everyone* can understand and enjoy. It will advance the love of opera at home and enhance the fame of Britain abroad.'[58]

By and large the popular press supported this assessment. Scott Goddard was left with 'an impression of great beauty, warmly lyrical music, many moments of compelling passion, and a general sense of power. This is music that lingers in one's memory and haunts one's imagination'.[59] Charles Reid in the London *Evening Standard* was even more enthusiastic:

> Most English operatic composers fumble shyly when required to write love music. Sir William Walton is an exception to this sorry rule. After composing nothing but platform music for 30 years he has given us a three-act tragic opera . . . which makes as big a commotion about love as Verdi, Gounod or Tchaikovsky ever did. I came away from last night's performance at Covent Garden actually humming some of the more salient love scenes. In the first act Troilus (Richard Lewis) sang a lilting Ode to Cressida . . . which 40 years ago would have been selling at 1s 6d a copy in the ballad shops . . . [but] the libretto would do with pruning here and there. Cressida's father is an old bore who betrays Walton into writing neo-Wagnerian padding. Pandarus on the other hand is a brilliant creation as sung by Peter Pears.[60]

A week or so after the première the music critic of *The Times* (Frank Howes, though his column is unsigned) published a parallel between Walton's opera and

Wagner's *Tristan*.[61] Another week on a letter to the editor found 'the uncritical reception accorded to Sir William Walton's Troilus and Cressida is, for the Continental opera lover . . . something of an enigma. . . . There is, indeed, nothing "wrong" with it: apart, perhaps, from the – negligible – fact that, for Continental ears, it is half a century late'.[62]

The issue of the idiom Walton adopted in his opera would dog the work's reception for nearly half a century. But although in 1954 such questions appeared to matter, by the 1990s they were far less important in a more pluralistic musical world.

> There is no doubt that in *Troilus* Walton handles his traditional idiom with superb conviction and authority, so convincingly indeed that the opera almost succeeds as a perfect exercise in the grand style, perfectly executed. The composer is aided by a splendidly contrived libretto of Christopher Hassall, dramatically compact, concise and pungent . . . his own theatrical sense remains astonishing. In hardly any respect did *Troilus* strike me as a first opera; its total maturity was truly surprising. But here, I suggest, is the rub. For *Troilus* seems to me to be not at all a 'first' opera but one of the last in a long line stretching from Wagner to Strauss . . . *Troilus* is a success on one level, because it is wonderfully competent, dramatically effective, warm-hearted and sincere. It fails, I believe, because Walton only gains his success at the expense of his own individuality.[63]

Walton's opera reached La Scala, Milan, in an Italian translation, about a year later. This was an achievement Walton had been looking forward to with considerable anticipation, albeit some trepidation. He was right to be worried, for it was received with whistling and catcalls.

> Rarely has a performance taken such a beating at the hands of musical Italy's top critics . . . The gilt-and-gingerbread house was packed for the glittering first night. But the hooting from the 'gods' drowned the polite plaudits of the white tie, diamonds and mink set. . . . The critics are practically unanimous in condemning *Troilus and Cressida* as 'soulless' and 'inconsistent', 'ill-constructed', 'lacking in originality and personality', 'false'.[64]

When the opera was revived in 1963 one might have expected there to have been a sense of perspective in the critical reception. But in fact the reservations expressed earlier were still put forward, applied equally to the words and the music. In the *Sunday Telegraph* John Warrack wrote

> The odds against him show when we come to the big arias. It is significant that Christopher Hassall, whose plot is well constructed, could do nothing but serve Walton up words like 'Child of the wine-dark wave, mantled in beauty' and 'At the haunted end of the day your voice, dear love, your voice alone I hear'. What is a poor composer to do! All the same, the opera has lasted better than many feared, and it suits the Covent Garden company well.[65]

Other critics returned to this theme: 'If the central relationship between the lovers leaves the listener disturbingly cool, it is because the musical language of their big lyrical outbursts is as devalued a currency as Christopher Hassall's "poetic" diction, something that is no longer backed by emotional reality.'[66] That was Martin Cooper's view, and he took the opportunity to write an extended comparison of Walton's opera and Prokofiev's *Love of Three Oranges* which was revived in London at the same time. He concluded that 'both men were to make the common and natural compromise with the artistic past that they had at first mocked, but Walton made it when he was ten years younger than Prokofiev'.[67]

Speaking personally, the 1963 revival seemed a somewhat tired production, and the opera did not make an impact until 1976 when Walton revised the name part for Janet Baker, lowering Cressida's tessitura and simplifying the story. Walton remarked 'Christopher Hassall, who gave me the libretto, really had no idea, nor had I, what would go on the stage'.[68] Yet Walton's analysis of the words he was getting from his librettist was practical and sure-footed.

> Not that we really saw eye to eye about things. If he were still alive, I'd never have been able to re-write *Troilus*. Every time I took out a word there or a note, there was a row. I think his style had been ruined by Ivor Novello. He didn't take it at all well when I suggested that Ivor's influence should be subdued. I remember I put 'IN' all over his libretto. That didn't please him at all. I think the worst of those bits have gone now.[69]

The fact that the 1976 version has been recorded and issued first on LP and now on CD means that the music has been assessed not only by a wider audience but now with a 40-year perspective since it was first heard. This has all been to the benefit of Walton's conception, though not necessarily to Hassall's libretto.

When the LPs first appeared they were warmly received, the *Penguin Stereo Record Guide* noting, in 1977, that 'the result is superbly alive . . . setting a classical story in big, bold gestures against warmly lyrical, finely concentrated music. If anything the result is even more compelling on records . . .'.[70] Already stylistic problems associated with either the words or the music were beginning to fade, but because of the difficulty of finding a suitable artist to sing the role of Cressida, either at the lower pitch chosen for Baker or as originally written, the work was not produced again until taken up by Opera North for the Chandos recording in 1995. A 28-year-old director, Matthew Warchus, was chosen to produce the work, his first appearance in the opera house. His view of the opera had a Nineties perspective: 'What persuaded me was the enthusiasm of the conductor, Richard Hickox', explains Warchus '. . . he saw the work in terms of its energy and its Mediterranean feel . . . Christopher Hassall's text . . . also turned out to be stronger than expected . . . The music's fantastic. You get incredible colour and energy in the orchestra. Walton was a really accomplished dramatic composer . . . He's got a very vivid sense of private and public worlds colliding and pulling against each other'.[71]

The Chandos recording of the Opera North production, having solved the textual[72] and casting problems which may have contributed to earlier reservations about the work, now reveals a score to be appreciated on its own terms. Some of the artistic concerns of 20 to 40 years ago on which past reservations may have turned are now themselves seen as unacceptable to a later generation. Style is no longer an issue, what matters is quality, as the *Gramophone* critic remarked:

It is here powerfully presented as an opera for the central repertory, traditional in its red-blooded treatment of a big classical subject, with the composer revelling in big tonal melodies presented with many frisson-making modulations. Few if any operas since Puccini have such a rich store of instantly memorable tunes as *Troilus and Cressida*.[73]

After *Troilus*, Walton's one act comic opera *The Bear* has a quite different effect, and the music a totally different relationship with the words. As Peter Heyworth observed after the Aldeburgh Festival première, Walton 'for the first time in over 40 years indulged that wickedly accurate gift of parody which makes *Façade* one of the few genuinely funny pieces of music written in the twentieth century.'[74]

The Bear is after a vaudeville by Chekhov and Paul Dehn's libretto makes no bones about coarsening the play's texture. 'The song texts are frankly doggerel, to which Walton responds with a kind of musical doggerel of his own, part pastiche, part self-parody'[75] wrote Stephen Walsh in *The Times*. The librettist in his note for the Aldeburgh première explained:

> here, in the small compass of a one-acter, Chekhov's dialogue subtly breathes as much (if not more) about the war between the sexes as was ever exhaled in the entire works of Thurber or in Shakespeare's *The Taming of the Shrew*; and Thurber would have been the first to approve the fact that Chekhov's shrew . . . does most of the taming.[76]

Walton responds to this scenario in uninhibited fashion with a sustained, almost schoolboy delight in parody. Apart from a glance at Britten's own *A Midsummer Night's Dream*, the objects of Walton's humour are largely Russian with parodies of Tchaikovsky, Mussorgsky, Stravinsky, as well as Offenbach, Poulenc and others. When it was revived in 1990 at the Newcastle Playhouse in a double bill with Martinu's *Comedy on the Bridge*, the Walton appeared the stronger, more sharply characterized, work. This humour is perhaps typically English, and it is telling that in 1967 Peter Stadlen 'could not always laugh when I knew I ought to'.[77]

By and large Walton's songs and works for solo voice and accompaniment do not rate highly among his music. Yet there are two exceptions to this generalization, both written late in his career: *Anon in Love* and *A Song for the Lord Mayor's Table*, both set texts assembled for Walton by Christopher Hassall. The first of these, written for the 1960 Aldeburgh Festival and Peter Pears and the guitarist Julian Bream, is remarkable for its apparent spontaneity, and for the idiomatic fluency of the guitar accompaniment. Writing in *The Times*, their 'special correspondent' was enthusiastic: 'Some of Walton's recent works have been received with mixed feelings, but these settings of sixteenth and seventeenth century love poems must surely be universally welcomed . . . Walton has distilled the fruits of his experience into a potent and concentrated musical utterance, sometimes direct and sometimes curiously subtle.'[78]

Later, in 1971, Walton arranged – or more accurately, recast – the accompaniment for small orchestra, and in this form the work has an irresistibly typical Waltonian drive and *élan*. The orchestra was also the reason for the success of his second song cycle, *A Song for the Lord Mayor's Table*. Initially this had been written for voice and piano, introduced in 1962 by no less a partnership than Elisabeth Schwarzkopf and Gerald Moore. It was 1970 before the orchestral version appeared, and here the work really takes wing in its symphonic form. One says 'symphonic' advisedly as the sweep of the music, and the almost operatic scale of the voice for which Walton writes, are to my mind not well caught by a solo singer with piano. If it does not have the charm of the earlier love songs it is nevertheless the work of a composer who responded with invention and affection to happy evocations of the city where he had made his reputation and spent much of his early career.

Walton's occasional vocal music, particularly that for chorus, is often very effective but has very much a subsidiary feel to his major works. A case in point is the *Gloria*, 'in Sir William's most defiantly brash and brassy vein. It sets out to provide a big chorus something meaty and exciting to sing'.[79] That was Peter Heyworth writing after the first London performance in 1962, adding waspishly 'Sir William goes through his circus tricks like an old trouper. and a large audience showed that it appreciated them as much as ever'. In fact the work is one of several that demonstrably mine the manner of *Belshazzar's Feast* rather than respond with newly-minted invention to the demands of new words. The result is that whether it is hymning London in *In Honour of the City* in 1937 or hymning God 25 years later, they all sound like a pagan orgy, exciting but somehow coarse and lacking in sympathy.

Walton was the composer of some of the most memorable and individual melodies in twentieth-century music, yet he left no great tune indelibly associated with specific words.[80] Nevertheless his music written to accompany words is dramatic and effective, and many of his most popular works require voices. His music establishes a unique relationship with a wide variety of words, and Walton's music resonates in the mind long after a lesser composer's more conventional lyrics word-setting is forgotten. But it is certain that if he had received a more conventionally literary education and had not experienced the hot-house university of his extended *ménage* with the Sitwells he might well have written his music differently. There is no guarantee that we would be the richer for it. His output is one of the pillars of twentieth-century British music, and although he felt at the end that he 'should have done better',[81] who would not be proud to have achieved one-tenth of his output?

Notes

1.   Walton, S. (1988) *William Walton, Behind the Façade*, Oxford: OUP, pp. 57–8.
2.   Op. cit. p. 67.
3.   Sitwell, O. (1949) *Laughter in the Next Room being the fourth volume of Left Hand, Right Hand!* Basingstoke: Macmillan, The Reprint Society (1950), p. 182.
4.   Mitchell, D. (1957) 'The "Modernity" of William Walton', *The Listener*, 7 Feb., p. 245.

5. Pearson, J. (1994) 'Façade and the Twenties', in *The Sitwells and the Arts of the 1920s and 1930s*, Exhibition handbook, National Portrait Gallery, p. 80.

6. Pearson, J. (1978) *Façades: Edith, Osbert and Sacheverell Sitwell*, London: Macmillan, and London: Fontana (1980), p. 183.

7. Kennedy, M. (1989) *Portrait of Walton*, Oxford: OUP, p. 29.

8. Widdicombe, G. (1982) 'Behind Walton's *Façade*', *Observer Magazine*, 7 February, pp. 28–33.

9. Banfield, S. (1985) *Sensibility and English Song Vol. 2*, Cambridge: CUP, p. 371.

10. 28 Sept 1928 in *From Parry to Britten*, ed. Lewis Foreman (1987), London: Batsford, p. 134.

11. Hughes, S. (1946) *Opening Bars*, London: Pilot Press, p. 363.

12. The recording of 11 numbers featured Edith Sitwell reciting four and Constant Lambert the remainder. Issued on two Decca 78s (T 124/5), it reappeared without the Valse on the 7" EP supplied with the 1971 limited edition of the score. (See note 16.)

13. The Alhambra 1919 prospectus for 30 April to 22 July listed 40 'Symphonic Interludes' for the season, of which four were by British composers.

14. Fuller, R. (1973) 'Façade', *The Listener*, 7 June, p. 773.

15. Pearson, J. 'Façade and the Twenties', op. cit., pp. 77, 79.

16. Walton, Sir W. (1973) *Façade: an entertainment*, Oxford: OUP, pp. xiv, xv (limited edition).

17. Ford, B. (1994) *Benjamin Britten's Poems*, Manchester: Carcanet Press, new ed. 1996.

18. 'Gray, Walpole, West and Ashton, the Quadruple Alliance', *Times Literary Supplement*, 4 September 1919; 'Scott and Shakespeare', *Times Literary Supplement*, 6 August 1925; 'A Frisk', *Times Literary Supplement*, 6 August 1925.

19. Banfield, S. (1985), op. cit., vol. 1, p. 27.

20. Bliss, Sir A. *As I Remember*, London: Faber (1970), Thames Publishing (1989), p. 93.

21. Cooper, M. (1957) 'The Unpredictable Walton', *The Listener*, 25 July, p. 146.

22. Boden, A. (1992) *Three Choirs: a history of the festival*, Stroud: Alan Sutton, p. 199.

23. Drew, D. (1962) 'Royal Justice', *New Stateman*, 26 Jan., p. 136.

24. Bradbury, E. (1963) 'Modern British Composers' in Jacobs, A. *Choral Music – a symposium*, Harmordsworth: Penguin, pp. 339–40.

25. *The Listener*, 25 June 1970, p. 869.

26. Barrie, J. M. (1938) *The Boy David*, London: Peter Davies.

27. Op. cit. p. 104.

28. Ibid., p. 107.

29. Ibid., p. 122.

30. The *Macbeth* music, with sequences from *Richard III* and *Major Barbara*, are on Chandos CHAN 8841.

31. Manvell, R. and Huntley, J. (1957) *The Technique of Film Music*, revised and enlarged by Richard Arnell and Peter Day (1975), New York: Hastings House, p. 94.

32. Walton, S., op. cit., p. 95.

33. Zdenek Fibich (1850–1900) was, after Smetana and Dvořák, the most prominent Czech composer of his day. Noted for operas and orchestral music, he wrote a succession of melodramas both for the stage – *Hippodamie* (a trilogy after Sophocles and Euripides) – and for the concert room. Six of the Fibich melodramas with three by Ostrcil were recorded on LP on Supraphone 1112 2711-12G. A CD recording of *Hippodamie* is on Supraphone SU3037-2.

34. Corder, F. (1895) 'Recitation with Music', in *Voice, Speech and Gesture: a practical handbook to the elocutionary art*, by H. Campbell et al., edited with notes and introduction by R. D. Blackman, new and enlarged edition, London: Charles William Deacon & Co., 1904.

35. Stanley Hawley melodramas are recorded by Pamela Hunter on Discovery International DICD 920245.
36. Widdicombe, G. (1973) 'Christopher Columbus', *Financial Times*, 10 April.
37. MacNeice, L. (1944) *Christopher Columbus: a radio play*, London: Faber, p. 19.
38. Ibid., p. 89.
39. First broadcast in two parts on 25 and 26 November 1943. The music was recently arranged by Chris de Souza as a concert work with the title *The Rescue of Penelope*, with linking narrative taken from the play, and recorded by the Hallé Orchestra with Dame Janet Baker in the speaking part (Erato 0630-12713-2).
40. Sackville-West, E. (1945) *The Rescue: a melodrama for broadcasting based on Homer's Odyssey*, London: Secker and Warburg, p. 13.
41. Ibid., p. 16.
42. Calder, A. (1995) 'Britain's Good War?' *History Today*, May, p. 60.
43. Manvell, R. and Huntley, J., op. cit., p. 95. They are quoting Hubert Clifford in *Tempo*.
44. Olivier edited Shakespeare's play for the screen, not only deleting passages but making interpolations and additions of his own. The script was published in the Classic Film Script series 'Shakespeare, William: *Henry V: produced and directed by Laurence Olivier*', London: Lorrimer Publishing, 1984 (cover title: 'Laurence Olivier – Henry V').
45. The *Passacaglia on the Death of Falstaff* and *Touch her Soft Lips and Part*, for string orchestra, were first recorded on one side of a 12" 78 in 1945 (issued January 1946), HMV C 3480. The well-known set with Olivier appeared on 4 × 12" 78s (HMV C 3583/6).
46. Walton, Sir W. in Manvell and Huntley, op. cit., p. 93.
47. Cross, B. (1948) *The film Hamlet – a record of its production*, London: The Saturn Press, p. 64.
48. Ibid.
49. HMV ALP 1341/3.
50. Widdicombe, G. 'Troilus and Cressida', booklet with LPs, HMV SLS 997, p. 5.
51. Hassall, C. (1954) 'A New Cressida in a New Opera', *Radio Times*, 26 November, p. 5.
52. Widdicombe, G., op. cit.
53. Kennedy, M. (1989) *Portrait of Walton*, Oxford: OUP, pp. 152–3.
54. 'Synopsis', Opera North Programme for Royal Opera House Covent Garden, January 1995, p. 9.
55. Kennedy, M. (1989), op. cit., p. 152.
56. Blom, E. (1954) 'Walton's "Troilus and Cressida"', *The Observer*, 5 December.
57. Remastered for CD on EMI CDM 7 64199 2.
58. Smith, C. (1954) 'Music Comes off its High Horse', *Daily Express*, 4 December.
59. Goddard, S. (1954) 'Walton Has An Operatic Triumph', *News Chronicle*, 4 December.
60. Reid, C. (1954) 'Sir William Goes for the Love Scenes', *Evening Standard*, 4 December.
61. Howes, F. (1954) 'Walton's Opera – a parallel with Wagner', *The Times*, 10 December, p. 10.
62. Von Einsiedel, W. (1954) 'Troilus and Cressida: To the Editor of The Times', *The Times*, 17 December.
63. Mitchell, D. (1955) 'Troilus and Cressida', *Musical Times*, January, p. 36.
64. Barber, S. (1956) 'Rival Began Opera Boos, Says Walton', *News Chronicle*, 14 January.
65. Warrack, J. (1963) 'Not too Late for Romance', *Sunday Telegraph*, 28 April.
66. Cooper, M. (1963) 'Strength and Wit in Walton "Troilus"', *Daily Telegraph*, 24 April.
67. Cooper, M. (1963) 'Diverging Parallels', *Daily Telegraph*, 27 April.
68. Blyth, A. (1976) 'Troilus Simplified', *The Times*, 12 November.

69. Blyth, ibid.
70. March, I. (ed) (1977) 'Walton – Troilus and Cressida (opera) complete', in *The Penguin Stereo Record Guide*, 2nd ed., Harmondsworth: Penguin, p. 1149.
71. Whitley, J. (1995) 'First Love is True Love', *Daily Telegraph*, 30 January, p. 17.
72. Walton's cuts were so fragmentary Hickox was unable to restore them for the recording.
73. G[reenfield], E. (1995) 'Walton Troilus and Cressida', *Gramophone*, May, p. 115.
74. Heyworth, P. (1967) 'Shipwreck in Suffolk', *Observer*, 11 June.
75. Walsh, S. (1972) 'The Bear', *The Times*, 10 October.
76. Dehn, P. (1967) 'The Bear an extravaganza in one act', *The Twentieth Aldeburgh Festival of Music and the Arts* [programme book], Aldeburgh, p. 11.
77. Stadlen, P. (1967) 'Odysseus as Hero of Berkeley Opera', *Daily Telegraph*, 13 July.
78. 'Walton's New Love Songs', *The Times*, 22 June, 1960, p. 7.
79. Heyworth, P. (1962) 'Music and Musicians', *Observer*, 21 January.
80. Along with Gerard Hoffnung we might perhaps regard Walton's most long-remembered setting as the one word: 'slain!'!
81. Walton in Tony Palmer's film *At the Haunted End of the Day*.

Bibliography

Abbate, C. (1991) *Unsung Voices*, Princeton: University Press.
Alexander, P. F. (1986) 'The Process of Composition of the Libretto of Britten's *Gloriana'*, *Music and Letters*, 67, pp. 147–58.
Aprahamian, F. (1960) 'Walton and his New Symphony', *The Listener*, 25 August.
Aprahamian, F. (1972) 'Walton in Perspective', *Music and Musicians*, 20, p. 11.
Avery, K. (1947) 'William Walton', *Music &Literature*, 28, pp. 1–11.
Ballantine, Christopher (1983) *Twentieth Century Symphony*, London: Dobson.
Banfield, S. (ed.) (1995) *Music in Britain, Vol. 6: The Twentieth Century*, London: Blackwell.
Banks, P. (ed.) (1993) *Britten's Gloriana: Assays and Sources*, The Britten Pears Library.
Barker, F. G. (1954) 'Walton's Troilus and Cressida', *Opera News*, 19, p. 10.
Barker, F. G. (1963) 'Troilus Revisited', *Music and Musicians*, 11, pp. 37–8.
Bliss, A. (1970) *As I Remember*, London: Faber and Faber.
Blom, E. (1945) 'The later William Walton', *The Listener*, 20 Sept.
Boyden D. (1955) 'Troilus and Cressida', *Musical Quarterly*, 41, pp. 238–41.
Brett, P. (ed.) (1983) *Benjamin Britten: Peter Grimes*, Cambridge: Cambridge University Press.
Brian, Havergal (1986) 'Havergal Brian on Music', selections from his Journalism edited by Malcolm MacDonald. *Vol. 1: British Music*, London: Toccata.
Carpenter, H. (1981) *W. H. Auden: A Biography*, London: Allen and Unwin.
Carpenter, Humphrey (1992) *Benjamin Britten: a Biography*, London: Faber & Faber.
Cooper, M. (1957) 'The Unpredictable Walton', *The Listener*, 25 July.
Cox, D. (1967) 'Walton', in Simpson, R. (ed.) *The Symphony 2*, Harmondsworth: Penguin Books, pp. 189–96.
Craggs, S. R. (1977) *William Walton, A Thematic Catalogue of his Musical Works*, London: OUP.
Craggs, S. R. (1990) *William Walton: A Catalogue*, Oxford: Oxford University Press.
Craggs, S. R. (1993) *A Walton Source Book*, Aldershot: Scolar Press.
Dean, W. (1977) 'Troilus and Cressida', *Musical Times*, 118, p. 55.
Evans, E. (1944) 'William Walton', *Musical Times*, 85, pp. 329–32; 364–71.

Evans, E. (1935) 'Walton's Symphony', *Radio Times*, 1 November, p. 15.

Evans, P. (1959) 'Sir William Walton's Manner and Mannerism', *The Listener*, 20 August, p. 297.

Ferris, P. (ed.) (1963) *The Collected Letters of Dylan Thomas*, London: Dent.

Ferris, P. (1977) *Dylan Thomas*, London: Hodder and Stoughton.

Ford, B. (ed.) (1988) *The Cambridge Guide to the Arts in Britain, vol. ix: Since the Second World War*, Cambridge: CUP.

Ford, B. (ed.) (1989) *The Cambridge Guide to the Arts in Britain, vol. viii: The Edwardian Age and the Inter-War Years*, Cambridge: CUP.

Foreman, L. (1987) *From Parry to Britten: British Music in Letters, 1900–1945*, London: B. T. Batsford.

Foss, H. J. (1945) 'The Music of William Walton', *The Listener*, 17 May, p. 557.

Foss, H. J. (1940) 'William Walton', *MQ*, 26, pp. 456–66.

Frank, A. (1939) 'The Music of William Walton', *The Chesterian*, 20, pp. 153–6.

Goddard, Scott (1952) 'William Walton', in Hill, R. (ed.), *The Concerto*, pp. 386–99.

Goodwin, N. (1977) 'Troilus and Cressida', *Music and Musicians*, 25, pp. 34–6.

Gray, C. (1948) *Musical Chairs, or Between two Stools*, London: Home and Van Thal.

Greenfield, E. (1972) 'William Walton', *The Guardian*, 29 February, p. 10.

Groos, A. and Parker, R. (1986) *Giacomo Puccini: La Bohème*, Cambridge: Cambridge University Press.

The New Grove Dictionary of Music and Musicians (1980) ed. Stanley Sadie, 20 vols, London: Macmillan.

Haltrecht, M. (1975) *The Quiet Showman: Sir David Webster and the Royal Opera House*, London: Collins.

Harewood, The Earl of (1981) *The Tongs And The Bones: The Memoirs of Lord Harewood*, London: Weidenfeld and Nicholson.

Hassall, C. (1954a) 'And Now – Walton's First Opera', *Music and Musicians*, 3, p. 12.

Hassall, C. (1954b) *Troilus and Cressida: Opera In three Acts*, Oxford: Oxford University Press.

Hassall, C. (1959) *Edward Marsh: a biography*, London: Longman.

Hassall, C. (1976) *Troilus and Cressida: Opera in three acts* (revised edn.), Oxford: OUP.

Headington, C. (1992) *Peter Pears: A Biography*, London: Faber & Faber.

Hill, Ralph (ed.) (1952) *The Concerto*, Harmondsworth: Penguin.

Howes, F. (1965) *The Music of William Walton*, Oxford: Oxford University Press.

Howes, F. (1966) *The English Musical Renaissance*, London: OUP.

Howes, F. (1974) *The Music of William Walton*, 2nd ed., London: OUP.

Hughes, Spike (1946) *Opening Bars*, London: Pilot Press.

Hurd, M. (1990) *Portrait of Walton* reviewed by Michael Kennedy, *Music and Letters*, 71, pp. 282–3.

Hussey, D. (1954) 'William Turner Walton', in A. L. Bacharach (ed.), *The Music Masters, iv*, London: Cassell, pp. 411–18.

Hutchings, A. (1937) 'The Symphony and William Walton', *Musical Times*, 78, pp. 211–15.

Jacobs, A. (1963) 'Troilus and Cressida', *Opera*, 14, pp. 419–21.

Keller, H. and Walton, Sir W. (1966) 'Contemporary Music: its Problems and its Future', *Composer*, 20, pp. 2–4.

Keller, H. (1955) 'The Half-Year's New Music', *Music Review*, 16, pp. 62–3.

Kennedy, M. (1973) 'William Walton: a Critical Appreciation', in Craggs's *Thematic Catalogue* (1977).

Kennedy, M. (1982) *Portrait of Elgar*, Rev. ed., London: OUP, 1982.

Kennedy, M. (1983) 'Walton in Perspective', *The Listener*, 11 August, p. 30.

Kennedy, M. (1989) *Portrait of Walton*, Oxford: OUP.

Kerman, J. (1955) 'Troy at the Golden Gate', *Opera News*, 20, pp. 6–7 and 32.

Klein, J. W. (1956) 'A Decade of English Opera', *Musical Opinion*, 79, pp. 211 and 213.

Lambert, C. (1966) *Music, Ho! A Study of Music in Decline*, 3rd ed., London:

Lambert, C. (1936) 'Some Angles of the Compleat Walton', *Radio Times*, 7 August, p. 13.

Layton, R. (1962) 'Walton and his Critics', *The Listener*, 29 March, p. 577.

Lewis, C. S. (1958) *The Allegory of Love: A Study in Medieval Tradition* (2nd edn), Oxford: OUP.

Mason, C. (1946) 'William Walton', in A.L. Bacharach (ed.) *British Music of Our Time*, Harmondsworth: Penguin, pp. 137–49.

Mendelson, E. (1993) *W. H. Auden and Chester Kallman. Libretti and other dramatic writings by W. H. Auden, 1939–1973*, London: Faber & Faber.

Merrick, F. (1941) 'Walton's Concerto for Violin and Orchestra', *MR*, 2, pp. 309–18.

Mitchell, D. (1952) 'Some Observations on William Walton', *The Chesterian*, 26, pp. 35–8.

Mitchell, D. (1955) 'Opera in London: Troilus and Cressida', *Musical Times*, 96, p. 36.

Mitchell, D. (1955) 'Revaluations: William Walton', *Musical Opinion*, 78, pp. 539 and 541.

Mitchell, D. (1955) 'Troilus and Cressida', *Opera*, 6, pp. 88–91.

Mitchell, D. (1957) 'The "Modernity" of William Walton', *The Listener*, 7 February, p. 254.

Morrison, A. (1984) 'Willie: The Young Walton and his Four Masterpieces', *RCM Magazine*, 80, 3, pp. 119–27. (From a talk at the British Festival of Recorded Sound.)

Ottaway, H. (1951) 'Walton and the Nineteen-thirties', *Monthly Musical Record*, 81, pp. 4–9.

Ottaway, H. (1970) 'Walton and his Critics', *The Listener*, 25 June, p. 869.

Ottaway, H. (1972) *Walton*, Sevenoaks: Novello.

Ottaway, H. (1972) 'Walton's First Symphony: the Composition of the Finale', *Musical Times*, 113, pp. 254–7.

Ottaway, H. (1973) 'Walton's First and its Composition', *Musical Times*, 114, pp. 988–1001.

Ottaway, H. (1980) 'Walton', in *The New Grove Dictionary of Music and Musicians*, Vol. 20, London: Macmillan.

Palmer, C. Sleeve notes to 'William Walton *The Bear*', CHAN 9245.

Pirie, P. (1972) 'Walton at Seventy', *Music and Musicians*, 20, pp. 16 and 18.

Pirie, P. (1979) *The English Musical Renaissance*, London: Gollancz.

Rosenthal, H. (1958) *Two Centuries of Opera at Covent Garden*, London: Putnam.

Rosenthal, H. (1977) 'Troilus and Cressida', *Opera*, 28, pp. 101–3.

Routh, F. (1972) 'William Walton', in *Contemporary British Music: the 25 Years from 1945 to 1970*, London: MacDonald, pp. 23–42.

Rubbra, E. (1972) 'William Walton's 70th Birthday', *The Listener*, 23 March.

Rutland, H. (1957) 'Walton's New Cello Concerto', *Musical Times*, 98, pp. 69–71.

Saremba, M. (1994) *Elgar, Britten & Co: Eine Geschichte der britischen Musik in zwölf Portraits*, Zürich & St. Gallen: M & T Verlag.

Schaarwächter, Jürgen (1995) *Die britische Sinfonie 1914–1945*, Köln: Dohr Verlag.

Schafer, M. (1963) 'William Walton', in *British Composers in Interview*, London: Faber & Faber, pp. 18–23, 73–82 and 151.

Schwarzkopf, E. (1982) *On And Off The Record: A Memoir of Walter Legge*, London: Faber & Faber.

Searle, H. (1962) 'Are Twelve-Note Symphonies Possible?', *The Listener*, 29 November, p. 941.

Searle, H. and R. Layton (1972) *Twentieth-Century Composers*, London: Weidenfeld & Nicholson.

Shead, R. (1973) *Constant Lambert*, London: Simon Publications.

Shore, B. (1949) 'Walton's Symphony', in *Sixteen Symphonies*, London: Longman, Green & Co, pp. 372–87.

Simpson, R. (ed.) (1967) *The Symphony*, Vol. 2: Elgar to the Present Day, Harmondsworth: Penguin.

Skelton, G. (1975) *Paul Hindemith: The Man behind the Music*, London: Gollancz.

Slonimsky, N. (1971) *Music since 1900*, 4th ed., New York: Charles Scribner's Sons.

Sternfeld, F. W. (1973) *A History of Western Music*, London: Weidenfeld & Nicholson.

Stradling R. and M. Hughes (1993) *The English Musical Renaissance 1860–1940: Construction and Deconstruction*, London & New York: Routledge.

Tertis, L. (1974) *My Viola and I*, London: Elek.

Tierney, N. (1984) *William Walton: His Life and Music*, London: Robert Hale.

Tippett, M. (1991) *Those Twentieth Century Blues: An Autobiography*, London: Hutchinson.

Tovey, D. F. (1936) *Essays in Musical Analysis, Vol. 3: Concertos*, London: OUP.

Walton, S. (1988) *William Walton: Behind the Façade*, Oxford: OUP.

Walton, W.T. (1965) 'Sir William Walton talks about his First Symphony to Eric Roseberry', BBC Interval Talk, Music Programme, 3 October.

Warrack, J. (1968) 'Sir William Walton talks to John Warrack', *The Listener*, 8 August, pp. 176–8.

Warrack, J. (1954) 'Walton's Troilus and Cressida', *Musical Times*, 95, pp. 646–9.

Warrack, J. (1954) 'Walton's Troilus and Cressida', *Opera*, 5, pp. 724–9.

Warrington, J. (ed.) (1974) *Troilus and Criseyde* by Geoffrey Chaucer, London: Dent.

White, Eric Walter (1937) 'William Walton', in *Life and Letters*, 16, pp. 111–14.

White, E. W. (1983) *A History of English Opera*, London: Faber & Faber.

Widdicombe, G. (1977) Sleeve Notes to *Troilus and Cressida*, EMI SL5 997.

Widdicombe, G. (1977a) 'Troilus revised', *Music and Musicians*, 25, pp. 34–5.

Young, P. M. (1967) *A History of British Music: Symphonies and Concertos*, London: Benn.

Index of Walton's music

Reference is made to C numbers as used in S.R.Craggs *William Walton : A Catalogue* (OUP, 1990)

General index

263